The Gospel according to Moses

The Gospel according to Moses

*Theological and Ethical Reflections
on the Book of Deuteronomy*

DANIEL I. BLOCK

CASCADE *Books* · Eugene, Oregon

Cascade Books
An Imprint of Wipf and Stock Publishers
199 W. 8th Ave., Suite 3
Eugene, OR 97401

www.wipfandstock.com

ISBN 13: 9781498214766

Cataloging-in-Publication data

Block, Daniel Isaac, 1943–

The Gospel according to Moses : theological and ethical reflections on the book of Deuteronomy / Daniel I. Block.

xxiv + 370 pp. ; cm. — Includes bibliographical references and indexes.

ISBN 13: 9781498214766

1. Bible. O.T. Deuteronomy—Criticism, interpretations, etc. 2. Bible. O.T.—Theology. I. Title.

BS1275.52 B57 2012

Manufactured in the U.S.A.

*This book is dedicated
to all the undergraduate and graduate students
who for almost forty years have celebrated with me
the amazing grace of God
in the gospel according to Moses*

Contents

Illustrations

Tables

Preface

DESPITE CREEDAL STATEMENTS TO the contrary, for many Christians the Old Testament has no real authority. Although Protestants will be forever grateful to Martin Luther for his rediscovery of the gospel, specifically salvation by grace alone through faith alone in Christ alone, his emphasis on the contrast between law and gospel has left many Protestants with a truncated canon. A generally negative view of the Hebrew Scriptures is buttressed by New Testament statements, especially by Paul, of the deadening effect of the law, in contrast to the life offered by faith through the Spirit. As often as not the Old Testament is presented as a negative foil against which to interpret the New Testament, as if Old Testament faith was fundamentally problematic. Admittedly the New Testament's ubiquitous use of the Old Testament forces us back into the Hebrew Scriptures to try to make sense of New Testament statements, but seldom do we go there to discover its own life-giving message from the inside out. As a result of five centuries of focusing on the discontinuities between the Testaments within Protestantism, not only have we lost the only Bible Jesus had, but we have also lost sight of the history of redemption. Instead of interpreting the incarnation and the saving work of Christ as the climax of a single plan, it is viewed as an alternate plan, replacing the failed plan that God revealed to Israel. But we do not realize the theological implications of such notions. Has God really failed? Does the faith of the New Testament actually represent Plan B?

After five hundred years of concentrating on the vast gulf that is perceived to exist between the testaments, the time has come to focus on continuities. Although Christians find great delight in the Psalms—and well they should—to restrict our serious study to this

book and to Old Testament texts we understand to be messianic because they point to Christ is to obscure and miss out on the glorious
gospel that confronts readers in every book of the Hebrew Scriptures,
if not on every page. Although a name like *Deuteronomy,* which
translates as "second law," is scarcely inviting to modern readers, the
book we know by this name may yet hold the key to rediscovering the
gospel in the Old Testament. Cast as a series of addresses and poems
presented by Moses to the people of Israel immediately prior to his
death and their entrance into the promised land, from beginning to
end this book proclaims gospel. Moses concludes his first address
with a powerful reminder of YHWH's grace to Israel in the revelation
of his will (4:1–8), in the covenant relationship to which he called
Israel (4:9–31), and most dramatically in his rescue of Israel from
slavery in Egypt (4:32–40). This gospel confronts us on every page
of the book. Moses begins his second address (chapters 5–26, 28) by
reciting the Decalogue, which opens with a glorious summary of the
gospel (5:6), and brings it to a magnificent climax by recasting Israel's
story in semi-creedal form in 26:1–15. The third address (chapters
29–30) opens with a depressing picture of Israel's apparently inevitable failure, but the second half speaks sheer grace, as YHWH
promises to do for Israel what they as a nation could never do for
themselves. The judgment threatened by the curses of chapter 28
could not be the last word, for YHWH's commitment to his people,
and through them to the world, is irrevocable. Moses' final utterances
involve lofty poems celebrating divine grace, which persists despite
centuries of cynicism and rebellion. Grace wins!

The essays in this volume arise out of a decade of meditating on
the book of Deuteronomy. Although Pss 1:2 and 119:97 use different expressions for these ruminations,[1] in context they belong to the

---

1. Psalm 1:2 uses הָגָה, which refers naturally to the sounds made by creatures—
the cooing of doves (Isa 38:14; 59:11; Nah 2:8), the growl of lions (Isa 31:4), but is
also used of the sound of human utterance, whether private audible reading (Josh
1:8; Ps 1:2), rebellious plotting (Ps 2:1), or oral speech/proclamation (Pss 35:28;
37:30; 71:24; 115:7). Elsewhere in the Psalms this word is used of meditations on
YHWH himself (Ps 63:7 [Eng 6]) or his deeds (77:13 [Eng 12]; 143:5). Psalm 119:97
uses the rare noun, שִׂיחָה, "meditation" (elsewhere only in Job 15:4), but it is cognate
to a common denominative verb, שִׂיחַ, "to muse, complain, talk about." This is the
psalmists' preferred expression for "muse" (77:7 [Eng 6]) or meditate upon (77:13
[Eng 12]//הָגָה; 119:15, 23, 27, 48, 78, 148; 145:5), though it may also be used of oral
praise, singing (Ps 105:2 = 1 Chr 16:9).

same semantic field. While we normally associate meditation with devotional reading, for me the articles that follow represent deep literary and theological meditations that have been personally incredibly inspiring and transformative. We have attempted to produce a stylistically coherent volume, but reproducing them more or less as originally published precludes a smoothly flowing series of chapters. The articles in this volume are concerned with broad hermeneutical and theological issues raised by Deuteronomy. They range in focus from an introductory consideration of the theological message of the book to its original audience and to modern readers, to the theological message of the book, to how it might have been produced, to a consideration of how the book might aid Christians in their life of faith and enrich their worship of our gracious Redeemer. For more specific essays on particular texts in Deuteronomy, readers may consult the companion volume, *How I Love Your Torah, O LORD! Studies in the Book of Deuteronomy*.

Each essay in this collection was written to stand on its own. Since they arise from a ten-year conversation with Moses, and were originally presented orally and in print in widely different contexts, readers of the entire volume may notice some repetition. Commitments to the publishers of the earlier versions precluded eliminating redundancies with cross references and summary statements when material presented earlier resurfaces. Unless otherwise indicated, generally the English translations of biblical texts are my own. I have tried to be consistent in rendering dates as BCE ("before the common era") and CE ("common era"), which Christians may also interpret as "before the Christian era" and "Christian era," respectively. The presentation of the divine name—represented by the Tetragrammaton, יהוה—is a particular problem for scholars. The practice of rendering the divine name in Greek as κύριος (= Hebrew אֲדֹנָי, "Adonay") is carried over into English translations as "LORD," which reflects the Hebrew יהוה, and distinguishes it from "Lord," which reflects Hebrew אֲדֹנָי. But this creates interpretive problems, for the connotations and implications of referring to someone by name or by title are quite different. Traditionally, when rendered as a name, English translations have vocalized יהוה as "Jehovah," which combines the consonants of יהוה with the vowels of אֲדֹנָי. Today non-Jewish scholars generally render the name as "Yahweh," recognizing that "Jehovah" is an artificial construct. Grateful that YHWH expressly revealed his name to his people and invited them to address him by name (e.g., Exod 3:13–15), but recognizing the uncertainty of its original vocalization and in deference to Jewish sensibilities regarding the name, in this volume the divine name is rendered simply with the English letters of the Tetragrammaton, YHWH (except in direct quotations of English versions or secondary authors).

Behind the voice of Moses in the book of Deuteronomy we hear the voice of YHWH, for Moses repeatedly declares that all his instructions were given as YHWH his God had charged him. But YHWH, the God of Moses and Israel, is incarnate in Jesus Christ.[2] When Moses speaks of YHWH, he speaks of Jesus (cf. Luke 24:44). Deuteronomy was not only Jesus' favorite book in the Old Testament (judging by the frequency of quotations); he also stands behind the Torah left for our meditation and nurture by Moses. Although I do not expect all who read my essays to agree with me on all points of interpretation, I pray that my delight in the grace of God as revealed and recounted in the Torah of Moses will be contagious, and that readers will grasp the life-giving and life-transforming Torah of YHWH. May the gospel according to Moses—which is the word of Christ—dwell in us richly, leading us in paths of righteousness, filling our hearts with gratitude to God, and inspiring us to sing to one another with psalms, hymns, and spiritual songs (cf. Col 3:16).

2. Cf. Rom 10:13; 1 Cor 1:31; 2:16; 2 Cor 10:17; Phil 2:10–11. For further discussion of this matter, see Block, "Who do Commentators say 'the Lord' is?"

Acknowledgments

ALTHOUGH I AM RESPONSIBLE for this collection of essays on the book of Deuteronomy, this volume is the work of a community of friends and scholars who have inspired, nurtured, pushed, and corrected me and each other. Whereas in an earlier phase of my vocation I lived with Ezekiel in Babylon, for the past decade I have lived with Moses on the plains of Moab. However, the adventure represented by this volume began more than a quarter century ago, when I taught a Hebrew exegesis course on Deuteronomy for the first time. No matter how technical our explorations, when we read the Scriptures we must stand before the biblical text with reverence and awe, and let the voice of God transmitted through his authorized spokespersons penetrate our hearts and minds.

However, this conversation has not been a one-way monologue; it has been a lively dialogue. Sometimes when I read Deuteronomy and I hear the voice of Moses, I don't understand what I am hearing and I ask for clarification. Sometimes what I hear sounds so different from what my ears have been trained to hear and my mind has been taught to accept. This leaves me puzzled and confused. Sometimes I hear the message clearly, but I don't like what I hear and I protest. The word of God challenges my theology and my understanding of piety. Sometimes I hear Moses pleading with me to abandon my idols and to follow the Lord more fully, and I resist his plea. But his voice exposes my self-centeredness and my hypocrisy. I do not love the Lord with all my heart and mind, with all my being, and with all my resources, and I certainly do not love my neighbor as myself. But thank you, Moses, for revealing to me the way of freedom and forgiveness; for reminding me of God's relentless pursuit of his people and his lavish grace.

Along the way, while Moses has been speaking to me, there have been many who have aided him by supporting me in my research on this remarkable book. This volume of essays is dedicated to hundreds of undergraduate and graduate students and thousands of people in churches around the world. Many of these have sat through my lectures and seminars and offered welcome insights into the book, and helped me refine the ways in which I communicate my discoveries. Some have performed mundane tasks for me, scouring databases and libraries for secondary materials that might aid in our interpretation, or proofreading drafts for factual errors and stylistic infelicities. Specifically, I must acknowledge the assistance of Daniel Owens, whose diligence and extraordinary computer skills have saved me countless hours and immeasurable frustration and facilitated preparation of this collection for Cascade Books; Austin Surls, who read the page proofs and indexes; and Carmen Imes and my wife Ellen, who assisted in the tedious task of preparing the indexes.

Since most of the essays in this volume have been published elsewhere, I must express my deep gratitude to editors of journals and publishers of books for their grace and willingness to let us reprint what they had made available earlier. In keeping with our promise, we have acknowledged the original place of publication on a separate page below, as well as at the beginning of each reprinted article. The versions presented here retain the essence of the original publication. Naturally, to produce a coherent volume and to follow the stylistic standards of Cascade Books, we have had to modify these essays stylistically—some more than others. Where needed, we have corrected errors of substance or form in the original, and in a few minor details my mind has changed. But readers should find no dissonance between the present forms of these essays and the original publications.

Special thanks are due to Robin Parry and Christian Amondson, for their enthusiasm for this project and the efficiency with which they have handled all the business and editorial matters. From the first conversation at the annual meeting of the Society of Biblical Literature in Atlanta, they have encouraged us and offered all the help we needed to produce it to their specifications. I am grateful to the administrators and my faculty colleagues at Wheaton College, for the unwavering institutional support and encouragement they offer, not only by creating a wonderful teaching environment, but also for providing the resources for our research. I am deeply grateful to Bud and Betty Knoedler, who have given so generously to underwrite my professorial chair. It is a special grace to know them not only as supporters of Wheaton College, but also as personal friends. Ellen and I are grateful for their daily prayers on our behalf. I eagerly also acknowledge Ellen, the delight of my life, who has stood by me as a gracious friend and counselor for more than four decades. Without her love and wisdom, the work represented here would either never have been finished, or it would have taken a different turn.

Finally, we must give praise to God. Unlike others who serve gods of wood and stone, that have eyes but don't see, ears but don't hear, and mouths but don't speak, we have a God who speaks. By his grace he revealed himself to Israel by name and by deed, and by his grace he revealed to them his will (Deut 4:6–8). This God, who introduced himself to Israel as YHWH, has introduced himself to us in the person of Jesus Christ. If in the Torah of Deuteronomy we hear his voice, this is a supreme grace, mediated by Moses. But this grace has been surpassed in Jesus Christ. He does not merely mediate the grace of God; he embodies it (John 1:16–17), for he is YHWH incarnate (John 1:23). To him be ultimate praise and glory.

Credits

I HEREBY GRATEFULLY ACKNOWLEDGE PERMISSION to republish articles that have appeared elsewhere:

Chapter 1: "Deuteronomy: A Theological Introduction," was originally published as "Deuteronomy, Book of." In *Dictionary for the Theological Interpretation of the Bible*, edited by Kevin J. Vanhoozer, 165–73. Grand Rapids: Baker, 2005, and subsequently republished as "Deuteronomy." In *Theological Interpretation of the Old Testament: A Book-by-Book Survey*, edited by Kevin J. Vanhoozer, 67–82. Grand Rapids: Baker, 2008.

Chapter 2: "Recovering the Voice of Moses: The Genesis of Deuteronomy," was previously published in *Journal of the Evangelical Theological Society* 44 (2001) 385–408.

Chapter 4: "Preaching Old Testament Law to New Testament Christians," was previously published in *Hiphil (Scandinavian Evangelical E-Journal)* 3 (2006) 1–24, and subsequently published in three parts in *Ministry* 78.5 (2006) 5–11; 78.7 (2006) 12–16; 78.9 (2006) 15–18.

Chapter 5: "'You shall not covet your neighbor's wife': A Study in Deuteronomic Domestic Ideology," was previously published in *Journal of the Evangelical Theological Society* 53 (2010) 449–74.

Chapter 6: "All Creatures Great and Small: Recovering a Deuteronomic Theology of Animals," was previously published in *The Old Testament in the Life of God's People: Essays in Honor of Elmer A. Martens*, edited by Jon Isaak, 283–305. Winona Lake, IN: Eisenbrauns, 2009.

Chapter 7: "Other Religions in Old Testament Theology," was previously published in *Biblical Faith and Other Religions: An Evangelical Assessment*, edited by David W. Baker, 43–78. Grand Rapids: Kregel, 2004.

Abbreviations

AB	Anchor Bible
ABD	*Anchor Bible Dictionary.* Edited by D. N. Freedman. 6 vols. Garden City, NY: Doubleday, 1992.
AHw	*Akkadisches Handwörterbuch.* Edited by W. von Soden. 3 vols. Wiesbaden: Harrassowitz, 1965–81
AJT	*Asia Journal of Theology*
ANET	*Ancient Near Eastern Texts Relating to the Old Testament.* Edited by James B. Pritchard. 3rd ed. Princeton: Princeton University Press, 1969
AnOr	Analecta orientalia
AOAT	Alter Orient und Altes Testament
ASORDS	American School of Oriental Research Dissertation Series
ASV	American Standard Version
AUSS	*Andrews University Seminary Studies*
AV	Authorized Version
BA	*Biblical Archaeologist*
BAR	*Biblical Archaeology Review*
BASOR	*Bulletin of the American Schools of Oriental Research*
BDB	Brown, F., S. R. Driver, and C. A. Briggs. *A Hebrew and English Lexicon of the Old Testament.* Oxford: Oxford University Press, 1907
BECNT	Baker Exegetical Commentary on the New Testament
Bib	*Biblica*
BN	*Biblische Notizen*
BR	*Biblical Research*
BRev	*Bible Review*
BSL	Biblical Studies Library
BWANT	Beiträge zur Wissenschaft vom Alten und Neuen Testament
BZ	*Biblische Zeitschrift*

BZAW   Beihefte zur Zeitschrift für die alttestamentliche Wissenschaft

CAD   *The Assyrian Dictionary of the Oriental Institute of the University of Chicago.* Chicago: Oriental Institute, 1956–2011

CBOT   Coniectanea biblica Old Testament Series

CBQ   *Catholic Biblical Quarterly*

COS   *The Context of Scripture.* Edited by W. W. Hallo. 3 vols. Leiden: Brill, 1997–2002

DCH   *Dictionary of Classical Hebrew.* Edited by D. J. A. Clines. Sheffield: Phoenix, 1993–

DDD   *Dictionary of Deities and Demons in the Bible.* Edited by K. van der Toorn, B. Becking, and P. W. van der Horst. Rev. ed. Leiden: Brill, 1999

DJD   Discoveries in the Judaean Desert

DNWSI   *Dictionary of the North-West Semitic Inscriptions.* J. Hoftijzer and K. Jongeling. 2 vols. Leiden: Brill, 1995

EA   El-Amarna tablets. According to the edition of J. A. Knudtzon. *Die El-Amarna-Tafeln mit Einleitung un Erläuterungen.* Leipzig: J. C. Hinrichs, 1908–1915 Reprint, Aalen: Otto Zeller, 1964. Supplemented in A. F. Rainey, *El-Amarna Tablets 359–379.* 2nd ed. AOAT 8. Neukirchen-Vluyn: Neukirchener Verlag, 1978

EAJT   *East Asia Journal of Theology*

EncJud1 *Encyclopaedia Judaica.* 1st ed. 16 vols. Jerusalem: Keter, 1972

EncJud2 *Encyclopaedia Judaica.* 2nd ed. 22 vols. Edited by F. Skolnik. Farmington Hills, MI: Gale, 2007

EQ   *Evangelical Quarterly*

ErIsr   *Eretz-Israel*

ESV   English Standard Version

ETL   *Ephemerides theologicae lovanienses*

ExpTim *Expository Times*

HALOT   Koehler, L., W. Baumgartner, and J. J. Stamm, *The Hebrew and Aramaic Lexicon of the Old Testament.* Translated and edited under the supervision of M. E. J. Richardson. 4 vols. Leiden: Brill, 1994–1999

HCSB   Holman Christian Standard Bible

HdO	Handbuch der Orientalistik
HSM	Harvard Semitic Monographs
HSS	Harvard Semitic Studies
HUCA	*Hebrew Union College Annual*
ICC	International Critical Commentary
IDB	*The Interpreter's Dictionary of the Bible.* Edited by G. A. Buttrick. Nashville: Abingdon, 1964
Int	*Interpretation*
ISBE	*International Standard Bible Encyclopedia.* Rev. ed. 3 vols. Grand Rapids: Eerdmans, 1976–86
JAOS	*Journal of the American Oriental Society*
JB	Jerusalem Bible
JBL	*Journal of Biblical Literature*
JBLMS	Journal of Biblical Literature Monograph Series
JBTh	*Jahrbuch für Biblische Theologie*
JCS	*Journal of Cuneiform Studies*
JCS	*Journal of Cuneiform Studies*
JETS	*Journal of the Evangelical Theological Society*
JHS	*Journal of Hellenic Studies*
JJS	*Journal of Jewish Studies*
JNES	*Journal of Near Eastern Studies*
JQR	*Jewish Quarterly Review*
JSOT	*Journal for the Study of the Old Testament*
JSOTSup	Journal for the Study of the Old Testament Supplement Series
JTI	*Journal of Theological Interpretation*
KAI	*Kanaanäische und aramäische Inschriften.* H. Donner and W. Röllig. 2nd ed. Wiesbaden: Harrassowitz, 1966–69
LCC	Library of Christian Classics
LCL	Loeb Classical Library
LSJ	Liddell, H. G., R. Scott, and H. S. Jones. *A Greek-English Lexicon.* 9th ed., with revised supplement. Oxford: Oxford University Press, 1996
NAC	New American Commentary
NAS	New American Standard
NCB	New Century Bible

NIBC	New International Biblical Commentary
NICNT	New International Commentary on the New Testament
NICOT	New International Commentary on the Old Testament
NIDOTTE	*New International Dictionary of Old Testament Theology & Exegesis.* Edited by Willem VanGemeren. 5 vols. Grand Rapids: Zondervan, 1997
NIGTC	New International Greek Testament Commentary
NIV	New International Version
NIVAC	New International Version Application Commentary
NJB	New Jerusalem Bible
NJPSV	Tanakh: The Holy Scriptures: The New JPS Translation according to the Traditional Hebrew Text
NLT	New Living Translation
NRSV	New Revised Standard Version
NSBT	New Studies in Biblical Theology
NTL	New Testament Library
OBO	Orbis biblicus et orientalis
OBT	Overtures to Biblical Theology
OTL	Old Testament Library
OTS	Old Testament Studies
RHR	*Revue de l'histoire des religions*
RSV	Revised Standard Version
SAA	State Archives of Assyria
SBAB	Stuttgarter biblische Aufsatzbände
SBB	Stuttgarter biblische Beiträge
SBLDS	Society of Biblical Literature Dissertation Series
SBLSCS	Society of Biblical Literature Septuagint and Cognate Studies
SBLWAW	Society of Biblical Literature Writings from the Ancient World
SBS	Stuttgarter Bibelstudien
SBT	Studies in Biblical Theology
SBTJ	*The Southern Baptist Theological Journal*
SBTS	Sources for Biblical and Theological Study
ScrHier	Scripta hierosolymitana
SE	*Studia Evangelica*

STDJ	Studies on the Texts of the Desert of Judah
TDNT	*Theological Dictionary of the New Testament*. Edited by G. Kittel and G. Friedrich. Translated by G. W. Bromiley. 10 vols. Grand Rapids: Eerdmans, 1964–76
THAT	*Theologisches Handwörterbuch zum Alten Testament*. Edited by E. Jenni, with assistance from C. Westermann. 2 vols. Munich: Kaiser, 1971–76
TDOT	*Theological Dictionary of the Old Testament*. Edited by G. J. Botterweck and H. Ringgren. Translated by J. T. Willis, G. W. Bromiley, and D. E. Green. 15 vols. Grand Rapids: Eerdmans, 1964–76
TLOT	*Theological Lexicon of the Old Testament*. Edited by E. Jenni, with assistance from C. Westermann. Translated by M. E. Biddle. 3 vols. Peabody, MA: Hendrickson, 1997
TNIV	Today's New International Version
TOTC	Tyndale Old Testament Commentaries
UBL	Ugaritisch-biblische Literatur
VTSup	Vetus Testamentum Supplement Series
WBC	Word Biblical Commentary
WMANT	Wissenschaftliche Monographien zum Alten und Neuen Testament
WOO	Wiener Offene Orientalistik
WTJ	*Westminster Theological Journal*
WUNT	Wissenschaftliche Untersuchungen zum Neuen Testament
ZAW	*Zeitschrift für die alttestamentliche Wissenschaft*
ZTK	*Zeitschrift für Theologie und Kirche*

1

Deuteronomy
A Theological Introduction[1]

T HE THEOLOGICAL SIGNIFICANCE OF Deuteronomy can scarcely be overestimated. Inasmuch as this book offers the most systematic presentation of theological truth in the entire Old Testament, we may compare it to Romans in the New Testament. On the other hand, since Deuteronomy reviews Israel's historical experience of God's grace as recounted in Genesis Numbers, a comparison with the Gospel of John may be more appropriate. Having had several decades to reflect on the significance of the death and resurrection of Jesus, John produced a profoundly theological Gospel, less interested in the chronology and facts of the life of Christ, and more concerned with its meaning. Similarly, according to Deuteronomy's internal witness, Moses has had almost four decades to reflect on the significance of the exodus of his people from Egypt and YHWH's establishment of a covenant relationship with Israel at Sinai. Like the Gospel of John, the book of Deuteronomy functions as a theological manifesto, calling on Israel to respond to God's grace with unreserved loyalty and love.

---

1. This essay was originally published as "Deuteronomy, Book of," in *Dictionary for the Theological Interpretation of the Bible*, edited by Kevin J. Vanhoozer, 165–73. Grand Rapids: Baker, 2005. It was subsequently republished as "Deuteronomy," in *Theological Interpretation of the Old Testament: A Book-by-Book Survey*, edited by Kevin J. Vanhoozer, 67–82. Grand Rapids: Baker, 2008.

1

History of Interpretation

Deuteronomy is the fifth and final book of what Jewish tradition knows as the *Torah,* and Christians refer to as the Pentateuch. In popular Hebrew tradition the book is called סֵפֶר דְּבָרִים, "Book of Words," which is an adaptation of the official Hebrew name, אֵלֶּה הַדְּבָרִים, "These are the Words," the first two words of the book. In the third century BCE the LXX translators set the course for the history of its interpretation. Instead of translating the Hebrew title as Τὸ Βιβλίον τῶν Λόγων, "The Book of Words," or more simply οἱ Λόγοι, "The Words," they replaced this title with Τὸ Δευτερονόμιον, "second law." The form of the name seems to be derived from Deut 17:18, where Hebrew מִשְׁנֵה הַתּוֹרָה, "a copy of the Torah," is misinterpreted as τὸ δευτερονόμιον, "second law" (Latin: Deuteronomium). This Greek heading probably became determinative because the book reiterates many laws found in Exodus–Numbers, and in chapter 5 cites the Decalogue. But the name "Deuteronomy" overlooks the fact that the book presents itself *not* primarily as law but as *a series of sermons.* Much of the book reviews events described in the earlier books. Where laws are dealt with (e.g., the central sanctuary law in chapter 12), the presentation is often in the form of exposition, rather than a recital of the laws themselves.

Prior to the rise of the source critical method, both Jewish and Christian readers assumed Mosaic authorship of the book, a fact reflected in the common designation of the Pentateuchal books outside the English world as the Five Books of Moses. For Jews, as the work of Moses it came with profound authority.[2] Observing Jesus' manner of ministry and speech, some looked upon him as the eschatological prophet like Moses whom YHWH would raise up.[3] While Jesus himself rejected this interpretation (John 1:21), judging by the number of quotations from it in his teaching, Deuteronomy was his favorite book. This impression is reinforced by his distillation of the entire law into the simple command to love the Lord with one's whole being and to love one's neighbor as oneself (Matt 22:37; Mark 12:30; Luke 10:27). Although appeals for love for one's neighbor and the stranger occur earlier in the Pentateuch (Lev 19:18, 34), the command to love

---

2. Cf. Mark 10:3; 12:19; Luke 20:28; John 5:45; 9:28; etc.

3. Deut 18:15; cf. Matt 11:9; John 1:21, 25; 6:14; 7:40.

God occurs only in Deuteronomy (Deut 6:5; 11:1; 11:13; 13:4 [Eng 3]; 30:6).

Paul repeatedly cites Deuteronomic texts to buttress his positions.[4] However, it is clear that he interpreted the entire history of God's revelation and the book of Deuteronomy in particular in light of Christ and the cross.[5] Paul seems to have functioned as a second Moses, not only in providing a profoundly theological interpretation of God's saving actions in Christ, but also in reminding his readers that salvation comes by grace alone. In Romans and Galatians his argumentation addresses those who would pervert the "law" (a narrow legalistic interpretation of Hebrew *Torah*) into a *means of* salvation, rather than treating it as a *response to* salvation as Moses perceived it.[6] While on the surface Paul's responses to this heresy often appear to contradict Moses, these statements should be interpreted in context and as rhetorical responses to his opponents. In his own disposition toward the "law" he was in perfect step with Moses: obedience to the law was not a means for gaining salvation but a willing and grateful response to salvation already received. There is nothing new in Paul's definition of a true Jew as one who receives the praise of God because he is circumcised in the heart (Rom 2.28–29, cf. Deut 10:16–21; 30:6), nor in his praise of the Law as holy, righteous and good (Rom 7:12; cf. Deut 6:20–25), nor in his distillation of the whole law into the law of love (Rom 13:8–10; cf. Deut 10:12–21). Elsewhere Peter's characterization of Christians as a privileged people, "a chosen race," and "God's own possession" (1 Pet 2:9) echoes Moses' understanding of Israel's privileged relationship with YHWH.[7]

To the extent that the early church used the book of Deuteronomy, the church fathers and other spiritual leaders tended to follow Paul's lead in interpreting Deuteronomy christologically, but in their application of the laws they often resorted to spiritualizing the details. By marshaling the Shema' (Deut 6:4–5) to defend trinitarian doctrine,[8] they obscured its original contextual meaning.[9] In the Reformers we

4. Rom 10:19; 11:8; 12:19; 1 Cor 5:13; 9:9; Eph 6:2–3; etc.

5. Rom 10:6–8; 1 Cor 8:6; Gal 3:13.

6. Schreiner, *The Law and Its Fulfillment*; Wright, *Climax of the Covenant*.

7. Deut 4:20; 10:15; 14:2; 26:18–19.

8. For examples, see Lienhard et al., eds. *Exodus, Leviticus, Numbers, Deuteronomy*, 282–83.

9. Block, "How Many Is God?" 73–97.

witness two different dispositions toward the laws of Deuteronomy. Luther tended to read the laws of Deuteronomy through the lenses of Paul's rhetorical and seemingly antinomian statements (Rom 7:4–9; 2 Cor 3:6; Gal 3:10–25) and his own debilitating experience of works-righteousness within the Roman Catholic Church. Consequently, he saw a radical contrast between the law (which kills) and the gospel (which gives life). His emphasis on the dual function of the law (civic—to maintain external order on earth; theological—to convict people of sin and drive them to Christ)[10] missed the point of Deuteronomy. This book presents the law as *a gift of grace* to guide the redeemed in the way of righteousness, leading to life (cf. Deut 4:6–8; 6:20–25). Like Luther, Calvin insisted that no one can be justified by keeping the law. However, through the gift of the law, Israel is instructed on how to express their gratitude for their redemption and bring glory and delight to God.[11]

These two approaches tended to dominate the disposition of interpreters of Deuteronomy until the Enlightenment, when the attention of critical scholars shifted from the theological value of Deuteronomy to hypotheses concerning the origin of the book. By the second half of the nineteenth century the documentary approach to Pentateuchal studies was firmly entrenched, and Deuteronomy had been isolated as a source separate from J, E, and P. Julius Wellhausen proposed that chapters 12–26 represent the original core of the book, written by a prophet (some suggest Jeremiah) ca. 622 BCE (cf. 2 Kgs 22–23) to promote reform of Israel's religious practices (2 Chr 34–35) and centralize the cult in Jerusalem. The prophet presumably wrote the book as a manual for reform and hid it in the temple so that it would be found. The book was completed after the exile and combined with Genesis–Numbers (an amalgam of J, E, and P sources) to create the Pentateuch more or less as we know it.

Convinced that the book of Joshua completed the story of the Pentateuch, Wellhausen and others preferred to interpret Deuteronomy within the context of the Hexateuch. Deuteronomy was crucial for Gerhard von Rad's theology of the Old Testament, which found in 26:5–9 an ancient Credo confessing the essentials of

10. Cf. Lohse, *Martin Luther's Theology*, 270–74.

11. Calvin, *Commentaries on the Four Last Books of Moses*, 1:363.

Israelite faith.[12] Martin Noth went in the opposite direction, cutting Deuteronomy off from Genesis–Numbers and treating this book as the paradigmatic theological prologue to the Deuteronomistic history work (Joshua–Kings). This large document provided a theological explanation for the events surrounding 722 BCE and 586 BCE, now viewed as the direct result of Israel's persistent apostasy and worship of strange gods.

Modern scholars attribute the bulk of Deuteronomy variously to country Levites writing shortly before 701 BCE,[13] prophetic circles of northern Israel,[14] or sages in the Jerusalem court.[15] Critical scholars generally tend to interpret the core of the book as a sort of manifesto, written in support of Josiah's efforts to centralize the religion of Israel in Jerusalem. According to Weinfeld, Deuteronomy is not only a remarkable literary achievement, but represents a profound monument to the theological revolution advocated by the Josianic circles. This revolution involved attempts to eliminate other shrines and centralize all worship of YHWH in Jerusalem, as well as to "secularize," "demythologize," and "spiritualize" the religion. It sought to replace traditional images of divine corporeality and divine enthronement in the Temple with more abstract, spiritual notions reflected in its "name theology." In this new religious world sacrifices were no longer institutional and corporate but personal expressions of faith, and the tithe was no longer "holy to YHWH" but remained the possession of the owner (14:22–27).[16]

Recognizing the strengths of each of these positions, most recently some have proposed that a coalition of dissidents (scribes, priests, sages, aristocrats) originally produced Deuteronomy. According to Richard D. Nelson,[17] the book has its roots in a time of crisis (seventh century), when loyalty to YHWH was undermined by the veneration of other gods. At this time the well-being of many was

12. Von Rad, "The Form-Critical Problem of the Hexateuch" in *The Problem of the Hexateuch and Other Essays*, 1–78.

13. E.g., von Rad, *Studies in Deuteronomy*.

14. E.g., Nicholson, *Deuteronomy and Tradition*, 58–82.

15. E.g., Weinfeld, *Deuteronomy 1–11*; Weinfeld, *Deuteronomy and the Deuteronomic School*.

16. Weinfeld, "Deuteronomy, Book of," 1775–78.

17. Nelson, *Deuteronomy*, 4–9; cf. Albertz, *History of Israelite Religion*, 1:194–231.

being jeopardized by exploitative royal policies, and the prophetic institution was out of control, and this is why we find Deuteronomy calling for tests of authenticity and limitation of influence. The inconsistencies and ambiguities in the Deuteronomic legislation reflect the varying interests of the dissident groups. Virtually all critical scholars agree that Deuteronomy either provides the occasion for or is the result of the Josianic reform. They also agree that the speeches in Deuteronomy are pseudepigraphical, fictionally attributed to Moses to support the parties whose interests are represented in the book.[18]

Not all are willing to date Deuteronomy this late. J. G. McConville[19] and others argue that the religious and political vision of the book does not fit the Josianic period as described in 2 Kings. On the contrary, "Deuteronomy, or at least a form of it, is the document of a real political and religious constitution of Israel from the premonarchic period."[20] As such it challenges prevailing ancient Near Eastern royal-cultic ideology, replacing this with a prophetic vision of YHWH in direct covenant relationship with his people and a people governed by Torah. Through the Torah the prophetic authority of Moses, the spokesperson for YHWH, extends to the community. The "Book of the Torah," deposited next to the Ark and formally read before the assembly, provides a constant reminder of the will of the covenant Lord and a guide for expressing its loyalty to him. As for the theological revolution envisioned by Weinfeld, this interpretation is coming under increasingly critical scrutiny.[21]

Deuteronomy presents itself as a record of addresses delivered orally by Moses on the verge of Israel's crossing over into the Promised Land, a series of speeches that were immediately committed to writing (31:9).[22] However, in accordance with ancient Near Eastern literary convention, strictly speaking the book as we have it is anonymous. We can only speculate when the individual speeches

18. Cf. Sonnet, *Book within the Book*, 262–67.

19. McConville, *Deuteronomy*, 33–40.

20. Ibid., 34.

21. For example, it is argued that the "name theology" of the book does not represent an abstraction of the real presence of YHWH, but an emphasis on worshiping at the divinely authorized place. See Wilson, *Out of the Midst of the Fire*; Richter, *The Deuteronomistic History and the Name Theology*; Vogt, *Deuteronomic Theology and the Significance of Torah*.

22. Block, "Recovering the Voice of Moses," 21–51, below.

of Moses were combined, arranged, and linked with their present narrative stitching. Certain stylistic and literary features, the content of a series of historical notes in the book, and the resemblances of the present structure of the book to second millennium BCE Hittite treaty documents suggest that this happened much earlier than critical scholars admit.

Hearing the Message of Deuteronomy

Because of a pervasive latent Marcionism and adherence to theological systems that are fundamentally dismissive of the OT in general and the book of Deuteronomy in particular, the message of this book has been largely lost to the church. This is a tragedy, not only because—more than any other book in the OT—the message of Deuteronomy lies right on the surface of the text, but also because few books in the OT proclaim such a relevant word to the church today. But how can readers today rediscover the message of the book?

First, it is important to "hear" the word of Deuteronomy. At significant junctures Moses appeals to his people to "hear" the word he is proclaiming (5:1; 6:3–4; 9:1; 20:3). In 31:9–13 he charges the Levitical priests to read the Torah that he has just transcribed (i.e., his speeches) before the people every seven years at the Feast of Booths. This statement assumes canonical status for the Torah Moses has just proclaimed and highlights the critical link between hearing his words in the future and the life of the people of God. This link may be represented schematically as follows:

Reading ⇨ Hearing ⇨ Learning ⇨ Fearing ⇨ Obeying ⇨ Living

A similar relationship between reading/hearing the words of "this Torah" and one's future well-being is expressed in 17:19, where Moses explicitly charges future kings to read the Torah for themselves so that they may embody the covenant fidelity he has espoused in his addresses to the people on the plains of Moab.

Second, to hear the message of Deuteronomy, we must recognize its genre and form. At one level, Deuteronomy represents the final major segment of the biography of Moses that began in the first chapter of Exodus.[23] Accordingly, Deuteronomy may be inter-

---

23. Knierim, *The Task of Old Testament Theology*, 355–59, 372–79.

preted as narrative in which a series of lengthy speeches have been embedded.

At another level, the manner in which the first two speeches have been arranged is reminiscent of ancient Near Eastern treaty forms, especially second-millennium Hittite suzerainty treaties.[24] Recognizing the fundamentally covenantal character of Deuteronomy has extremely significant implications for the message we hear in the book. YHWH is the divine suzerain who graciously chose the patriarchs and their descendants as his covenant partner (4:37; 7:6–8). He demonstrated his covenant commitment (אָהֵב, "love") by rescuing them from Egypt (4:32–40), entering into an eternal covenant relationship with them at Sinai (4:9–32), revealing to them his will (4:1–8), providentially caring for them in the desert (1:9—3:29), and is now about to deliver the promised land into their hands (1:6–8; 7:1–26). As a true prophet of YHWH, Moses challenges Israel to respond by declaring that YHWH alone is their God (6:4), and by demonstrating unwavering loyalty and total love for him through acts of obedience to him (6:5–19; 10:12—11:1; etc.). Moses realistically anticipates Israel's future rebellion against her suzerain, leading ultimately to her banishment from the land promised on oath to Abraham. Nevertheless, YHWH's compassion toward his people and the irrevocable nature of his covenant mean that exile from the land and dispersion among the nations cannot be the last word; YHWH will bring them back to himself and to the land (4:26–31; 30:1–10). Indeed Moses perceives the covenant that he is having them renew with YHWH as an extension of the covenant made with Israel at Sinai (28:69 [Eng 29:1]), and ultimately an extension and fulfillment of the covenant made with the ancestors (29:9–12 [Eng 10–13]).

At a third level the book of Deuteronomy presents itself as a series of addresses by Moses to Israel immediately before they enter the land of Canaan and prior to his own decease. The narrative preamble (1:1–5) should determine how we hear its message. Although in later chapters Moses will integrate many prescriptions given at Sinai into his preaching, contrary to prevailing popular opinion Deuteronomy does not present itself as legislation, that is, a book of laws. This is prophetic preaching at its finest. The preamble identifies Moses'

24. For commentaries that highlight the treaty form of the book, see Thompson, *Deuteronomy*; Craigie, *Book of Deuteronomy*.

words as הַתּוֹרָה הַזֹּאת, "this Torah." The word תּוֹרָה, *tôrâ*, should not be understood primarily as "law" (the book includes much that is not legal), but as "instruction." The word תּוֹרָה, *tôrâ*, is derived from the hiphil verb הוֹרָה, "to teach," and the expression סֵפֶר הַתּוֹרָה (e.g., Deut 29:20 [Eng 21]; Josh 1:8; etc.), means "Book of the *Instruction*," rather than "Book of the Law." The expression was applied to specific aspects of the will of YHWH revealed to Israel earlier (e.g., Exod 12:49; 24:12; Lev 7:1; Num 19:14; etc.). Nevertheless, the Torah that YHWH commanded Joshua himself to read and obey fully in Josh 1:7–8, and which he read to the people of Israel as part of the covenant-renewal ceremony at Shechem (Josh 8:30–35), was probably the collection of Moses' sermons that constitute the bulk of the present book of Deuteronomy. Eventually, the scope of the term *Torah* was expanded to include the narrative sections (1:1–5; 27:1–10; 34:1–12; etc.), that is, the entire book of Deuteronomy more or less as we have it. It is widely accepted that the document referred to as "the book of the Torah" (סֵפֶר הַתּוֹרָה, 2 Kgs 22:8; 2 Chr 34:15) and "the book of the Torah of YHWH by the hand of Moses" (2 Chr 34:14), discovered by Josiah's people in the course of renovating the Temple, was some form of the book of Deuteronomy.

Although the covenant principles developed in Deuteronomy applied to all Israelites generally, in Deut 17:14–20 Moses declares that kings in particular were to write and read this Torah. Hearing the voice of God through the words of the Torah would be the key to their own fear of God, their obedience to him, their humility before their fellow Israelites, and their tenure as kings of Israel. This was probably what David had in mind when he charged his son Solomon to keep all the ordinances of YHWH his God according to what was written "in the Torah of Moses" (1 Kgs 2:3–4). The author of 1 and 2 Kings evaluates the monarchs of Israel and Judah on the basis of their adherence to or departure from the Torah. He commends some (Hezekiah, 2 Kgs 18:6), but condemns most (e.g., Manasseh, 2 Kgs 21:1–9). In the end both the northern kingdom of Israel (2 Kgs 17:1–18) and the southern kingdom of Judah were destroyed because they rebelled against YHWH. Sadly in their rebellion the kings led the way. The book of Deuteronomy represents the heart of the Torah, which priests were to teach and model,[25] which psalmists praised

25. Deut 33:10; 2 Chr 15:3; 19:8; Mal 2:6, 9; cf. Jer 18:18; Ezek 7:26; Ezra 7:10.

(Ps 19:8–15 [Eng 7–14]; 119), to which the prophets appealed (e.g., Isa 1:10; 5:24; 8:20; 30:9; 51:7), by which faithful kings ruled,[26] and righteous citizens lived (Ps 1). In short, this book provides the theological base for virtually the entire OT and the paradigm for much of its literary style.

Deuteronomy obviously incorporates prescriptive and motivational material deriving from the Sinai revelation (in the Decalogue, 5:7–21; the so-called Deuteronomic Code, 12:1—16:15; the covenant blessings and curses, 28:1–69 [Eng 29:1]). Nevertheless, lists of specific prescriptions analogous to the forms of other ancient Near Eastern law codes tend to be concentrated in only seven chapters (19–25),[27] but even these are punctuated by strong rhetorical appeals and a fundamental concern for righteousness rather than mere legal conformity. The remainder, even of the second address, bears a pronounced homiletical and pastoral flavor. Both the book of Deuteronomy and the word *torah* are represented much more accurately by Greek διδασκαλία, "teaching, instruction," and διδαχή, "teaching, instruction," as used in the New Testament, than by νόμος, "law."

This does not mean that what Moses declares in these speeches is any less authoritative than the laws given by YHWH at Sinai. In 1:4 the narrator declares that in these addresses Moses functions as the authorized spokesman for YHWH—he delivers these speeches at and according to the command of YHWH. Nevertheless, here Moses' role is that of pastor, not lawgiver. Like Jacob in Gen 49, Joshua in Josh 24, and Jesus in John 13–16, knowing that his death is imminent, Moses gathers his flock and delivers his final homily, pleading with the Israelites to remain faithful to YHWH. Deuteronomy is therefore to be read primarily as discourse on the implications of the Israelite Covenant for a people about to enter the land promised to the ancestors under the Abrahamic Covenant (cf. Gen 15:7–21; 26:3; Exod 6:2–8).

But hearing the message of Deuteronomy involves more than hearing the words and correctly identifying the genre of the material one hears; it also involves interpreting the book correctly, grasping its theology, and making appropriate application to life. According to the internal witness of the book, with these addresses Moses sought

---

26. 1 Kgs 2:2–4; 2 Kgs 14:6; 22:11; 23:25.

27. On legal lists as a genre, see Watts, *Reading Law*, 36–45.

to instill in the minds of the generation that was about to claim the Promised Land a deep sense of gratitude for the grace that YHWH had lavished on them. At the same time he guided them in applying the principles of the covenant made at Sinai to the new situation that faced them on the other side of the Jordan. While the Canaanites posed a formidable military threat, the spiritual threat they represented was much more serious. Accordingly, throughout the book the emphasis is on exclusive devotion to YHWH, demonstrated in a life of grateful obedience. If they would do so, Moses envisioned the people of Israel and the land they would occupy flourishing under the blessing of YHWH.

How are Christians to read the book today? The following principles may guide us in this enterprise. First, rather than beginning with what the New Testament says about Deuteronomy, we should read the book as an ancient Near Eastern document that addresses issues current a thousand years before Christ in idioms derived from that cultural world. Although the New Testament church accepted this book, along with the rest of the Old Testament, as its authoritative Scripture, the book sought to govern the faith and life of Israel, a nation composed largely of ethnic descendants of the patriarchs.

Second, we should recognize the book as a written deposit of eternal truth. Some of these verities are cast in explicit declarative form, as in "YHWH is God; there is no other [god] besides him" (4:35, 39). Others are couched in distinctive Israelite cultural dress, for which we need to identify the underlying theological principle. For example, "When you build a new house, you shall make a parapet for your roof" (22:8 NRSV). This represents a specific way of demonstrating covenantal commitment ("love") to the well-being of one's neighbor. The validity of specific commands for the Christian may not be answered simply by examining what the New Testament explicitly affirms. On the contrary, unless the New Testament explicitly declares a Deuteronomic ordinance to be rendered passé, we should assume minimally that the principle underlying the command remains valid.

Third, after we establish the meaning of a Deuteronomic passage in its original context, we must reflect on the significance of the passage in the light of Christ, who has fulfilled the law (and the prophets, Matt 5:17). This means not only that he is the perfect embodiment of all that the law demands, and its perfect interpreter, but also that he represents the climax of the narrative. The message of the New Testament is that the One who spoke then is none other than Jesus Christ, YHWH incarnate in human form.

Deuteronomy and the Canon

The written copies of Moses' last addresses to Israel were recognized as authoritative and canonical *from the very beginning*. Not only did Moses prohibit addition to or deletion from his words (4:2), but he also commanded the Levites to place the written Torah beside the ark of the covenant. There it was to remain perpetually as a witness against Israel and as the norm by which the nation's conduct in the Promised Land would be measured. The fact that this Torah, which was written down by Moses, was placed *beside* the Ark, rather than *in* it (unlike the Tablets containing the Decalogue [10:1–9], which were written down by God himself [5:22]), does not suggest a lesser authority, but a different significance. The tablets of stone containing the Decalogue represented the actual covenant document (4:13; 10:1–4), placed in the Ark as a reminder to God of his covenant with Israel. The Deuteronomic Torah was Moses' commentary on the covenant, whose terms included not only the Ten Principles, declared directly by God himself, but also the "ordinances and statutes" (חֻקִּים וּמִשְׁפָּטִים) revealed to Moses at Sinai and then passed on to the people. Moses' instructions on the covenant were fully inspired and authoritative, for he spoke to Israel "according to all that YHWH had commanded him [to declare] to them" (1:3).

The theological stamp of Deuteronomy is evident throughout the Old Testament canon and into the New Testament. If in Deuteronomy the term *torah* applies expressly to the speeches of Moses, eventually it was applied to the entire Pentateuch, for which Deuteronomy represents the conclusion. Many treat Deuteronomy as a dangling legal appendix to the narratives of the Patriarchs, Israel's exodus from Egypt, the establishment of YHWH's covenant with Israel at Sinai, and the desert wanderings. Still some divorce the book from the Pentateuch altogether. However, critical scholars are increasingly recognizing a Deuteronomic flavor in many of the narratives, so much so that for some the classical JEDP source hypothesis of Pentateuchal origins has collapsed into a theory of two sources. One of these is Deuteronomic (which includes most of what was previously attributed to Yahwist and Elohist sources), and the other is the reactive P source.[28]

The stamp of Deuteronomy on the so-called "Deuteronomistic History" (Joshua–Kings) is evident not only in the style of these books (many of the embedded speeches sound like Deut 1—Josh 24; 1 Sam 12; etc.), but also especially in their theology.[29] Specifically, Solomon's emphasis on the temple as a place for the "name of YHWH" to dwell (1 Kgs 8) harks back to Deut 12 *et passim*. More generally, if and when the nation of Israel and her monarchy are destroyed, it is because they have failed in their covenant relationship with YHWH as outlined in Deuteronomy. The influence of Deuteronomy is less obvious on Chronicles and Ezra-Nehemiah, but in the Latter Prophets one hears echoes of Moses' orations throughout. In Hosea and Jeremiah, in particular, the links are so direct that scholars often debate which came first, Deuteronomy or the prophet. Prophetic pronouncements of judgment and restoration appear often to be based on the covenant curses of Deut 28 and promises of renewal in chapter 30. Indeed the canonical collection of prophets as a whole and the book of Malachi specifically (Mal 3:22–24 [Eng 4:4–6]) end with a call to return to the "*torah* of my servant Moses," which has its base in the revelation at Sinai, but strictly speaking refers fundamentally to Moses' exposition of that revelation.

In the Psalms, Deuteronomic influence is most evident in the so-called "Torah" Psalms (1, 19, 119), which highlight the life-giving purpose of the law, but also in the "wisdom" psalms, with their emphasis on the fear of YHWH (111:10; cf. 34:8–12). Weinfeld has argued that Deuteronomy bears many verbal and conceptual affinities with Proverbs (e.g., emphasis on fearing YHWH, and presentation of two ways—life/blessing and death/curse)—which supposedly point to wisdom influence in the book.[30] However, it seems more likely that the influence was in the opposite direction.

28. Cf. Albertz, *History of Israelite Religion*, 464–93.

29. See McConville, *Grace in the End*.

30. Weinfeld, *Deuteronomy 1–11*, 62–65; Weinfeld, *Deuteronomy and the Deuteronomic School*, 244–319.

New Testament texts like Luke 24:44 suggest that by the time of Christ the expression תּוֹרַת מֹשֶׁה, "Torah of Moses,"[31] served as the standard designation of the first part of the Jewish canon (alongside "the Prophets" and "the Psalms"). As noted earlier, the Pentateuchal location of Deuteronomy, which serves as a theological exposition of the events narrated in the previous books, may have influenced the canonical location of John, the most overtly theological of the Gospels. However, whereas Christ himself is presented as YHWH incarnate, the person whose role most closely resembles that of Moses in Deuteronomy is Paul. Like Moses, this apostle was specially called not only to lead the community of faith in mission, but also to interpret God's saving actions and instruct God's people in the life of covenant faith. In so doing he responded sharply to those who insisted that adherence to the law of Moses was a prerequisite to salvation. Like Deuteronomy, often Paul's epistles divide readily into two parts, the first being devoted to theological exposition (cf. Deut 1–11), and the second to drawing out the practical and communal implications of the theology (cf. Deut 12–26).

Deuteronomy and Theology

As an overall theme to the book of Deuteronomy we propose the following: A call to Israel for covenantal faithfulness in the land, in response to the grace that God has lavished on them (cf. 6:20–25). In developing this theme Moses presents a theology that is remarkable for both its profundity and scope.

First, Israel's history begins and ends with God. Deuteronomy instructs Israel and all subsequent readers on his absolute uniqueness,[32] eternality (33:27), transcendence (7:21; 10:17; 32:3), holiness (32:15), justice and righteousness (32:4; cf. 10:18), passion (jealousy) for his covenant and his relationship with his people,[33] faithfulness (7:9), presence,[34] compassion (4:31), and especially his covenant love.[35] But none of these are mere abstractions. YHWH lives in relationship with human beings, which explains why Moses never tired of speaking

31. Josh 8:31–32; 23:6; 2 Kgs 14:6; 23:25; Neh 8:1; Mal 3:22 [Eng 4:4].

32. Deut 4:32–39; 6:4; 10:17; 32:39; 33:26.

33. Deut 4:24; 5:9; 6:15; 9:3; 32:21.

34. Deut 1:41; 4:7; 6:15; 7:21; 31:17.

35. Deut 4:37; 7:7, 8, 13; 10:15, 18; 23:6 [Eng 5].

of God's grace—expressed in many different concrete actions toward Israel: his election of Abraham and his descendants (4:37; 7:6), his rescue of Israel from the bondage of Egypt (4:32–36), his establishment of Israel as his covenant people,[36] his providential care (1:30–33; 8:15–16), his provision of a homeland (6:10–15; 8:7–14), leadership (16:18—18:22), and victory over their enemies (7:17–24).

Second, Deuteronomy offers a comprehensive picture of the community of faith. Externally the community that stands before Moses consists largely of descendants of Abraham, and the first-generation offspring of those who had experienced the exodus from Egypt. These are the chosen people of YHWH. In Deuteronomy, the doctrine of divine election plays a prominent role. The book speaks of the divine election (בָּחַר, "to choose") of the place for YHWH's name to be established and to which the Israelites are invited to come for worship and communion with him (12:5 *et passim*). It also speaks of the divine election of Israel's king (17:15), whose primary function was to embody covenant righteousness, and of the Levitical priests (18:5, 21:5). However, YHWH's election of Israel to be his covenant people receives special attention. Lest his hearers have any illusions about the grounds of their election, Moses emphasizes that YHWH's election of Israel was based on neither exceptional physical nor spiritual qualifications. Israel was not granted favored status with YHWH because of their significance as a people among the nations, for they were the least (7:6–8), nor because of their superior moral behavior vis-à-vis the nations, for their past is characterized by rebellion (9:1–24). On the contrary, their election was an act of *sheer grace*, grounded in YHWH's love for the ancestors and (4:32–38) and in his inexplicable love for their descendants (7:6–8). In so doing, Deuteronomy presents Israel as an incredibly privileged people. Of all the peoples, they alone have experienced the strong redeeming hand of YHWH (4:32–40), have participated in a covenant ceremony in the presence of the living God (4:9–31), and enjoy vital communion with him. YHWH not only hears them whenever they cry out, but in an unprecedented act of revelation has made his will known to them (4:1–8; 6:20–25). Their standing with God is characterized directly as that of his covenant partners (26:16–19) and a holy people belonging to him alone (7:6; 14:2; 26:19; 28:9). Metaphorically, they

36. Deut 4:9–31; 5:1–22; 26:16–19.

are counted as his adopted sons (14:1; cf. the portrayal of God as their father in 1:13; 8:5; 32:6, 18) and his treasured possession (סְגֻלָּה, 7:6; 14:2; 26:18). However, although YHWH had called the nation as a whole to covenant relationship, the true community of faith consisted of persons who loved YHWH with their entire being. They demonstrate that love through righteousness (צְדָקָה, 6:25), which involves repudiating all other gods and compassionately pursuing justice toward others (10:16–20).

Third, no other book in the Old Testament presents as thorough a treatment of covenant relationship as Deuteronomy. Though some draw sharp lines of distinction between the Abrahamic covenant and the covenant made with Israel at Sinai, Deuteronomy perceives these to be organically related and united. The covenant YHWH made with Israel at Sinai/Horeb represents the fulfillment of the covenant he had made with Abraham and an extension of his commitment to his descendants (cf. Gen 17:7). In Deuteronomy Moses provides an exposition of the covenant to which the present generation binds itself (26:16–19). Chapters 29–30 do not envision a new covenant, but the present generation's recommitment to and extension of the old.

It is within this covenantal context that we must understand the nature and role of the law and the importance of obedience: (1) Obedience to the law was not viewed as a burden, but as a response to the unique privilege of knowing God's will (Deut 4:6–8), in contrast to the ignorance of nations who worshiped gods of wood and stone (4:28; Ps 115:4–8). (2) Obedience to the law is not a way of or precondition to salvation, but the grateful response of those who had already been saved (6:20–25). (3) Obedience to the law is not primarily a duty imposed by one party on another, but an expression of confident covenant relationship (26:16–19). (4) Obedience to the law is the external evidence of the circumcision of one's heart and the internal disposition of fearing and loving God (10:12—11:1; 30:6–9). (5) Obedience to the law involves a willing subordination of one's entire being to the authority of the gracious divine suzerain (6:4–9; 10:12–13) (6) While obedience to the law is not a prerequisite to salvation, it is evidence of righteousness, which is a precondition to Israel's fulfillment of the mission to which they have been called and the precondition to their own blessing (4:24–25; chs. 11, 28) (7) Obedience to the law is both reasonable and achievable (30:11–20).

The last point demands further comment, especially since the book seems to view Israel's failure as inevitable.[37] Part of the answer to this dilemma may be found in the frequent alternation between the singular and the plural forms of direct address in the book. The shifts between "you" singular and "you" plural serve a rhetorical function, recognizing that though YHWH entered into covenant relationship with the nation, in the end fidelity cannot be legislated and must be demonstrated at the personal and individual level. Yet, this device also recognizes the existence of two Israels. On the one hand, there was a physical Israel, consisting of descendants of Abraham, Isaac, and Jacob. On the other hand, there was a spiritual Israel, consisting of those persons (like Moses, Joshua, and Caleb) with circumcised hearts who demonstrated unqualified devotion to YHWH. For the latter, obedience was not only possible; it was a delight. But Deuteronomy is both pessimistic and realistic about the former, anticipating a future rebellion that will lead eventually to the destruction and exile of the nation. According to 30:16 this problem of national infidelity will only be resolved in the distant future, when the people come to their senses and repent, and YHWH brings the people back and circumcises their hearts.

Fourth, Deuteronomy presents a highly developed theology of land. Moses' cosmic awareness is expressed by his appeal to heaven and earth to witness Israel's renewal of the covenant (4:26; 30:19; 31:28). But corresponding to YHWH's love for Israel within the context of the nations, in 11:12 he declares that the land currently occupied by the Canaanites, but set aside for Israel, is the special object of YHWH's perpetual care (דָּרֵשׁ). YHWH is delivering this land into the hands of the Israelites as their special grant (נַחֲלָה, 4:21 *et passim*) in fulfillment of his oath to the ancestors (1:8 *et passim*), though the onus is placed on the nation to engage the Canaanites and wrest it from their hands (7:1, *et passim*). Even so, the Israelites are challenged to engage the Canaanites, drive them out (9:3), and utterly destroy them and their religious installations (7:1–5; 12:2–3). However, this land is not given to Israel as a reward for moral superiority (9:1–24), but granted to them as an act of grace.

Deuteronomy describes the nation's relationship to the land within the context of the tripartite association of Deity-land-people.

37. Deut 4:24; 5:29; 29:13 [Eng 14]–30:1; 31:16–21; 32:14–27.

Accordingly, the response of the land to Israel's occupation will depend entirely upon the people's fidelity. If they are faithful to YHWH, the land will yield bountiful produce (7:11–16; 11:8–15; 28:1–14). But if they prove unfaithful, not giving YHWH the credit for their prosperity and going after other gods, then the land will stop yielding its bounty and he will sever the tie with it.[38] When the Israelites will be removed from the land because of their sin (which in Moses' mind appears inevitable), this will not represent a cancellation of the covenant, but its fulfillment and the application of its fine print (cf. Dan 9:4–16). Because of YHWH's immutable covenant commitment to Abraham and his descendants (4:31) he must and will bring Israel back to the land and to himself (30:1–10). Accordingly, within their present literary contexts and within the context of the history of God's covenant relationship with Israel, the "new" covenant of which Jeremiah speaks (31:31–34) and the eternal covenant of which Ezekiel writes (Ezek 16:60; cf. 34:25–31) should not be interpreted as absolutely new. Instead, they represent anticipations of the full realization of God's single original covenant made with Abraham, ratified and fleshed out at Horeb and renewed on the Plains of Moab. This covenant envisioned a time when the boundaries of physical and spiritual Israel will finally be coterminous.[39] Accordingly, Israel's exile cannot be the final word on the land. Because of YHWH's compassion and the irrevocability of his covenant with Israel (4:31), when the people repent he will regather them from the lands where they are scattered and bring them back to the land originally given to them (30:1–5). However, the book is clear: Israel's occupation of the land and her prosperity in it are contingent on fidelity to YHWH.

Fifth, Deuteronomy presents a remarkable approach to government. Although the kingship of YHWH receives scant explicit attention (cf. 33:5), from beginning to end, it presents Israel as a theocracy, with YHWH as their divine suzerain. The book provides for judicial officials appointed by the people (1:9–15; 16:18), and kings, priests, and prophets appointed and/or raised up by YHWH (17:14—18:22).

---

38. Deut 4:25–28; 8:17–20; 11:16–17; 28:15–26.

39. The NT development of this theme in the context of the Lord's Supper (Luke 22:20; 1 Cor 11:25) and in Hebrews (8:8–13; 9:15; 12:24) recognizes that ultimately God's covenant relationship with his people is possible only because of the mediatorial and sacrificial work of Christ.

Indeed many scholars interpret 16:18—18:22 as a sort of state "constitution" (*politeia*) for Israel designed to reinforce the centralization of power in Jerusalem under Josiah.[40] However, this interpretation is extremely problematic, first because 17:14–20 presents the monarchy as optional, and interest in the king's real power over the people is eclipsed by concern for his primary role as a paradigm of covenant faithfulness—a disposition quite at odds with the nature of Israelite kingship historically. But the "constitution" interpretation of 16:18—18:22 is even more problematic because it tends to overlook the primary concern of the book—to establish a people under the authority of Torah and governed by "righteousness" (צְדָקָה).[41]

Conclusion

For modern readers plagued by a negative view of the OT in general and OT law in particular, the book of Deuteronomy offers a healthy antidote. Through the work of Christ not only is Israel's relationship made possible, but the church, the new Israel of God, is grafted into God's covenant promises. As was the case with Israel, access to these promises remains by grace alone, through faith alone. However, having been chosen, redeemed, and granted covenant relationship with God, his people will gladly demonstrate whole-hearted allegiance to him with whole-bodied obedience (cf. Rom 12:1–12). Deuteronomy remains an invaluable resource for a biblical understanding (1) of God, especially his grace in redeeming those bound in sin; (2) of appropriate response to God, entailing love for God and for our fellow human beings; and (3) of the sure destiny of the redeemed.

40. Cf. McConville, *Deuteronomy*, 78–79.

41. Contrary to most English translations, which render צֶדֶק צֶדֶק in 16:20 something like "Justice, only justice" (NIV), the root צדק never carries a narrowly judicial sense elsewhere in Deuteronomy. God is "righteous" (צַדִּיק, 32:4), and so are his "ordinances and laws" (צַדִּיקִם, 4:8; cf. צִדְקַת יְהוָה, "the righteous [will] of YHWH," 33:21). Righteous behavior includes compassion for the poor person (24:13), offering righteous sacrifices (וְבִחֵי־צֶדֶק, 33:19). Living according to the covenant standards is considered "righteousness" (צְדָקָה, 6:25; 24:13); those who do so are "righteous" (צַדִּיק [as opposed to "guilty," רָשָׁע], 25:1). Those who claim to be righteous but resist YHWH's will (9:4–6) are rebellious (מַמְרִים, 9:7, 23, 24), wicked (רָשָׁע, 9:27), and sinful (חַטָּאת, 9:16, 27). True weights are "accurate" (שְׁלֵמָה) and "righteous" (צֶדֶק). Honorable judges "judge righteously" (שָׁפַט צֶדֶק, 1:16). As elsewhere, the root connotes righteousness, defined as "right behavior/standing as specified by the terms of YHWH's covenant with Israel."

More than any other book in the OT (if not the Bible as a whole), Deuteronomy concretizes faith in real life. Inasmuch as the NT identifies Jesus Christ with the God of Israel's redemption, in the spiritual, moral, and ethical pronouncements of Deuteronomy we find fleshed both the first and great commandment (Matt 22:34–40) and "the law of Christ" (Gal 6:2). A church that has discovered this book will have its feet on the ground, resisting the tendency to fly off into realms of platonic ideas and inward subjectivity so common in Western Christianity.

2

Recovering the Voice of Moses

The Genesis of Deuteronomy[1]

BACK IN 1999, WHEN I was reflecting on the significance of the last year of a millennium, it struck me that the tradition that Moses wrote the Pentateuch is actually more than three thousand years old. Of course, Christian adherence to this tradition is based on three pillars: (1) the internal evidence of the book of Deuteronomy, which specifically speaks of Moses writing the Torah (31:9, 24); (2) the frequent references to "the book of the Torah of Moses" (Josh 8:31, 32; 23:6; 2 Kgs 14:6; Neh 8:1), "the book of Moses" (Neh 13:1; 2 Chr 25:4; 35:12), "the Torah of Moses,"[2] "the book of the Torah of YHWH by the hand of Moses" (2 Chr 34:14, 15), and "the words of YHWH by the hand of Moses" (2 Chr 35:6), in the OT; (3) and NT references to "the νόμος of Moses,"[3] "Moses" used as a substitute for ὁ νόμος,[4] "the book of Moses" (Mark 12:26), Moses' "writings" (John 5:47), vaguer references to laws that Moses commanded,[5] statements like "Moses

---

1. This essay was previously published in *Journal of the Evangelical Theological Society* 44 (2001) 385–408.

2. 1 Kgs 2:3; 2 Kgs 23:25; 1 Chr 23:18; 30:16; Ezra 3:2; 7:6; Dan 9:11, 13; Mal 3:22.

3. Luke 2:22; 24:44; John 7:23; Acts 13:39; 15:5 (cf. "the manner of Moses" in v. 1); 28:23; 1 Cor 9:9; Heb 10:28.

4. Luke 16:29, 31; 24:27; John 5:45, 46; Acts 6:11; 21:21; 26:22; 2 Cor 3:15.

5. Matt 8:4; 19:7, 8; 22:24; Mark 1:44; 7:10; 10:3, 4; Luke 5:14; John 8:5; Acts 6:14.

wrote/writes,"[6] "Moses says" (Rom 10:19), and "customs that Moses delivered to us" (Acts 6:14). In the Gospels Jesus himself frequently refers to Moses as a recognized authority in Jewish tradition and as an authority behind his own teachings.

Luke 16:19–31 and John 5:19–47 illustrate the enormous stature of Moses in the tradition of Judaism at the turn of the ages. In the Torah the Jews heard Moses' prophetic voice, and in the Torah they read what he wrote, which raises the question I propose to address in this chapter: How did the Torah, particularly the book of Deuteronomy, come to be viewed as the book of Moses? More specifically, how did the oral proclamation of Moses become the written book of Deuteronomy? In my search for the answers to these questions I shall begin by describing the problem and by briefly surveying the solutions that have been proposed. But the bulk of this chapter will consist of an inductive consideration of the evidence for the genesis of the book of Deuteronomy within the book itself. I shall conclude with a few reflections on the implications my conclusions have for our understanding of Scripture and the process of its inspiration.

I. The Problem

Like the first four books of the OT, Deuteronomy poses a problem for scholarly investigation, because it has come to us as an anonymous composition. Nowhere does the author identify himself. But then, this is not that remarkable, especially if we consider that this problem applies to virtually all of the OT.[7] Although few would doubt that the book of Amos contains the authentic words of this eighth-century prophet, the fact is we do not know who was responsible for transcribing, gathering, and arranging his oracles in their present form. The narrative preamble (1:1) at least appears to come from a different hand.

But there is a second reason why we should not be puzzled by the anonymity of Deuteronomy. This accords perfectly with what we know (or do not know!) of the composition of literary texts in the ancient Semitic world. Although ancient Mesopotamian documents tend to reflect great concern to identify scribes who copied tradi-

---

6. Luke 20:28, referring to Deut 25:5; Rom 10:5.

7. A point made also by Waltke, "Oral Tradition," 30.

tional and economic texts, those that explicitly identify their authors
are extremely rare. In 1957 W. G. Lambert could cite only two literary texts that mention the name of the author: [8] the myth of "Erra
and Ishum," which claims to be the divinely inspired composition
of Kabti-ilani-Marduk,[9] and "The Babylonian Theodicy," a complex
autobiographical acrostic poem consisting of twenty-seven stanzas
each made up of eleven lines beginning with the same syllable.[10] Our
understanding of the authorship of ancient Mesopotamian literature
has not changed much since 1957,[11] and no additional compositions
naming their authors have been discovered.[12] The reticence of ancient
authors of literary texts to identify themselves presumably derives
from their placement of a higher value on the message of their compositions than on the identity of the composer. Whatever the reason,
the same phenomenon is evident in the OT. Not a single book names
its author. But this has not stopped readers from trying to answer
what is ultimately unanswerable. Indeed, until the recent awakening
of interest in literary approaches to biblical texts, critical scholarship
was preoccupied with trying to answer questions of authorship and
provenance.

8. Lambert, "Ancestors, Authors, and Canonicity," 1. For a discussion of an ancient text that lists the names of several authors, see idem, "A Catalogue of Texts
and Authors," 59–77.

9. For English translations, see Dalley, in *COS* 1:404–16; Foster, *Before the
Muses*, 2:771–805. Kabti-ilani-Marduk's name has also surfaced in the "Catalogue
of Texts and Authors" from the library of Ashurbanipal published by Lambert, "A
Catalogue of Texts and Authors," 65. Cf. his comments on ibid., 73–74.

10. The author does not identify himself outrightly, but when the opening sylla-
bles of each stanza are pieced together they yield the sentence "I, Sagilkinamubbib,
am adorant of god and king." See the translation by Foster in *COS* 1:492–95; *Before
the Muses*, 2:709–98. For the Akkadian text, translation, and commentary, see
Lambert, *Babylonian Wisdom Literature*, 63–89.

11. We have learned that the legendary Adapa was recognized as the author of
written texts, presumably by dictation from a god, and that the Etana Epic is attributed to a certain Lunanna. See Lambert, "A Catalogue of Texts and Authors," 67. Cf.
his discussion, pp. 72–76.

12. For a discussion of the present awareness of ancient authors, see Foster,
Before the Muses, 19–21.

II. A Brief Survey of Solutions Proposed

As already noted, in pre-critical Jewish and Christian traditions the predominant interpretation ascribed the authorship of the Pentateuch as a whole and of Deuteronomy in particular to Moses. In fact, many maintained that the entire Torah was dictated by God to Moses,[13] and this remains the position held by many preachers in evangelical churches, not to mention the lay people in the pews—though some would concede that a later writer (perhaps Joshua) may have added Deut 34.

While many evangelical scholars today argue for at least a more nuanced understanding of the book's origins,[14] virtually all critical scholars reject this interpretation. In the nineteenth century two Germans, W. M. L. De Wette and Julius Wellhausen, provided the impetus for more critical approaches. In his 1805 doctoral dissertation,[15] the former proposed that Deuteronomy was the recently written law book used by Josiah as the basis of his religious reforms. This thesis was picked up and developed by Julius Wellhausen who argued that chapters 12–26, the core of the book, were written by a prophet (some suggest Jeremiah) ca. 622 BCE (cf. 2 Kgs 22–23) to promote the reform of Israel's religious practices (2 Chr 34–35), specifically by centralizing the cult in Jerusalem and by removing the "high places" in the land (Deut 12). The prophet presumably wrote the book as a manual for reform and hid it in the Temple in such a way that it would be found. Thus Hilkiah's discovery became the basis for the reformations. Eventually Deuteronomy was added to the Tetrateuchal corpus to create the Pentateuch.[16]

13. Helpful surveys of the history of interpretation of the book of Deuteronomy are found in the introductions to most commentaries. See Tigay, *Deuteronomy*, xix–xxiv; Merrill, *Deuteronomy*, 22–23; Weinfeld, *Deuteronomy 1–11*, 9–57; Miller, *Deuteronomy*, 2–10; Mayes, *Deuteronomy*, 81–108; Craigie, *The Book of Deuteronomy*, 24–32; Thompson, *Deuteronomy*, 47–68; Driver, *A Critical and Exegetical Commentary on Deuteronomy*, xxxiv–lxvi. See also the detailed discussion by Harrison, *Introduction to the Old Testament*, 1–82, 495–542, 637–53.

14. Cf. the discussion by Christensen and Narucki, "The Mosaic Authorship of the Pentateuch," 465–71. But Merrill, *Deuteronomy*, 22, for example, fails to distinguish between Moses' transcription of his sermons on the Plains of Moab and the authorship of the book.

15. *Disertatio qua Deuteronomium a priorbus Pentateuchi libris diversum alius cuisdam recentioris auctoris opus esse demonstratur* (Jena, 1805).

16. Wellhausen, *Prolegomena to the History of Israel*, 9, *et passim*; Wellhausen, *Die Composition des Hexateuchs* (1889), 76, *et passim*.

Today many of Wellhausen's specific points have been rejected, but his central thesis, that Deuteronomy is a late work associated with Josiah's reforms, continues to be assumed by most higher critical studies. But this does not mean that scholars are agreed in their explanations for the origin of the book. In 1943 Martin Noth turned a century of scholarship upside down by proposing that Joshua–2 Kings is a single work written by a Judaean historian to explain the demise of Israel, and that Deuteronomy was added as a paradigmatic prologue.[17] Recent scholarly efforts have worked hard to fix the origins of the book more precisely. Gerhard von Rad argued that Deuteronomy was written by country Levites shortly before 701 BCE;[18] E. W. Nicholson attributes the book to prophetic circles of northern Israel;[19] Moshe Weinfeld maintains that the book derives from the Jerusalem court and is the work of wise men, sages, and scribes, such as were commonly employed in ancient Near Eastern courts.[20] Claiming the best of all worlds, Patrick Miller finds in the book the evidences of priestly interest cited by von Rad, the prophetic spirit recognized by Nicholson, and the humaneness and social morality of the teachers of wisdom identified by Weinfeld.[21] However, the denial of Moses as a literary figure is such an entrenched tenet of higher critical ortho-

17. Noth, *Überlieferungsgeschichtliche Studien*, literally *Historical Studies in Tradition*, available in English as *The Deuteronomistic History*, 43–52. This is a translation of the second edition published in German at Tübingen by Max Niemeyer, 1957. For a survey of recent variations of this theory see McKenzie, "Deuteronomistic History," 2:160–68.

18. The book supposedly reflects the rise of country priests who competed for influence with the official priestly establishment of Jerusalem and tried to reawaken the old spirit of Yahwism, displaying a martial spirit in their interpretation and application of the ancient law (cf. Deut 7:16–29; 9:1–6). Von Rad, *Studies in Deuteronomy*, 66–67; Von Rad, *Deuteronomy*, 23–30. For a recent revival of this thesis, see Miller, *The Origins of the Bible*, 58–66.

19. After the fall of Samaria to Assyria in 722 BCE, these northern prophets had fled to Judah where they formulated their old (northern) traditions and integrated them with those of the south into a program of reform intended for Judaean authorities. See Nicholson, *Deuteronomy and Tradition*.

20. Among the reasons Weinfeld arrives at this position are the facts that the book is dominated by what most consider typical "wisdom vocabulary" (e.g., "counsel," "fear," "Hear!" etc.) and develops many themes and motifs found in Israelite wisdom literature. See his detailed presentation of his theory on the origins of Deuteronomy in *Deuteronomy 1–11*, 1–84. For a summary statement see Weinfeld, "Deuteronomy," 2:168–83.

21. Miller, *Deuteronomy*, 5–10.

doxy that Miller cannot consider the possibility that the only person in Israel's history who might have represented all three interests was Moses.[22] Many scholars who have investigated the OT from a canonical perspective do indeed recognize in the production of the book of Deuteronomy the first stage in the growth of the canon,[23] and everyone recognizes the putative voice of Moses in the book. However, in the words of Michael Fishbane, "this voice—pseudepigraphic in the Book of Deuteronomy—is a composite of many teaching voices, deriving from the many teachers of the Deuteronomic tradition."[24]

The wide range of results produced by the classical critical approaches raises fundamental questions concerning the methods employed, but scholars who operate by a more conservative hermeneutic and try to let ancient documents speak for themselves are regularly marginalized. Surveys of the history of interpretation rarely interact seriously with the work of those with a more positive disposition toward the authenticity, integrity, and reliability of the information communicated in the biblical texts. In his 1992 introduction to the Pentateuch, Joseph Blenkinsopp dismisses evangelical scholarship with a single sweeping generalization: "For the fundamentalist churches in the English-speaking world and elsewhere, Mosaic authorship has, of course, remained a basic article of faith."[25] But thanks to the work of scholars like Gordon McConville,[26] the weaknesses of these various critical approaches are being exposed and the development of alternative methods are being placed on more secure foundations. My aim in the remainder of this paper is to take a fresh look at the internal evidence of the book to see if it yields any clues to its own genesis.[27]

---

22. Cf. the recent study by Watts, "The Legal Characterization of Moses and the Rhetoric of the Pentateuch," 415–26, in which he argues that the Pentateuch characterizes Moses as a king, a prophet, and a scribe.

23. See Blenkinsopp, *Prophecy and Canon*, 24–53.

24. Fishbane, *Biblical Interpretation in Ancient Israel*, 436.

25. See Blenkinsopp, *The Pentateuch: An Introduction to the First Five Books of the Bible*, 13.

26. See McConville, *Grace in the End*; McConville, *Law and Theology in Deuteronomy*.

27. Leiman, *The Canonization of Hebrew Scripture*, 16–26, argues convincingly that Israel did indeed have canonical books and law corpora long before Josiah's time.

At the outset I acknowledge my indebtedness to a recent work by Jean-Pierre Sonnet.[28] Sonnet rightly recognizes that the book of Deuteronomy offers us more clues concerning its composition as a literary document than any other book in the OT. After analyzing in detail every piece of evidence in the book, Sonnet concludes, "Deuteronomy claims to represent not only history but foundational history—deeds and words which underlie Israel's existence for all generations to come."[29] But this history is the creation of an omniscient narrator who presents Moses first as a great orator and then as a scribe who puts his orations into writing. "The words" that Moses *spoke* have become the words that Moses *wrote* and, by extension, the authority of his speeches now extends to the present book. But after a masterful presentation of his case, in the last five pages Sonnet tips his hand, declaring that all this is staged. The speeches in the book capitalize on the tradition of Moses as a guardian and teacher of Torah but in reality retroject upon him the interests of later scribes. He writes, "Particularly salient in Deuteronomy is the use of Moses' valedictory speech to 'voice' the revising and updating of a previous legal tradition."[30]

When I read Sonnet's work, I began to wonder if his conclusion was not predetermined by specific historical and hermeneutical presuppositions, and what would happen if, like students of ancient extra-biblical literature, one let the chips fall where they wanted, instead of rearranging them according to the prevailing historical reconstruction. It is to that task that I now turn.

III. An Alternative Interpretation

1. The Voices in Deuteronomy

We begin our search for the origins of the book of Deuteronomy by identifying the voices that we hear in the book. The preamble (1:1–5) introduces us to two of these, the voice of Moses and the voice of YHWH: "Moses spoke . . . according to all that YHWH had commanded him" (v. 3).[31] And since it is the narrator who tells us that

28. Sonnet, *The Book within the Book*.

29. Ibid., 259.

30. Ibid., 265.

31. The preamble (1:1–5) presents a telling view of the book's perspective on itself. On the one hand, it answers the generic question. The book is presented as

behind Moses' voice is the voice of God, and accompanying Moses are elders and Levites, the voice of God reaches the reader of the book through a four-stage process that may be represented like this:

YHWH ⇨ Moses ⇨ Narrator ⇨ Reader.[32]

We shall examine each of these voices briefly in turn.[33]

a. *The voice of YHWH*. In a composition devoted to the communication of divine truth it is remarkable that the voice of God is heard directly only in five short speeches found in 31:14b, 31:16b–21, 31:23b, 32:49–52, and 34:4b. Each of these speeches is formally introduced with something like, "And YHWH said."[34] Although YHWH's *scribal* work is read in 5:6–21, his voice is never heard directly before chapter 31, not even in chapters 12–26, which as a piece is generally interpreted as a law code of divine origin. The Song preserved in 32:1–43 is presented as YHWH's song, apparently dictated to Moses inside the tent of meeting (cf. 31:14, 19), but the Israelites heard it from the lips of Moses. On the other hand, God is often identified as the voice behind Moses' speech, contributing to the image of Moses as the greatest prophet of YHWH in Israel's history (cf. 18:14–22).

---

(1) "the words that Moses spoke" (v. 1); (2) a deliberate Mosaic undertaking (v. 5; the auxiliary verb הוֹאִיל expresses initiative and boldness; cf. Weinfeld, *Deuteronomy 1–11*, 128); (3) an "exposition" (v. 5; Hebrew בָּאֵר means to incise, cut, bore, inscribe: 27:8, i.e., to inscribe clearly. Here it is used abstractly of declaring clearly, making clear, providing exposition); (4) this Torah (v. 5; the expression הַתּוֹרָה הַזֹּאת, "this Torah," will occur many times in the book). The LXX name for the book, δευτερο νόμος, "second law," suggests it is a revised version of the original law (cf. Mishnaic מִשְׁנֶה הַתּוֹרָה, "repeated law," "second law"). Specifically, it seems to be based on 17:18 where we find the expression τὸ δευτερονόμιον τοῦτο, "this second law," for מִשְׁנֶה הַתּוֹרָה הַזֹּאת, "a copy of this Torah." This misunderstanding has been determinative for contemporary misinterpretation of the book. On the other hand, the preamble declares the source and/or authority of the address to follow: "Moses spoke to the descendants of Israel according to all that YHWH had commanded him." What follows is presented as the instruction of YHWH through his mediator.

32. According to contemporary postmodern hermeneutical theory, the voice of the last is the most important determinant of meaning.

33. For documentation of the voices of YHWH, Moses, and the narrator, respectively, see Excursus A below.

34. For discussion of divine speech markers in the OT, see Meier, *Speaking of Speaking*.

b. *The voice of Moses.* The bulk of Deuteronomy is taken up with Moses' speeches. Specifically the book contains three major addresses and two poems. The addresses are preserved in 1:6—4:40; 5:1b—26:19; 28:1-69 [Eng 29:1];[35] and 29:1 [Eng 2]–30:20. The poems consist respectively of "The Song of Moses" (32:1-43) and "The Blessing of Moses" (33:2-29).[36] In addition to these major blocks, we hear the voice of Moses in chapter 27 in two short speeches that Moses issued jointly with others (the elders of Israel: 27:1;[37] Levitical priests: 27:9-10),[38] and a third in which he dictates the curses that are to be recited and responded to in Israel's covenant renewal ceremony (27:12-26). Finally, in 32:46b-47 we hear the voice of Moses in an exhortation embedded in the narrative conclusion to the Song of Moses.

35. That chapter 28 originally followed immediately after 26:19 seems likely on several grounds: (1) Whereas the transition from chapter 27 to chapter 28 is extremely abrupt, the opening וְהָיָה is natural after 26:19; (2) on form-critical grounds the blessings and curses of chapter 28 are awkward if not redundant after the ceremonial curses in chapter 27, but they follow logically if read after 26:19; (3) specifically, the reference to YHWH putting Israel high above the nations in 28:1 links directly with 26:19; (4) 28:58-61 link "the words of this Torah written in this book," whose aim is to teach fear of the awesome name of God, and "every sickness and plague not written in the book of this Torah" seem to refer to 5:1b—26:19 and 28:1-68. Chapter 27 appears to be a secondary interpolation of narrative and declarative material whose covenantal content links more logically with Moses' third speech (29:1b[Eng 2b]—30:20). Whether it should have come before or after is unclear, though the specific instructions for renewing the covenant within the land of Canaan seem to belong more logically after Moses' challenge. On possible reasons for the insertion of chap. 27 at this point, see below.

36. Most scholars treat 4:44—28:69 [Eng 29:1] as a single address, but chapter 27 seems to have been secondarily inserted between chapters 26 and 28, thus disrupting an otherwise coherent transition. As we shall see, 27:1-10 consists of two speeches issued conjointly by Moses and the elders (27:1-8) and Moses and the Levitical priests (27:9-10). The curses in 27:12-26 are formulaic and seem to be linked to the ceremony prescribed in 27:1-8. While the covenant curses in chapter 28 were probably originally presented as the conclusion to the second address, the present arrangement of the book presents them as a sequel to (exposition of ?) the ceremony of curses in 27:11-26.

37. Now Moses and the elders of Israel commanded the people, saying, "Keep all the commandment that I command you this day . . ." (RSV).

38. And Moses and the Levitical priests said to all Israel, "Keep silence and hear, O Israel: this day you have become the people of the LORD your God. You shall therefore obey the voice of the LORD your God, keeping his commandments and his statutes, which I command you this day" (RSV).

c. *The voice of the narrator.* That Moses is portrayed as the voice behind the speeches is clear. However, in the book that has come down to us, that is, in the selection, arrangement, and shaping of the materials, we hear the voice of the final author/editor/narrator.[39] Although the book contains an exceptionally high proportion of direct speech, it is in fact a narrative composition. But the book is distinguished from most biblical narrative by the fact that the narrator's voice is heard directly in only sixty-four verses.[40] This voice may be recognized through several clues.

Most obviously, in contrast to the addresses, where Moses always refers to himself in the first person, whenever he is identified by name or with the third person pronoun we may detect the hand of the narrator.[41] This is not unexpected in the preamble (1:1–5) and the epilogue (34:1–4a; 5–12), which frame the book as a whole and fix the context of the addresses. But his voice is also heard in narrative frame texts on both sides of "this Torah" (4:41–43; 32:44–46a), a separate preamble to "this Torah" (4:44—5:1a), notes coordinating speeches in preparation for the ceremony of transcription of the Torah and the covenant curses (27:1a, 9a, 11), a preamble to Moses' third address (28:69—29:1a [Eng 29:1–2a]), notes coordinating the speeches of Moses and YHWH in chapter 31 (vv. 1–2a, 7a, 9–10a, 14a, 14c–16a, 22–23a, 24–25, 30), and notes embedding the poems, the Song of Moses/YHWH (32:1–43) and the Blessing of Moses (33:2b–29) in their literary environment.

Second, while not quite as distinct, the narrator's voice may be recognized in a series of historical notes in the first address, updating what might have been misunderstood by his immediate readers (2:10–12, 20–23; 3:9, 11, 13b–14), and a parenthetical comment in

---

39. Nowhere does the book of Deuteronomy explicitly credit the selection, arrangement, and shaping of the contents to Moses; but then, nor does it exclude his role in these literary activities either.

40. Deut 1:1–5; 2:10–12, 20–23; 3:9, 11, 13b–14; 4:41—5:1a; 10:6–9; 27:1a, 9a, 11; 28:69—29:1a [Eng 29:1–2a]; 31:1–2a, 7a, 9–10a, 14a, 14c–16a, 22–23a, 24–25, 30; 32:44–46a, 48; 33:1–2a; 34:1–4a, 5–12. Polzin, *Moses and the Deuteronomist,* 29, mistakenly counts only fifty-six.

41. Of course, one's reference to oneself does not *a priori* preclude one's being the author of the text. The use of the third person is common in early histories. See Xenophon's *Anabasis* and Julius Caesar's *The Gallic Wars.* But the shift to third person at least invites the reader to look at Moses from another perspective.

the second address on the nature of Levitical authority as custodians of the covenant document placed inside the Ark (10:6–9).

But the narrator's voice is also heard indirectly in the material he chooses to include in or exclude from the book, as well as in his arrangement of the materials. In the end, it is the narrator's point of view that determines the permanent canonical meaning of the text.

2. From Spoken Word to Canonical Text: The Evidence

Deuteronomy presents itself largely as a record of oral addresses. But the question arises, "How did Moses' purported addresses on the plains of Moab become the present book of Deuteronomy?" As I have already noted, scholars have answered this question in radically different ways: from "Moses wrote every word," to "the book is a pseudepigraph, ascribed to one of the most revered figures of Israelite legend/fiction." But what evidence of its growth as a literary text does the book of Deuteronomy itself present?[42]

a. *Israel's earliest canon.* The internal evidence of the book of Deuteronomy suggests that the "Torah" contained in this book was not the first canonical text possessed by the Israelites.[43] Four texts (4:12–14; 5:22; 9:9–17; 10:1–5) point unequivocally to the Decalogue as a pre-existent canonical Scripture.[44] An examination of these four passages together yields a series of interesting observations:

42. For documentation of the evidence discussed in the following, see Excursus B below.

43. We follow Leiman's definition of canon (*Canonization of Hebrew Scripture,* 14): "A canonical book is a book accepted . . . as authoritative for religious practice and/or doctrine, and whose authority is binding . . . for all generations. Furthermore, such books are to be studied in private and in public."

44. The canonical status of the Decalogue is clearly implied in the covenant ratification ceremony at Sinai described in Exod 24:1–11. After recounting to the people all the words of YHWH and all the laws, and hearing the people's unreserved declaration of obedience, Moses wrote down all the words (vv. 3–4). Later he took the covenant document (סֵפֶר הַבְּרִית) and read it to the people, followed by their third declaration of unreserved obedience (cf. 19:8). By the "words of YHWH" (דִּבְרֵי יְהוָה) the narrator undoubtedly means the ten principles of covenant relationship outlined in the Decalogue (cf. Exod 20:1), and by "the laws" (הַמִּשְׁפָּטִים) he means the specific application of these principles as declared in 21:1—23:33 (cf. 21:1). Although the text used in this covenant ceremony appears to have been produced by Moses, the narrator of Exodus (Exod 32:16; 34:28) agrees with Moses in Deut 10:1–5 that the copy of the Decalogue that was later placed inside the Ark of the Covenant was written by God himself.

- The contents of the Decalogue represented the only revelation the Israelites received directly from God (4:10–14; 5:1–5, 22; cf. Exod 20:18–21).

- Although Israel received the Decalogue as an oral communication, it was transcribed and preserved as a written text from the beginning.

- The Decalogue was not written by human hands, but by the finger of God (9:10; 10:1–5; cf. Exod 31:18).

- The contents of the Decalogue were strictly defined: There were ten words at the beginning, and there would never be more than ten words on this document (4:13; 10:4; cf. Exod 34:28).[45]

- The form of the Decalogue was fixed: it has always consisted of a preamble followed by the ten principles governing the relationship between YHWH and his people.

- The Decalogue was written by God but placed into human custody (5:22; 9:10; 10:4) for the people's instruction and use (cf. 30:11–20).

- The Decalogue was considered "the covenant document" from the beginning (4:13; 9:9, 11).[46]

- The Decalogue was written on two tablets of stone, in accordance with the ancient custom of providing a written copy for all parties to a treaty.[47]

- The Decalogue was treated as a canonical text from the beginning, containing the will of God for the generation that received it, the generation that stood before Moses (5:1–15), and all generations to come. A special container, the Ark, was

45. Note especially 5:22, where Moses declares, "He (God) added no more," suggesting it was not subject to comment, or commentary, and could not be revised. When the first copy was destroyed, a second was produced exactly like the first (10:1–5). The fixed form of the Decalogue probably explains Exod 32:15, which notes that tablets were inscribed on both sides, leaving no room for addition.

46. Note the description לוּחֹת הַבְּרִית אֲשֶׁר־כָּרַת יְהוָה עִמָּכֶם, "tablets of the covenant which YHWH cut with you." Like previous Biblical covenants, this covenant is YHWH's covenant (not Israel's, nor "ours") and contains his decreed will for his covenant partners. This is a suzerainty (not parity) covenant. YHWH is the divine Lord, who by an act of sheer grace elects Israel as the covenant partner and by his sovereign will declares its terms.

47. Cf. Weinfeld, *Deuteronomy and the Deuteronomic School*, 63–64.

constructed to house the Decalogue,[48] and a tribe, the Levites, were designated its custodians.

- The Decalogue is referred to by various expressions (the Ten words, the stone tablets, the tablets of the covenant), but Deuteronomy never refers to it as "the Torah," or "this Torah," or "the book of the covenant," or "the book of the Torah," or by the term סֵפֶר, "written document."[49] Based on these observations and the absence of any contrary evidence for written traditions prior to the exodus in the OT, we may conclude that the Decalogue represented Israel's first Scripture.[50]

b. *The Torah of Moses—first edition.* We begin our search for the Mosaic roots of the book of Deuteronomy by observing that the word *Torah* occurs twenty-two times in the book.[51] But what is "this

48. Note that according to 10:1–9 the highlighted function of the Ark is not a place of atonement, nor a palladium for holy war, as elsewhere. Although its deposit in the Ark does not mean that the document was never to be read by humans, it appears that Moses recites the Decalogue from memory in 5:6–21.

49. Exod 24:7 has Moses reading the text of סֵפֶר הַבְּרִית, "the covenant document," as part of the original covenant ratification ceremony at Sinai. Cf. note 48 above. Exod 24:12 refers to the Decalogue as "the tablets of stone and the Torah and the commandment which I have written for your instruction" (לֻחֹת הָאֶבֶן וְהַתּוֹרָה וְהַמִּצְוָה אֲשֶׁר כָּתַבְתִּי לְהוֹרֹתָם). Incidentally, this document is never called "The Ten Commandments" in Deuteronomy or in Exodus (cf. 34:28).

50. Deuteronomy says nothing about סֵפֶר הַבְּרִית, "the covenant document" (usually rendered anachronistically as "the Book of the Covenant") mentioned in Exod 24:7. Within the book of Deuteronomy the Decalogue functions as a "written document" within a written document, "a book within a book." It was important for Israel to have a written record of the covenant YHWH made with them at Sinai for several reasons. First, a written record highlights and provides permanent testimony to the moment of divine revelation and the entrance of Israel into covenant relationship with YHWH. Second, a written record fixes the boundaries of belief and practice. It provides a standard against which human theology, thinking, and conduct may be judged, thereby guarding against an esoteric, abstract, and subjectively defined religion. Third, a written document provides a public record of the divine will. In this regard the Israelite experience represents a drastic contrast to that of the surrounding nations, a fact not lost on Moses in Deut 4:5–8. Of all the nations, only Israel has a deity who has revealed his will to his people, which contrasts with the secret "Tablet of Destinies" written by Marduk of Babylon. For a helpful discussion of the effect of writing on religious belief and practice, see Goody, *The Logic of Writing and the Organization of Society*, 1–44. In a later chapter, Goody examines the effect of writing on the practice of law (ibid., 127–70).

51. Deut 1:5; 4:8, 44; 17:11, 18, 19; 27:3, 8, 26; 28:58, 61; 29:20[Eng 21], 28[Eng 29]; 30:10; 31:9, 11, 12, 24, 26; 32:46; 33:4, 10.

Torah"? In response to this question we offer the following observations. Negatively, we note, first, that whatever it is, it is never referred to as the Torah of YHWH. YHWH's Torah is indeed referred to in 33:10, but this occurs in the appended blessing of Moses (33:4, 10), which, as we shall see, is not included in the first or second edition of the Torah.

Second, we recognize that the book speaks of an *oral Torah* and a written Torah. The oral Torah is referred to by the narrator in 1:5[52] and by Moses as speaker in 4:8.[53] This Torah that Moses sets before the people by declaring it to them includes minimally the historical summary of YHWH's past actions on behalf of Israel (chapters 1–3) and the paraenetic sequel (4:1–40). The narrative preamble to Moses' second address in 4:44–45 appears to function as a formal heading for the *written Torah*: "This is the Torah that Moses set before the descendants of Israel; these are the stipulations, the decrees, and the laws, which Moses spoke to the descendants of Israel when they came out of Egypt." While the term *Torah* (תּוֹרָה), "instruction, teaching," applies generally to the entire address from 5:1b to 26:19, verses 44–45 appear to offer a broad outline for the address. Accordingly, the "Torah" of verse 44 may be seen to consist of Moses' hortatory instruction in chapters 5–11, and the triad of expressions, "covenant stipulations" (הָעֵדֹת), "decrees" (הַחֻקִּים), and "laws" (הַמִּשְׁפָּטִים), may refer to chapters 12–26, the so-called Deuteronomic Code.

Third, the second address contains several specific indications that it is indeed written Torah.[54] We shall discuss each of these briefly in turn.

6:6–9 and 11:18–21. These two texts refer specifically to writing "these words" on the doorposts of houses and city gates. In isolation the written text referred to in 6:6–9 seems to refer to the Shema', but the broader context may suggest the entire Torah or an abbreviation thereof. Binding them on the hands and foreheads as signs also

---

52. "Beyond the Jordan, in the land of Moab, Moses undertook to explain this Torah, saying . . ."

53. "And what great nation is there, that has statutes and ordinances so righteous as all this Torah which I set before you this day?"

54. For a discussion of the meaning of the word תּוֹרָה, "instruction, teaching," see Sanders, *Torah and Canon*, 1–5; on its use in Deuteronomy, see Blenkinsopp, *Prophecy and Canon*, 35–39.

assumes a written copy.[55] Moses obviously expects that, when he is through speaking, a written form of his words will be available.

17:18–20. According to this Mosaic מִשְׁפַּט הַמֶּלֶךְ, "Charter for Kingship," in the future the reigning king is to write for himself a copy of "this Torah" on a סֵפֶר, a written document. This statement not only presupposes royal literacy, but the expression, "copy of this Torah" (מִשְׁנֵה הַתּוֹרָה), also assumes a *Vorlage* from which the king is to copy. Presumably "this Torah" refers to the words that Moses is currently speaking, that is, the second address. The Levitical priests, who in 10:6–9 were assigned the role of custodians of the Decalogue, are now presented as custodians of the Torah from whom the king receives the copy and in whose presence he copies it. The king is to read this Torah throughout his life and treat it as his own personal guide of appropriate religious disposition (fear YHWH) and conduct (he is to keep all the words of this Torah). Indeed, by governing his life according to "this Torah" the king is to embody all that is spiritual and right within the covenant community and thereby secure his own future.[56]

28:58–61. The next reference to a written Torah to be considered occurs in chapter 28, which is generally recognized as the Deuteronomic version of the covenant blessings and curses found in Leviticus 26.[57] Whether the people experience the blessing of YHWH or the curses

55. Putting them on the hearts represents a figurative expression for indelibly imprinting the Torah on the hearts of the Israelites. Cf. Ps 37:31; 40:8–9 [Eng 7–8]; 119:11; Isa 51:7; Jer 31:33; 2 Cor 3:3.

56. The Israelite king may be chosen by God and distinguished from the people, but one of the functions of the written Torah is to keep him from separating himself from them. He is one brother in this community of brothers (cf. 15:1–18). In this regard Moses' Torah differs radically from Hammurabi's law code, whose concern was to govern the conduct of his subjects, not himself. The closest extra-biblical analogue to Deut 17:14–20 is found in the early first-millennium BCE Babylonian document named by W. G. Lambert "Advice to a Prince" (Lambert, *Babylonian Wisdom Literature*, 110–15). This document does indeed contain instructions for a prospective king. However, neither here nor in any other ancient Near Eastern document do we find a king enjoined to write "for himself" a copy of the laws given to the entire nation to rein in his own exercise of power.

57. Apparently these blessings and curses represent the conclusion to Moses' second address, but they have been cut off from 26:19 by the editorial insertion of chapter 27. In their present location, coming after the curses of 27:11–26, the curses of chapter 28 function as an exposition of what is meant by the word "curse."

cited in the present chapter will depend entirely upon their scrupulous observance (by doing) of all the words of "this Torah written in
this book."[58] Obviously this edition of the written Torah includes the
covenant curses.

27:1–8. Inserted between chapters 26 and 28, chapter 27 seems intrusive. As noted earlier, Moses' second address is apparently interrupted
by speeches issued jointly with the elders (27:1–8) and the Levitical
priests (27:9–10), followed by a series of formulaic curses to be recited antiphonally in a ceremony in the valley between Mounts Ebal
and Gerizim (27:11–26). The speech issued by Moses and the elders
prescribes that as part of a sacred ritual "the words of this Torah" be
transcribed on to large stones covered with lime (vv. 2–3, 8) at Mount
Ebal.[59] The purpose of this act is not stated, but one may surmise
these inscribed stones' function is to testify publicly to the terms of
Israel's occupation of the Promised Land and their covenantal pledge
of devotion to YHWH.[60] In any case, the instructions presuppose
minimally that the Israelites will carry a copy of Moses' second address across the Jordan.

58. As in 17:18–20, Moses recognizes a direct correlation between reading the
Torah, the fear of YHWH, obedience to the divine will, and long life in the land.
The people are to know that if they should hold the covenant Lord in contempt
and refuse to live according to this Torah, YHWH would be absolved of all pa-
tronly obligations to them and Israel would find itself in the same category as the
Canaanites—the objects of divine wrath.

59. Transcribing this Torah is presented as a sacred act, accompanied by the
construction of an altar after the instructions of Exod 20:5, offering whole burnt
offerings, sacrificing and eating peace offerings, and rejoicing before YHWH. Like
ancient treaties (cf. Sefire) and law stelae (Hammurabi) the words of this Torah are
to be inscribed, in this instance clearly on stones covered with lime. The call for
stones covered with lime is presumably based on the need to do it quickly (that very
day). Thus Sonnet, *Book within the Book*, 91.

60. The present act finds an analogue in Exod 24:4, where Moses transcribes
all the words of YHWH on a סֵפֶר, "document," which is then used in the covenant
ratification ceremony. Whereas the covenant ceremony at Sinai had tied people and
Torah together, this one links deity, people, Torah, and land. And whereas Moses
had supervised the entire procedure at Sinai, this covenant renewal ceremony must
necessarily transpire in two phases: Moses' own call for commitment in Moab
(chaps. 29–30), and the reading of the Torah in the land. In effect, the written Torah
functions as a replacement for Moses himself (cf. 31:14–22).

29:13-28 [Eng 14-29]. Chapters 29–30 represent a record of Moses' third address, proclaimed as the first phase of a covenant renewal ceremony initiated by Moses but to be completed under Joshua's leadership in the Promised Land.[61] In 29:19 and 26 [Eng 20 and 27] the written record is called a סֵפֶר, "written document"; in verse 20 [Eng 21] it is "this document of the Torah" (בְּסֵפֶר הַתּוֹרָה הַזֶּה, v. 20 [21]). As in 28:58–61, here the focus is on "all the curses of the covenant written in this document of the Torah" (כֹּל אָלוֹת הַבְּרִית הַכְּתוּבָה בְּסֵפֶר הַתּוֹרָה הַזֶּה), confirming that chapter 28 was considered part of the Torah document from the beginning. The written record of these imprecations declares to foreigners, future generations, and the witnesses appealed to by Moses in 30:19 the consequences of Israel's covenantal performance.

30:8-11. These verses promise the obverse to the preceding, namely, if Israel will adhere with heart and soul to the written demands of her covenant Lord she will surely enjoy the blessings of covenant relationship with YHWH as spelled out in the Torah document. In this instance the contents of "this written record of the Torah" are said to include YHWH's commandments (מִצְוֹת), his decrees (חֻקֹּת), and his "laws" (מִשְׁפָּטִים, cf. v. 16), which apparently refer specifically to chapters 12–26, and generally to 5–11 as well (cf. 4:45 and 5:1). According to verse 20 it was the voice of God that was mediated to this generation through the voice of Moses, but it will be mediated to future generations through the written text. In order for all this to transpire, the speech of Moses had to be transcribed immediately upon its utterance.[62] To this point the text gives no indication regarding who might have done the actual transcription.

c. *The Torah of Moses—second edition.* Critical approaches to Deuteronomy have tended to dismiss chapter 31 as a confused collection of text fragments that contribute little to the storyline.[63]

---

61. Note the narrator's comment in 28:69—29:1a[Eng 29:1-2a]. The covenant in question includes both "this covenant" (הַבְּרִית הַזֹּאת) and "this curse" (הָאָלָה הַזֹּאת, 29:13 [Eng 14]).

62. While the process of recording the speech would have involved considerable effort and taken some time, the immediate transcription of a prophetic word is well documented in ancient Near Eastern records. Cf. Millard, "La prophetie et l'ecriture—Israël, Aram, Assyrie," 125–44.

63. According to G. von Rad (*Deuteronomy*, 190) the chapter contains the "debris of traditions," but offers little real advance in the narrative. In 1962 N. Lohfink

However, Sonnet's more holistic and respectful interpretation recognizes a deliberate patterning in the sequence of speeches,[64] designed to establish the emergence of Joshua as authorized leader in Moses' place (cf. the similarity between vv. 7–9 and 23–25). But here we are concerned with what happens to the written Torah.

Although there have been several earlier references to a written Torah (29:19, 20, 26 [Eng 20, 21, 27]; 30:10), in 31:9 we encounter the first notice of Moses actually writing.[65] After noting that Moses encouraged the people (vv. 2–6) and Joshua (vv. 7–8) to be strong and courageous, the narrator observes that Moses wrote (וַיִּכְתֹּב) and handed (וַיִּתְּנָהּ) the transcribed Torah to the Levitical priests and elders.[66] He then charged the Levites and elders to read this Torah in front of all the people every seven years in connection with the remission of debts during the Feast of Booths at the place that YHWH would choose. The purpose of the reading of the Torah is clearly spelled out. As in 17:18–20:

("Der Bundesschluss im Land Moab: Redaktionsgeschichtliches zu Dt 28,69–32,47," 32–56) characterized the chapter as "confused, disjointed, and unreal," a montage of speeches organized according to systematic/aesthetic principles. Thirty years later Lohfink attempts to reconstruct the order of events reflected in the text, rather than the order of narration ("Zur Fabel in Dtn 31–32," 255–79), but this is accomplished only by reconstructing and rearranging the material on the basis of his own definitions.

64. Sonnet (*The Book within the Book*, 125–82) recognizes a chiastic pattern in the arrangement of the speeches:

A	To the people (vv. 2–6)	By Moses
B	To Joshua (vv. 7–8)	By Moses
C	To the Levites and elders (vv. 10–13)	By Moses
D	To Moses (v. 14)	By YHWH
D'	To Moses (vv. 16–21)	By YHWH
C'	To Joshua (v. 23)	By YHWH
B'	To the Levites (vv. 26–28)	By Moses
A'	To the people (32:1–43)	By Moses

65. The similarities extend to the use of the converted imperfect. With Sonnet (ibid., 138), the converted imperfect should probably be interpreted as a pluperfect: Moses had written this Torah. For a discussion of Moses' scribal role see Watts, "The Legal Characterization of Moses in the Rhetoric of the Pentateuch," 422–26.

66. In the light of 17:18–20 the reference to the former as custodians of the Torah is not unexpected. But the reference to elders is, though this links their involvement with 5:23, where they had asked Moses to mediate between God's voice and themselves. The lethal face-to-face oral encounter of the former context is past; now they receive the life-giving written communication from God (cf. 30:15).

Reading ⇨ Hearing ⇨ Learning ⇨ Fearing ⇨ Obeying ⇨ Living.[67]

In verse 14 the narrative takes a surprising turn. YHWH calls Moses and Joshua into the Tent of Meeting, where he apparently dictates to them what is commonly called "the Song of Moses," but is more accurately read as "the Song of YHWH." In anticipation of the people's apparently inevitable apostasy after the death of Moses, YHWH commanded Moses and Joshua to write this song for themselves,[68] and then he instructed Moses (note the singular) to teach the song to the people by putting it on their lips, combining written transcription with oral recitation. The declared function of the song is to serve as a witness against Israel when they prosper in the land, feel smug, and apostatize, breaking YHWH's covenant and provoking him to impose his curse on them. Thus the song will join heaven and earth (30:19) as an objectified third party, testifying to God's covenant grace and Israel's failed response. The narrator notes that as a faithful covenant mediator Moses wrote down the words of the song that very day and taught it to the people, and verse 30 reiterates that Moses recited all the words of this song before the people until it was complete.

From the very beginning this song is ascribed canonical status. (1) It was dictated by YHWH, Israel's God. (2) It was immediately transcribed as a permanent written record. (3) It was intended to serve as a witness in the future, after the land has been conquered, the people have prospered, they have apostatized, and experienced the curses of the covenant. (4) The parenthetical comment in verse 21 specifically demands that it not be forgotten by the descendants of the present generation standing before Moses. Conclusion: This song

---

67. This statement clearly assumes canonical status for this Torah: (1) It was given to the Levites who carry the Ark of the Covenant of YHWH, hence associated with the Decalogue. (2) It was given to the elders who are charged to read the Torah before the people. (3) It was to be read at one of the annual festivals every seven years. (4) It was to be read at the place God would choose. (5) It was deemed applicable to all: men, women, children, and aliens. (6) It was to be read as long as they would dwell in the land; if they would be obedient, this meant forever.

68. Verse 19, כְּתְבוּ לָכֶם. Compare 17:18, though here the plural has all Israel in view. The pattern of theophany followed by verbal revelation recalls Israel's experience at Horeb. But this time YHWH's knowledge of the people's imminent rebellion precipitates the divine disclosure. This is the first time in the book anyone is commanded by God to write down anything.

is presented as Israel's national anthem. It is to stand in for Moses after his death, as a permanent witness to the grace of God and a perpetual challenge to Israel's covenantal fidelity.

Critical scholars tend to look at verses 24–29 as an editorial interpolation, but with Sonnet it is preferable to treat it as a description of another phase of the original event.[69] YHWH's aim here is to supplement the previously proclaimed and transcribed Torah, that is, Moses' second address. The fact that YHWH called Moses and Joshua into the Tent of Meeting to hear the words of this supplement and then to write them down highlights its importance. When they had completed the task, the song preserved in chapter 32 was attached to the original Torah (5:1b—26:19; 28:1–69 [Eng 29:1]) to produce the second edition of the Torah.[70] The supplementation accounts for the emphatic construction of verse 24, which has Moses writing down the [new] Torah until it was complete.[71]

According to verse 26, Moses commanded the Levites to receive "this Torah document" (סֵפֶר הַתּוֹרָה הַזֶּה) and place it beside the Ark of the Covenant. This statement reaffirms its canonical status and its divine authority/origin, but it distinguishes this Torah from the Decalogue, which was placed inside the Ark (10:5). By extension, the song's function as a permanent witness for YHWH and against Israel now applies to the entire Torah. After embedding the poem, the narrator announces that Moses taught the people all the words of this song and then challenged them to heed carefully all the words of this [supplemented] Torah, for in the Torah there is life.

---

69. See the detailed discussion by Sonnet, *The Book within the Book*, 158–67.

70. The emphatic construction compares with 5:22, where Moses notes that when YHWH declared the Decalogue, he added no more.

71. Moses finished writing the words of this Torah on a document until they (the words) were perfect (כְּכַלּוֹת מֹשֶׁה לִכְתֹּב אֶת־דִּבְרֵי הַתּוֹרָה־הַזֹּאת עַל־סֵפֶר עַד תֻּמָּם).

3. *From Spoken Word to Canonical Text: The Reconstruction*

Having examined all the internal factual evidence for the transcription of Moses' orations on the plains of Moab, we may now propose a reconstruction of the stages involved in the genesis of the book of Deuteronomy, paying particular attention to what the book actually tells us about its committal to writing.

a. According to the data provided by Deuteronomy, from their beginnings as the covenant people, the Israelites were "a people of the book." The evidence available suggests that the Decalogue was Israel's first "Bible," the nation's original canonical text.[72]

b. Following Moses' second address, which incorporated the Decalogue and consisted of 5:1b—26:19 and 28:1-68, this speech was transcribed in written form in its entirety in a סֵפֶר. This document was known from the beginning as "the Torah," or "this Torah." This was the document that future kings were to copy in the presence of the Levitical priests and read to restrain their pride (17:14-20).

---

72. Deuteronomy is silent on how the rest of the constitutional revelation at Sinai was received and/or transcribed. Exodus 24:1-11 highlights the role of a written "covenant document" (presumably Exod 20:22—23:33) in the covenant ratification ceremony at Sinai, but this is the only explicit clue. Exodus–Numbers leave few hints concerning how and under what circumstances the design of the Tabernacle (Exod 25-31), the sacrificial rituals and the laws regarding ceremonial cleanness (Lev 1-15), the "Holiness Code" (Lev 16-27), the miscellaneous regulations preserved in Numbers (4:1—11:10), and other ordinances scattered throughout the book, were committed to writing. However, it seems reasonable to suppose that when the Israelites left Sinai, they carried with them a series of written documents, all of which were deemed normative and canonical, and which were eventually combined with additional narrative materials and the speeches of Deuteronomy to produce the present Pentateuch. This interpretation of the transcription of the Sinai revelation is bolstered by occasional explicit references to Moses' scribal/writing activity in other contexts: Exod 17:14 (recording the victory over Amalek); Num 33:2 (keeping a journal of Israel's travels and camping places in the desert). The combination of transcription and recitation in the former recalls what Moses does with the Song of Moses/YHWH in Deut 31:14-22. For analogous ancient Mesopotamian examples of the accompaniment of written texts with oral recitation, see Waltke, "Oral Tradition" 22-23. Leiman (*Canonization of Hebrew Scripture*, 22) rightly notes that at times Deuteronomy presupposes the existence of the Sinai legislation (cf. 24:8 and Lev 13:1—14:57), but the book speaks explicitly only of the document that was recognized from the beginning to have been written by God himself (cf. Exod 34:1). All the remaining comments regarding the Torah and its transcription relate to Moses' addresses on the plains of Moab.

c. After another theophanic visitation and the divine dictation of the Song of YHWH (32:1–43), this document was transcribed and added to the Torah. The revised document became the new Torah, and was deposited beside the Ark in the custody of the Levitical priests. This was probably the Torah that Moses commanded Joshua to follow (Josh 1:7), "this book of the Torah" (סֵפֶר הַתּוֹרָה הַזֶּה) on which YHWH admonished Joshua to meditate day and night and to do according to everything written therein (1:8), the textual base of his sermon in Josh 23 (cf. v. 6), and the base for his covenant renewal ceremony at Shechem in Josh 24 (cf. vv. 26–27).

d. Although the book of Deuteronomy nowhere alludes to the transcription of Moses' first (1:6—4:40) and third (28:69 [Eng 29:1]–30:20) speeches, it is reasonable to suppose that they underwent a similar transcriptional/compositional history as the second speech for which hard data regarding the process are provided. Written versions of these addresses probably also existed separately for a time, and as a record of the speeches of Moses were probably stored beside the Ark of the Covenant as well.

e. As was the custom in the ancient world,[73] Moses issued his eloquent benediction for each of the tribes immediately prior to his death (33:2–29). This document was initially recorded on a separate scroll and stored separately from the rest of the book. When the compositional unit presently consisting of Exodus–Numbers was produced, the narrator of this material composed the narrative framework around the Benediction of the Tribes (32:48–52; 34:1–12) and added this unit to the large composition to complete the story of Moses, the principal figure, and making this the ending to the book of Numbers.[74]

---

73. Cf. Jacob's final benediction of his sons in Gen 49. It is reasonable to suppose that a written version of this blessing was produced prior to the time of Moses, but firm conclusions regarding this and other text units from Genesis are precluded by the absence of specific evidence of literary activity in the book.

74. Several considerations may be marshaled in support of this interpretation. (1) The form of the divine speech marker opening the literary unit in Deut 32:48 (וַיְדַבֵּר יְהוָה אֶל־מֹשֶׁה . . . לֵאמֹר), "and YHWH spoke to Moses . . . saying") is identical to Num 35:1 (and 34:1), but contrasts with the form of the divine speech marker elsewhere in Deuteronomy (וַיֹּאמֶר יְהוָה אֶל־מֹשֶׁה, "and YHWH said to Moses," 31:14, 16). (2) The content of Deut 32:48—34:12 provides a natural sequel to Num

f. The narrative preambles and conclusions were added to Moses' addresses, probably separately, that is before they were brought together in a single volume. 1:1–5 and 4:41–43 were composed as a narrative frame for the first address. 4:44—5:1a was added to the second address. 31:1–30 and 32:44–47 were composed as a narrative frame for the Song of Moses and inserted in the second address. 28:69—29:1a [Eng 29:1–2a] was added to the third address. 27:1–26 was composed to clarify the context of the covenantal renewal ceremony on Mount Ebal prepared for by Moses' third address. Later this chapter was inserted between chapters 26 and 28. This completed the process whereby Moses' final speeches on the plains of Moab (1:1—32:47) were transcribed, assembled, and united through narratorial stitching to produce the present form.

g. As the final stage in the genesis of Deuteronomy, this document (1:1—32:47) was inserted between Num 36:13 and Deut 32:48 to finalize the shape of the Pentateuch.

This reconstruction is complex and admittedly speculative. As an alternative, one may argue that a single editor/narrator collated the three independent speeches, added the narrative preambles to each speech, as well as the interpolations, including chapters 27 and 31. By this reconstruction 1:1–5 serves as a preamble not just for the first address but also for the entire book. This same editor could have been responsible for the parenthetical historical notes in the first speech,

---

36:13. (3) This conclusion to the block of material encompassing Exodus through Numbers (which is essentially a biography of Moses), consisting of an announcement of Moses' impending death (Deut 32:48–52), his blessing of the tribes (33:1–29), and the narrative of his death (34:1–12) creates a remarkable parallel with the ending of the patriarchal narratives in Genesis, which consists of an announcement of Jacob's impending death (Gen 47:27–31), his blessing of his sons (49:1–28), and the narrative of his death (49:29–33). With its focus on Joseph, Genesis 50 functions anticlimactically.

Although we reject Mark S. Smith's late dating of the book of Deuteronomy in particular and the Pentateuch as a whole, this interpretation compares with his hypothesis that by the priestly redaction of the Pentateuch the insertion of Deuteronomy at this point moved "the old story of Moses' death from the end of the old material in Numbers . . . to the end of Deuteronomy" (Smith, "Matters of Space and Time in Exodus and Numbers," 203). Cf. Weinfeld's proposal (*Deuteronomy 1–11*, 10) that Deut 32:48–52 represents a priestly passage that recaptures the priestly tradition of Moses' death in Num 27:12–14.

the notice of Moses' setting aside the cities of refuge in 4:41–43,[75] the note regarding the Levites and the Ark (10:6–9), and the account of Moses' death (32:48–52; 34:1–12).

Whatever the genesis of the book of Deuteronomy, contrary to Martin Noth and those who follow in his train, as those who have investigated issues of canon have recognized, the book does not function primarily as a preamble to the Deuteronomistic history. Rather, this book represents the final chapter in the story of God's call and deliverance of Israel, and the ending to the biography of Moses. Indeed, Deuteronomy ends the narrative begun in Gen 1:1.[76] This integration with the Pentateuch is evident not only in its logical and chronological placement after Numbers, but in the numerous intra-Pentateuchal textual connections.[77] In my view, the final narrator of Deuteronomy was probably the final narrator of the entire Pentateuch. This would account for the "deuteronomic" tone of much of Genesis–Numbers that critical scholars are finally beginning to recognize.[78] And if later historiographic works in the canon sound

75. Since Moses could not cross the Jordan, he appears to have taken special measures to ensure that the regulations previously revealed on the plains of Moab (Num 35) were fulfilled. But he had to leave it to Joshua to fulfill this command in Canaan.

76. Cf. Smith, "Matters of Space and Time in Exodus and Numbers," 182–207. J. W. Watts ("The Legal Characterization of Moses in the Rhetoric of the Pentateuch," 420) concludes, "the rhetorical structuring of the whole Pentateuch casts Deuteronomy as the concluding sanctions to the preceding stories (Genesis–Exod 19) and lists (Exod 20–Numbers)." This position is argued more fully by Watts in "Rhetorical Strategy in the Composition of the Pentateuch," 3–22.

77. Limitations of space prevent us from developing this theme more fully, but for a beginning Sonnet cites Deut 34:9, which refers back to Num 27:18, and 34:11, which echoes expressions from Exodus (Sonnet, *The Book within the Book*, 21–24).

78. Whereas in the past the separation of J and E strata and the early dating of these sources relative to Deuteronomy (usually tenth to ninth century BCE for J; eighth century BCE for E) were key tenets of critical orthodoxy, recent Pentateuchal scholarship recognizes significant links between Deuteronomy and JE. Indeed, some go so far as to deny the existence of J and E altogether. According to Blum, *Studien zur Komposition des Pentateuch*, 77–88, Deut 31:14–15, 23 and 34:10(–12) belong to a larger constellation including Exod 33–34 and Num 11–12. These texts derive from the so-called *D-Komposition*, a post-Deuteronomistic composition of the Pentateuch in the tradition of Deuteronomism. Blum's work has been influential for Albertz, *A History of Israelite Religion in the Old Testament Period*, 466–80, who recognizes only two traditional sources behind Genesis-Deuteronomy, and views the present Pentateuch as a compromise text between non-priestly and priestly traditional materials. The former (KD) consisted of the book of Deuteronomy and

like Deuteronomy, this is not because they were written by the same author, or because Deuteronomy was composed as a theological prologue to the Deuteronomistic History. Rather it is because their authors had been schooled in the "book of the Torah of Moses." As prophets after the order of Moses (Deut 18:14–22), later historians evaluated Israel's performance based upon the Mosaic Torah, and adopting the style and vocabulary of Deuteronomy.[79]

IV. Concluding Reflections

Limitations of time and space prevent us from exploring the time and circumstances in which the book of Deuteronomy as we know it might have been produced. Scholars divide on the question of the role that Moses might have had in the final production of the book. But I conclude this chapter by asking what effects a study like this might have for our understanding of the inspiration and authority of Scripture that 2 Tim 3:16 and our confessional statements claim for the entire OT. I would suggest several implications.

(1) We affirm the truthfulness of all that the Scriptures declare. When we interpret the Scriptures as they are intended to be understood, we will find them to be completely reliable preservers of truth. But this high view of the Scriptures means that we must let them say what they want to say, refusing on the one hand to diminish their affirmations, and on the other to exaggerate their claims. Moses' warning in Deut 4:2 to those who would be tempted to modify his own oral declarations extends to the entire written record: "You shall not add to the word that I command you, nor take from it; that you may keep the commandments of YHWH your God, which I command you."[80] Deuteronomy purports to preserve the *speeches* of Moses, and there is no reason to question this. But the truth is the author of the book did not leave his name. Expressions like "Book of Moses," and "Torah of Moses," do not demand that Moses' own

---

major portions of what the previous generation of scholars attributed to J and E. On the Deuteronomic character of much of JE see also Blenkinsopp, *The Pentateuch*, 186–94.

79. For an analysis of the distinctly Deuteronomic school of style and message and its persistence through the centuries evaluated against comparable stylistic traditions in Assyrian royal literary traditions, see Niehaus, "The Deuteronomic Style."

80. The NT book of Revelation ends with a similar prohibition (Rev 22:18–19).

hand produced the book. We do not doubt the historicity of Moses, the authenticity of his speeches, nor the fundamentally Mosaic authority behind the entire Pentateuch, any more than we question the authenticity of the speeches of Jesus in the Gospels. Nor do we doubt the fundamental Mosaic authority behind the entire book of Deuteronomy as we have it.

(2) We affirm that if Peter's characterization of prophecy as divine utterances by "men moved by the Holy Spirit" who "spoke from God" (2 Pet 1:21) applied to OT prophets in general, this was particularly true of Moses, the prophet *par excellence*.[81] And we affirm with 2 Tim 3:16 that the orations Moses delivered to the Israelites on the plains of Moab were inspired by God. At Sinai Moses himself recognized that he spoke for God (5:1–5), and the narrator of Deuteronomy explicitly extends that same divine inspiration to the context of his final addresses (28:69 [Eng 29:1]). Moses explicitly expressed his awareness of his own prophetic status (18:14–22); he declared to the people that he communicated with YHWH on a regular basis (3:23–29; 10:1); and the manner in which he spoke demonstrated that he viewed his own voice to be the voice of God (30:1–20).

(3) Whether we are considering the oral event or the written record, we must abandon tight mechanical theories about the process of inspiration. The truth is that inspiration covers a broad range of communicative activities. Most obviously, the notion of inspiration covers oral messages that YHWH himself declared to the people and texts that he himself delivered in written form. The Decalogue came to the people as written text, written by the finger of God.[82] But the notion of inspiration clearly also applies to texts that were dictated by God. Deuteronomy 32, mislabeled "Song of Moses," is really the "Song of YHWH," which God delivered orally to Moses and Joshua inside the tent of meeting, and then commanded Moses to record its words and to teach them to the people (31:19). The narrator notes that Moses complied perfectly in both respects. Indeed, it appears that when he emerged from the tent, he came out with the written text of the Song in his hands (31:24), and then taught it verbatim to

---

81. For a brief discussion of and bibliography on Moses' prophetic role, see Watts, "Moses in the Rhetoric of the Pentateuch," 418–22.

82. Deut 4:13; 10:2; cf. Exod 31:18; 32:15–16; 34:1, 28.

the people (31:30; cf. 32:44). Furthermore, the notion of inspiration applies to texts that purport to be spoken on God's behalf, even in the absence of explicit prophetic formulae. Formulae like "Thus has Adonai YHWH declared" (כֹּה־אָמַר אֲדֹנָי יְהוָה, the citation formula), "The word of YHWH came to me saying" (וַיְהִי דְבַר־יְהוָה אֵלַי לֵאמֹר, the word-event formula), and "the declaration of Adonai YHWH" (נְאֻם אֲדֹנָי יְהוָה, the signatory formula) are ubiquitous in the prophets, but they are never found in Deuteronomy. Nor do we ever find the formula, "Then YHWH spoke to Moses saying," so common in the narrative line of Exod 25–Num 19. But inspired messages [and texts] are not limited to utterances and writings that contain these "inspirational" formulae.[83] The notion of inspiration extends to the written record of inspired oral events. This includes the transcripts of the oral messages (Moses' three speeches and the poems in Deuteronomy) and the interpretive narrative framework around those transcripts. The book of Deuteronomy never claims for itself the inspiration claimed by the author of the poem of Erra and Ishum at the end of the composition: "The one who put together the composition about him [Erra] was Kabti-ilani-Marduk son of Dabibi. He [some god] revealed it to him in the middle of the night, and when he recited it upon waking, he did not miss anything out, nor add a single word to it. Erra heard it and approved it, and it was pleasing to Ishum who marches in front of him. All the other gods gave praise with him."[84]

Nevertheless, Moses himself recognized that he was not the last of the inspired prophets (18:14–22). Surely the narrator of the book, on whom we are ultimately dependent for our own assessment of Moses, was a "prophet like Moses."[85] Moses' biographer has provided the inspired narrative filter through which to understand the man and his message. If one of the tests of a true prophet was conformity to the Mosaic revelation, this test certainly applied to the canonical author/editor of the book. In view of these considerations, we affirm that the process of inspiration encompasses YHWH's original guidance of the thoughts of Moses, Moses' oral communication of the

83. This has implications for our understanding of Paul's words in 1 Cor 7:6, 25 and 2 Cor 8:8.

84. As translated by Dalley, *COS* 1:415.

85. Cf. Polzin's extension of the "prophet like Moses" to the narrator of the Deuteronomic History (*Moses and the Deuteronomist*, 61).

message to the people, Moses' transcription of the message to text, and finally the collation and editing of those texts.[86]

(4) We do well to distinguish between inspiration and canonicity. With Paul we affirm that all canonical Scripture is inspired (literally "God-breathed"), but this does not mean that all inspired messages were deemed canonical, to be preserved in writing as normative for the community of faith for all time. According to 1 Chr 28:11–19, YHWH revealed to David in detail the plan of the Temple and he made him understand it in writing by his hand upon him (v. 19). This plan was obviously inspired, but it has not been preserved either as a separate document or as an embedded text. It is possible, if not probable, that in his last days with the people Moses delivered more than three addresses on the Plains of Moab, and that the three speeches preserved in Deuteronomy are actually condensations of longer addresses. The narrator makes no claim to have preserved every word that Moses spoke on the plains of Moab. But under the inspiration of God he has preserved the essence of Moses' preaching.

(5) The notion of "autographs," an expression that theologians apply to "the first or original copies of the biblical documents,"[87] is not as tidy as many claim. On the one hand, the Masoretic Text that provides the base for our biblical study is the product of a millennium of copying after the OT canon was closed, and, if our dating of the composition of Deuteronomy is correct, more than two millennia of copying since the book was produced.[88]

This raises an important question: Is the task of textual criticism to establish the text as it stood at the time the canon was closed, or as it stood when the book of Deuteronomy as a unitary literary work was composed and accepted as normative for Israel's faith, cult, and conduct? On the other hand, even if autographs are defined as "the first or original copies of the biblical documents," what do we mean by "biblical documents"? Does the expression refer to the individual speeches of Moses transcribed on separate parchment scrolls by Moses' own hand and recognized immediately to be canonical?

86. Compare the NT declaration in John 20:30–31.

87. Cf. Grudem, *Systematic Theology*, 96.

88. This contrasts with many of the documents the archaeologists' spades have unearthed.

Or the collection of the three speeches on one scroll? Or the edited version of the book of Deuteronomy, complete with its narratorial stitching? Or the grammatically updated version of the book? Or the Pentateuch as we have it, with Deuteronomy as the last book? The complexity of the process whereby biblical books were produced complicates the issue.

(6) In the revelation of YHWH at Sinai and the scribal activity of Moses we witness an oft-overlooked but extraordinary providential moment. Historians have often observed that among the reasons the gospel was able to spread so rapidly in the first century were the establishment of Greek as the language of international intercourse and the Roman construction of a system of roads throughout the empire. Similarly, students of the Reformation have noted that Luther's radical ideas would never have taken root in Europe had the printing press with movable type not just been invented to make the rapid and wide dissemination of his ideas possible. When we look back on the history of civilization we must recognize in the timing of God's self-revelation at Sinai and in his call of Moses as the agent through whom his grace would be mediated a moment of equal providential significance.

A previous generation of scholars objected to the Mosaic authorship of the Pentateuch on the grounds that it required a level of literacy inaccessible to him. It is true that the complexity of hieroglyphics in Egypt and cuneiform in Mesopotamia, both of which took a lifetime to learn, guaranteed literacy for only a privileged few. But what is often overlooked by students of culture is that "in the fullness of time," in the middle of the second millennium BCE, at precisely the right time, the Canaanites were developing a system of writing whereby all the sounds of their language could be represented in writing by fewer than two dozen symbols. To quote the judgment of W. F. Albright, this meant that "the 22 letter alphabet could be learned in a day or two by a bright student and in a week or two by the dullest; hence it could spread with great rapidity. I do not doubt for a moment that there were many urchins . . . who could read and write as early as the time of the Judges."[89] Albright went on to express doubt that the

---

89. Albright, *Discussion*, 122–23. For a superb discussion of the date and circumstances of the invention of the alphabet see G. J. Hamilton, "Alphabet," an unpublished and undated paper based on his unpublished doctoral dissertation,

script was used for formal literature until later. But Alan Millard has effectively dispelled such doubts. After examining the extra-biblical evidence from the Late Bronze Age, Millard concludes, "There was literary activity in the Levant covering a wide range of texts and the scribes were clearly capable of producing books."[90] This is remarkable. God was using the Canaanites to prepare the way for his appearance at Sinai and for Moses' scribal work. By an act of uncommon grace YHWH, Israel's "uniquely communicative Deity,"[91] chose the very people the Israelites were to destroy to be the agents that would make possible the transcription and mass communication of his revelation and Moses' interpretation thereof. In the providence of God, the same people who provided Israel with the linguistic vehicle of communication, "the lip of Canaan" (Isa 19:18), also provided them with the graphic vehicle for the dissemination of his truth.

Debate concerning the provenance and authorship of all of the books of the OT will continue until we discover the names of the persons whose hands actually produced the biblical books. Given the Israelites' apparent disinclination to erect permanent memorials to any of their achievements and the more general hesitation of ancient Near Eastern poets and authors to identify themselves, this prospect is highly unlikely. In the meantime we are left at the mercy of the internal witness of the texts themselves. The book of Deuteronomy is unequivocal in declaring that Moses' voice is to be heard in the speeches of the book. It is equally clear in its assertion of Mosaic involvement in the transcription of at least one of those speeches.

If one can accept these basic facts and acknowledge that the person responsible for producing the book of Deuteronomy was a prophet "like unto Moses," then later Israelites who spoke of the "Book of the Torah of Moses," accurately recalled the source and authority of the book of Deuteronomy. No one in the history of the nation, save our Lord Jesus Christ himself, ever spoke with such authority. No one in the history of the nation, save our Lord Jesus Christ, had such access to the mind of God. No one in the history of the nation, save

---

"Development of the Early Alphabet." I am grateful to my colleague Peter Gentry for drawing this study to my attention.

90. "Books in the Late Bronze Age in the Levant," 179.

91. An epithet employed by A. R. Millard in "Mass Communication and Scriptural Proclamation," 70. Cf. Deut 4:5–8, 11–14; *et passim*.

our Lord Jesus Christ, left a more authoritative legacy of truth for the world. No one in the history of the nation, save our Lord Jesus Christ, had a more profound influence in shaping the vocabulary of spiritual speech for the people of God. With the Israelites of old and the Jewish rabbis of our own time we give praise to God for the man Moses, and the written record of his valedictory addresses on the Plains of Moab.

The book of Deuteronomy is the heart of the Torah, which the priests were to teach and model,[92] which psalmists praised,[93] to which the prophets appealed,[94] by which faithful kings ruled,[95] and righteous citizens lived (Ps 1). In short, this book provides the theological base for virtually the entire Old (and New) Testament and the paradigm for much of its literary style.[96] May we in our day discover anew in the book of Deuteronomy the divinely breathed, hence living and transforming, Scripture of which the NT Moses, the Apostle Paul, spoke in 2 Tim 3:16. And may we, like Paul, find in the "Book of the Torah of Moses" a sure and effective instrument of teaching, reproof, correction, training in righteousness, and equipping for every good work to the glory of God.

---

92. Deut 33:10; 2 Chr 15:3; 19:8; Mal 2:6, 9; cf. Jer 18:18; Ezek 7:26; Ezra 7:10.

93. Pss 19:8–15 [Eng 7–14]; 119; etc.

94. Isa 1:10; 5:24; 8:20; 30:9; 51:7.

95. 1 Kgs 2:2–4; 2 Kgs 14:6; 22:11; 23:25.

96. Lest some miss the point, our interpretation of the genesis of Deuteronomy differs sharply from the higher critical conclusions proposed by Wellhausen, von Rad, et al., on several significant counts: (1) We date the book as a whole at least four centuries earlier than prevailing scholarship ascribes to the earliest part of the book, the so-called Deuteronomic Code (12:1—26:19). (2) We accept that Moses was a historical figure as described in the Pentateuch, and that the book of Deuteronomy actually preserves his speeches. (3) We take the internal evidence of the book seriously and reject a pseudepigraphic interpretation. In trying to let the text say what it wants about its own genesis, our interpretation is in complete accordance with Paragraph 4 of "A Short Statement" that precedes the "Articles of Affirmation and Denial" in "The Chicago Statement on Biblical Inerrancy": "Being wholly and verbally God-given, Scripture is without error or fault . . . in what it states . . . about its own literary origins under God." See "Appendix," in Geisler, *Inerrancy*, 494.

Excursus A

The Voices in Deuteronomy (RSV modified)

I. YHWH's Voice in Deuteronomy

31:14b   And YHWH said to Moses, *"Behold, the days approach when you must die; call Joshua, and present yourselves in the tent of meeting, that I may commission him."*

31:16b–21 ¹⁶And YHWH said to Moses, *"Behold, you are about to sleep with your fathers; then this people will rise and play the harlot after the strange gods of the land, where they go to be among them, and they will forsake me and break my covenant which I have made with them. ¹⁷Then my anger will be kindled against them in that day, and I will forsake them and hide my face from them, and they will be devoured; and many evils and troubles will come upon them, so that they will say in that day, 'Have not these evils come upon us because our God is not among us?' ¹⁸And I will surely hide my face in that day on account of all the evil which they have done, because they have turned to other gods. ¹⁹Now therefore* **write** *this song, and teach it to the people of Israel; put it in their mouths, that this song may be a witness for me against the people of Israel. ²⁰For when I have brought them into the land flowing with milk and honey, which I swore to give to their fathers, and they have eaten and are full and grown fat, they will turn to other gods and serve them, and despise me and break my covenant. ²¹And when many evils and troubles have come upon*

them, this song shall confront them as a witness (for it will
live unforgotten in the mouths of their descendants); for I
know the purposes which they are already forming, before I
have brought them into the land that I swore to give."

31:23b   And YHWH commissioned Joshua the son of Nun and
said, *"Be strong and of good courage; for you shall bring
the descendants of Israel into the land which I swore to give
them: I will be with you."*

32:49–52   [48]And YHWH spoke to Moses that very day, [49]*"Ascend this
mountain of the Abarim, Mount Nebo, which is in the land
of Moab, opposite Jericho; and view the land of Canaan,
which I give to the people of Israel for a possession; [50]and
die on the mountain which you ascend, and be gathered
to your people, as Aaron your brother died in Mount Hor
and was gathered to his people; [51]because you broke faith
with me in the midst of the people of Israel at the waters of
Meribath-kadesh, in the wilderness of Zin; because you did
not revere me as holy in the midst of the people of Israel.
[52]For you shall see the land before you; but you shall not go
there, into the land which I give to the people of Israel."*

34:4b   And YHWH said to him, *"This is the land of which I swore
to Abraham, to Isaac, and to Jacob, 'I will give it to your
descendants.' I have let you see it with your eyes, but you
shall not go over there."*

II. Moses' Voice in Deuteronomy

A. Moses' Lone Voice

1:6—4:40	Moses' First Address: Historical Background to the Covenant
4:44—26:19 28:1–69 [Eng 29:1]	Moses' Second Address: The Stipulations of the Covenant
27:11–26	Moses' Short Imprecatory Address: The Covenant Blessings and Curses
29:1 [Eng 2]—30:20	Moses' Third Address: The Call for Covenant Renewal
32:1–43	The Song of YHWH: Israel's National Anthem
32:46b–47	Moses' Final Exhortation
33:2–29	The Blessing of Moses

B. Moses' Accompanied Voice

27:1–8	Now Moses and the elders of Israel commanded the people, saying, *"Keep all the commandment which I command you this day . . ."*
27:9–10	And Moses and the Levitical priests said to all Israel, *"Keep silence and hear, O Israel: this day you have become the people of YHWH your God. ¹⁰You shall therefore obey the voice of YHWH your God, keeping his commandments and his statutes, which I command you this day."*

III. The Narrator's Voice in Deuteronomy

1:1–5	¹These are the words that Moses spoke to all Israel beyond the Jordan in the wilderness, in the Arabah over against Suph, between Paran and Tophel, Laban, Hazeroth, and Dizahab. ²It is eleven days' journey from Horeb by the way of Mount Seir to Kadeshbarnea. ³And in the fortieth year, on the first day of the eleventh month, Moses spoke to the

people of Israel according to all that YHWH had given him in commandment to them, [4]after he had defeated Sihon the king of the Amorites, who lived in Heshbon, and Og the king of Bashan, who lived in Ashtaroth and in Edrei. [5]Beyond the Jordan, in the land of Moab, Moses undertook to explain this Torah, saying, . . .

2:10–12   [10](The Emim formerly lived there, a people great and many, and tall as the Anakim; [11]like the Anakim they are also known as Rephaim, but the Moabites call them Emim. [12]The Horites also lived in Seir formerly, but the sons of Esau dispossessed them, and destroyed them from before them, and settled in their stead; as Israel did to the land of their possession, which YHWH gave to them.)

2:20–23   [20](That also is known as a land of Rephaim; Rephaim formerly lived there, but the Ammonites call them Zamzummim, [21]a people great and many, and tall as the Anakim; but YHWH destroyed them before them; and they dispossessed them, and settled in their stead; [22]as he did for the sons of Esau, who live in Seir, when he destroyed the Horites before them, and they dispossessed them, and settled in their stead even to this day. [23]As for the Avvim, who lived in villages as far as Gaza, the Caphtorim, who came from Caphtor, destroyed them and settled in their stead.)

3:9   (The Sidonians call Hermon Sirion, while the Amorites call it Senir.)

3:11   (For only Og the king of Bashan was left of the remnant of the Rephaim; behold, his bedstead was a bedstead of iron; is it not in Rabbah of the Ammonites? Nine cubits was its length, and four cubits its breadth, according to the common cubit.)

3:13b–14   (The whole of that Bashan is called the land of Rephaim. [14]Jair the Manassite took all the region of Argob, that is, Bashan, as far as the border of the Geshurites and the

Maacathites, and called the villages after his own name, Havvothjair, as it is to this day.)

4:41–43 ⁴¹Then Moses set apart three cities in the east beyond the Jordan, ⁴²that the manslayer might flee there, who kills his neighbor unintentionally, without being at enmity with him in time past, and that by fleeing to one of these cities he might save his life: ⁴³Bezer in the wilderness on the tableland for the Reubenites, and Ramoth in Gilead for the Gadites, and Golan in Bashan for the Manassites.

4:44—5:1a ⁴⁴This is the Torah which Moses set before the descendants of Israel; ⁴⁵these are the covenant stipulations, the ordinances, and the laws which Moses spoke to the descendants of Israel when they came out of Egypt, ⁴⁶beyond the Jordan in the valley opposite Bethpeor, in the land of Sihon the king of the Amorites, who lived at Heshbon, whom Moses and the descendants of Israel defeated when they came out of Egypt. ⁴⁷And they took possession of his land and the land of Og the king of Bashan, the two kings of the Amorites, who lived to the east beyond the Jordan; ⁴⁸from Aroer, which is on the edge of the valley of the Arnon, as far as Mount Sirion (that is, Hermon), ⁴⁹together with all the Arabah on the east side of the Jordan as far as the Sea of the Arabah, under the slopes of Pisgah. ⁵:¹ And Moses summoned all Israel, and said to them, . . .

10:6–9 ⁶(The people of Israel journeyed from Beeroth Benejaakan to Moserah. There Aaron died, and there he was buried; and his son Eleazar ministered as priest in his stead. ⁷From there they journeyed to Gudgodah, and from Gudgodah to Jotbathah, a land with brooks of water. ⁸At that time YHWH set apart the tribe of Levi to carry the ark of the covenant of YHWH, to stand before YHWH to minister to him and to bless in his name, to this day. ⁹Therefore Levi has no portion or inheritance with his brothers; YHWH is his inheritance, as YHWH your God said to him.)

27:1a   Now Moses and the elders of Israel commanded the people, saying, . . .

27:9a   Moses and the Levitical priests said to all Israel, . . .

27:11   And Moses charged the people the same day, saying, . . .

28:68   These are the words of the covenant which YHWH commanded Moses to make with the people of Israel in the land of Moab, besides the covenant which he had made with them at Horeb. [Eng 29:1]

29:1   And Moses summoned all Israel and said to them, . . . [Eng 29:2a]

31:1–2a   So Moses continued to speak these words to all Israel. ²And he said to them, . . .

31:7a   Then Moses summoned Joshua, and said to him in the sight of all Israel, . . .

31:9–10a And Moses *wrote* this Torah, and gave it to the priests the sons of Levi, who carried the ark of the covenant of YHWH, and to all the elders of Israel. ¹⁰And Moses commanded them, . . .

31:14a   And YHWH said to Moses, . . .

31:14c–16a And Moses and Joshua went and presented themselves in the tent of meeting. ¹⁵And YHWH appeared in the tent in a pillar of cloud; and the pillar of cloud stood by the door of the tent. ¹⁶And YHWH said to Moses, . . .

31:22–23a So Moses *wrote* this song the same day, and taught it to the people of Israel. ²³And YHWH commissioned Joshua the son of Nun and said, . . .

31:24–25 When Moses had finished *writing* the words of this Torah in a book, to the very end, ²⁵Moses commanded the Levites who carried the ark of the covenant of YHWH, saying, . . .

31:30   Then Moses spoke the words of this song until they were finished, in the ears of all the assembly of Israel, . . .

32:44–46a Moses came and recited all the words of this song in the hearing of the people, he and Joshua the son of Nun. [45]And when Moses had finished speaking all these words to all Israel, [46]he said to them, . . .

32:48   And YHWH spoke to Moses that very day, . . .

33:1–2a   This is the blessing with which Moses the man of God blessed the descendants of Israel before his death. [2]He said, . . .

34:1–4a   And Moses went up from the plains of Moab to Mount Nebo, to the top of Pisgah, which is opposite Jericho. And YHWH showed him all the land, Gilead as far as Dan, [2]all Naphtali, the land of Ephraim and Manasseh, all the land of Judah as far as the Western Sea, [3]the Negeb, and the Plain, that is, the valley of Jericho the city of palm trees, as far as Zoar. [4]And YHWH said to him, . . .

34:5–12   So Moses the servant of YHWH died there in the land of Moab, according to the word of YHWH, [6]and he buried him in the valley in the land of Moab opposite Bethpeor; but no man knows the place of his burial to this day. [7]Moses was a hundred and twenty years old when he died; his eye was not dim, nor his natural force abated. [8]And the people of Israel wept for Moses in the plains of Moab thirty days; then the days of weeping and mourning for Moses were ended. [9]And Joshua the son of Nun was full of the spirit of wisdom, for Moses had laid his hands upon him; so the people of Israel obeyed him, and did as YHWH had commanded Moses. [10]And there has not arisen a prophet since in Israel like Moses, whom YHWH knew face to face, [11]none like him for all the signs and the wonders which YHWH sent him to do in the land of Egypt, to Pharaoh and to all his servants and to all his land, [12]and for all the mighty power and all the great and terrible deeds which Moses wrought in the sight of all Israel.

Excursus B

Evidence for Writing in the Book of Deuteronomy

I. The Decalogue: Israel's Earliest Canon

4:12–14   [12]"Then YHWH spoke to you out of the midst of the fire; you heard the sound of words, but saw no form; there was only a voice. [13]And he declared to you his covenant, which he commanded you to perform, that is, the *ten words*; and he *wrote* them upon two tables of stone. [14]And YHWH commanded me at that time to teach you statutes and ordinances, that you might do them in the land which you are going over to possess."

5:22   "These words YHWH spoke to all your assembly at the mountain out of the midst of the fire, the cloud, and the thick darkness, with a loud voice; and he added no more. And he *wrote* them upon two tables of stone, and gave them to me."

9:9–17   [9]"When I went up the mountain to receive the tables of stone, the tables of the covenant which YHWH made with you, I remained on the mountain forty days and forty nights; I neither ate bread nor drank water. [10]And YHWH gave me the two tables of stone *written* with the finger of God; and on them were all the words which YHWH had spoken with you on the mountain out of the midst of the fire on the day of the assembly. [11]And at the end of forty days and forty nights YHWH gave me the two tables of stone, the tables of the covenant. [12]Then YHWH

59

said to me, 'Arise, go down quickly from here; for your people whom you have brought from Egypt have acted corruptly; they have turned aside quickly out of the way which I commanded them; they have made themselves a molten image.' ¹³Furthermore YHWH said to me, 'I have seen this people, and behold, it is a stubborn people; ¹⁴let me alone, that I may destroy them and blot out their name from under heaven; and I will make of you a nation mightier and greater than they.' ¹⁵So I turned and came down from the mountain, and the mountain was burning with fire; and the two tables of the covenant were in my two hands. ¹⁶And I looked, and behold, you had sinned against YHWH your God; you had made yourselves a molten calf; you had turned aside quickly from the way which YHWH had commanded you. ¹⁷So I took hold of the two tables, and cast them out of my two hands, and broke them before your eyes."

10:1–5 ¹"At that time YHWH said to me, 'Hew two tables of stone like the first, and come up to me on the mountain, and make an ark of wood. ²And I will *write* on the tables the words that were on the first tables which you broke, and you shall put them in the ark.' ³So I made an ark of acacia wood, and hewed two tables of stone like the first, and went up the mountain with the two tables in my hand. ⁴And he *wrote* on the tables, as at the first writing, the *ten words* which YHWH had spoken to you on the mountain out of the midst of the fire on the day of the assembly; and YHWH gave them to me. ⁵Then I turned and came down from the mountain, and put the tables in the ark which I had made; and there they are, as YHWH commanded me.

II. The Torah of Moses: First Edition

A. *References to the Written Torah in Moses' Second Address (Deut 5–26; 28)*

6:6–9   ⁶"And these words which I command you this day shall be upon your heart; ⁷and you shall teach them diligently to your children, and shall talk of them when you sit in your house, and when you walk by the way, and when you lie down, and when you rise. ⁸And you shall bind them as a sign upon your hand, and they shall be as frontlets between your eyes. ⁹And you shall *write* them on the doorposts of your house and on your gates."

11:18–21   ¹⁸"You shall therefore lay up these words of mine in your heart and in your soul; and you shall bind them as a sign upon your hand, and they shall be as frontlets between your eyes. ¹⁹And you shall teach them to your children, talking of them when you are sitting in your house, and when you are walking by the way, and when you lie down, and when you rise. ²⁰And you shall *write* them upon the doorposts of your house and upon your gates, ²¹that your days and the days of your children may be multiplied in the land which YHWH swore to your fathers to give them, as long as the heavens are above the earth."

17:18–20   ¹⁸"And when he sits on the throne of his kingdom, he shall *write* for himself in a book a copy of this Torah, from that which is in the charge of the Levitical priests; ¹⁹and it shall be with him, and he shall read in it all the days of his life, that he may learn to fear YHWH his God, by keeping all the words of this Torah and these decrees, and doing them; ²⁰that his heart may not be lifted up above his brethren, and that he may not turn aside from the commandment, either to the right hand or to the left; so that he may continue long in his kingdom, he and his children, in Israel."

28:58–61   ⁵⁸"If you are not careful to do all the words of this Torah which are *written* in this book, that you may fear this glo-

rious and awful name, YHWH your God, [59] then YHWH
will bring on you and your offspring extraordinary afflictions, afflictions severe and lasting, and sicknesses griev-
ous and lasting. [60] And he will bring upon you again all the
diseases of Egypt, which you were afraid of; and they shall
cleave to you. [61] Every sickness also, and every affliction
which is not *written* in the book of this Torah, YHWH
will bring upon you, until you are destroyed."

B. References to the Written Torah in Deuteronomy 27

27:1–8   [1] Now Moses and the elders of Israel commanded the
people, saying, "Keep all the commandment which I
command you this day. [2] And on the day you pass over
the Jordan to the land which YHWH your God gives
you, you shall set up large stones, and plaster them with
plaster; [3] and you shall *write* upon them all the words of
this Torah, when you pass over to enter the land which
YHWH your God gives you, a land flowing with milk and
honey, as YHWH, the God of your fathers, has promised
you. [4] And when you have passed over the Jordan, you
shall set up these stones, concerning which I command
you this day, on Mount Ebal, and you shall plaster them
with plaster. [5] And there you shall build an altar to YHWH
your God, an altar of stones; you shall lift up no iron tool
upon them. [6] You shall build an altar to YHWH your God
of unhewn stones; and you shall offer burnt offerings on
it to YHWH your God; [7] and you shall sacrifice peace offerings, and shall eat there; and you shall rejoice before
YHWH your God. [8] And you shall *write* upon the stones
all the words of this Torah very plainly."

C. References to the Written Torah in Moses' Third Address (Deut 29–30)

29:13–18   [Eng 14–19] [14] "Nor is it with you only that I make this
sworn covenant, [15] but with him who is not here with us
this day as well as with him who stands here with us this

day before YHWH our God. [16]You know how we dwelt in the land of Egypt, and how we came through the midst of the nations through which you passed; [17]and you have seen their detestable things, their idols of wood and stone, of silver and gold, which were among them. [18]Beware lest there be among you a man or woman or family or tribe, whose heart turns away this day from YHWH our God to go and serve the gods of those nations; lest there be among you a root bearing poisonous and bitter fruit, [19]one who, when he hears the words of this sworn covenant, blesses himself in his heart, saying, 'I shall be safe, though I walk in the stubbornness of my heart.' This would lead to the sweeping away of moist and dry alike. [20]YHWH would not pardon him, but rather the anger of YHWH and his jealousy would smoke against that man, and the curses *written* in this book would settle upon him, and YHWH would blot out his name from under heaven. [21]And YHWH would single him out from all the tribes of Israel for calamity, in accordance with all the curses of the covenant *written* in this book of the Torah."

[22]"And the generation to come, your children who rise up after you, and the foreigner who comes from a far land, would say, when they see the afflictions of that land and the sicknesses with which YHWH has made it sick— [23]the whole land brimstone and salt, and a burnt-out waste, unsown, and growing nothing, where no grass can sprout, an overthrow like that of Sodom and Gomorrah, Admah and Zeboiim, which YHWH overthrew in his anger and wrath—[24]yea, all the nations would say, 'Why has YHWH done thus to this land? What means the heat of this great anger?' [25]Then men would say, 'It is because they forsook the covenant of YHWH, the God of their fathers, which he made with them when he brought them out of the land of Egypt, [26]and went and served other gods and worshiped them, gods whom they had not known and whom he had not allotted to them; [27]therefore the anger of YHWH was kindled against this land, bringing upon it all the curses *written* in this book; [28]and YHWH

uprooted them from their land in anger and fury and great wrath, and cast them into another land, as at this day.' ²⁹The secret things belong to YHWH our God; but the things that are revealed belong to us and to our children for ever, that we may do all the words of this Torah."

30:8–14   ⁸"And you shall again obey the voice of YHWH, and keep all his commandments which I command you this day. ⁹YHWH your God will make you abundantly prosperous in all the work of your hand, in the fruit of your body, and in the fruit of your cattle, and in the fruit of your ground; for YHWH will again take delight in prospering you, as he took delight in your fathers, ¹⁰if you obey the voice of YHWH your God, to keep his commandments and his decrees which are *written* in this book of the Torah, if you turn to YHWH your God with all your heart and with all your soul. ¹¹For this commandment which I command you this day is not too hard for you, neither is it far off. ¹²It is not in heaven, that you should say, 'Who will go up for us to heaven, and bring it to us, that we may hear it and do it?' ¹³Neither is it beyond the sea, that you should say, 'Who will go over the sea for us, and bring it to us, that we may hear it and do it?' ¹⁴But the word is very near you; it is in your heart, so that you can do it."

III. The Torah of Moses: Second Edition (Deut 31:1—32:47)

31:1–8   ¹"So Moses continued to speak these words to all Israel. ²And he said to them, "I am a hundred and twenty years old this day; I am no longer able to go out and come in. YHWH has said to me, 'You shall not go over this Jordan.' ³YHWH your God himself will go over before you; he will destroy these nations before you, so that you shall dispossess them; and Joshua will go over at your head, as YHWH has spoken. ⁴And YHWH will do to them as he did to Sihon and Og, the kings of the Amorites, and to their land, when he destroyed them. ⁵And YHWH will give them over to you, and you shall do to them according to all the commandment which I have commanded you. ⁶Be strong and of good courage, do not fear or be in dread of them: for it is YHWH your God who goes with you; he will not fail you or forsake you." ⁷Then Moses summoned Joshua, and said to him in the sight of all Israel, "Be strong and of good courage; for you shall go with this people into the land which YHWH has sworn to their fathers to give them; and you shall put them in possession of it. ⁸It is YHWH who goes before you; he will be with you, he will not fail you or forsake you; do not fear or be dismayed."

31:9–13 ⁹And Moses *wrote* this Torah, and gave it to the priests the sons of Levi, who carried the ark of the covenant of YHWH, and to all the elders of Israel. ¹⁰And Moses commanded them, "At the end of every seven years, at the set time of the year of release, at the feast of booths, ¹¹when all Israel comes to appear before YHWH your God at the place which he will choose, you shall read this Torah before all Israel in their hearing. ¹²Assemble the people, men, women, and little ones, and the sojourner within your towns, that they may hear and learn to fear YHWH your God, and be careful to do all the words of this Torah, ¹³and that their children, who have not known it, may hear and learn to fear YHWH your God, as long as you live in the land which you are going over the Jordan to possess."

31:14–22 ¹⁴And YHWH said to Moses, "Behold, the days approach when you must die; call Joshua, and present yourselves in the tent of meeting, that I may commission him." And Moses and Joshua went and presented themselves in the tent of meeting. ¹⁵And YHWH appeared in the tent in a pillar of cloud; and the pillar of cloud stood by the door of the tent. ¹⁶And YHWH said to Moses, "Behold, you are about to sleep with your fathers; then this people will rise and play the harlot after the strange gods of the land, where they go to be among them, and they will forsake me and break my covenant which I have made with them. [17]Then my anger will be kindled against them in that day, and I will forsake them and hide my face from them, and they will be devoured; and many evils and troubles will come upon them, so that they will say in that day, 'Have not these evils come upon us because our God is not among us?' [18]And I will surely hide my face in that day on account of all the evil which they have done, because they have turned to other gods. [19]Now therefore *write* this song, and teach it to the people of Israel; put it in their mouths, that this song may be a witness for me against the people of Israel. [20]For when I have brought them into the land flowing with milk and honey, which I swore to give to their fathers, and they have eaten and are full and grown fat, they will turn to other gods and serve them, and despise me and break my covenant. [21]And when many evils and troubles have come upon them, this song shall confront them as a witness (for it will live unforgotten in the mouths of their descendants); for I know the purposes which they are already forming, before I have brought them into the land that I swore to give." [22]So Moses *wrote* this song the same day, and taught it to the people of Israel.

31:23   [23]And YHWH commissioned Joshua the son of Nun and said, "Be strong and of good courage; for you shall bring the descendants of Israel into the land which I swore to give them: I will be with you."

31:24–29   [24]When Moses had finished *writing* the words of this Torah in a book, to the very end, [25]Moses commanded the Levites who carried the ark of the covenant of YHWH, [26]"Take this book of the Torah, and put it by the side of the ark of the covenant of YHWH your God, that it may be there for a witness against you. [27]For I know how rebellious and stubborn you are; behold, while I am yet alive with you, today you have been rebellious against YHWH; how much more after my death! [28]Assemble to me all the elders of your tribes, and your officers, that I may speak these words in their ears and call heaven and earth to witness against them. [29]For I know that after my death you will surely act corruptly, and turn aside from the way which I have commanded you; and in the days to come evil will befall you, because you will do what is evil in the sight of YHWH, provoking him to anger through the work of your hands."

31:30   [30]Then Moses spoke the words of this song until they were finished, in the ears of all the assembly of Israel.

3

Will the Real Moses Please Rise?

An Exploration into the Role and Ministry of Moses in the Book of Deuteronomy [1]

Introduction

IN THE 1960S THERE was a popular television show in the United States in which a host would interview four characters, three of whom pretended to be the mystery person and the fourth who actually was. Based on the comments of these individuals the audience would have to identify which of the candidates was the actual celebrity of the night. After the verdict of the people was in, the host would announce: "Will the real so-and-so please stand up?" As I have been poring over the book of Deuteronomy for the last ten years I have frequently found myself waiting for the host to call out: "Will the real Moses please stand up?"

The question is appropriate to this investigation, inasmuch as the Hebrew expression, קוּם, "to rise," (hiphil, הֵקִים) is applied to Moses several times in the book of Deuteronomy. In 18:15 Moses says, "YHWH your God will raise up (הֵקִים) for you a prophet like me from among you, from your brothers." And in the epitaph at the end, the narrator observes, "Never has a prophet like Moses risen (קוּם) in Israel." So when we ask, "Will the real Moses please stand up?" we actually get our cue for framing the question from the biblical text.

---

1. An earlier version of this paper was presented to the Pentateuch Section of the Evangelical Theological Society in Atlanta, November 18, 2010.

68

But how should we answer the question? While scholars generally recognize that Moses played many roles,[2] if one asks, "Who is the Moses we encounter in the book of Deuteronomy?" most will say his primary role was that of Israel's lawgiver. This was the answer of the producers of the six-part, 360 minute-long 1974 miniseries, *Moses the Lawgiver* directed by Gianfranco De Bosio and James H. Hill, and starring Burt Lancaster, among others. This is also the view of visual artists, who typically depict him holding massive tablets on which were inscribed the ten foundational words of the covenant.[3] And it is the perception of who write about Moses, whether they be populist authors like Thomas Keneally or Julius Leibert,[4] on the one hand, and biblical scholars like George W. Coats, on the other. In a focused study on Moses, Coats wrote, "in the book of Deuteronomy and in the Deuteronomistic Historian, the operative image of Moses builds on issues of power and authority. Moses is the lawgiver."[5] This view has a long history. Among the many names the rabbis had for Moses we find Měhōqēq (*Baba Bathra* 15a). The epithet is based on Deut 33:21, where the pual participle מְחֹקֵק, from חָקַק, "to decree, legislate,"[6] occurs in Moses' blessing of Gad, presumably with the sense of "legislator," even though it does not refer to Moses himself.[7]

The book of Deuteronomy offers some support for the perception of Moses primarily as a legal figure. First, the name of the book, "Deuteronomy," which goes back to the Septuagint's Τὸ Δευτερονόμιον, "second law," suggests a legal document. Since Moses was the primary hand behind the book, he is naturally viewed as the lawgiver. Second, critical junctures in the book invite readers to expect legislation:

2. Roles suggested include king, prophet, scribe, intercessor, covenant mediator, legislator, and hero. For the most recent discussion, see Miller, "The 'Biography' of Moses in the Pentateuch."

3. For discussions of Moses in the media, see Britt, *Rewriting Moses*; Spronk, "The Picture of Moses in the History of Interpretation," 253–64.

4. Keneally, *Moses the Lawgiver*; Leibert, *The Lawgiver*.

5. Coats, *Moses*, 162. According to Römer, "Moses outside the Torah and the Construction of a Diaspora Identity," article 15 page 3. Cf. Watts, "The Legal Characterization of Moses in the Rhetoric of the Pentateuch," 415–26.

6. Meaning "what is decreed." This root is the closest biblical Hebrew comes to our word, "legislate, enact/pass laws." The qal form bears this sense in Isa 10:1, where the prophet pronounces woe on all who pass iniquitous ordinances (הַחֹקְקִים חִקְקֵי־אָוֶן).

7. Isa 33:22 reserves this role (מְחֹקֵק) for Yahweh.

- 4:1a: "And now, Israel, listen to the ordinances (הַחֻקִּים) and the regulations (הַמִּשְׁפָּטִים) that I am teaching you."

- 4:5: "See, I have taught you ordinances (חֻקִּים) and regulations (מִשְׁפָּטִים), as YHWH my God commanded me."

- 4:45: "These are the [covenant] stipulations (הָעֵדֹת), the ordinances (הַחֻקִּים) and the regulations (הַמִּשְׁפָּטִים) that Moses spoke to the people of Israel when they came out of Egypt."

- 5:1: "Hear, O Israel, the ordinances (הַחֻקִּים) and the regulations (הַמִּשְׁפָּטִים) that I speak in your hearing today."

- 5:31: "But you, stand here by me, and I will tell you the whole commandment (הַמִּצְוָה) and the ordinances (הַחֻקִּים) and the regulations (הַמִּשְׁפָּטִים) that you shall teach them."

- 6:1: "Now this is the commandment (הַמִּצְוָה), the ordinances (הַחֻקִּים) and the regulations (הַמִּשְׁפָּטִים) that YHWH your God commanded me to teach you."

- 6:20: "In the future, when your son asks you, 'What is the meaning of the [covenant] stipulations (הָעֵדֹת) and the ordinances (הַחֻקִּים) and the regulations (הַמִּשְׁפָּטִים) that YHWH our God has commanded you?'"

- 7:11: "You shall therefore be careful to do the commandment (הַמִּצְוָה) and the ordinances (הַחֻקִּים) and the regulations (הַמִּשְׁפָּטִים) that I command you today."

- 8:11: "Take care lest you forget YHWH your God by not keeping his commandments (מִצְוֹתָיו) and his regulations (מִשְׁפָּטָיו) and his ordinances (חֻקֹּתָיו), which I command you today."

- 11:1: "You shall therefore love YHWH your God and keep his charge (מִשְׁמַרְתּוֹ), his ordinances (חֻקֹּתָיו), his regulations (מִשְׁפָּטָיו), and his commandments (מִצְוֹתָיו) always."

- 11:32: "You shall be careful to do all the ordinances (הַחֻקִּים) and the regulations (הַמִּשְׁפָּטִים) that I am setting before you today."

- 12:1: "These are the ordinances (הַחֻקִּים) and the regulations (הַמִּשְׁפָּטִים) that you shall be careful to do in the land that YHWH, the God of your fathers, has given you to possess."

- 26:16: "This day YHWH your God commands you to do these ordinances (הַחֻקִּים) and these regulations (הַמִּשְׁפָּטִים)."

- 30:15–16: "See, I have set before you today life and good, death and evil. If you obey the commandments of YHWH your God that I command you today, by loving YHWH your God, by walking in his ways, and by keeping his commandments (מִצְוֹתָיו) and his ordinances (חֻקֹּתָיו), his regulations (מִשְׁפָּטָיו), then you shall live and multiply, and YHWH your God will bless you in the land."

The frequent association of these expressions with the verb "to command" (צָוָה),[8] Moses' assembly of the people to proclaim divine decrees,[9] and his promulgation of instructions that do in fact have a legal flavor, particularly in chapters 19–25, reinforce this impression.

Nevertheless, if persons who had never been exposed to the history of interpretation would encounter the book of Deuteronomy on its own for the first time, especially if they heard it read orally, with the clarity, passion, and force commended by the text itself, it is unlikely they would characterize the one whose voice they hear as a lawgiver. The purpose of this essay is to explore the matter further. How does the book of Deuteronomy present Moses? This question will be answered by examining how the narrative framework characterizes Moses, and how Moses characterizes himself in the addresses.[10] At the end I will summarize the significance of the findings for

8. Deut 6:2; 8:11; 10:13; 28:15, 45; 30:16.

9. With the root קָהַל, "to assemble": Deut 4:10; 5:22; 9:10; 10:4; 18:16; 31:12, 28, 30; with the root קָרָא, "to summon" (5:1; 29:1[Eng 2]; 31:7).

10. If we treat the book of Deuteronomy holistically as a literary text, intentionally composed, the answers to these questions will not be affected greatly by our hermeneutical predispositions toward the book. I have argued elsewhere for the authenticity of Moses' addresses, that is, the speeches faithfully represent the essence of a series of valedictory addresses that Moses actually delivered to his people on the Plains of Moab immediately prior to his death. Block, "Recovering the Voice of Moses," chapter 2 in this book. However, Arnold ("Deuteronomy as the *Ipsissima Vox* of Moses," 61–62) misconstrues my views by suggesting I believe the speeches in the book represent the *ipsissima verba* of Moses. I suggest only that the speeches in the book have their origin in what Moses said and wrote, and that in the book we hear his voice—which is a metaphor for his message. An *ipsissim verba* stance precludes intentional changes in the text, a stance that is unnecessarily literalistic. The book is preserved in seventh–eight century Jerusalem dialect Hebrew (akin to Jeremiah). While the history of the ancient Hebrew language remains a mystery, it

understanding both the nature of the book of Deuteronomy and its authority for Christian readers.

Moses' Role in the Narrative Framework of Deuteronomy

Consisting primarily of purported direct speech, the book of Deuteronomy is dominated by three formal addresses (1:6—4:40; 5:1b—26:19 + 28:1–68; 29:1b[Eng 29:2b]—30:20), and two lengthy poetic texts: Israel's national anthem (32:1–43) and Moses' blessing of the tribes (33:2–29). To these major blocks we should add three shorter addresses in chapter 27: instructions by Moses and the elders regarding the ceremony by which the land will be incorporated into the tri-partite covenantal relationship (27:1b–8), a short exhortation to faithfulness by Moses and the Levitical priests (27:9b–10), and an imprecatory charge by Moses (27:12–26). In 31:1–29, 32:44–52, and 34:1–12 we find additional short speeches by Moses and YHWH, but these are more thoroughly integrated into the narrative framework. Apart from embedded speech, strictly speaking we hear the voice of the narrator in only sixty-four verses,[11] a mere 560 words out of a

---

is obscurantist to insist that Moses' voice should be understood in this way. Indeed, given the evolution of other languages and dialects (e.g., English) it would have been extremely difficult, if not impossible, for Moses and Jeremiah to have engaged in meaningful oral conversation. Apparently the language of Deuteronomy, including its vocabulary and syntax, have been updated over time to preserve a meaningful text. Rabbinic perceptions of a sacrosanct written text developed much later. Arnold's own reconstruction of the origins of the book (ibid., 68–74) is much more speculative than what I have proposed. Critical reconstructions of the evolution of the text and theories of pseudepigraphy notwithstanding, all must agree that without exception all early textual witnesses to the book accept it as a coherent whole. Scholars may find it interesting and even significant to excavate the document for stages and layers of composition, but the scholarly interpretation is often grounded in modern Western assumptions of coherence and literary unity. Even if chapters 4 and 30 are exilic or post-exilic additions, which we doubt, both their meaning and their significance for readers are determined by the literary contexts in which they occur. I recognize the complexity of the literary issues, but as Ekhart Otto reminded us in a recent paper presented to the Society of Biblical Literature, in the end we need to read the legal documents in the light of the narrative contexts within which they are embedded (Otto, "Revisions in the Legal History of Covenant Code, Deuteronomy, Holiness Code and the Legal Hermeneutics of the Torah").

11. Deut 1:1–5; 2:10–12, 20–23; 3:9, 11, 13b–14; 4:41—5:1a; 10:6–9; 27:1a, 9a, 11; 28:69—29:1a[Eng 29:1–2a]; 31:1–2a, 7a, 9–10a, 14a, 14c–16a, 22–23a, 24–25, 30; 32:44–46a, 48; 33:1–2a; 34:1–4a; 5–12. Polzin (*Moses and the Deuteronomist*, 29) mistakenly counts 56.

total of 14,294 (< 4 percent). But what does the narrator have to say about Moses?

First, he identifies Moses by name thirty-eight times. In the concluding death narratives he characterizes him with three additional epithets: "man of God" (אִישׁ הָאֱלֹהִים; 33:1), "servant of YHWH" (עֶבֶד־יהוה; 34:5), and "prophet" (נָבִיא; 34:10). While Moses is called "the man of God" elsewhere (Josh 14:6; Ps 90:1 [Psalm title]; Ezra 3:2; 1 Chr 23:14), in later texts the expression functions as a title for prophets generally,[12] and was also used of David (Neh 12:24, 36). Referring to the book of Deuteronomy, 2 Chr 30:16 and Ezra 3:2 speak of "the Torah of Moses the man of God" (תּוֹרַת מֹשֶׁה אִישׁ־הָאֱלֹהִים). The phrase "man of God" refers primarily to a person's official standing with YHWH, but it may also describe his character: Moses was a "godly man." Given YHWH's characterization of Moses as one who had broken faith with him and had not treated him as holy (32:51), the epithet may reflect the narrator's attempt to rehabilitate his reputation. It was as "man of God" that Moses blessed the tribes (33:1), and ironically was buried on foreign (i.e., unholy) soil. However, it was also as "man of God" that God personally buried him (34:5–6).[13]

The notion that human beings could function as servants of deities was widespread in the ancient Near East. It is reflected especially in theophoric names that employ the root, like עֶבֶד, "servant," in Hebrew.[14] Although the word "servant" may denote menial status, references to court officials as "servant of the king" (עֶבֶד הַמֶּלֶךְ) demonstrate that in contexts like this it bears honorific significance (2 Kgs

---

12. 1 Sam 9:7–10; 1 Kgs 12:22; 13:4–31 (14x); 17:18; 20:28; 2 Kgs 1:9–13 (5x); 4:7–40 (10x). Targum Neofiti reads "prophet of Yahweh."

13. On Moses as "the man of God," see Schmid, *Die Gestalt des Mose*, 73; on the significance of the expression in its ancient Near Eastern context, see Dijkstra, "Moses, the Man of God," 17–36.

14. E.g., Obadiah, "one who serves Yahweh." For Mari, see Huffmon, *Amorite Personal Names in the Mari Texts*, 118–19, 189; the Amarna Letters, see Hess, *Amarna Personal Names*, 7–13, 244; Phoenician texts, see Benz, *Personal Names in the Phoenician and Punic Inscriptions*, 371; Ugarit, see Gröndahl, *Die Personennamen der Texte aus Ugarit*, 80, 105; Aramaic, see Maraqten, *Die semitischen Personennamen in den alt-und reischsaramäischen Inschriften aus Vorderasien*, 94, 192.

25:8).[15] While "servant of YHWH" is used of other persons as well,[16] the suffixed form of the title ("my/his/your servant") is frequently applied to prophets.[17] Moses is the prophetic servant *par excellence*.[18]

Within the Old Testament's rich vocabulary of prophecy,[19] נָבִיא is the most common designation. While the etymology of this word remains uncertain,[20] the word refers to "one summoned by God."[21] The primary role of prophets was to proclaim to the intended audiences messages they had received from the deity (cf. Exod 7:1–2). According to Jer 23:16–22, true prophets in Israel stood before YHWH as members of the divine council and were sent out by him to declare his messages. In 18:15–22 Moses will claim the title of נָבִיא for himself and announce the perpetuation of the institution in Israel cast in his image.

Apart from these titles and epithets, the narrator attributes a variety of actions to Moses. Verbs of motion have him "coming" (בּוֹא, 32:44) to the people and "going" (הָלַךְ, 31:14) to God; "going out" of Egypt (יָצָא, 4:46), together with the people; "going up"

15. See *HALOT* 775. This interpretation is reinforced by archaeologists' discovery of dozens of seals from ancient Palestine referring to the bearer of the seal generally as "servant of the king" or servant of a specific king, as in the famous seal of "Shamaʿ servant of Jeroboam" and the Edomite seal of "Qausʿanal servant of the king." Slaves did not have seals.

16. The full epithet is used elsewhere of Moses in Josh 1:1, 13, 15; 8:31, 33; 11:12; 12:6; 13:8; 14:7; 18:7; 22:2, 4–5; 2 Kgs 18:12; 2 Chr 1:3 (cf. the suffixed form in Exod 14:31 and Num 12:8); of Joshua, Josh 24:29; Judg 2:8; of David, Ps 18:1[Eng title]; 36:1[Eng title]. But note also the common expressions, "my/his/your servants." For references, see *HALOT* 774–76.

17. 2 Kgs 9:7; 17:13; Jer 7:25; 25:4; 26:5; 35:15; 44:4; Ezek 38:17; Amos 3:7; Zech 1:6; Dan 9:6, 10; Ezra 9:11.

18. On which see Miller, "'Moses My Servant,'" 245–55; Schmid, *Gestalt des Mose*, 71–73.

19. Prophets are referred to variously as seer (רֹאֶה; 1 Sam 9:9), "visionary" (חֹזֶה; Mic 3:7), "man of God" (אִישׁ הָאֱלֹהִים; 2 Kgs 4:7), "servant of YHWH" (עֶבֶד יְהוָה; 2 Kgs 17:13), "messenger/envoy of YHWH" (מַלְאַךְ יְהוָה; Isa 44:26; 2 Chr 36:15, 16).

20. The word is cognate to Akkadian *nabû*, "to call, name." *AHw*, 697b, 699b. Cf. *HALOT*, 659. The form is best understood as an I–class passive from a hypothetical root, נבא, "to call," analogous to many other official terms: מָשִׁיחַ, "anointed one, messiah"; נָגִיד, "promoted one, ruler"; נָשִׂיא, "raised one, prince"; נָזִיר, "consecrated one, Nazirite"; פָּקִיד, "appointed one, overseer"; שָׂכִיר, "hired one, hireling."

21. See further, Huehnergard, "On the Etymology and Meaning of Hebrew *nābîʾ*," 88*–93*. Contra Fleming, "The Etymological Origins of the Hebrew *nābîʾ*," 217–24, who relates the Hebrew word to Syrian *nābû*, "to name."

(עָלָה, 34:1) Mount Pisgah; and together with Joshua "stationing him-self" (הִתְיַצֵּב, 31:14) in the tent of meeting before YHWH. None of these movements was private or leisurely; throughout Moses operat-ed in an official capacity, either before YHWH, whom he represented before the people, or before the people, whom he represented before God. His official role is also is reflected in his performance of specific actions. He "performed" (עָשָׂה, 34:11) signs and wonders in Egypt,[22] "defeated" (הִכָּה, 1:4; 4:46) Sihon of Heshbon and Og of Bashan;[23] "set apart" (הִבְדִּיל, 4:41) three cities of refuge in the Transjordan; su-pervised the covenant ratification rituals (כָּרַת הַבְּרִית) according to YHWH's charge (צִוָּה: 28:69[Eng 29:1]); and ordained Joshua as his successor by laying his hands on him (סָמַךְ מֹשֶׁה אֶת־יָדָיו עָלָיו, 34:9). It seems the only personal event involving Moses was a non-act; he died (מוּת, 34:5, 7).[24]

The narrator also highlights Moses' role as author and scribe. He "wrote" down (כָּתַב, 31:9, 24) the *tôrâ* that he proclaimed to the people and "handed it over" (נָתַן, 31:9) to the Levitical priests as its custodians (31:10–13, 26) and to the elders (31:9). Later he wrote down the words of the national anthem, which functioned as a poetic supplement to the Torah (31:19, 22). Although Moses often referred to the act of writing in his addresses,[25] he never spoke of his own

---

22. Remarkably this is the only place in the Old Testament where the miracles associated with the exodus are attributed to him. In his speeches Moses always attributes these awesome feats to YHWH (Deut 4:34; 6:22; 7:19; 26:8; 29:1[Eng 2]). Exodus 11:10 attributes the wonders to Moses and Aaron. On Moses "the Magician," see Römer, "Moses outside the Torah," 4–6.

23. Although in 4:46 the verb הִכָּה has a compound subject (involving the people as well), as in 1:4 this verb is singular, as if to focus attention on Moses' role. Remarkably in the next verse, וַיִּירְשׁוּ, is plural: "and they possessed the land."

24. To these we might add "arising" (קוּם, 34:10) as prophet. Technically, the verb is attributed to other prophets, denying that any has risen in Israel like Moses. However, the comparison seems to assume the rise of Moses. Similar considerations apply to the use of the hiphil from of this verb (הֵקִים) in 18:18. While this verb normally expresses physical movement, in 34:10 it is employed metaphorically; Moses emerged as prophet, rising to a status unequalled when the conclusion to the book was composed.

25. YHWH wrote the ten words of the covenant on the tablets of stone (4:13; 5:22; 10:2, 4); the Israelites are to write "these words" on the doorposts of their houses and the gates of their towns (6:9; 11:20); the king is to write for himself a written copy of this Torah before the Levitical priests (17:18); the Israelites are to write all the words of this Torah on the stones at Shechem as part of the covenant

scribal activity.[26] Deuteronomy 31:9–13 has him transcribing the *tôrâ*, but critical scholars dismiss the narrator's attribution of the Torah's transcription to Moses as a part of a late legend of Moses as scribe and author.[27]

Despite all these actions, the narrative framework casts Moses primarily in the role of *speaker* before an audience.[28] Verbs of communication dominate: Moses "said" (אָמַר: 1:5; 31:2; 32:46); he "spoke" (דִּבֶּר: 1:1; 4:45; 27:9; 31:1; 32:44, 45); he "summoned" (קָרָא: 5:1; 29:1[Eng 2]; 31:7); he "charged/commanded" (צִוָּה: 27:1; 31:10; 31:25);[29] he "taught" (לִמַּד: 31:22); he "blessed" (בֵּרַךְ: 33:1); he ratified the covenant (הוֹאִיל בֵּאֵר: 1:5) by orally proclaiming the Torah; and he "set" (שִׂים: 4:44) the Torah before the people. Because "the words that Moses spoke to all Israel" (1:1) he spoke "according to all that YHWH charged him [to say] to them" (כְּכֹל אֲשֶׁר צִוָּה יְהוָה אֹתוֹ אֲלֵהֶם) his words were coterminous with God's words.[30]

---

renewal ceremony (27:3, 8). Note also the references to written divorce documents (סֵפֶר כְּרִיתֻת) in 24:1, 3.

26. However, his references to "the words of this Torah written in this document" (דִּבְרֵי הַתּוֹרָה הַזֹּאת הַכְּתוּבִים בַּסֵּפֶר הַזֶּה; 28:58) and related expressions obviously assume his addresses will be available in written form—though without identifying who will perform this service.

27. See Sonnet, *The Book within the Book*. Sonnet suggests (ibid., 264) that "Deuteronomy is the product of scribal activity, especially of scribal continuous writing and rewriting of the book," with Moses playing the role, not of author, but of scribe. According to van der Toorn, *Scribal Culture and the Making of the Hebrew Bible*, 166–70, the scribes responsible for the book of Deuteronomy view themselves as heirs and successors of Moses. Arnold proposes an *ipsissima vox* approach to the book in order to avoid "the exegetical problems raised by a *verba* approach to *hattôrâ hazô't*, 'this law,' in 31:9, and "other interpretive dilemmas" (Arnold, "Deuteronomy as the *Ipsissima Vox* of Moses, 73). But the dilemmas are heightened for those who refuse to let the text say what it wants to say and prefer much more complex and multi-layered speculation about the evolution of the text.

28. The audience is referred to variously as "all Israel" (1:1; 5:1; 27:9; 29:1[Eng 2]; 31:1; 32:45; 34:12); "sons of Israel" (1:3; 4:44, 45, 46; 28:69[Eng 29:1]; 31:22; 33:1); the assembly (קָהָל) of Israel (31:30); or simply "the people" (הָעָם: 27:1, 11; 32:44).

29. In Deut 27:1 together with the elders. What follows in each case has the character of instructions rather than laws.

30. Thus Miller, "Moses My Servant," 246. Moses' eloquence as interpreter of the Exodus and the earlier revelation at Sinai in the book not only portrays him continuing in his role as the transmitter of divine revelation, but also stands in sharp contrast to the man who in the narratives protests to YHWH that he is not "a man of words" (אִישׁ דְּבָרִים), but has a "heavy mouth and a heavy tongue" (כְּבַד־פֶּה וּכְבַד לָשׁוֹן, Exod 4:10).

In Deut 31:30 and 32:44 the narrator expressly notes that he spoke all the words of the Song (chapter 32) "in the ears of" (בְּאָזְנֵי) the people. Twice the narrator notes that he performed actions while the Israelites look on as spectators: he encouraged Joshua (31:7) and he performed the signs and wonders (34:12) "before the eyes of" (לְעֵינֵי) the people. But Moses also worked confidently with specific elements within the population. He involved the elders in the speech of 27:1b–8 (though the verb is singular: וַיְצַו), and collaborated with the Levitical priests in speaking to all Israel in 27:9 (singular verb, וַיְדַבֵּר).[31] In 31:7–8 the people observed him relating directly to Joshua, appealing for courage (cf. also v. 23), and in 31:9–13 he handed the written copy to the Levitical priests and the elders of Israel. He reinforced the instructions for the Levitical priests in verses 25–29, charging them again to place it beside the ark and specifying its function as witness against the people. We may imagine that as he blessed his people with his final benediction (33:1–29) he turned successively to each of the tribes. Although Moses recounted some of his two-way conversations with YHWH (3:23–28; 9:26–29), remarkably the narrator never has him addressing YHWH—even though YHWH spoke freely to him (31:14, 16; 32:48; 34:4).[32]

But what does the narrator say Moses intends to do with his words? Speech act theory becomes significant here.[33] According to speech act theory, the words used in communication represent the *locution*. This is what we have on the page in front of us when we read Deuteronomy. What the speaker hopes to accomplish with those words we refer to as the *illocution*. This issue is critical for reading Deuteronomy. Is this legislation? Are these the terms of a covenant? Is this propaganda?[34] Is this a literary fabrication? Or is this a record of hortatory addresses? How we view the book affects how we in-

31. If the verb precedes a compound subject it frequently agrees with the gender and number of the first subject, which is nearer to it. GKC §146*f*.

32. Cf. references to Moses speaking "as YHWH commanded him" (1:3; 34:9).

33. On which, see Austin, *How to Do Things with Words*; Searle, *Speech Acts: An Essay in the Philosophy of Language*; Briggs, "Speech-Act Theory"; Briggs, *Words in Action: Speech Act Theory and Biblical Interpretation*; Vanhoozer, *Is There a Meaning in This Text?*, 201–80.

34. Critical scholars tend to read Deuteronomy as a propagandistic treatise written to bolster support for Josiah's religious reforms at the end of the seventh century BCE.

terpret it. Finally, in speech act theory the response of the audience/
readers to the speech is referred to as the *perlocution*. Moses' perlocutionary goals in delivering these speeches and his goals for future
hearers of these speeches are reflected in a series of verbs that appear
several times in the book: "Read [this book of the Torah] that they
may hear, that they may learn, that they may fear, that they may obey,
that they may live" (17:19–20; 31:11–13). Although both Moses and
YHWH express pessimism concerning the people's future response
(31:16–21, 27–29), the desired perlocution is clear (10:12—11:1).

But how did the narrator perceive the illocutionary goals and
the perlocutionary response? According to the introduction (1:1–5),
in his oral performance Moses' speech act is represented by the verb
דָּבָר, "to speak" (vv. 1, 3), and involved "words" (דְּבָרִים, v. 1) and "instruction" (תּוֹרָה, v. 5), with the illocutionary goal of confirming a
covenantal relationship between Israel and YHWH. Although the
clause, הוֹאִיל מֹשֶׁה בֵּאֵר אֶת־הַתּוֹרָה הַזֹּאת לֵאמֹר, (v. 5), is usually rendered
something like "he began to expound this law," the verb בֵּאֵר speaks of
more than verbal exposition. It points to a speech act whereby Moses
"puts in force" YHWH's covenant with the generation about to enter
the land promised to the ancestors long ago (Gen 15:1–21 *et passim*)
and to the exodus generation (Exod 6:2–9; 23:20–33). Through the
proclamation of the Torah that follows and the performance of the
covenant renewal rituals underlying the book, the Israelite covenant
ratified at Horeb[35] is put into effect with this generation.[36] The narrator's colophonic ending to the second address reinforces this interpretation: "These are the words (דְּבָרִים) of the covenant that YHWH

---

35. Consistent with the common designations of the other biblical covenants
(Abrahamic/Patriarchal covenant, Noachian/Cosmic covenant, Davidic covenant),
throughout I shall refer to this covenant as the Israelite covenant. The covenant
made at Sinai was not made *with* Moses, but *through* him; Moses was not the
covenant partner.

36. The verb בֵּאֵר (D–stem), which occurs elsewhere only in 27:8 and Hab
2:2, is related to Akkadian *burru*, "to confirm," that is "put a legal document in
force." See Schaper, "The 'Publication' of Legal Texts in Ancient Judah," 230; Braulik
and Lohfink, "Deuteronomium 1,5 *B'R 'T-HTWRH HZ'T*," 49. The common
interpretation, "to make clear, explain," derives from postbiblical Hebrew, where
the word means "to expound, provide exposition." See Jastrow, *Dictionary of the
Targumim, Talmud Babli, Yerushalmi and Midrashic Literature*, 135. However, for
defense of the traditional interpretation, "to make clear, explain," see Otto, "Mose
der erste Schriftgelehrte," 273–84.

commanded Moses to make (כָּרַת) with the people of Israel in the land of Moab, besides [the words of] the covenant that he had made (כָּרַת) with them at Horeb" (28:69[Eng 29:1]).

As for the word תּוֹרָה, this is a didactic term, derived from ירה (hiphil), "to teach," and so is best rendered "instruction," rather than "law."[37] The *tôrâ* that follows includes historical recollections (1:6—3:22); personal anecdotes (3:23–29); enthusiastic appeals for the people to guard themselves (4:1–31); calls for reflection (4:32–40); recitation of a sacred text (5:1—6:3); exposition of the first principle of covenant relationship (6:4—11:32); invitations to the presence of God (12:1–14; 14:22—16:17; 26:1–15), promises of blessing as a reward for fidelity (7:12–16; 11:13–25; 28:1–14) and stern warnings against defection (12:28—13:19[Eng 12:28—13:18]; 28:15–69[Eng 28:15—29:1]; 29:1–28[Eng 2–29]); invitations to delight in life itself through dietary provisions (12:15–28; 14:1–21); provision of administrative institutions to ensure the promotion of righteousness (16:18—18:22); instructions regarding every conceivable ethical situation (19:1—25:19); promises of a future when the covenant relationship will be in full force (30:1–20); a national anthem (32:1–43); and a blessing for the tribes (33:1–26). Laws in the strict sense actually play a very minor role in the book. The translators of the Septuagint sent the interpretation of the book of Deuteronomy down an extremely unfortunate track when they named the book Τὸ Δευτερονόμιον, "second law,"[38] instead of translating the Hebrew title, הַדְּבָרִים, as οἱ Λόγοι or סֵפֶר הַדְּבָרִים as Τὸ Βιβλίον τῶν Λόγων, "The Book of Words," and when they decided to translate the Hebrew word תּוֹרָה as νόμος rather than διδαχή or διδασκαλία, "teaching, instruction."[39] Whether or not νόμος meant "law" in the second century BCE,[40] later readers have

---

37. By the second century BCE the Pentateuch as a whole was being referred to as "the Torah" (Greek ὁ νόμος). See the Prologue to the Wisdom of Ben Sirach.

38. The form of the name seems to be derived from Deut 17:18, where Hebrew מִשְׁנֵה הַתּוֹרָה, "a copy of the Torah," is misinterpreted as τὸ δευτερονόμιον, "second law."

39. Deut 1:5; 4:8, 44; 17:11, 18, 19; 27:3, 8, 26; 28:58, 61; 29:20, 28 [Eng 29:21, 29]; 30:10; 31:9, 11, 12, 24, 26; 32:46; 33:4, 10.

40. It is not clear whether νόμος actually bore the narrow sense of "law" in the third century BCE, or whether its scope was broader, more akin to Hebrew תּוֹרָה. See Gutbrod, "Nomos," 1046–47.

treated this book primarily as a legislative document and overlooked its true nature and intent.

If the introduction (1:1–5) orients readers to the genre and illocutionary intent of Moses' speeches and Deuteronomy as a book, the conclusion suggests these speeches also performed a pastoral function;[41] they represent a collection of Moses' valedictory addresses prior to his death on Mount Nebo.[42] This complex death story reflects both the narrator's ambivalence toward Moses and his demise, and the divine perspective on the man. On the one hand, Moses may blame only himself for his death outside the Promised Land. The narrator's report of YHWH's final speech reminds readers that at a critical moment Moses and Aaron had acted treacherously (מָעַל) against YHWH and failed to respect his sanctity at Meribah-Kadesh (32:48–52). For this reason Moses was barred entrance into the land; he could only see it from across the Jordan (v. 52; 34:4; cf. 3:27). On the other hand, the narrator expresses extreme admiration for Moses. As the head of this "the house of Israel," Moses prepared for his death not by setting up monuments of himself or his accomplishments, but he set the household in order, encouraging the people (31:2–6) and his successor (31:7–8, 23) to carry on with courage, hope, and fidelity. His notion of a lasting legacy was a people devoted fully to YHWH. To that end he provided a written transcript of his addresses (31:9–13) and taught the people a song that should have kept them on track spiritually after his departure (31:14—32:47).

This is a picture of a man who, despite forty years of frustration with the people, never abandoned them or lost his passion for their spiritual well-being. The narrator's esteem is obvious in the final statements: (1) Moses had earned the title, "the servant of YHWH"; (2) Moses had received the ultimate honor—being bur-

---

41. This conclusion is confirmed by the pervasively hortatory style of the addresses and the verbs used to describe Moses' verbal action in the book: לְמַד, "to teach" (4:1, 5, 14; 6:1; 31:19, 22); דִּבֶּר, "to speak" (1:1, 3, 18; 4:45; 5:1, 31; 31:30); as for the Israelites, they are to "learn" (לָמַד) them: 4:10; 5:1; 17:19(?); 31:12; and "teach" (לְמַד) them: 5:31; 11:19; שָׁנַן (6:7).

42. The death narrative of Moses (chapters 31–34) involves a series of actions intended to get his "house" in order (31:2, 14, 29; 32:48–52; 34:1–12). Chapters 32 and 33, which consist of two long poems, are embedded in the narrative as fundamental elements of that picture. See further Cribb, *Speaking on the Brink of Sheol*, 185–227.

ied by YHWH—though the narrator adds to the mystique by noting that only God knew the location of his grave; (3) Moses died an extraordinarily robust physical figure, living 120 years with no diminution of his senses;[43] (4) Moses' death precipitated a season of mourning that put the people's advance into the Promised Land on hold for thirty days; (5) Moses laid hands on Joshua, resulting in his endowment with the spirit of wisdom, and the people's acceptance of his authority; (6) Moses had established the standards for the people's conduct, receiving and passing on to them YHWH's revelation; (7) In the history of the prophetic institution, Moses' stature was unequalled. At the time the book was composed in its final form, no prophet had matched him for his intimacy with YHWH, his performance of signs and wonders before the Egyptians, or his awesome power demonstrated before all the Israelites (34:5–12). Through Moses' addresses and the songs at the end the narrator teaches hearers and readers that there is no God but YHWH, but he also teaches that Moses is his prophet.[44] In the history of the prophetic institution, Moses towered so high above the rest that the eighth-century BCE prophet Hosea subsumed even his deliverer role under that of prophet:

> I am YHWH your God [who brought you out]
> from the land of Egypt;
> I will again make you dwell in tents,
> as in the days of the appointed feast [Sukkoth].
> And I spoke to the prophets,
> as the one who multiplied visions,
> and through the prophets gave parables[45] . . .
> By a prophet YHWH brought Israel up from Egypt,
> and by a prophet he was preserved.
> (Hos 12:10–11, 14[Eng 9–10, 13])

Just as David set the bar by which all later kings would be measured, so Moses established the standard for prophets of Israel. But

43. Apparently Moses did not die of natural causes. His physical condition contrasts with that of the exodus generation, who had plenty to eat and whose clothing and shoes did not wear out in the desert (8:4), but whose bodies gave out. YHWH had sustained Moses supernaturally all these years.

44. Cf. Nohrnberg, *Like Unto Moses*, 33.

45. The verb דָּמָה, "to make comparisons, speak with figurative language" (from דָּמָה, "to compare, be like"), probably alludes to חִידֹת, "riddles," in Num 12:8.

the narrator of Deut 34 did not invent the notion of Moses as an extraordinary prophet. In Num 12:6–8 YHWH contrasts him with other
(ordinary) members of the profession: whereas he (YHWH) spoke to
them through visions, dreams, and riddles, he spoke with his faithful
servant Moses directly (mouth to mouth) in plain speech. Despite
the fact that Aaron was the first person in the Exodus–Numbers to be
designated a נָבִיא (Exod 7:1), Moses' role as prophet originated in the
divine call (Exod 3–4). Remarkably in Deuteronomy neither the narrator nor Moses ever alluded to this event. Unlike Paul in Galatians 1,
Moses never had to defend his apostolic authority; YHWH did it for
him (Exod 4:1–9; 19:9; Num 12:6–8). To the narrator, Moses' activities all fall under the rubric of prophecy.

Moses in His Own Addresses and Poems

But how did Moses view his role? While the narrator was ultimately
responsible for the content and shape of embedded speeches, the
speeches themselves offer another lens through which to grasp the
narrator's view of Moses' role. The questions that concern us now are
"Who does Moses think he is?" and "What does Moses think he is
doing in these addresses?"

Moses' Role in the First Address (1:6—4:40)

In the first address Moses portrays himself playing several roles. *First,
Moses functioned as Israel's [first] historian.* The discourse signal,
עַתָּה יִשְׂרָאֵל שְׁמַע אֶל־הַחֻקִּים וְאֶל־הַמִּשְׁפָּטִים, "And now Israel, listen to
the ordinances and regulations," in 4:1 divides the speech into two
parts. However, despite this heading, the entire speech is generically
united by a concern for past events. While the historian's agenda is
more obvious in 1:6—3:29, Moses' recollections of past events divide
into three phases: Israel's experiences since Mount Sinai (1:6—3:29),
Israel's experiences at Sinai (4:1–31), and Israel's experiences in Egypt
(4:32–40). While the space allotted to each phase decreases, so that
events fresh in the people's memory receive the greatest attention,[46]
Moses actually told Israel's story backwards. Indeed within the last

---

46. The first segment (1:6—3:29) subdivides further into experiences of the
exodus generation (1:6—2:1) and the experiences of the present generation (2:2—
3:29).

section he looks back as far as YHWH's election of the ancestors (4:37). In his recollections Moses is not a dispassionate lecturer or legislator, nor a detached biographer of a nation. Rather, he presents Israel's history as his story; he is both a participant and a driving force. More so than anywhere else in Deuteronomy, he wrestles with the implications of the nation's experiences for his own fate.

Second, Moses functioned as the senior administrator of the people of Israel. He appointed judges to assist him and charged them with their responsibilities (1:9–18); he announced the time to take the Promised Land and tried to encourage the people (1:19–21); he determined whether or not to send scouts ahead to survey the land (1:22–25); he chastised the people for faithlessness and disobedience (1:26–46); he communicated YHWH's orders to leave Mount Seir and travel on, as well as YHWH's instructions on how to treat the people they will encounter (2:1–23); he sent messengers to negotiate peace with Sihon of Heshbon (2:26–30); he led the Israelites in battle against Sihon and Og (2:31—3:11); he allotted the Transjordanian territory to Reuben, Gad, and the half tribe of Manasseh (3:12–17);[47] he demanded that the men of these tribes accompany the rest of the Israelites across the Jordan and fight with them until the land was conquered (3:18–20); he commissioned his successor (3:21–22; cf. 31:7–8; 34:9). As the head of an entire nation, Moses exercised moral and political power that Israelites would later recognize in their king.[48]

Third, Moses functioned as the spokesman for God. The address opens with a citation of divine speech (1:6–8), but direct quotations

---

47. That Moses should have cast the event entirely as his own decision and action raises doubts about its wisdom. The narrative of Num 32 does not allay these doubts. Despite numerous references to YHWH in peoples' speech, particularly the Reubenites' and Gadites' comment, "As YHWH has said to your servants, so we will act" (Num 32:31), YHWH seems not to have been involved in the decision (though see Josh 22:25). History (beginning in Josh 22) would prove how problematic the decision was; these territories proved the most vulnerable to foreign invaders.

48. Although Moses cast an impressive physical shadow (34:7), his moral power was limited. In the end he was unable to secure the fidelity of his people (31:14–22, 29), to convince YHWH to relent and let him enter the land, or even to secure his own burial. All he could do was leave a written deposit of his Torah on a scroll and the national anthem on the people's lips, and a final benediction ringing in their ears. The effectiveness of these actions would depend upon the people's disposition and YHWH's grace. For a discussion of issues of power in Deuteronomy, see Polaski, "Moses' Final Examination," 29–41.

of YHWH's words[49] and indirect references to past divine speech[50] punctuate the entire text. Moses declared explicitly that he followed YHWH's orders in specific actions (2:1) and in his instruction (4:5).

Fourth, Moses functioned as an overloaded pack animal. Adopting the language of his father-in-law in Exod 18:18–23, in Deut 1:9–12 Moses admitted he could not carry (נְשָׂא) the nation alone; they were a "burden" (טֹרַח)[51] and "load" (מַשָּׂא). Whereas YHWH had carried Israel like a father carries a child (1:31), Moses felt like a donkey that has fallen down under its load (22:4).[52] To assist him, particularly in judicial matters, he appointed capable and trustworthy administrators, but this did not prevent him becoming increasingly resentful. At the outset he complained of the burden of the people themselves and their contentiousness (רִיב, 1:12). Later he accused them of stubborn rebellion against YHWH at Kadesh-barnea; refusing to enter the Promised Land, they groused (וַתֵּרָגְנוּ) in their tents (1:26–28). Reminiscent of Exod 14:11–12, they accused YHWH of hating them and bringing them out of Egypt to destroy them at the hands of the Amorites; his gracious plan of salvation was actually a diabolical plot of deceit and murder. Despite Moses' assurance that YHWH would fight for them and reminders of his care in the desert, they refused to trust him (v. 32). Moses' description of the second phase of this fiasco was even more direct. Instead of heeding his warning not to attack the Amorites on their own, they refused to listen to him and rebelled against YHWH, presumptuously (וַתָּזִדוּ) launching their attack (v. 43). The absence of specific complaints in chapters 2–3 suggests a more positive disposition toward the new generation (cf. 4:3–4).

Nevertheless, with remarkable transparency, three times Moses inserted into his recollections a troubling and troubled general note:[53]

---

49. Deut 1:42; 2:2–7, 9, 13a, 18–19, 24–25, 31; 3:2; 3:26b–28; 4:10b.

50. Deut 1:19, 41; 2:1, 14; 4:5, 14.

51. The word occurs elsewhere only in Isa 1:14, where YHWH speaks of Israel's religious performances as an intolerable burden. Note the references to pack animals in Exod 23:5 (donkey); 2 Kgs 5:17 (two mules); 8:9 (forty camels).

52. Jethro had asserted that Moses would be able to "stand" (עָמַד) if he accepted his counsel (Exod 18:23).

53. For insightful discussion of these texts, see Polzin, *Moses and the Deuteronomist*, 36–43.

- 1:37: Even with me YHWH was angry on your account (גַּם־בִּי הִתְאַנַּף יְהוָה בִּגְלַלְכֶם), and said, "You also shall not go in there."
- 3:26: But YHWH was angry with me because of you (וַיִּתְעַבֵּר יְהוָה בִּי לְמַעַנְכֶם), and would not listen to me.
- 4:21: And YHWH was angry with me because of you (וַיהוָה הִתְאַנַּף־בִּי עַל־דִּבְרֵיכֶם).

The first two are awkwardly inserted, as if Moses could not think about the events he was recounting without stewing over the personal cost to him. And the last is part of a heated conversation he had with YHWH, in which he begged to be admitted to the Promised Land, but YHWH would not relent. As a consolation prize he told him to climb Mount Pisgah and look over the land. But even this would have been a bitter moment, for it concretized the extent and intensity of Moses' loss. These three outbursts arose from the soul of a man embittered by the people whom he had carried and for whom he cared. It was their fault that he could not complete his mission and enjoy the blessings of the land.

On the surface, the words are not true, YHWH refused Moses entrance into Canaan because of his own sin (32:49–52). However, technically Moses is correct. If the Israelites had entered the land from Kadesh-barnea, the incident that precipitated Moses' sin would never have occurred, and by now he would have enjoyed the blessings of the land for thirty-eight years.[54] These are the laments of a bitter old man, frustrated with God and angry with his people. Moses might have been tempted to see himself as a "suffering servant,"[55] as an innocent bearer of the judgment that rightly belongs to others, but YHWH had none of this. If he failed to enter the land, like Israel, he bore the punishment of his own sin, no one else's.[56]

54. In his otherwise thorough discussion of Deuteronomy's perspective[s] on the reason for Moses not entering the land, Lim ("The Sin of Moses in Deuteronomy," 250–66) seems oblivious to this fundamental chronological datum. Cf. Lee, "The Exclusion of Moses from the Promised Land," 217–39.

55. Contra Miller, "Moses My Servant," 253–54.

56. These inserted comments reinforce the authenticity and originality of Moses' addresses in Deuteronomy. A later pseudepigraphist would scarcely have painted Israel's most heroic figure in such negative colors.

Fifth, Moses functioned as Israel's pastor-teacher. The narrator recognized Moses' teaching role in 31:22, but Moses acknowledged it four times in chapter 4:

- 4:1: And now, Israel, hear the ordinances and regulations I am *teaching* (מְלַמֵּד) you to observe so that you may live and go in and take possession of the land that YHWH, the God of your fathers, is giving you.

- 4:5: See, I have *taught* (לִמַּדְתִּי) you ordinances and regulations, as YHWH my God commanded me that you may do them in the land that you are entering to take possession of it.

- 4:9: What great nation is there, that has ordinances and regulations as righteous as this entire Torah that I am *placing before* (נֹתֵן לִפְנֵיכֶם) you today?

- 4:14: And YHWH commanded me at that time to *teach* (לְלַמֵּד) you ordinances and regulations, that you might do them in the land that you are going over to possess.

Verse 10 reinforces the pedagogical tone of the address: At Horeb YHWH had told Moses, "Gather the people to me, that I may let them hear my words, so they may *learn* (יִלְמְדוּן) to fear me all the days that they live on the earth, and so they may *teach* (יְלַמֵּדוּן) their children." Remarkably, in each instance "the ordinances and regulations" (חֻקִּים וּמִשְׁפָּטִים) are the subjects of instruction. In Deuteronomy this pair of words refers to the constitutional material revealed at Horeb,[57] along with supplements before (Exod 12–13) and after (Num 15:1–31; 18–19; 28–30; 34–36).[58] Moses' pedagogical role would later be assumed by the Levites (Deut 33:10; cf. Ezra 7:10). But the ordinances that Moses teaches are not his own; they are the commands of YHWH (מִצְוֹת יְהוָה, 4:2) that he taught precisely as YHWH God commanded (4:5, 14). Moses deemed his instructions as canonical as the original ordinances and regulations (4:2), but saw himself neither as the source of nor the authority behind this instruction. He was indeed the agent by which the laws were transmitted at Sinai,

---

57. Including the "book of the covenant" (סֵפֶר הַבְּרִית), the "manual on worship" (Lev 1–16), and the "instructions on holiness" (Lev 17–26).

58. Perhaps the Decalogue would also have been included, but this document is usually referred to as "the [ten] words" (עֲשֶׂרֶת הַדְּבָרִים). Cf. Exod 20:1; 24:3; 34:28; Deut 4:13; 10:4. Exodus 24:12 calls the document "the *torah*, that is the commandment" (וְהַתּוֹרָה וְהַמִּצְוָה).

and in Deuteronomy he functioned as the authoritative teacher/interpreter of the laws. However, technically he was not a "lawgiver," if by this term we mean legislator[59]—that role was reserved for YHWH. Instead, Moses served YHWH and the people as their pastor-teacher.

In the earlier narrative of Joshua's induction as leader of the people, Moses expressed his awareness of his pastoral role: "May YHWH, the God of the spirits of all flesh, appoint someone over the congregation who will go out before them and come in before them, who will lead them out and bring them in, so the congregation of YHWH may not be like sheep without a shepherd" (רֹעֶה, Latin *pastore*; Num 27:16–17). His pastoral role was demonstrated in his response to the people's infidelity at Kadesh-Barnea (1:19–46), but his performance became more and more pastoral as he moved through this speech. This climaxes in chapter 4, which is fueled by his homiletical passion.

First, as a pastor he begins by calling his congregation to attention ("And now, Israel, hear . . .") to the instruction to follow. Like Paul's οὖν, "therefore," in Rom 12:1, the opening deictic particle, וְעַתָּה, "and now," signaled to his audience a turning point in the address, from a recital of past experiences of divine grace to the presentation of the implications of those experiences.[60] Second, the chapter is dominated by appeals to active obedience,[61] diligent self-watch,[62] to remember/not to forget (4:9, 23, 31), positive and negative motive clauses,[63] causal clauses,[64] and specific exhortations against violation of the first command of the Decalogue (4:9–24). Moses' first address reached a homiletical crescendo in 4:32–40, as he invited the audience to conduct exhaustive research to see if YHWH's actions on

59. Arnold ("Deuteronomy as the *Ipsissima Vox* of Moses," 53–74]) is inconsistent in his portrayal of Moses. First he rightly observes, "[I]n Deuteronomy, Moses is not a lawgiver but an exegete of the law—a law interpreter" (ibid., 58), but later he asserts that "Deuteronomy is . . . the result of ancient Israel's method for an evolving *tradition* while respecting the *traditum* of the great lawgiver" (ibid., 74).

60. On וְעַתָּה, "and now," signaling a turning point, see 10:12 and 1 Sam 12:13. Cf. van der Merwe, Naudé, and Kroeze, *A Biblical Hebrew Reference Grammar*, §44.6. Although the Septuagint usually translates the expression literally with καὶ νῦν, here וְעַתָּה functions similarly to οὖν, "therefore," as in Rom 12:1.

61. "To listen/obey" (שָׁמַע): 4:1, 6, 10, 12, 28, 30; "to do/act" (עָשָׂה): 4:1, 5–6, 13–14; "keep" (שָׁמַר): 4:2, 6, 40.

62. הִשָּׁמֶר וּשְׁמֹר (4:9); וְנִשְׁמַרְתֶּם (4:15); הִשָּׁמְרוּ (4:23).

63. Positive: 4:1, 40; negative; 4:9, 16, 19, 23.

64. Deut 4:3, 6, 22, 24, 31, 37.

Israel's behalf had any parallels or equals in the history or literature of humankind (4:32). He alternated descriptions of YHWH's unprecedented actions (vv. 33–34, 36–38) with observations on the theological implications of those actions (vv. 35, 39), and then culminated with an appeal to willing obedience to the will of the divine suzerain and promises of the rewards for doing so (v. 40). Far from presenting Moses as "lawgiver," this is prophetic and pastoral preaching at its best. Patrick Miller observes rightly, "Moses seeks at every turn to convey, explain, and also stir the heart to respond to the divine instruction, to follow the way that is set forth."[65]

Moses' Role in the Second Address

By word count Moses' second address is four times the length of the first address.[66] The speech divides into three major sections. The first two are signaled by formal invitations to hear the "ordinances and regulations" (הַחֻקִּים וְהַמִּשְׁפָּטִים) that the people are to observe (5:1; 12:1), and the last (chapter 28) is separated from the preceding sections by chapter 27. The former raise expectations for a recitation of the laws revealed at Sinai—perhaps the "book of the covenant" or the "instructions on holiness," but this does not happen. Instead Moses began the first section (Deut 5–11) by reciting the "Ten Words" (עֲשֶׂרֶת הַדְּבָרִים) of the Decalogue, which he followed up with a series of mini-homilies on the first principle of covenant relationship—no other God but YHWH. While 12:1 signals a literary break, Moses continued the homiletical style of 6:4—11:32. These homiletical features are best treated separately.

MOSES' ROLE IN 5:1b—11:32

As in the first address, especially chapter 4, Moses functioned as a pastor-teacher delivering another address to a congregation that has assembled before him. He appeared not as a legislator drawing up laws for the people, or even standing before YHWH to receive the laws, as he had at Sinai,[67] or as the renowned Hammurabi stela

---

65. Miller, "Moses My Servant," 247.

66. The first address is ca. 2,260 words; the second ca. 9,040 words.

67. After YHWH's direct communication of the Decalogue to all the people, virtually all the laws and regulations revealed at Sinai are cast as divine speech to

portrays the king standing before Shamash to receive laws for ancient Babylon. The narrator's introduction and Moses' opening line
set the stage: "Moses summoned (קָרָא) all Israel, and said to them,
'Hear, O Israel, the ordinances and regulations that I am declaring
to you today; you shall learn them and observe them diligently.'" The
introduction offers guidance for interpreting the address and for
understanding Moses' role. First, the assembly involves all Israel, presumably including men, women, children, and aliens in their midst
(cf. 12:12; 31:12). Second, this introduction signals the beginning of
a formal address. When the people had gathered Moses called them
to attention, "Hear, O Israel!" (שְׁמַע יִשְׂרָאֵל). Third, Moses' address is
characterized as "speech," rather than legislation. The narrator uses
the verb אָמַר, "to say," and Moses the verb דִּבֶּר, "to speak." Moses' task
was to transmit and interpret ordinances and regulations, not create them. Fourth, by adding "in your ears" (בְּאָזְנֵיכֶם) he highlighted
the aural (rather than textual) nature of his performance. Fifth, his
declared immediate goal was pedagogical—that they might learn
(לָמַד)—but his ultimate goal was transformational and ethical: that
Israel might keep the ordinances and regulations by doing them.[68] The
remainder of the preamble to the second address (vv. 2–5) reinforces
this agenda. Moses' locutionary acts of speaking the ordinances and
regulations were intended to achieve a covenantal illocutionary goal.
His intention was not to impose laws on people, but to create (כָּרַת)
a covenantal relationship with YHWH.[69] This is critical because a
community governed by covenant differs fundamentally from a community governed by laws (Table 1). Covenant relationship inspires
fidelity; laws coerce conformity.

Moses, which he is to "say" (אָמַר) to the Israelites (Exod 20:22; etc.), "set before
them" (שִׂים לִפְנֵיהֶם, 21:1), and "tell them" (דִּבֶּר אֶל, 25:2 + more than two dozen
times).

68. The construction, וּשְׁמַרְתֶּם לַעֲשֹׂתָם, "and you shall keep by doing," contrasts
with 4:6, which uses finite verbs for both, "keep and do." This form occurs repeatedly
in the book (5:29; 6:3, 25; etc.). The construction is reminiscent of Gen 18:19, where
Yahweh calls on Abraham's descendants to "keep the way of Yahweh by doing
justice and righteousness." On this gerundive use of the infinitive construct, see
WO §36.2.3e; Joüon §124o.

69. Verses 2–3; cf. 26:16–19; 28:69[Eng 29:1]; 29:9–12[Eng 10–13].

TABLE 1: A Comparison of Societies Founded on Covenant and Societies Founded on Law[70]

	Covenant	Law
Purpose	Creates a community where none existed before, by establishing a common relationship to a common lord.	Presupposes a social order in which it serves as an instrument for maintaining an orderly freedom and security.
Basis	Gratitude: response to benefits already received, usually by grace	Social fear: attempts to protect society from disruption and attack by threat of force.
Enactment	By voluntary act in which each individual willingly accepts the obligations presented.	By competent social authority, obligating all individuals by virtue of status as members of the social organization, usually by birth.
Validity	Binding upon each person without regard to social context; as universally applicable as God himself, reflecting a vision of the "omnipresence of God."	Dependent upon social boundary lines; irrelevant to those who cross the boundary of the social order.
Sanctions	Not controlled by social organizations, but connected with cause-and-effect concepts in human history; includes both positive and negative sanctions.	Enforced by social organization through its chosen authorities; sanctions are largely negative though nonpolitical organizations use economic and prestige motivations to obtain conformity.
Norms	Typically presented as verbal abstractions, the definition of which is an obligation of persons in concrete circumstances and expression of the "fear of God"; conformity based on commitment to seeking the interest of the next person, whether God or fellow citizens.	Defined by social authority in advance, usually with specific sanctions defined for specific violations; arbitrary and formal in nature, since only visible actions may be assessed in courts of law; conformity based on self-interest.

70. Adapted from Mendenhall, "The Conflict between Value Systems and Social Control," 211. For his full discussion, see ibid., 169–80.

Orientation	Toward the future—promotes reliable individual behavior, thereby providing a basis for both private and public security; predictions of consequences extend to four generations in case of violation (the definition of a household).	Toward the past: attempts to punish violations of the public order to make that public order more secure; it is oriented toward the future only in the sense that it gives advance warning of penalties the society has power to impose upon violators. Very short attention span (statute of limitations).
Social Aspect	Obligations individual, but consequences (blessings and curses) are of necessity social, since they are "acts of God"—drought, epidemic, defeat in war, etc.; powerfully reinforces individual responsibility to society, and social responsibility to refrain from protection of the guilty.	Obligations defined by society are binding upon all members, but sanctions are imposed only upon guilty individual, involving adversarial procedures and rites; a form of warfare pitting society against the guilty.
Evolution	Forms basis for social custom especially in early stages. As social control takes over, may degenerate into mere ritual reinforcement of a social solidarity.	Presupposes a customary morality that it attempts to protect, but cannot create. Tends to become increasingly rigid in formal definition, and increasingly devoid of real ethical content.
Continuity	Since it is not produced by society, it cannot be guaranteed by society; essentially private, individual, independent of roles, encouraged through persons with no legislative authority: prophets, the Christ, apostles. Destruction of a particular social control system, therefore, does not mean the end of the value system.	Cannot exist apart from social institutions—king, priest, political officers, legislative, executive, judicial; ceases to exist when political structures fall.

In considering what strategies Moses employed to achieve this goal we observe first that Deut 5–11 bears few if any marks of law, but sermonic features pervade. Structurally this part of the second address begins with a recitation of a base text, the Decalogue (5:6–21), referred to variously elsewhere: "the Ten Words" (עֲשֶׂרֶת הַדְּבָרִים, 4:13; 10:4), "the words of the covenant" (דִּבְרֵי הַבְּרִית, Exod 34:28), the "tablets of the [covenant] stipulations" (לֻחֹת הָעֵדֻת, Exod 31:18; 32:15; 34:29), or "the tablets of the covenant" (לוּחֹת הַבְּרִית, Deut 9:9, 11, 15), which were stored in "the ark of the covenant of YHWH" אֲרוֹן בְּרִית־יְהוָה, Deut 10:8; etc.). The modifications to the Exod 20 version of the Decalogue demonstrate that Moses was interested less in legal precision than in the spirit of the document.[71] Following a review of the circumstances in which the document was revealed (5:22–31), in chapters 6–11 he expounded on the first principle of covenant relationship: exclusive devotion to YHWH.

Few texts in Scripture are as sermonic as this. First, Moses continued the Decalogue's "I–you" form of address, rather than employing the less personal and more legal casuistic third person forms found for example in the "book of the covenant" (Exod 21:1—23:19). His alternation of singular and plural forms reinforced its homiletical tone. Although some treat these alternations as evidence of different textual layers, this feature served an important rhetorical function. When Moses conceived of Israel as a collective he used the singular, but his use of the plural reminded his hearers (and modern readers) that ethics and faith cannot be legislated; they must be applied individually.[72] Whether or not the masses would heed his challenge, individuals were responsible for their own courses.

Second, chapters 5–11 are laced with hortatory features. In addition to 5:1, twice more Moses called his audience to listen with "Hear, O Israel" (6:4; 9:1), and in 10:12 he asked, "And now, what does YHWH your God ask of you?" (וְעַתָּה יִשְׂרָאֵל מָה יְהוָה אֱלֹהֶיךָ שֹׁאֵל מֵעִמָּךְ). Despite having warned his audience earlier not to add to or subtract from his commands (4:2), twice Moses

---

71. Which was captured by Jesus, who summarized the entirety of the divine expectation in a single two-clause sentence: "You shall love YHWH your God with all your inner being, your whole person, and your resources, and you shall love your neighbor as yourself" (Mark 12:30–31).

72. The literature on this problem is vast. See especially McConville, "Singular Address in the Deuteronomic Law and the Politics of Legal Administration," 19–36.

himself adds "as YHWH your God commanded you" (כַּאֲשֶׁר צִוְּךָ
יְהוָה אֱלֹהֶיךָ) to YHWH's own words in the Decalogue (5:12, 16).
Beyond this we note repeated appeals to right knowledge, especially
knowledge of YHWH (7:9; 8:2–3, 5; 9:3, 6), to remember Israel's past
and YHWH's grace (5:15; 6:12; 7:18; 8:2, 11, 14, 18–19; 9:7, 27), to
be diligent in obedience,[73] to adopt the right attitude, especially to
love and fear YHWH,[74] to be committed to YHWH with one's entire
heart/mind (לֵבָב) and being (נֶפֶשׁ, 6:5; 10:12; 11:13, 18), to circumcise
one's heart and to stop stiffening the neck (10:16). A series of positive
and negative motive clauses[75] and triadic constructions (e.g. 6:4–9)
contribute to the sermonic nature of the address. Additional rhetorical features include appeals to and quotations of divine speech,[76]
recollections of past events,[77] and the introduction of interlocutors
and prescribed responses.[78] Moses' speech reached a crescendo in
10:12—11:1:

> And now, Israel, what does YHWH your God require of you,
> but to fear YHWH your God, to walk in all his ways, to love
> him, to serve YHWH your God with all your heart and with
> all your soul, and to keep the command and ordinances of
> YHWH, which I am commanding you today for your good?
> See, to YHWH your God belong heaven and the heaven of
> heavens, the earth with all that is in it. Yet YHWH set his
> heart in love on your fathers and chose their offspring after
> them, you above all peoples, as you are this day.

73. וְשָׁמַרְתָּ לַעֲשׂוֹת, "and you shall keep by doing . . ." and variations: Deut 5:1, 32;
6:3, 25; 7:12; 8:1; 11:32.

74. אָהֵב, "love" 6:5; 11:1, 13; יָרֵא, "fear," 6:2, 24; 10:12, 20.

75. Positive: 5:33; 8:1; 11:9. Negative: 6:12, 15; 7:22, 25; 8:11–12, 17; 9:28; 11:16.

76. Apart from the Decalogue, Moses quotes divine speech in 5:28b–31; 9:12–
14; 10:1–2, 11.

77. Deut 5:2–33; 6:16; 8:2–4, 14–16; 9:6—10:11; 11:2–6. Although Moses did
not claim to function as an intercessor for the assembly on the Plains of Moab, in
9:7—10:11 he recalled in detail an earlier event at Sinai (the golden calf incident)
when he had wrestled with YHWH for forty days and nights on the people's behalf.
While his intercession then involved deprivation—forty days and nights without
food and water (9:9, 18, 25)—unlike the narrative in Exod 32:30–33, Moses did
not recall that he had offered to make atonement for the people's sin by having his
own name blotted from YHWH's book, if only he would forgive (and take back)
his people.

78. Deut 6:20–21; 7:17–18; 8:17–18; 9:4–5.

> Circumcise therefore the foreskin of your heart, and stop being stubborn. For YHWH your God is God of gods and Lord of lords, the great, the mighty, and the awesome God, who is not partial and takes no bribe. He executes justice for the fatherless and the widow, and loves the sojourner, giving him food and clothing. So love the sojourner, for you were sojourners in the land of Egypt.
>
> You shall fear YHWH your God. You shall serve him and hold fast to him, and by his name you shall swear. He is your praise. He is your God, who has done for you these great and awesome things that your eyes have seen. Your fathers went down to Egypt seventy persons, and now YHWH your God has made you as numerous as the stars of heaven.
>
> So you shall love YHWH your God and keep his charge, his ordinances, his regulations, and his command always.

This is scarcely the stuff of law, nor merely a call to obedience to the law. Moses' concern was not legal, but *personal, spiritual, and pastoral*; he appealed for undivided devotion to YHWH demonstrated in acts of piety and fidelity to him and covenant commitment to one's fellow citizens.

MOSES' ROLE IN 12:1—26:19; 28:1–69 [ENG 28:1—29:1]

The style and tone of chapters 5–11 continue in the second address. Commonly misidentified as the Deuteronomic Law Code, critical scholars typically treat Deut 12–26 like an onion, whose layers may be peeled off until one arrives at an original legal core, which then becomes the focus of interpretation.[79] While often differing in substance, the resulting code bears striking resemblances stylistically to the Book of the Covenant (Exod 21:1—23:19) and Holiness Code

---

79. Martin Rose represents an extreme view. He identifies four strata in these materials: Stratum I (the legal core) derives from the time of Hezekiah (715–696 BCE or slightly later). Stratum II modifies the laws slightly and is dated to the time of Josiah (639–609 BCE or slightly later). Stratum III represents the older deuteronomistic edition from the time of the destruction of Jerusalem (587 BCE) and the exilic situation. This "preacher," recognizable by the use of the plural, fixes the law in a historical situation, prior to crossing the Jordan, and emphasizes obedience to God. Stratum IV represents the younger deuteronomistic edition from the end of the Babylonian exile (539 BCE) to the early post-exilic period. This "preacher" concretizes the prohibitions on local cult sites and emphasizes the need for their destruction in the sharpest tones. Rose, *5. Mose 12–25*. Cf. also Seitz, *Redaktionsgeschichtliche Studien zum Deuteronomium*.

(Lev 17–26). However, this approach completely neuters the second part of Moses' second address of its rhetorical force, and runs against the grain of the literary reality, and perhaps even of the historical reality. Given the theological trajectory and rhetorical/paraenetic nature of Deuteronomy 6–11, the fuel energizing chapters 12–26 is not the underlying laws, but a fundamental covenant theology. Whereas in the former Moses had grounded his call for exclusive allegiance to YHWH in the Decalogue, in the latter he marshaled previously revealed חֻקִּים וּמִשְׁפָּטִים, "ordinances and regulations," to serve that same theology, though with an increasing emphasis on fidelity in worship (chapters 12–13, 16, 26) and the horizontal ethical implications of covenant relationship.[80] In a recent address Ekhart Otto suggested that the legal texts in the Pentateuch should be read in the light of the narrative contexts within which they are embedded rather than in isolation from their contexts.[81] This counsel should also apply to legal statements embedded in the so-called Deuteronomic Code. We hear the voice of Moses most clearly when we attend to the theological bed in which they rest.

If we adopt a more holistic hermeneutic,[82] we quickly discover that the style and tone of Moses' second address do not change appreciably after chapter 11. Pronouncements that actually look like laws are sprinkled throughout chapters 12–18, but concentrations of such statements do not occur until chapters 19–25. However, even here the motive clauses and God-talk that punctuate this section contribute to a profoundly theological and paraenetic flavor. Deuteronomy

---

80. The clause כַּאֲשֶׁר צִוְּךָ יְהוָה אֱלֹהֶיךָ, "as YHWH your God commanded you," in 5:12, 16 signals dependence on the Exodus version of the Decalogue; in 20:17 the same clause suggests that the Deuteronomic *ḥerem* ordinance was also grounded in some earlier law—though it is never explicitly stated as law. However, note that Exod 23:20–33, a supposed E text, antedates Deuteronomy. Some such law seems to be assumed in Lev 27:29; Deut 2:34 and 3:6, and Saul's treatment of the Amalekites in 1 Sam 15 and the Gibeonites in 1 Sam 21. Similarly Milgrom ("Profane Slaughter and a Formulaic Key to the Composition of Deuteronomy," 6–9), who also suggests that חֻקִּים וּמִשְׁפָּטִים "laws and norms" can only refer to the Covenant Code, and that D is also dependent on P.

81. Otto, "Revisions in the Legal History of Covenant Code, Deuteronomy, Holiness Code and the Legal Hermeneutics of the Torah."

82. As advocated by Greenberg, "The Vision of Jerusalem in Ezekiel 8–11," 143–64.

24:6–22, one of the most "secular" passages, illustrates the point. Of eight topics, only one (v. 16) lacks paraenetic commentary:

> No one shall take a mill or an upper millstone in pledge, *for that would be taking a life in pledge.* If someone is caught kidnapping another Israelite, enslaving or selling the Israelite, then that kidnaper shall die. *So you shall purge the evil from your midst.*
>
> Guard against an outbreak of a leprous skin disease by being very careful; you shall carefully observe whatever the Levitical priests instruct you, just as I have commanded them. *Remember what YHWH your God did to Miriam on your journey out of Egypt.*
>
> When you make your neighbor a loan of any kind, you shall not go into the house to take the pledge. You shall wait outside, while the person to whom you are making the loan brings the pledge out to you. If the person is poor, you shall not sleep in the garment given you as the pledge. You shall give the pledge back by sunset, *so that your neighbor may sleep in the cloak and bless you; and it will be to your credit before YHWH your God.*
>
> You shall not withhold the wages of poor and needy laborers, whether other Israelites or aliens who reside in your land in one of your towns. You shall pay them their wages daily before sunset, *because they are poor and their livelihood depends on them; otherwise they might cry to YHWH against you, and you would incur guilt.*
>
> Parents shall not be put to death for their children, nor shall children be put to death for their parents; only for their own crimes may persons be put to death.
>
> You shall not deprive a resident alien or an orphan of justice; you shall not take a widow's garment in pledge. *Remember that you were a slave in Egypt and YHWH your God redeemed you from there; therefore I command you to do this.*
>
> When you reap your harvest in your field and forget a sheaf in the field, you shall not go back to get it; it shall be left for the alien, the orphan, and the widow, *so that YHWH your God may bless you in all your undertakings.*
>
> When you beat your olive trees, do not strip what is left; it shall be for the alien, the orphan, and the widow. When you gather the grapes of your vineyard, do not glean what is left; it shall be for the alien, the orphan, and the widow. *Remember*

*that you were a slave in the land of Egypt; therefore I am com-
manding you to do this.* (NRSV, modified)

Beyond theological and motivational insertions like those featured here, chapters 12–26 contain all the rhetorical features found
in chapters 5–11: (1) The "I-you" form of direct address, rather than
the less personal and definitely more legal casuistic third person
forms;[83] (2) alternation of singular and plural forms; (3) appeals
to the Israelites to keep alive the memory of their own past and
YHWH's past grace;[84] (4) references to past divine commands ("as
YHWH your God commanded you," כַּאֲשֶׁר צִוְּךָ יְהוָה אֱלֹהֶיךָ, 20:17) or
promises ("as YHWH your God promised you," כַּאֲשֶׁר דִּבֶּר־לָךְ, 12:20;
15:6; 18:2; 26:18, 19), or oaths ("as he swore to you/your ancestors,"
כַּאֲשֶׁר נִשְׁבַּע־לָךְ, 13:18[Eng 17]; 19:8; also 28:9); (5) exhortations to
be on their guard and to diligence in obedience ("and you shall keep
by doing," וְשָׁמַרְתָּ לַעֲשׂוֹת, and variations);[85] (6) appeals to adopt the
right attitude, especially to love (13:4[Eng 3]) and fear YHWH,[86]
and for wholehearted[87] and full-bodied (נֶפֶשׁ, 13:4[Eng 3]; 26:16)
devotion; (6) a vast array of positive and negative motive clauses.[88]
Other rhetorical features continue as well: appeals to and quotation
of divine speech (17:16),[89] recollections of past events (23:5–6 [Eng
4–5]; 25:17 18; 26:5–9), and the introduction of interlocutors and
prescribed responses.[90]

But chapters 12–26 also include some new features. Moses'
(and YHWH's) pastoral sensitivity toward the people is reflected in

83. This is not to deny the presence of casuistic statements. See, for example,
21:15–17, 18–21; 22:5, 13–18, 28–30; 23:11–12 [Eng 10–11]; 24:1–7; 25:1–3, 5–10.

84. Deut 15:15; 16:3, 12; 24:9, 18, 22; 25:17–19.

85. Deut 12:1, 13, 19, 28, 30; 13:1–3, 19 [Eng 12:32—13:2]); 15:5, 9; 16:12; 17:10,
19; 19:9; 23:10, 24 [Eng 9, 23]; 24:8; 26:16–18; 28:1, 9, 13, 15, 45, 58.

86. Deut 13:5, 12 [Eng 4, 11], 11; 14:23; 17:13, 19; 19:20; 21:21; 25:18; 28:58;
31:12–13.

87. The word לֵבָב/לֵב occurs frequently: Deut 13:4 [Eng 3]; 15:7, 9–10; 17:17, 20;
18:21; 20:3, 8; 26:16; 28:47, 65, 67.

88. Positive with לְמַעַן, "in order that": Deut 12:25, 28; 13:18 [Eng 17]; 14:23, 29;
16:20; 17:19–20; 22:7; 23:21 [Eng 20]; 24:19; 25:15. Negative with פֶּן, "lest": Deut
12:13, 19, 30; 15:9; 19:6; 20:5–7; 22:9; 25:3.

89. Apart from the Decalogue, Moses quotes divine speech in 5:28b–31; 9:12–
14; 10:1–2, 11.

90. Deut 12:20; 15:9; 17:14; 18:21; 20:3; 26:3, 5–10, 13–15.

his response to their desires, expressed particularly with the phrase, אַוַּת נַפְשֶׁךָ, "your personal desire." With remarkable magnanimity, in 12:15 Moses opens the door to the consumption of meat away from the central sanctuary as wide as he can: "Go ahead, slaughter and eat meat in any of your towns, as much as you desire (בְּכָל־אַוַּת נַפְשְׁךָ), according to the blessing of YHWH your God that he has given you. The unclean and the clean may eat of it, like they eat the meat of the gazelle and the deer." This tone continues in Deut 12:20–23:

> When YHWH your God enlarges your territory, as he has promised you, and you say, "I would like to eat meat," because you crave meat (כִּי־תְאַוֶּה נַפְשְׁךָ לֶאֱכֹל בָּשָׂר), you may eat meat whenever you desire (בְּכָל־אַוַּת נַפְשְׁךָ). If the place that YHWH your God will choose to put his name is too far away for you, then you may kill any of your herd or your flock, which YHWH has given you, as I have commanded you, and you may eat within your towns whenever you desire. Just as the gazelle or the deer is eaten, so you may eat of it. The unclean and the clean alike may eat of it. Only be sure that you do not eat the blood, for the blood is the life, and you shall not eat the life with the flesh.

In 14:24–26 Moses makes it as convenient as possible for people who live far from the central sanctuary to bring the tithes of their crops, permitting them to bring the equivalent value in silver shekels:

> If the way is too long for you, and you are unable to carry the tithe, when YHWH your God blesses you, because the place that YHWH your God chooses to set his name is too far away, then you may convert its value to money. With the money secure in your hand you may go to the place that YHWH your God chooses and spend the money for whatever you desire (אֲשֶׁר־תְּאַוֶּה נַפְשְׁךָ בְּכֹל)—oxen or sheep or wine or strong drink, whatever your appetite craves. And you may eat there before YHWH your God and celebrate, you and your household.

In 18:6–8 Moses extends the same magnanimity to the Levites: "If a Levite leaves any of your towns out of all Israel, from wherever he lives to the place that YHWH will choose, he may do so whenever he desires (בְּכָל־אַוַּת נַפְשׁוֹ). Then he may minister in the name of YHWH his God, like all his fellow Levites who stand to minister there before YHWH, and he may have equal portions to eat, besides what he receives from the sale of his patrimony."

Although the expression is missing in 17:14–15, Moses accedes to the people's desire for a king with equal magnanimity: "When you come to the land that YHWH your God is giving you, and you possess it and dwell in it and then you say, 'I would like to set a king over me, like all the nations that are around me,' then go ahead, set a king over yourself, [only be sure that] he is the one YHWH your God will choose. You may install over yourself a king from among your brothers. You may not put a foreigner over you, who is not your brother."

Although this permission is granted within the context of a series of official appointments (judges, 16:18–19; priests, 18:1–8; prophets, 18:9–22), none of these texts is cast in the form of a law. These are Moses' instructions regarding the nation's leadership to ensure that "righteousness, only righteousness" (צֶדֶק צֶדֶק) prevails in the land.[91]

The pastoral nature of chapters 12–26 is suggested by the framework of this large section. Commentaries and English translations often refer to the opening pericope as "the altar law" (12:2–14). However, not only does the text not speak of an altar at all, this label obscures the exciting provisions for worship Moses announced here. If the critical verbs in verses 5–14 are translated modally, rather than as imperatives, the passage takes on a different flavor:

> But you may repair to the place that YHWH your God will choose out of all your tribes to put his name and establish it there. There you may come, and there you may bring your burnt offerings and your sacrifices, your tithes and the contribution that you present, your votive offerings, your freewill offerings, and the firstborn of your herd and of your flock. And there you may eat before YHWH your God, and you may rejoice, you and your households, in all that you undertake, in which YHWH your God has blessed you . . .
>
> When you cross the Jordan and live in the land that YHWH your God is giving you as a grant, and when he gives you rest from all your enemies around, so that you live in safety, then to the place that YHWH your God will choose to establish his name, there you may bring all that I command you: your burnt offerings and your sacrifices, your tithes and

91. Most commentators and translations mistakenly render the phrase "justice, only justice," but this gives the expression too legal a flavor and obscures the scope of the instructions that follow.

the contribution that you present, and all your finest votive offerings that you vow to YHWH. And you may rejoice before YHWH your God, you and your sons and your daughters, your male servants and your female servants, and the Levite that is within your towns, since he has no portion or grant of land with you. Take care that you do not offer your burnt offerings at any place that you see, but at the place that YHWH will choose in one of your tribes, there you may offer your burnt offerings, and there you may do all that I am commanding you. (12:5–14)

This is not law; this is an invitation to an ongoing relationship with YHWH through feasting and fellowshipping in his presence. The same is true of the instructions at the end of this large unit:

When you come into the land that YHWH your God is giving you for an inheritance and have taken possession of it and live in it, you shall take some of the first of all the fruit of the ground, which you harvest from your land that YHWH your God is giving you, and you shall put it in a basket, and you shall go to the place that YHWH your God will choose, to make his name to dwell there. And you shall go to the priest who is in office at that time and say to him, "I declare today to YHWH your God that I have come into the land that YHWH swore to our fathers to give us." Then the priest shall take the basket from your hand and set it down before the altar of YHWH your God.

And you shall respond before YHWH your God, saying, "My father was a wandering Aramean. He went down into Egypt and sojourned there, only a handful in number, and there he became a nation, great, mighty, and populous. But the Egyptians treated us harshly and humiliated us and laid on us hard labor. Then we cried out to YHWH, the God of our fathers, and YHWH heard our voice and saw our affliction, our toil, and our oppression. And YHWH brought us out of Egypt with a mighty hand and an outstretched arm, with great deeds of terror, with signs and wonders. And he brought us into this place and gave us this land, a land flowing with milk and honey. Now see, I bring the first of the fruit of the ground, which you, O YHWH, have given me." And you shall set it down before YHWH your God and worship before YHWH your God. And you may rejoice in all the good that YHWH your God has given to you and to your house, you, and the Levite, and the sojourner who is among you.

> When you have finished paying all the tithe of your pro-
> duce in the third year, which is the year of tithing, giving it
> to the Levite, the sojourner, the fatherless, and the widow, so
> that they may eat within your towns and be filled, then you
> shall say before YHWH your God, "I have removed the sa-
> cred portion from my house, and I have given it to the Levite,
> the sojourner, the fatherless, and the widow, according to all
> your command that you have commanded me. I have not
> transgressed any of your commands, nor have I forgotten
> them. I have not eaten of the tithe while I was mourning, or
> removed any of it while I was unclean, or offered any of it to
> the dead. I have obeyed the voice of YHWH my God. I have
> done according to all that you have commanded me. Look
> down from your holy habitation, from heaven, and bless your
> people Israel and the ground that you have given us, as you
> swore to our fathers, a land flowing with milk and honey.
> (26:1–15)"

This is not law. These are the instructions of a pastor about to leave, challenging his congregation never to forget YHWH's saving and providential grace, and never to forget the economically mar-ginalized in the community. Moses ended his third address with a passionate appeal to fidelity, describing again Israel's privileged role as YHWH's people and the conditions necessary to enjoy the benefits that come with the role, and then with severe warnings against infi-delity (28:1–68). Like chapters 12–26, chapter 28 is driven by pastoral concerns, setting before the people two ways: the way of life through joyful obedience to YHWH (vv. 1–14), and the way of death through disobedience and persistent rebellion against YHWH (vv. 15–58). Brent Sandy rightly observes with reference to the curses that "this was language designed to get the hearers' attention, to warn of serious consequences, to arouse fear, to imagine what it would be like to be sinners in the hands of an angry God."[92]

Moses' Role in the Third Address

The image of Moses the pastor climaxes in the third address. In this speech he reviewed the significance of the events that had transpired on the plains of Moab,[93] reminded Israel of the ongoing need for fidel-

---

92. Sandy, *Plowshares and Pruning Hooks*, 89.

93. Israel's covenant relationship had been confirmed (29:1–13[Eng 2–14]).

ity and the frightening consequences of infidelity (29:14–28[Eng 15–29]), and promised them that should they fail, which seemed to him inevitable, divine judgment would not be the last word. Reiterating and expanding on the ending to the first address (4:29–31), he painted a picture of Israel's ultimate restoration to YHWH and the land (30:1–10), and then concluded with an altar call (30:15–20): "See, I have set before you today life and good, death and evil . . . So choose life, that you and your offspring may live, by loving YHWH your God, obeying his voice and holding fast to him, for he is your life and length of days, that you may dwell in the land that YHWH swore to your fathers, to Abraham, to Isaac, and to Jacob, to give them."

The liturgical event represented by the three addresses ended with the pastor encouraging the people and his successor for the challenges that lay ahead (31:1–8, 23), providing them with a written text of his final sermons to ensure their ongoing memory of divine grace and this covenantal moment (31:9–13, 24–29), teaching the people a closing song that would serve as the nation's national anthem (31:14–22, 30–32:47), and pronouncing the benediction over all the tribes (33:1–29). With this act Moses' final pastoral acts ended.

Conclusion

It is unfortunate that biblical scholars, pastors, and lay readers denigrate the fifth book of Moses by mislabeling it as "the second law" (Latin, *deuteronomium*) and the primary speaker in the book as a lawgiver. Some have recognized the book as a series of prophetic, liturgical, and military orations.[94] Others have acknowledged that as Torah the book is not primarily law, but a program of catechesis, intended to educate or socialize "a new generation in the community's tradition." As catechesis it is (1) theologically centered, (2) humanly adaptable, (3) form-critically inclusive, (4) socially transformative, and (5) communally oriented.[95] Dennis Olson is certainly correct in assuming that the book was intended to provide the basis for the identity and life of the community that survived the exile. However, even if the book as we have it was produced later, the book itself wants us to read it as oral and transcribed speeches by Moses intended to pro-

94. See "The Orations," in Weinfeld, *Deuteronomy and the Deuteronomic School*, 10–58.

95. Olsen, *Deuteronomy and the Death of Moses*, 7–14.

vide the basis for the identity and life of the community that crossed the Jordan River many centuries earlier. Therefore Deuteronomy is much more than a manifesto on polity[96] or a legal code establishing the boundaries of Israel's behavior. It is above all a pastoral manifesto for a community of faith whose identity and status are summarized in 14:1–2: "Sons you are to YHWH your God . . . You are a people holy to YHWH your God, and YHWH has chosen you out of all the peoples who are on the face of the earth to be his people, his treasured possession" (14:1–2). In 26:19 Moses declared YHWH's intention for Israel: to "set you high above all nations that he has made, for [his] praise, fame, and honor; and that you shall be a consecrated people to YHWH your God." Moses summarized the required ethical response in 10:12–13: "And now, Israel, what does YHWH your God require of you, but to fear YHWH your God, to walk in all his ways, to love him, to serve YHWH your God with all your heart and with all your soul, to keep YHWH's command and his ordinances, which I am commanding you today for your good?"

This is not law; this is *pastoral exhortation arising from gospel!* Deuteronomy presents Moses first and foremost as Israel's pastor, passionate in keeping the gospel ever before his congregation, and passionate in his call for unconditional and unqualified devotion to their Redeemer. Obviously he could not anticipate every conceivable ethical or spiritual situation that the people would encounter in Canaan. Therefore he tried to instill in his people a theological and theocentric worldview, a way of thinking that guarantees that every decision arises from a covenant commitment to YHWH and to one's fellow citizens,[97] and thereby ensure the success of Israel's mission as agent of divine grace to the nations.

---

96. See McBride, "Polity of the People of God," 229–44. McBride's perception of Deuteronomy as "the archetype of modern western constitutionalism" (243) is grounded in Josephus' view of תּוֹרָה as πολιτεία (i.e., a national "constitution") rather than νόμος. Cf. *Antiquities* 4.184, 193, 198, 302, 310, 312.

97. This is the reverse of the rabbinic tradition that cites YHWH as saying, "Would that they would abandon Me but keep my Torah" (commenting on Jer 6:11; 9:12–14). See Neusner, *The Treasury of Judaism*, 2:77.

4

Preaching Old Testament Law to New Testament Christians[1]

Introduction

I AM KEENLY AWARE THAT in proposing to address this subject I have guaranteed for myself a limited hearing. There are many reasons why there is little interest in preaching Old Testament law in our churches, whether they are mainline Protestant, charismatic, fundamentalist, or generic evangelical. This aversion toward Old Testament law arises from a series of "mythconceptions" concerning the law. First, we are deluded by the *ritualistic* myth, that is, that Old Testament law is preoccupied with boring ritualistic trivia, declared to be obsolete with Christ's final sacrifice on the cross. Second, we are driven away by the *historical* myth, that is, that Old Testament law concerns the times and cultural context of nations so far removed from our own that, unless one has purely academic or antiquarian interests, what it has to say about the human condition is hopelessly out of date. Third, we are repelled by the *ethical* myth: the OT law reflects a standard of ethics that is rejected as grossly inferior to the law of love announced by Jesus and the high stock placed on tolerance in our enlightened age. Fourth, we are confused by the *literary* myth, that is, that the Old Testament laws are written in literary forms that are so

1. This essay was previously published in *Hiphil* (*Scandinavian Evangelical E-Journal*) 3 (2006) 1–24, and subsequently published in three parts in *Ministry* 78.5 (2006) 5–11; 78.7 (2006) 12–16; 78.9 (2006) 15–18.

different from modern literature that we cannot understand them. Fifth, we are indoctrinated by the *theological* myth, that is, that Old Testament law presents a view of God that is utterly objectionable to modern sensitivities. So long as these "mythconceptions" determine the disposition of preachers and pastors toward Old Testament law there is little hope that they will pay much attention to those parts of the Old Testament that we refer to as Israel's constitutional literature.

Contributing to these "mythconceptions" are fundamental ideological and theological prejudices against Old Testament law. The essentially antinomian stance of contemporary Western culture may represent the most important factor, especially in our post-Christian and increasingly secular culture. But these will hardly explain why *within the church* the law has had such a bad rap for such a long time. The roots of the aversion to Old Testament law within the church may be traced back almost two thousand years to the second-century heretic Marcion. Marcion proclaimed a radical discontinuity between Old and New Testaments; Israel and the church; the God of the Old Testament and the God of the New. In his canon he rejected all of the Old Testament and accepted only those New Testament books that highlighted the discontinuity of the church from Israel, which left him with radically edited versions only of the Gospel of Luke and ten Pauline Epistles (minus the pastorals and Hebrews). This is not so different from American evangelical Christianity, which bears a distinctly Pauline stamp (cf. the Eastern Church), and hears only Paul's criticism of Old Testament law.

In Western Protestantism we observe two traditional specific streams of antipathy toward Old Testament law. The first is associated with Lutheranism, with its fundamental law-gospel contrast. In his epochal discovery of the "gospel of grace" in the course of his study of Romans, Luther came to identify the ritualism and works-oriented approach to salvation of Roman Catholicism with the Old Testament law. But in Christ believers are declared to be free from the law! The grace of the gospel in Christ has replaced the bondage of the law under Moses. The second is associated with extreme forms of dispensationalism. In its division of human history into seven dispensations, a radical change in the divine economy is seen to have occurred in the transition from the Old to the New Testament. We are now in the church age, which is fundamentally the dispensation of grace, in contrast to the age of Israel, ruled by the dispensation of law. To these two traditional sources of the problem of Old Testament law within American evangelical Christianity we must now add a third, more recent development, namely the influence of New Covenant Theology. This movement, which has its roots in Reformed theology but exhibits a radically different view toward the Old Testament than Calvin himself did, insists that since the "Mosaic Covenant" [sic][2] has come to an end in Christ, it has no claim on Christians. We are subject only to the law of Christ.[3] This dichotomy is remarkable, especially in the face of the New Testament's repeated and emphatic identification of Jesus Christ with YHWH.

Consequently, if one hears preaching from Old Testament law at all (which is rare!), the preaching tends to take one of three approaches.[4] First, since through his atoning work Jesus Christ has abolished the law as a way of life, Old Testament law has no bearing on the Christian at all. In fact, the blessed gospel of grace liberates us from the curse of the law.[5] Second, interpreting the word τέλος in Rom 10:4 as the "fulfillment" rather than the "end" of the law, Jesus Christ is seen as the culminative fruit of Old Testament law, and since his righteousness is imputed to us, we are not under obligation to any external code. Third, since the Ten Commandments and some of the ethical injunctions of the Torah are thought to have some binding force on Christians, the operative question with respect to Old Testament law is, "Do I have to keep this law?" Careful attention is paid to distinguishing among the ceremonial, civil, and moral laws. A fourth theonomist option, which views the Old Testament law fun-

---

2. "Mosaic covenant" is a misnomer. Unlike the Abrahamic and Davidic covenants, which are rightly named after the person whom God graciously chose to be his covenant partner, the covenant made at Sinai was not made with Moses. He served as the mediator between the two covenant partners, YHWH and Israel. Since no other biblical covenants are named after the place where they were established, "Sinai covenant" is no better. Following the paradigm of the Abrahamic and Davidic covenants, it is best referred to as the "Israelite covenant," or "neo-Abrahamic covenant," inasmuch as through this ceremony Israel as a nation was formally recognized as the heir of Abraham (cf. Gen 17:7–8).

3. See Wells and Zaspel, *New Covenant Theology*.

4. Cf. Bergen's summary of the three basic positions represented in New Testament scholarship on the disposition of the early church to the law in "Preaching Old Testament Law," 55–56.

5. Rom 3:21; 6:14; 7:4; 10:4; Gal 2:19–21; 3:23–26; 4:21–31; Heb 7:12.

damentally to be in force even for the church, receives scant attention these days.

So long as the first three perspectives determine the relationship of Old Testament law to New Testament Christians we can hardly expect to hear much preaching from the law. But how Christians can tolerate this antinomian stance remains a mystery to me, especially in the light of Jesus' own statements that he came *not to abolish* the law, but to *fulfill* it, and his own declarations of its permanent validity (Matt 5:17–20); in the light of his declaration that love for him is demonstrated first and foremost by keeping his commands (John 14:15; cf. 15:10), and Paul's assertion that "it is not the hearers of the law who are righteous before God, but the doers of the law who will be justified" (Rom 2:13).

"All Scripture is breathed out by God and profitable for teaching, for reproof, for correction, and for training in righteousness, that the person of God may be competent, equipped for every good work" (2 Tim 3:16–17). Does this statement really mean that "while believers were not obliged to carry out all the demands of the Mosaic law, they *could* nevertheless draw from the O[ld] T[estament], read paradigmatically, lessons for Christian living."[6] They "*could*" draw lessons? Does it have no more moral force than an invitation to read it as an optional sourcebook for optional lessons? Should C. G. Kruse not have said at least, "they *should* nevertheless draw from the O[ld] T[estament], read paradigmatically, lessons for Christian living"? In order to move beyond this typical trivializing of the Old Testament we probably need to take a closer look at Old Testament law, particularly as the Old Testament law presents itself. I propose to do so under four headings:

A. The Designations for "Law" in the Old Testament

B. The Literary Contexts of Laws in the Old Testament

C. The Significance of the Laws of the Old Testament for Old Testament Saints

D. The Significance of the Laws of the Old Testament for New Testament Saints

I will conclude with some reflections on the implications of these observations for our preaching today.

6. Thus Kruse, "Law," 636.

A. The Designations for "Law" in the Old Testament

The Old Testament uses a series of expressions to refer to the laws of God. Perhaps the most explicit is the term מִצְוָה, "command," from the verb צִוָּה, "to command." But the term "command" should not be construed as synonymous with "law." In day to day life we often give orders that need to be carried out immediately or in a given circumstance, but this is not the same as an ordinance by which our church or company must operate until further ordinances are handed down.

The laws in the Pentateuch are often referred to by the standardized word pair חֻקִּים וּמִשְׁפָּטִים, often translated "decrees/ordinances and judgments." On etymological grounds one may surmise that the former expression, singular חֹק, "ordinance," derives from a root חָקַק, "to inscribe, incise," and refers to "inscribed" laws, that is laws that have been prescribed by a superior and recorded by incising a clay tablet with a reed stylus, or a wax-covered writing board with a metal stylus, or even a stone with a chisel. The form of the second expression, מִשְׁפָּטִים, "laws" (literally, "judgments"), apparently originates in case law. Judgments previously made in judicial contexts become laws in a prescriptive sense. When originating with YHWH they represent his "judgments" concerning Israel's conduct in the pursuit of righteousness (צְדָקָה). While some have argued that חֻקִּים relate primarily to religious regulations and מִשְׁפָּטִים to civil law,[7] within the book of Deuteronomy at least these distinctions cannot be maintained.

To this list we should also add פִּקּוּד (pl. פִּקּוּדִים), "obligation, regulation, procedure," from פָּקַד, "to muster, commission," which occurs twenty-four times in the Psalms.[8] A fifth expression is הָעֵדֹת, "the stipulations." Based on the assumption of a derivation from the same root as עֵד, "testimony," the New International Version follows the traditional rendering of the word with "testimonies."[9] However, since we usually think of "testimony" as the utterance of a witness in a court of law or some less formal context in which a particular event is being debated or discussed, this interpretation is misleading.[10] It is true that in the case of a person who had sworn an oath to keep an

---

7. See Liedke, "חקק einritzen, festsetzen," *THAT* 1:631.

8. *HALOT* 959.

9. Thus LXX (μαρτύρια), Vulgate, the Targums.

10. Hague (*NIDOTTE* 1:502) notes that "the translation of עֵדוּת as 'testimony' is reasonable, as long as we understand the testimony as *the law* that is the seal of the Lord's covenant with Israel."

agreement but was being brought to court for violating it, the written document could certainly be produced as a standard against which to measure his behavior, hence to serve as a *witness*. However, the possibility of an etymological link with the Akkadian word for "covenant/ treaty" and "loyalty oath,"[11] strengthens the case for interpreting עֵדֹת (plural of עֵדוּת) as a general designation for the stipulations of the covenant. This interpretation is confirmed in Deut 4:45, which clarifies the sense of הָעֵדֹת, "the stipulations," by adding הַחֻקִּים וְהַמִּשְׁפָּטִים, "the ordinances and laws."[12] The fact that all these expressions have the article suggests a specific and identifiable body of laws is in mind. In accordance with our conclusions regarding the significance of הַחֻקִּים וְהַמִּשְׁפָּטִים, "the ordinances and laws," stated earlier, the covenant stipulations refers to the specific body/bodies of prescriptions revealed by YHWH through Moses at Sinai, and periodically prior to the present addresses (cf. Num 36:13), an interpretation supported by the addition of "when they came out of Egypt."

These five words do indeed often refer to the specific laws and regulations prescribed by YHWH at Sinai and elsewhere. While the expressions above tend to be associated with specific kinds of laws, the expression most often associated with "law" itself is תּוֹרָה. The noun תּוֹרָה derives from the verb הוֹרָה, "to teach."[13] On occasion תּוֹרָה may be legitimately translated as "law." However, its everyday meaning is illustrated by the book of Proverbs, which applies the term to the instruction that the wise provide for the community (13:14), parents provide for children (1:8 [mother]; 4:1–11), and the woman of the household to those under her influence (31:26). Its theological meaning is illustrated most clearly by the book of Deuteronomy, which, contrary to the Greek (and English) name of the book (δευτερονόμιον, "second law"), does not present itself as "law," but as

11. On the meaning and significance of *adē* see Parpola and Watanabe, *Neo-Assyrian Treaties and Loyalty Oaths*, xv–xxv.

12. This interpretation is strengthened by the observation that what Moses will call the "ark of the covenant of YHWH" (אֲרוֹן בְּרִית־יְהוָה, Deut 10:8; 31:9, 25–26) is referred to elsewhere as the "the ark of the stipulation" (אֲרֹן הָעֵדֻת, Exod 25:22; 26:33–34; 30:6, 26; 31:7; 39:35; 40:3, 5, 21; Num 4:5, 16; 7:89). The present triad of terms recurs in Deut 6:20 (with הָעֵדֹת preceding the present pair). הָעֵדֹת appears between מִצְוֹת and חֻקִּים in 6:17. On the meaning and significance of עֵדֹת/עֵדֻת, see Simian-Yofre, *TDOT* 10:514–15.

13. *HALOT* 436–37.

a series of pastoral addresses (Deut 1:1–5; 4:40). Admittedly Moses repeats and adapts many of the ordinances previously prescribed by YHWH, but the first eleven and the last nine chapters contain little that we would classify as "law" in a legal sense, and even the so-called "Deuteronomic Code" (Deut 12–26) has a predominantly pastoral and didactic (rather than legal) flavor. In fact, in the book of Deuteronomy the semantic range of תּוֹרָה, is much better captured in Greek by διδασκαλια or διδαχη, rather than νομος as the Septuagint renders the term in 202 of 220 occurrences.[14]

This conclusion regarding the meaning of תּוֹרָה, is confirmed when we observe how easily its scope was extended to the rest of the Pentateuch, despite the fact that at least two-thirds of Genesis–Numbers is narrative; that is, the story of YHWH's grace in election, salvation, and providential care for Israel, and his establishment of his covenant first with Abraham and then with the patriarch's descendants at Sinai. When the psalmist declares that the godly delight in the תּוֹרָה of YHWH (Ps 1:2), surely he did not have in mind only the laws of Sinai, for apart from the surrounding narrative the laws provide no occasion for joy.

B. The Literary Contexts of Laws in the Old Testament

Before we preach from Old Testament law we need to remind ourselves that there is law in the Old Testament and there is law. Since the groundbreaking work of Albrecht Alt,[15] many scholars have recognized two major types of laws:[16] laws in the conditional form dealing with specific cases, and laws in the unconditional form. The former typically involve a protasis introduced with "When/If" (Hebrew כִּי or אָם in subordinate cases) describing a specific circumstance, fol-

---

14. Both expressions are common in the New Testament. For *didaskalia*, see Matt 15:9; Mark 7:7; Rom 12:7; 15:4; Eph 4:14; Col 2:22; 1 Tim 1:10; 4:1, 6, 13, 16; 5:17; 6:1, 3; 2 Tim 3:10, 16; 4:3; Tit 1:9; 2:1, 7. For *didachē*, see Matt 7:28; 16:12; 22:33; Mark 1:22, 27; 4:2; 11:18; 12:38; Luke 4:32; John 7:16–17; 18:19; Acts 2:42; 13:12; 17:19; Rom 6:17; 16:17; 1 Cor 14:6, 26; Eph 4:14; 1 Tim 4:6; 2 Tim 4:2; Tit 1:9; Heb 6:2; 13:9; 2 John 9–10; Rev 2:14, 15, 24.

15. Alt, "The Origins of Israelite Law," 101–71.

16. Alt's classification of these laws as "casuistic" and "apodictic" has recently been criticized as too simplistic, not allowing enough room for mixed forms, and even misnamed. See Sonsino, "Forms of Biblical Law," 252–53.

lowed by an apodosis outlining the required response. These may be cast in third person ("If a person . . .") or second person ("If you . . ."). The latter are typically cast as direct commands in the second person, though third person jussives are not uncommon. Apodictic laws subdivide further into positive prescriptions ("Honor your father and mother"), or negative prohibitions ("You shall not murder"). The differences between the two types are obvious when specific examples are juxtaposed as in the following synopsis:

TABLE 2: A Comparison of Conditional and Unconditional Law

Conditional Law	Unconditional Law
Exodus 21:28 If an ox gores a man or woman to death, the ox shall surely be stoned and its flesh shall not be eaten; but the owner of the ox shall go unpunished.	Exodus 20:3 You shall have no other gods before me.
Exodus 22:25–26 [Eng 26–27] If you ever take your neighbor's cloak as a pledge, you are to return it to him before the sun sets, for that is his only covering; it is his cloak for his body. What else shall he sleep in?	Exodus 20:16 You shall not bear false witness against your neighbor.
Features	**Features**
Conditional	Unconditional
Declarative mood	Imperative mood
In third (or second) person	In second person
Specific: based on actual cases, often with motive or exception clauses	General: without qualification or exception
Usually positive in form	Often negative in form
Begin with "If" or "When"	Begin with the verb (in the imperative)

The Pentateuch contains a great deal of prescriptive material through which YHWH sought to govern every aspect of the Israelites' lives. Maimonides, a twelfth-century Jewish rabbi and philosopher, established that the commandments scattered throughout the Pentateuch numbered 613.[17]

Beyond recognizing the basic formal differences between individual laws, preachers do well also to recognize the differences among the series of specific documents within the Pentateuch that might qualify as law. These may be grouped in two classifications. On the one hand, we note the focused instructions, usually involving cultic and liturgical matters: "Instructions Concerning the Passover" (Exod 12–13), "Instructions Concerning the Tabernacle" (Exod 25–31), "Instructions Concerning Sacrifice" (Lev 1–7). On the other hand, we note the collections of ordinances and regulations governing a wide range of human activity: the Decalogue (Exod 20:2–17; Deut 5:6–21), the "Book of the Covenant" (סֵפֶר הַבְּרִית, Exod 20:22—23:19, cf. 24:7), the "Instructions on Holiness" (Lev 17–26),[18] and the so-called "Deuteronomic Torah" (Deut 12–26, 28). Although these documents all represent collections of prescriptions whose scope covers all of life, each has its own distinctive flavor.

1. The Decalogue

In both Exodus 20 and Deuteronomy 5 the Decalogue is presented as the only speech of YHWH addressed directly to the Israelites. Contrary to modern practice, the Scriptures never refer to the Decalogue as the "Ten Commandments." The genre of the document is identified in both contexts as "all these words" (כָּל־הַדְּבָרִים הָאֵלֶּה, Exod 20:1; Deut 5:22) that YHWH "spoke" (דִּבֶּר), rather than "these commandments" that YHWH "commanded." In fact, whenever this document is identified by title it is always referred to as "the Ten *Words*" (עֲשֶׂרֶת הַדְּבָרִים, Exod 34:28; Deut 4:13; 10:4), and never "the Ten *Commandments*." At this point we would do well to follow the Septuagint in referring to this document as the Decalogue (δέκα λόγοι, literally "Ten Words"), or, since the Hebrew word דָּבָר is capable of a broad range of meaning, "the Ten Principles" of covenant relationship. That this document is perceived as the foundational written record of YHWH's covenant with Israel is demonstrated not only in the fact that two copies (one for each party) of this

---

17. See Reines, "Commandments, The 613," 760–83.
18. Referred to by scholars as the "Holiness Code."

document alone were stored in the "ark of the covenant of YHWH" (אֲרוֹן בְּרִית־יְהוָה, Deut 10:1–5), but also Moses' explicit reference to this document as "his covenant" (בְּרִיתוֹ, Deut 4:13). The structure of the narratives introducing the Decalogue reinforces the covenantal nature of the Decalogue. Indeed in both Exodus and Deuteronomy it is cast in the pattern of an ancient Near Eastern suzerainty treaty:

(a)   The Preamble (Exod 20:1; Deut 5:1–5) sets the stage for the document.

(b)   The Historical Prologue (Exod 20:2; Deut 5:6) introduces the divine suzerain and summarizes the history of the relationship of the parties to the covenant to this point: "I am YHWH your God who brought you out of the land of Egypt, out of the house of slavery."

(c)   The Covenant Principles (Exod 20:3–17; Deut 5:7–21) specify the fundamental obligations placed upon the human vassal. The Principles of Covenant Relationship were reduced to ten presumably to facilitate commitment to memory and to match the number of fingers on our hands. Their unconditional form invests them with an absolutist flavor. Inasmuch as the terms of the Decalogue are addressed to potential perpetrators of offenses it may be interpreted as ancient Israel's version of the "Bill of Rights." However, unlike modern Bills of Rights, the Decalogue is not concerned to protect *my* rights but the rights of the next person. According to the arrangement of the stipulations of the Decalogue the *next person* involves two parties: YHWH, the divine Suzerain, and fellow members of the vassal community.[19] In fact, as Jesus and Paul recognized in their reduction of all the commandments to the command to love YHWH and one's neighbor (Luke 10:27; Rom 13:9), the objec-

---

19. The vertical dimensions of covenant (Exod 20:1–11) respectively call for a recognition of YHWH's right to: (a) exclusive allegiance; (b) the definition of his image; (c) honor and true representation; (d) govern human time. The horizontal dimensions of covenant (20:8–17) respectively call for a recognition of (a) the members of the household's right to humane treatment (cf. Deut 5:12–15); (b) parents' right to respect from children; (c) the right of all to life; (4) the right of all to a pure and secure marriage; (5) the right to personal property; (6) the right to an honest reputation; (7) the right to security. The terms add up to eleven because the fourth is transitional. The Exodus version highlights the Sabbath as a creation ordinance; the Deuteronomic version highlights its humanitarian character.

tive of the Decalogue is to encourage love for God and for one's neighbor,[20] the kind of behavior that puts the interests of the next person ahead of one's own.

(d) The Declaration of the People's Response (Exod 20:18–21; Deut 5:22–33) reports the people's acceptance of the document and a recognition of its revelatory significance. The latter text ends with a summary blessing as a reward for obedience (vv. 31–33), also common to ancient treaty forms.

2. The "Book of the Covenant" (Exod 20:22—23:19)

Although the Decalogue obviously functioned as the official covenant document, this does not mean that it exhausted the terms of YHWH's covenant. Indeed the other collections of laws may be interpreted as elaborations and practical explications of the Decalogue. The "Book of the Covenant," encompassing Exod 20:21—23:33, derives its name from Exod 24:7, according to which, as part of the covenant ratification ceremony Moses took the סֵפֶר הַבְּרִית (literally, "written document of the covenant") and read it in the hearing of all the people, precipitating their third declaration of "All that YHWH has spoken we will do." Unlike the Decalogue, which is referred to as דְּבָרִים ("words") declared directly by YHWH to the people, this document is formally introduced as מִשְׁפָּטִים ("judgments, regulations") that Moses is to set before the people (Exod 21:1). Furthermore, whereas the Decalogue consists entirely of unconditional statements in the second person, the Book of the Covenant consists largely of conditional statements in the third person. Taken as a whole the Book of the Covenant may be divided into six parts arranged in an artful, chiastic order:

A Introduction (20:22, placing Israel's response to covenant in the present context of divine revelation)

　B Principles of Worship (20:23–26, highlighting Israel's cultic expression of devotion to Yahweh)

　　C Casuistic Laws (21:1—22:20, highlighting Israel's ethical expression of devotion to Yahweh)

---

20. Cf. Childs, *The Book of Exodus*, 439.

C' Apodictic Laws (22:20 [Eng 21]—23:9, highlighting
Israel's ethical expression of devotion to Yahweh)

B' Principles of Worship (23:10–19, highlighting Israel's cultic
expression of devotion to Yahweh)

A' Conclusion (23:20–33, placing Israel's response to covenant in the
future context of divine action)

Notice that prescriptions for Israel's worship frame the prescriptions governing daily life. The purpose of worship is to inspire devotion to YHWH and to create an ethical community of faith. Worship and ethics are tightly linked.

3. The "Instructions on Holiness" (Lev 17–26)

What distinguishes this "Code" from other similar texts, such as the Book of the Covenant (Exod 20:22—23:33), is its emphasis on *holiness*. First, YHWH identifies himself as the Holy One (קָדוֹשׁ, Lev 19:2; 20:26; 21:8). Second, YHWH identifies himself as the one who makes Israel holy (קָדַשׁ, "sanctifies them," 20:8; 21:8, 15, 23; 22:9, 16, 32; cf. הַבְדִּיל, 20:24, 26) Third, Israel is challenged to "Sanctify yourselves" (הִתְקַדֵּשׁ, 20:7) and "Be holy" (קְדֹשִׁים תִּהְיוּ, 19:2; 20:7, 26 [to YHWH]; 21:6a, 6b [cf. 7, 8]). Fourth, many of the articles and persons discussed in this section are described as holy (קֹדֶשׁ): YHWH's name, 20:3; 22:3, 32; sacrificial food, 19:8; ordinary food, 19:24; sacred bread, 21:22; 24:9; food dedicated to YHWH, 22:2–4, 6, 10, 14–16; convocations, 23:2–4, 7–8, 21, 24, 27, 35–37; a place (tabernacle), 24:9; a time (Year of Jubilee) 25:12. As for the content of this long section, it provides a summary catch-all of moral exhortations, cultic regulations, and legal prescriptions. What use was made of this "Holiness Code" in ancient Israel we may only speculate. D. N. Freedman suggests it may have served "as a catechism for some sanctuary school, or as a guide for priests and Levites in their work as teachers of the people."[21] We may view this document as an exposition of the expressions "a kingdom of priests" and "holy nation" in Exod 19:5.

That this is viewed as an exposition of the nature of Israel's covenant relationship with YHWH is demonstrated by the eighteen-fold occurrence of YHWH's self introduction as "I am YHWH your

---

21. Freedman, "Pentateuch," 722.

God,"[22] which represents an adaptation of the covenant formula, "I am your God and you are my people" (cf. 20:26; 26:12). Looking far ahead to the time when the Israelites will be settled in the land that YHWH has promised them, this document seeks to govern the life of the Israelites as YHWH's vassals (עֲבָדִים, Lev 25:42, 55) living in YHWH's land (25:23). The covenantal nature of this document is affirmed by the addition of chapter 26. This chapter not only refers to the covenant six times,[23] but its presence here accords with the pattern of ancient Near Eastern Hittite treaties, which typically followed up the stipulations with declarations of blessings as a reward for obedience.[24]

4. The "Deuteronomic Torah" (Deut 12–26, 28)

It has become customary for scholars to refer to the long section of text encompassing Deuteronomy 12–26, 28 as the Deuteronomic Law Code. This seems justified on several grounds. First, it is formally framed by references to the laws of God:

> *Introduction:* "These (אֵלֶּה) are the ordinances (הַחֻקִּים) and laws (הַמִּשְׁפָּטִים) that you shall keep (תִּשְׁמְרוּן) by doing (לַעֲשׂוֹת) [them] in the land that YHWH, the God of your fathers, has given you to possess, all the days that you live on the earth." (12:1)

> *Conclusion:* "YHWH your God commands you this day to follow these (הָאֵלֶּה) ordinances (הַחֻקִּים) and the laws (הַמִּשְׁפָּטִים), and you shall keep (וְשָׁמַרְתָּ) and do (וְעָשִׂיתָ) them." (26:16)

Second, Moses repeatedly refers explicitly to "ordinances" (חֻקִּים),[25] "laws" (מִשְׁפָּטִים),[26] "command"/"commands" (הַמִּצְוָה/מִצְוֹת),[27] "instruction" (תּוֹרָה, usually rendered "law"),[28] and "covenant stipulations" (הָעֵדֹת, usually rendered "testimonies"), if one may refer back

22. Lev 18:2, 4, 30; 19:3–4, 10, 25, 31, 34, 36; 20:7, 24; 23:22, 43; 24:22; 25:17, 38, 55.

23. Verses 9, 15, 25, 42, 44–45.

24. See Kitchen, *On the Reliability of the Old Testament*, 283–89.

25. Deut 16:12; 17:19; 26:16–17.

26. Deut 26:16–17.

27. Deut 13:5, 19 [Eng 4, 18]; 15:5; 17:20; 19:9; 26:13, 17–18; cf. 27:1; 30:11; 31:5.

28. Deut 17:18–19; cf. 4:44; 28:61; 29:20, 28 [Eng 21, 29]; 30:10; 31:9, 11–12, 24, 26.

to 4:45, which functions as a heading for the second half of Moses' second speech. Third, within this large block of material we do indeed find several series of regulations that have the appearance of legal lists, especially in chapters 22–25. Fourth, the types of issues dealt with in these chapters often correspond to those found in codes of law outside the Old Testament.[29]

Recently it has become fashionable to argue that Moses' presentation of the covenant obligations in Deuteronomy 12–26 is structured after the Decalogue. Stephen Kaufman, for example, has argued that the Deuteronomic Code derives from a single redactor, who has organized the entire Code after the model provided by the Decalogue as a whole.[30] It is apparent throughout that Moses has the Principles of Covenant Relationship as outlined in the Decalogue in mind, but this system seems quite forced, and can be achieved only by resorting to extraordinary exegetical and redactional gymnastics.[31] Moses seems here to have been inspired by other aspects of the Sinai revelation as well. Although there are also strong links with Exodus 34:11–28,[32] Bernard Levinson argues more plausibly that the Deuteronomic Code represents a revision of the Covenant Code (Exod 21–23).[33] The links are recognized not only in the details, but also in the broad structure of the text, as the synopsis in Table 3 illustrates:

---

29. The links have been noted frequently. For a helpful collection of ancient Near Eastern law codes, see Roth, *Law Collections from Mesopotamia and Asia Minor*.

30. "The Structure of Deuteronomic Law," 105–58. For a variation of this approach, see Braulik, *Die deuteronomischen Gesetze und der Dekalog*; idem, "Die Abfolge der Gesetze," 252–72. Merrill follows this approach in his commentary, *Deuteronomy*, 31.

31. It is an unlikely stretch, for example, to interpret Moses' instructions regarding administrative institutions in 16:18—18:22 as an exposition of the commandment to honor father and mother in 5:16. This approach is also rejected by Tigay, *Deuteronomy*, 226 n. 19, and Otto, *Das Deuteronomium*, 226.

32. So also Lohfink, "Zur deuteronomischen Zentralizationsformel," 324–26.

33. Levinson, *Deuteronomy and the Hermeneutics of Legal Innovation*, 144–50.

TABLE 3: A Synopsis of the Structures of
Exodus 20:22—23:19 and Deuteronomy 12:2—26:15

Exodus 20:22—23:19	Deuteronomy 12:2—26:15
A Principles of Worship (20:23–26) Highlighting Israel's cultic expression of devotion to Yahweh	A Principles of Worship (12:2–16:17) Highlighting Israel's cultic expression of devotion to Yahweh
B Casuistic and Apodictic Laws (21:1—23:9) Highlighting Israel's ethical and civil expression of devotion to Yahweh	B Casuistic and Apodictic Laws (16:18—25:15) Highlighting Israel's ethical and civil expression of devotion to Yahweh
A′ Principles of Worship (23:10–19) Highlighting Israel's cultic expression of devotion to Yahweh	A′ Principles of Worship (26:1–15) Highlighting Israel's cultic expression of devotion to Yahweh

Moses' flow of thought is best grasped, not by forcing it into some sort of Decalogic pattern, but by outlining chapters 12:2—26:15 on the basis of content and without reference to any external document. This lengthy document also displays strong links with the Holiness Code. Most striking is the addition of the lists of covenant blessings and curses in chapter 28, which echoes the addition of Leviticus 26 to the Instructions on Holiness.[34]

Despite these links with the Book of the Covenant, in tone and style much of Deuteronomy 12–26 bears a closer resemblance to chapters 6–11 than it does to the Sinai documents[35] on which they are based. In fact, there is no appreciable shift in style and tone as one moves from chapter 11 to chapter 12 and beyond. While scholars are quick to recognize in the speeches of the book of Deuteronomy the voices of a prophet or a scribe, or even a priest,[36] the concerns and style of the speaker are better understood as the addresses of a pastor who knows that his own tenure as shepherd of YHWH's sheep

34. Chapter 28 seems originally to have been attached directly to chapter 26, before chapter 27 was inserted.

35. The Book of the Covenant (Exod 20:22—23:33), the so-called Holiness Code (Lev 17–26).

36. For a helpful discussion of the prophetic and scribal voices, see Watts, *Reading Law*, 112–21; on the priestly voice, see von Rad, *Deuteronomy*, 23–27.

is about to come to an end.[37] As pastor, Moses is concerned not only about civil and liturgical matters, but especially with the spiritual and physical well-being of the people. He expresses particular passion about the people's relationship with God, a relationship that, on the one hand, is to be treasured as an incredible gift, and on the other hand is to be demonstrated in a life of grateful obedience to their divine Redeemer and Lord.

C. The Significance of the Laws of the Old Testament for Old Testament Saints

Even though we have clarified the forms and genres of the major constitutional documents in the Pentateuch, the chances are rather good that we have still not overcome the prejudices that inhibit preaching from these texts. In order to do so we probably need to wrestle a little more with the significance of these laws, particularly as Moses and the genuinely pious in ancient Israel understood them. As we try to resolve this issue we must keep in mind two important principles of interpretation. First, whenever we interpret a biblical text, the most important clues to its meaning must be derived from the immediate literary context, not later comments on the text. Second, biblical texts must always be interpreted in the light of the broader cultural context from which they derive, not the culture of a later time, let alone pervasive modern understandings of these texts.

I begin by drawing attention to a very important question raised by Moses in his second farewell pastoral address to his people, the Israelites, as quoted in Deut 6:20:

כִּי־יִשְׁאָלְךָ בִנְךָ מָחָר לֵאמֹר מָה הָעֵדֹת וְהַחֻקִּים וְהַמִּשְׁפָּטִים אֲשֶׁר צִוָּה
יְהוָה אֱלֹהֵינוּ אֶתְכֶם:

> "When your son asks you in time to come, 'What is the meaning of the covenant stipulations and the ordinances and the laws that YHWH our God has commanded you?'"

37. Moses gives most eloquent expression to this understanding of his role in Num 27:15–17: "Moses spoke to Yahweh, saying, 'Let Yahweh, the God of the spirits of all flesh, appoint a man over the congregation who shall go out before them and come in before them, who shall lead them out and bring them in, that the congregation of Yahweh may not be as sheep that have no shepherd.'"

The form in which Moses casts the question, arises out of the everyday experience of parents trying to raise their children. I shall never forget the evening when we as a family were gathered around the table enjoying our supper. As is often the case with teenage children, we were engaged in a rather warm discussion. Suddenly our son burst out, "Why do we have to live in such a prehistoric family?" While his motives left something to be desired, I took this as a compliment: at least he recognized that our household was run by counter-cultural norms.

The point Moses raises is that succeeding generations will not have memory of the experiences that the people in his audience have shared, either of YHWH's revelation at Sinai or his present discourses on that revelation on the plains of Moab. Therefore, it will be necessary for this and all subsequent generations to be very intentional in transmitting their faith to the next generation. As in every social context and every age, the children will watch the way their parents live, and, especially when faced with the challenge of competing cultures, they will be curious about the nature and rationale behind their own traditions. Moses assumes that the children will ask their parents for an explanation of their way of life.

The specific question Moses anticipates here concerns the covenant stipulations (הָעֵדֹת), ordinances (הַחֻקִּים), and regulations (הַמִּשְׁפָּטִים) that YHWH has commanded Israel to observe. These three expressions function as shorthand for the totality of the will of God as it had been revealed primarily at Horeb and to a lesser degree en route to the Promised Land. The question assumes a package: all the moral, ceremonial, and civil regulations that God has prescribed as the appropriate response to his salvation and the privilege of covenant relationship. As illustrated so impressively in Leviticus 19, this revelation refused to divide life into the sacred and the ordinary. When the children observe how their parents conduct their private and family lives, how they carry on their social and economic relations, how they worship, how they conduct themselves within the family, then they will inquire concerning the meaning of it all. Of course, what the children's question calls for is not a detailed exposition of each of the 613 laws in the Pentateuch identified by Maimonides, but an explanation of the significance of the entire package. In short, "Why is it that our lives are governed by this set of principles?" and "What is the significance of this set of laws?"

If we were asked today, "What is the significance of the stipulations, the ordinances, and laws that God commanded the Israelites to observe?" we would probably respond with several different answers. If we were actually to read the laws some of us would probably shake our heads in bewilderment, and wonder seriously whether there is any point to these laws at all. Look at Lev 19:19: "You shall keep my statutes. You shall not let your cattle breed with a different kind. You shall not sow your field with two kinds of seed, nor shall you wear a garment of cloth made of two kinds of material." Or consider Lev 11:3–6:

> Whatever parts the hoof and is cloven-footed and chews the cud, among the animals, you may eat. Nevertheless, among those that chew the cud or part the hoof, you shall not eat these: The camel, because it chews the cud but does not part the hoof, is unclean to you. And the rock badger, because it chews the cud but does not part the hoof, is unclean to you. And the hare, because it chews the cud but does not part the hoof, Is unclean to you.

If we are not truly bewildered by these kinds of laws, we may actually feel sorry for the Israelites. What a burden they were called upon to bear! Surely many must have looked on the other nations with envy that they weren't saddled with this load.

Some with cultural and antiquarian interests, especially those interested in the history of law and culture, might say these laws offer the modern reader an interesting window into the society of ancient Israel. Readers familiar with the Near Eastern legal world of the second millennium BCE might even conclude that these laws represent a significant advance on those found in the law code of Hammurabi, king of Babylon in the nineteenth century BCE.

My suspicion, however, is that many of us would not have answered the question in either of these ways. In our day, especially in contemporary Western evangelicalism, when asked about the significance of the law for Israel, many would answer that for Israel the law was the way of salvation. Whereas in the New Testament people are saved by grace, under the old covenant people were saved by keeping the law.

The problem with this explanation is that it flies in the face of Paul's explicit statements that even in the Old Testament, people (like

Abraham) were justified by faith rather than through obedience to the law (Rom 4; Gal 3:1–12). In fact, many view the law, not as a way of salvation, but as the way of death. And they quote Paul to buttress their position, for does he not say in Rom 4:15, "The law brings about wrath"; and in Rom 7:6, "But now we have been released from the law, having died to that by which we are bound"; and according to Gal 3:10–13, "as many as are of the works of the law are under a curse," and "the law is not of faith," and "Christ has redeemed us from the curse of the law"; and Gal 3:23–24, "Before faith came we were kept in custody under the law, being shut out from the faith that was later revealed, therefore the law has become our tutor"; and in Gal 4:21–31, speaking of the law, Paul writes that Mount Sinai (who is Hagar) bears children who are slaves, in contrast to Jerusalem, our mother, who has borne free children.

These verses seem to offer a rather clear answer to the question that Moses raised: The significance of the law lay in its power to bind those who are under the law, to subject them to the curse and the wrath of God, and to demonstrate their desperate need of a Savior. While on the surface this seems to be the way the New Testament perceives the law, it raises serious questions concerning both the justice and mercy of God. How and why would God rescue the Israelites from the burdensome and death-dealing slavery of Egypt (cf. Exod 20:2) only to impose upon them an even heavier burden of the law, which they in any case were unable to keep, and which would sentence them to an even more horrible fate—damnation under his own wrath? When you look at the exodus this way, it turns out not to be such a good deal after all.

One of the most important principles for the interpretation of Scripture is to interpret Scripture with Scripture. And this is indeed what we are doing when we appeal to Paul for the answer to Moses' question. But sometimes we move too quickly to later texts, especially the New Testament, and we forget the primacy of the immediate context in determining the meaning of any word or statement in Scripture. When we seek to understand the significance of the regulations and ordinances that God prescribed for his people, from the outset we need not only to explore seriously their function in the original settings, but also to distinguish between the ideal and the real; between the role of the laws in the lives of the Israelites as intended by God and Moses, and the way the Israelites actually used the laws.

First, God and Moses perceived obedience to the laws, not as a way of or precondition to salvation, but as the grateful response of those who had already been saved. In the New Testament Paul demonstrates this point by appealing to Abraham (Rom 4), but he might just as well have cited the experience of the nation of Israel, whose deliverance from Egypt becomes paradigmatic of a person's experience of salvation. God did not reveal the law to the Israelites in Egypt and then tell them that as soon as they had measured up to this standard he would rescue them. On the contrary, by grace alone, through faith, they crossed the Red Sea to freedom. All that was required was belief in the promise of God that he would hold up the walls of water on either side and see them safely through to the other shore. The chronological priority of Israel's salvation *vis-à-vis* the revelation of the law is illustrated clearly by Exod 19:4–6 and Deut 6:20–25:

> When your son asks you in time to come, "What is the meaning of the testimonies and the statutes and the rules that YHWH our God has commanded you?" then you shall say to your son, "We were Pharaoh's slaves in Egypt. And YHWH brought us out of Egypt with a mighty hand. And YHWH showed signs and wonders, great and grievous, against Egypt and against Pharaoh and all his household, before our eyes. And he brought us out from there, that he might bring us in and give us the land that he swore to give to our fathers. And YHWH commanded us to do all these statutes, to fear YHWH our God, for our good always, that he might preserve us alive, as we are this day. And it will be righteousness for us, if we are careful to do all this commandment before YHWH our God, as he has commanded us."

Second, God and Moses perceived obedience to the law not primarily as a duty imposed by one party on another, but as an expression of covenant relationship. Before God revealed his will to his people "he brought them to himself." Israel's primary commitment was not to be to a code of laws but to the God who graciously called Israel to covenant relationship with himself; they were to obey "his voice." In fact, he does not reveal his will to the people until he hears their declaration of complete and unconditional servitude to him as covenant lord (Exod 19:8). Every one of the so-called "law codes" listed above must be interpreted within the context of redemption and covenant.

Third, God and Moses perceived obedience to the law not as the precondition for salvation, but as the precondition to Israel's fulfillment of the mission to which she had been called and the precondition to her own blessing. The first point is highlighted in Exod 19:5–6: if Israel will keep YHWH's covenant and obey his voice she will be God's special treasure, his kingdom of priests, his holy nation (cf. Deut 26:16–19). The second is spelled out in detail in Lev 26:1–13 and Deut 28:1–4.

Fourth, God and Moses perceived God's revelation of the law to Israel as a supreme and unique privilege (Deut 4:6–8), in contrast to the nations who worshiped gods of wood and stone that never spoke (4:28; Ps 115:4–8). Contrary to prevailing contemporary evangelical opinion, for the genuinely faithful in Israel obedience to the law was *a delight*, in part because of their deep gratitude for God's grace experienced in salvation and covenant relationship, but also because they knew that God would respond to their obedience with favor (Deut 6:20–25; Ps 24:3–6). Moses alludes to this extraordinary fact in Deut 4:1–8:

> And now, O Israel, listen to the ordinances and the laws that I am teaching you, and do them, that you may live, and go in and take possession of the land that YHWH, the God of your fathers, is giving you. You shall not add to the word that I command you, nor take from it, that you may keep the commandments of YHWH your God that I command you. Your eyes have seen what YHWH did at Baal-peor, for YHWH your God destroyed from among you all the men who followed the Baal of Peor. But you who held fast to YHWH your God are all alive today. See, I have taught you ordinances and laws, as YHWH my God commanded me, that you should do them in the land that you are entering to take possession of it. Keep them and do them, for that will be your wisdom and your understanding in the sight of the peoples, who, when they hear all these ordinances, will say, "Surely this great nation is a wise and understanding people." For what great nation is there that has a god so near to it as YHWH our God is to us, whenever we call upon him? And what great nation is there, that has ordinances and laws as righteous as this whole Torah that I set before you today?

To help us understand the significance of the Torah I draw attention to a prayer, written in Sumerian, and probably dating back to the second millennium, but preserved in the library of Ashurbanipal, one of the seventh-century BCE emperors of Assyria.[38] The text is repetitious, but to get the point we need to read the entire piece.

Prayer to Every God[39]

May the fury of my lord's heart be quieted toward me.[40]
May the god who is not known be quieted toward me;
May the goddess who is not known be quieted toward me.
May the god whom I know or do not know be quieted toward me;
May the goddess whom I know or do not know
be quieted toward me.
May the heart of my god be quieted toward me;
May the heart of my goddess be quieted toward me.
May my god and goddess be quieted toward me.
May the god [who has become angry with me][41]
be quieted toward me;
May the goddess [who has become angry with me]
be quieted toward me. (10) (lines 11–18 cannot be restored
with certainty)
In ignorance I have eaten that forbidden of my god;
In ignorance I have set foot on that prohibited by my goddess. (20)

38. According to Stephens (*ANET*, 391–92),

> This prayer is addressed to no particular god, but to all gods in general, even those who may be unknown. The purpose of the prayer is to claim relief from suffering, which the writer understands is the result of some infraction of divine law. He bases his claim on the fact that his transgressions have been committed unwittingly, and that he does not even know what god he may have offended. Moreover, he claims, the whole human race is by nature ignorant of the divine will, and consequently is constantly committing sin. He therefore ought not to be singled out for punishment.

39. Adapted from *ANET*, 391–92.

40. According to Stephens (ibid.), the Sumerian is rendered literally, "of my lord, may his angry heart return to its place for me." The phrase "return to its place," a figurative expression for "to settle down," suggests the imagery of a raging storm or of water boiling in a kettle.

41. The restoration is based on line 32, after Langdon, *Babylonian Penitential Psalms*, 39–44.

O Lord, my transgressions are many;
great are my sins.
O my god, (my) transgressions are many;
great are (my) sins.
O my goddess, (my) transgressions are many;
great are (my) sins.
O god, whom I know or do not know,
(my) transgressions are many;
great are (my) sins;
O goddess, whom I know or do not know,
(my) transgressions are many;
great are (my) sins.
The transgression that I have committed, indeed I do not know;
The sin that I have done, indeed I do not know.
The forbidden thing that I have eaten, indeed I do not know;
The prohibited (place) on which I have set foot,
indeed I do not know.
The lord in the anger of his heart looked at me; (30)
The god in the rage of his heart confronted me;
When the goddess was angry with me, she made me become ill.
The god whom I know or do not know has oppressed me;
The goddess whom I know or do not know
has placed suffering upon me.
Although I am constantly looking for help,
no one takes me by the hand;
When I weep they do not come to my side.
I utter laments, but no one hears me;
I am troubled;
I am overwhelmed;
I can not see.
O my god, merciful one, I address to you the prayer,
"Ever incline to me";
I kiss the feet of my goddess;
I crawl before you. (40)
(lines 41–49 are mostly broken and cannot be restored with
certainty)
How long, O my goddess, whom I know or do not know,
before your hostile heart will be quieted? (50)
Man is dumb; he knows nothing;
Mankind, everyone that exists—what does he know?
Whether he is committing sin or doing good,
he does not even know.
O my lord, do not cast your servant down;
He is plunged into the waters of a swamp; take him by the hand.

The sin that I have done, turn into goodness;
The transgression that I have committed let the wind carry away;
My many misdeeds strip off like a garment.
O my god, (my) transgressions are seven times seven;
remove my transgressions;
O my goddess, (my) transgressions are seven times seven;
remove my transgressions; (60)
O god whom I know or do not know,
(my) transgressions are seven times seven;
remove my transgressions;
O goddess whom I know or do not know,
(my) transgressions are seven times seven;
remove my transgressions.
Remove my transgressions (and) I will sing your praise.
May your heart, like the heart of a real mother,
be quieted toward me;
Like a real mother (and) a real father may it be quieted toward me.

Is this not a pathetic piece? And what an indictment this prayer is on the religious systems of the world around ancient Israel! To be sure, with his keen sense of sin and his awareness of ultimate accountability before deity, this person expresses greater enlightenment than many in our own day. However, he cannot escape the fact that he is faced with three insurmountable problems. First, he does not know which god he has offended. Second, he does not know what the offense is. Third, he does not know what it will take to satisfy the god/gods. It is against this backdrop that we must interpret Moses' statements in Deut 4:1–8. With their clear knowledge of the will of YHWH, the faithful in Israel perceived themselves as an incredibly privileged people and the envy of the nations. Unlike other peoples, whose gods of wood and stone crafted by human hands neither saw nor heard nor smelled (Deut 4:28; cf. Ps 135:15–17), YHWH hears his people when they call upon him (Deut 4:7). And unlike the nations, whose idols have mouths but they do not speak (Ps 135:16), Israel's God has spoken. By his grace he has given his people statutes and judgments that are perfect in righteousness (Deut 4:8), because: (1) they reveal with perfect clarity who he is; (2) they reveal with perfect clarity what sin is; and (3) they reveal with perfect clarity how that sin may be removed and a relationship of peace and confidence with him established/maintained. This explains why, when David experiences forgiveness for his sins, he can exclaim, "Oh the joy/privilege of the one whose transgression is forgiven, whose sin is covered!"

Fifth, God and Moses perceived true obedience to the law to be the external expression of an inward disposition of fear and faith in God and covenant love toward him. True biblical religion has always been a matter of the heart. This internal transformation is referred to metaphorically as a circumcised heart (Lev 26:41; Deut 10:16; 30:6–10; Jer 4:4), a heart transplant (Jer 24:7; 32:39; Ezek 11:19; 36:26), the placement of God's Spirit within a person (Ezek 11:19; 36:26), and the writing of God's תּוֹרָה (tôrâ) in the heart (Jer 31:32). While these are occasionally viewed as future eschatological events to be experienced by all Israel, it is clear that they have always been true of the remnant of true believers in ancient Israel (e.g., Caleb, Num 14:24; also Pss 19:8–15 [Eng 7–14]; 37:31; 40:8 [Eng 7]; 51:18–19 [Eng 16–17]; 119:11; Isa 51:7).

Sixth, both God and Moses perceived the laws holistically, viewing all of life as under the authority of the divine suzerain. Whereas modern interpreters tend to discuss the ethical relevance of the laws by classifying them according to moral, civil, and ceremonial categories, these categories are not very helpful and in any case do not reflect the nature and organization of the laws themselves. Christopher Wright has moved the discussion forward by recognizing five categories of Israelite law: criminal law, civil law, family law, cultic law, and compassionate law.[42] Even so we must realize that the documents themselves do not make these distinctions. This is illustrated most impressively in Leviticus 19, which, with its more than four dozen commandments, refuses to classify, let alone arrange in order of importance, civil, ceremonial, and moral laws.

Seventh, both God and Moses perceived the laws as comprehensible and achievable (30:11–20). God did not impose upon his people an impossibly high standard, but revealed to them in great detail a system of behavior that was uniquely righteous and gracious at the same time (Deut 4:6–8). The genuinely pious in Israel, transformed in heart by the Spirit of God, lived by faith and by the promise, assured that if they would conduct their lives according to the covenant they would live (Deut 6:20–25). However, God also had a realistic

---

42. Wright, *An Eye for an Eye*, 148–59; Wright, *Walking in the Ways of the Lord*, 114.

view of his people. Recognizing their propensity to sin, he provided a means of forgiveness and communion through the sacrificial and ceremonial ritual. There was no time in Israel's history when every Israelite was truly devoted to YHWH in this sense. For this reason, within the new Israelite covenant, Jeremiah anticipates a time when the boundaries between physical Israel and spiritual Israel will be coterminous and all will love God and demonstrate with their lives that his תּוֹרָה has been written on their hearts (Jer 31:31–34).

Of course, these facts did not prevent later Israelites from perverting obedience to the law as a condition for blessing into a condition for salvation. The prophets constantly railed against their people for substituting true piety, which is demonstrated first in moral obedience, with the external rituals prescribed by the law (Isa 1:10–17; Hos 6:6; Amos 5:21–24; Mic 6:6–8), thinking that if they performed these rituals God was obligated to receive them favorably. Nor did these facts prevent the Israelites from perverting their possession of the law as a privilege into a divine right and an unconditional guarantee of God's protection (Jer 7:1–10, 21–26; 8:8–12), as if the covenant only obligated God to them and not them to God. Nor did YHWH's desire that his people have his word written on their hearts prevent Israelites from being satisfied with, nay taking pride in the external law that they possessed, but forgetting to write the law on their hearts. Nor did the fact that God and Moses considered all of life as holy prevent the Israelites from perverting the law by placing great stock in divinely prescribed rituals while disregarding God's ethical and communal demands. Instead of heeding the examples of Cain and Abel, and acknowledging that God looks upon our religious expressions through the lenses of our hearts and everyday lives, they imagined that God looked upon their hearts through the lenses of their sacrifices ("To obey is better than sacrifice," 1 Sam 15:22). So they violated the moral laws with impunity even while they continued to observe the ceremonial regulations (Isa 1; Jer 7).

D. The Significance of Old Testament Law for New Testament Christians

By now we should have grasped the Old Testament understanding of the relationship between law and grace within the divine plan of salvation and sanctification. The Scriptures are consistent in asserting that no one may perform works of righteousness sufficient to merit the saving favor of God. In the words of Isaiah:

> All of us have become like one who is unclean,
> and all our righteous acts are like filthy rags;
> we all shrivel up like a leaf,
> and like the wind our sins sweep us away.
> (Isa 64:4 [Eng 6])[43]

In the words of David,

> Against You, You only, have I sinned
> and done what is evil in Your sight,
> so that you are proved right when You speak
> and justified when You judge.
> Surely I was sinful at birth,
> sinful from the time my mother conceived me.
> (Ps 51:6–7 [Eng 4–5])

And in the New Testament words of Paul, "All have sinned and fall short of the glory of God" (Rom 3:23).

However, within the gospel of salvation by grace alone through faith alone, YHWH graciously reveals the standard of righteousness by which His redeemed people may live and be confident of His approval. There is no conflict here between law and grace. The Torah is a gracious gift. It provided his people with an ever-present reminder of YHWH's deliverance, his power, his covenant faithfulness, and the way of life and prosperity.

1. The Problem: Paul versus Moses

But how is this perspective to be reconciled with Paul's outspoken statements regarding the death-dealing effect of the law in contrast to the life that comes by the Spirit (Rom 2:12–13; 4:13–15; 7:8–9; 8:2–4; 10:4–5; 1 Cor 3:6; Gal 3:12–13, 21–24; 5:18)? In answering the question we need to keep in mind several important considerations.

First, Moses' statement concerning the life-giving/sustaining effects of the law is consistent with Moses' teaching in 30:15–20, and is of a piece with the teaching of the Old Testament elsewhere. In Lev 18:5, YHWH declares, "Keep my ordinances and laws, for the man

---

43. Compare the repeated assertions of the psalmists that (apart from relationship with Yahweh) there is none who does good: 14:1, 4; 53:2, 4 [Eng 1, 3].

who obeys them will live by them. I am YHWH." Similar statements are found in Ezek 20:11, 13 and Neh 9:29. The Psalter begins with an ode to the life-giving nature of the law (1:1–6), and Psalm 119, by far the longest piece in this collection, is devoted entirely to the positive nature of the law. References to the relationship between keeping the law and well-being are common: vv. 17, 40, 77, 93, 97, 116, 144, 156, 159, 175. The basic Old Testament stance is summarized by Habakkuk in 2:4, which, in context, is best interpreted, "As for the proud one, his person (נֶפֶשׁ) is not right on the inside; but the righteous in his faithfulness shall live." Ezekiel offers an extended exposition of this notion in 18:1–23. After describing the ethical behavior of a man, on behalf of YHWH, he declares, "He is righteous; he shall surely live" (v. 9). After describing the unethical behavior of his son he declares, "He has committed all these abominations; he shall surely be put to death" (v. 13). Later he declares that if a wicked man turns from his wickedness and observes all of YHWH's ordinances, and practices righteousness and justice, "he shall surely live" (vv. 21–23).[44] The assumption in each case is that the outward actions reflect the inner spirit of the person,[45] on the basis of which a judgment concerning the spiritual status of the person may be made and the sentence of life or death rendered.

Second, from a hermeneutical and theological perspective, later revelation cannot correct earlier revelation, as if there were some defect in it. Later revelation may be more precise and more nuanced, but it cannot be more true. Accordingly, Paul cannot be interpreted as correcting Moses, as if Moses was wrong or there was some kind of error in his teaching. If Paul appears to declare something different from Moses, who celebrates the life-giving/sustaining function of the law (cf. Lev 18:5), then we need to ask whether or not he is addressing the same issues as Moses was. His statements must be interpreted both in the light of Moses and in the context of particular arguments. In both Romans and Galatians Paul was responding to those who insist that salvation comes by the works of the law, as represented by circumcision. To those who represent this view he replies that if one looks to the law as a way of salvation, it will lead to death. On the other hand, if one looks to the law as a guide for those already saved,

44. For detailed discussion of this chapter, see Block, *Ezekiel 1–24*, 554–90.

45. This principle is operative also in Jesus' teaching: Matt 7:15–23.

it yields life (cf. Gal 5:13–25). On this matter Moses and Paul are in perfect agreement. In fact, Paul himself says, "It is not the hearers of the law who are righteous before God, but the *doers* of the law who will be justified" (Rom 2:13). The notion of "the obedience of faith," that is, a faith that is demonstrated through acts of obedience, is common to Old and New Testaments. Both testaments attest to the same paradigm:

- YHWH's gracious (i.e., unmerited) saving actions yields the fruit of a redeemed people.
- A redeemed people yields the fruit of righteous deeds.
- Righteous deeds yield the fruit of divine blessing.

It is evident from the New Testament that in the light of Christ, Christians do indeed have a new disposition toward the law. Not only do they see him as its fulfillment and through their union with him delight in its fulfillment themselves, but the law of God is written on Christians' hearts even as it was written on the hearts of true believers in the Old Testament. But we should not imagine that the law written on our hearts is different from the law revealed under the old covenant. Jesus said, "If you love me you will keep my commandments" (John 14:15), and "Whoever has my commandments and keeps them, he it is who loves me. And he who loves me will be loved by my Father, and I will love him and manifest myself to him" (14:21). In lifting these statements right out of Deuteronomy Jesus identifies himself with YHWH in the Old Testament. Furthermore, his use of the plural τὰς ἐντολάς μου, "my commandments," presupposes a specific body of laws with which the disciples are familiar. Here Jesus does not say generically and vaguely, "If you love me you will do as I say," as if this refers to marching orders for the future.

Accordingly, when we reflect on whether or not Christians need to keep any or all of the Old Testament laws, perhaps we have been asking the wrong question all along. When we are confronted with a specific commandment from the Pentateuch, instead of asking, "*Do I* as a Christian have to keep this commandment?" perhaps we should be asking, "*How* can I as a Christian keep this commandment?" Of course, when we read the commands concerning the sacrifices, we recognize that the blood of bulls and goats could never by itself take away sin (Heb 10:4), but we keep these laws by celebrating the fact that when the Old Testament rituals were performed in faith by those who walked with God, the sacrifice of Christ, slain before the foundation of the world (1 Pet 1:18–20),[46] was applied to them, and that this sacrifice has been offered for us, once and for all. When we approach the laws concerning the civil administration of Israel we analyze the functions and objectives of those laws and translate them into equivalent goals for the people of God in our context. When we encounter criminal laws, we interpret the drastic responses required as reflective of the heinousness of the crimes in the eyes of God. When we read the family laws we hear the voice of God affirming the sanctity of this institution and the responsibilities of all members for the maintenance of the household. And when we hear the pleas for compassion to the poor and the marginalized members of society, we remember the words of the Old Testament sage:

> Whoever oppresses a poor man insults his Maker,
> but he who is generous to the needy honors him.
> (Prov 14:31)

> Whoever mocks the poor insults his Maker;
> he who is glad at calamity will not go unpunished.
> (Prov 17:5)

2. The Solution

How then are New Testament Christians to apply the Old Testament law to their own lives? It is evident from the deliberations and the decisions of the Jerusalem Council in Acts 15:1–21 that in the light of the cross and the redemptive work of Christ, Gentile Christians are not subject to the laws of the old covenant in the same way that Jewish Christ-believers were; particularly that conformity to the ritual laws (specifically circumcision) was not to be viewed as a precondition to salvation (v. 1). On the other hand, the Council did not absolve Gentile Christians of any and all accountability to God as outlined in previous revelation. On the contrary, the demand that Gentile believers "abstain from the things polluted by idols, and from sexual immorality, and from what has been strangled, and from blood" (v. 20; cf. 29) assumes not only familiarity with the Old Testament

---

46. Cf. Matt 25:34; Eph 1:4; Heb 4:3; 9:26; Rev 13:8; 17:8.

laws, but also a continued relevance of some of those laws for New Testament believers.[47] These prohibitions may be viewed as shorthand for Deuteronomic calls for exclusive allegiance to YHWH/ Christ, scrupulous ethical purity, and the respect for the sanctity of all life, including that of animals whose flesh we may legitimately consume as food.

How then should Christians approach the Old Testament laws? Let me offer a few suggestions.

First, Christians must take 2 Tim 3:15–17 as the starting point, recognizing that this statement not only affirms the reliability of the Old Testament as divinely breathed Scripture, but especially that it is ethically relevant and through its application God creates a transformed people. This means also that before we impose the Old Testament laws on others, we must adopt the commitments of Ezra as our own, setting our hearts to study, to apply, and to teach it to God's people (Ezra 7:10).

Second, while we recognize that with the sacrifice of Christ all the Old Testament sacrifices have been terminated, we also recognize the essential theological and ethical unity of the two Testaments, a unity that is summarized in Jesus' call for covenantal commitment (love) to God and to one's fellow human beings. This means that the redeemed scrupulously seek to please God in all of life (1 Cor 10:31; Col 3:17, 23; cf. Lev 19), and they compassionately always put the welfare of others ahead of their own (Phil 2:3–4). At the same time we look to the New Testament for guidance on which Old Testament laws have been rendered obsolete in Christ. Most Western evangelical Christians assume that unless the New Testament expressly affirms the continued relevance of an Old Testament ordinance, we may assume it has been abrogated in Christ. One should probably rather adopt the opposite stance: unless the New Testament expressly declares the end of an Old Testament ordinance (e.g., the sacrifices), we assume its authority for believers today continues.

---

47. For further discussion of this issue, see Davidson, "Which Torah Laws Should Gentile Christians Obey?"; Richard Bauckham, "James and the Jerusalem Church," in *The Book of Acts in Its Palestinian Setting*, vol. 4 of *The Book of Acts in Its First Century Setting* (Grand Rapids: Eerdmans, 1995) 459–67; idem, "James and the Gentiles (Acts 15:13–21)," in *History, Literature, and Society in the Book of Acts*, ed. Ben Witherington, III (Cambridge: Cambridge University Press, 1996) 172–78. I am grateful to Robin Parry for drawing these Bauckham texts to my attention.

Third, we recognize that without the background of Old Testament law, Paul's call for obedience to the "law of Christ" (1 Cor 9:21; Gal 6:2) and Jesus' call for adherence to the "commandments" remain vague and empty, subject to anybody's personal and subjective interpretation. Familiarity with the Old Testament laws is indispensable for an understanding of Jesus' and Paul's ethical exhortations.

Fourth, even as we accept the fundamental theological and ethical unity of the testaments, we must respect the distinctions among different categories of Old Testament law.[48] By "categories" here I do not mean the classical distinctions of moral, ceremonial, and civil laws, which in any case are not biblical categories, but the laws governing criminal, civic, family, cultic, and social affairs. In some of these the relevance for New Testament believers is on the surface (Deut 6:4–5), but in others it may be couched in culturally specific terms. This is the case, for example, in the law concerning houses with parapets (Deut 22:8). In arguing for the ongoing relevance of this commandment we obviously do not mean that Christians must build houses with parapets. Rather, we recognize and live by the theological principle illustrated by this law: heads of households must ensure the well-being of all who enter their homes. In the context of a modern city like Chicago, this translates into an appeal to keep the sidewalk leading up to the house clear of ice and snow in the winter.

This leads to the fifth suggestion, namely to investigate carefully not only the features of Old Testament laws, but especially their social function and theological underpinnings. Many of the specific regulations (e.g., haircuts, tattoos, and gashing the body, Lev 19:27–28) represent responses to specific pagan customs, whose nature can only be determined by careful consideration of the cultural context out of which these ordinances arose and which they seek to address. In Deuteronomy in particular we observe a fundamental concern to protect the weak and vulnerable from abuse and exploitation at the hands of those with economic and political power. The principles obviously have permanent relevance.

Sixth, seize the underlying principles of those that are culturally and contextually specific and apply those principles to the contexts

---

48. In the following comments I am heavily indebted to Christopher J. H. Wright. See especially his four methodological principles outlined in *Walking in the Ways of the Lord*, 114–16.

in which we live. It is impossible to establish the particular kind of haircut Lev 19:27 seeks to ban, but it is not difficult to identify parallel contemporary practices that need to be reined in. While hairstyles change from generation to generation, and even from year to year, surely the principle applies to all forms of dress that represent ungodly values.

The problem of applying Old Testament laws to contemporary contexts is much more complex than these few summary statements would imply. However, the time has come for us to reexamine the fundamental assumptions that we bring to the matter. Hear me carefully. I am *not* hereby advocating any kind of works salvation, that is, a view that if we keep the laws the right way we will have merited salvation. No one has ever been saved by works. Salvation is made possible only through the unmerited grace and mercy of God in Jesus Christ. Salvation is a gift to be received by faith, not earned by human effort. But we are concerned about a salvation that works, that is, that results in a life that conforms to the will of God. At issue is the believer's sanctification. While obedience is not a prerequisite to salvation, it is the key to the blessing of the redeemed. The relationship between obedience to the law and the believer's well-being is declared by the Lord Jesus Christ himself, the Sage *par excellence* of the New Testament:

> Then the King will say to those on his right, "Come, you who are blessed by my Father, inherit the kingdom prepared for you from the foundation of the world. For I was hungry and you gave me food, I was thirsty and you gave me drink, I was a stranger and you welcomed me, I was naked and you clothed me, I was sick and you visited me, I was in prison and you came to me."
>
> Then the righteous will answer him, saying, "Lord, when did we see you hungry and feed you, or thirsty and give you drink? And when did we see you a stranger and welcome you, or naked and clothe you? And when did we see you sick or in prison and visit you?"
>
> And the King will answer them, "Truly, I say to you, as you did it to one of the least of these my brothers, you did it to me." (Matt 25:34–40, ESV)

5

"You shall not covet your neighbor's wife"

A Study in Deuteronomic Domestic Ideology[1]

Introduction

IN 1990 THE RENOWNED Jewish scholar Moshe Greenberg published a short but insightful article that has not received the notice it deserves, "Biblical Reality toward Power: Ideal and Reality in Law and Prophets."[2] In this essay Greenberg argues that the foundations of the *social program* of the Torah are clear: while all power belongs ultimately to God, he distributes the exercise of power to human agents—kings, judges, priests, elders, tribal chiefs—for the purpose of maintaining the moral order. Although the Torah calls on all to treat those in authority with due honor and respect,[3] it is intentional

---

1. This essay was previously published in *Journal of the Evangelical Theological Society* 53 (2010) 449–74.

2. In *Religion and Law*, 101–12.

3. Children are to honor parents (Exod 20:12; 21:15, 17; Lev 19:3; Deut 5:16; 21:18–21; 27:16); tribal chiefs (נָשִׂיא) are not to be cursed (Exod 22:27[Eng 28]): "You shall not revile God, or curse a leader of your people." Leviticus 19:32 calls for respect for the elder: "You shall rise before the aged, and defer to the elder (זָקֵן); and you shall fear your God: I am YHWH." Cf. the sapiential counsel in Eccl 10:20, "Do not curse the king, even in your thoughts, and do not curse the rich, even in your bedroom; for a bird of the air may carry your voice, or some winged creature tell the matter." Also Prov 24:21: "My son, fear YHWH and the king, and do not disobey

in dispersing power among various members of society. In contrast to the neighboring nations, where absolute power tended to be concentrated in the hands of the king and his officials, the Torah not only prevents the accumulation and concentration of power in individuals, but also takes deliberate steps to rein in the abuse of power by those who sit in seats of authority. According to the Mosaic paradigm for kingship as spelled out in Deut 17:14–20, kings were not to exploit their offices for personal gain, measured in the accumulation of horses, wives, and wealth "for himself" (thrice in verses 16–17). Indeed the only activity in which the king was permitted to engage "for himself" was writing a copy of "this Torah." This Torah was to be his constant companion; he was to read all the days of his life "that he may learn to fear YHWH his God, diligently observing all the words of this Torah and these statutes by doing them, in order that his heart may not be lifted up above his fellow citizens and that he not turn aside from the Supreme Command, either to the right or to the left."[4]

Elsewhere, by publicizing the standards for the administration of justice, the Torah reins in the power of those with legal authority.[5] References to these standards are distributed among the various constitutional documents.

Exodus 23:6–9 (The Book of the Covenant):

> You shall not pervert the justice due to your poor in their lawsuits. Keep far from a false charge, and do not kill the innocent and those in the right, for I will not acquit the wicked. You shall take no bribe, for a bribe blinds the clear-sighted [officials], and subverts the cause of those who are in the right.

---

either of them." According to Deut 17:12, presumptuous disregard for the verdict in a case presented before the priest at the central sanctuary was a capital offense.

4. For detailed study of Deut 17:14–20, see Block, "The Burden of Leadership," 118–39.

5. Greenberg notes (p. 108) that the Torah's oral publication of judiciary regulations arms those who feel victimized by the system with "a publicly known divine sanction." This contrasts with the wider ancient Near Eastern situation, symbolized by the code of Hammurabi, which was transcribed on a large stela to be sure, but it was written in esoteric cuneiform and located inside the temple, away from public view. Accordingly, Hammurabi's claim to fairness rings hollow: "Let any wronged man who has a lawsuit come before the statue of me, the king of justice, and let him have my inscribed stela read aloud to him, thus may he hear my precious pronouncements and let my stela reveal the lawsuit for him; may he examine his case, may he calm his (troubled) heart" (From the epilogue of the code, as translated by Roth, *Law Collections from Mesopotamia and Asia Minor*, 134).

> You shall not oppress an alien (גֵּר), for you know the feelings of the alien (גֵּר), having yourselves been aliens (גֵּרִים) in the land of Egypt.

Leviticus 19:15 (Instructions on Holiness)

> You shall not operate unjustly in a legal case (לֹא־תַעֲשׂוּ עָוֶל בַּמִּשְׁפָּט); you shall not be partial to the poor or defer to the great: with righteousness (צֶדֶק) you shall judge your neighbor.

Deuteronomy 10:17–19 (Torah of Deuteronomy)

> For YHWH your God is God of gods and Lord of lords, the great, the mighty, and the awesome God, who is not partial and takes no bribe. He executes justice for the fatherless and the widow, and loves the alien (גֵּר), giving him food and clothing. So you shall love the alien, for you were aliens in the land of Egypt.

Moses himself had demonstrated awareness of this paradigm already at Sinai, when he charged the newly appointed heads of the tribes of Israel on the march to Canaan as follows: "Hear the cases of your fellow citizens, and decide justly (שָׁפַט צֶדֶק) between any man and a fellow Israelite or an alien (גֵּר). You must not be partial in judging: hear out the small and the great alike; you shall not be intimidated by anyone, for the judgment is God's. Any case that is too hard for you, bring to me, and I will hear it" (Deut 1:16–18).

Similarly, the publication of priestly perquisites in Deut 18:1–5 and the specification of conditions under which priests disqualified themselves from divine service in Lev 21:13–23 have the effect of reining in the power and authority of religious officials. Institutions like the Year of Jubilee every fiftieth year (Lev 25), and the seventh year as the year of release for citizens who for reasons of poverty had given up their freedoms to a neighbor (Deut 15:1–18) were intended to curb excessive concentration of economic power. Deuteronomy 21:18–21 limits both the painful responsibilities of parents toward rebellious children, and their power over them. Parents of a disrespectful and insubordinate son were required to submit their case before the elders for final adjudication.

In keeping with these specific instructions regarding those who exercise power, the Book of the Covenant (Exod 22:20, 25[Eng 21, 26]; 23:12), the Instructions on Holiness (Lev 19:9–10, 13–14, 29,

33–34) and the Deuteronomic Torah exhibit remarkable coherence. All these constitutional documents are concerned with the
well-being of people at the economic and social margins, who are at
the mercy of persons with power.[6] Indeed, the charges "to love your
neighbor as yourself" and "to love the alien as yourself" mean that all
citizens—those with greater and those with lesser power—are always
to demonstrate their covenant commitment with actions performed
in the interests of the next person, rather than in one's own interests.[7]
If this was true for ordinary citizens, it was especially true for those in
authority. Israel's constitutional literature perceives the call to leadership, not primarily as an appointment to power, but to responsibility
to be exercised on God's behalf for the well-being of those they lead.[8]

For all that is to be learned from Greenberg's essay, this esteemed
scholar pays scant attention to the most common leadership position
of all—the role of the father in the בֵּית אָב, literally "a father's house."
The expression reflects the shamelessly patricentric structure of ancient Israelite families. Although men did indeed function as rulers
of households,[9] the Old Testament pays relatively little attention to
the power of the husband and father.[10] The only reference to a man's
status as ruler over his wife occurs in Gen 3:16, but here it highlights
the fundamentally negative effects of the fall on marital relations: as
a result of sin responsible headship degenerates to an inappropriate

---

6. Note the numerous contexts in which the plight of the widow, the fatherless
and the alien are addressed: Deut 10:18; 14:29; 16:11, 14; 24:19–21; 26:12–13; 27:19.

7. For a convincing discussion of אָהַב, "love," as an active and concrete, rather
than abstract, expression, see Malamat, "'You Shall Love Your Neighbor as Yourself.'"

8. Cf. Block, "Burden of Leadership," 125–39; Block, "Leadership, Leader, Old
Testament," 3:620–26.

9. Witness the references to a head of a household as its בַּעַל, "owner, master"
(Exod 22:8[Eng 7]) and אָדוֹן, "lord, sovereign," of his wife/wives (Gen 18:12), children, slaves, livestock, movable property, and land. For discussions of the former
term see J. Kühlewein, TLOT 1:247–51; for the latter see E. Jenni, TLOT 1:23–29. Cf.
also 1 Pet 3:6 in the New Testament. 1 Timothy 3:12 avoids the vocabulary of power
(ἄρχειν, "to rule"; e.g., Rom 15:12), preferring the vocabulary of management and
caring for (προΐστημι, literally "to stand before, be at the head").

10. The fourth command of the Decalogue (according to the Catholic and
Lutheran numeration; see Excursus C below) addresses a child's duty to honor parents, rather than parents' power to demand the respect of the child.

exercise of power over (מָשַׁל) the woman; patri*centrism* degenerates to patri*archy*.[11]

While this degeneracy is reflected in many Old Testament narratives,[12] we do a disservice to the biblical record if we focus on biblical narratives as the primary source for establishing normative/ ideal Israelite social patterns, and if we are preoccupied with the power the אָב, "father," wielded. In functional households the male head was neither despot nor dictator. On the contrary, since the family members were perceived as extensions of the progenitor's own life, the head's own interests depended upon the well-being of the household. Rather than evoking images of "ruler" or "boss," the term אָב should have expressed confidence, trust, security.[13] This emphasis

11. Taken out of context, Ps 105:21 could be interpreted as highlighting the authority of a father over his household ("He [YHWH] made him lord [אָדוֹן] of his house [בֵּיתוֹ], and ruler [מֹשֵׁל] over all his possessions [קִנְיָנוֹ]"), except that this statement refers to Joseph, whom the Pharaoh put in administrative charge of his kingdom. Elsewhere the verb מָשַׁל, "to rule," occurs in association with the government of a household only in Prov 17:2, which speaks of a wise servant ruling over a foolish son and sharing in the inheritance. But see also Isa 3:12, which speaks of an upside-down world in which children oppress and women rule the people of YHWH.

12. Including the narratives of the patriarchs and of David. For a study of the problem in the book of Judges see Block, "Unspeakable Crimes," 46–55. On the distinction between normative *patricentrism* and exploitative *patriarchy* see Block, "Marriage and Family in Ancient Israel," 40–45; Köstenberger, *God, Marriage, and Family.* For a contrary view, see Moore, "After Patriarchy, What?" 569–76.

13. This is evident in texts like Ps 68:6–7[Eng 5–6], which portray the father figure as the protector of orphans, defender of widows, host for the homeless, and savior of the prisoner; or Job 29:12–17, where, as one dressed in righteousness and justice, Job describes himself as a savior to the poor in distress, a helper for the orphan, a blessing to the perishing, a joy for the widow, eyes for the blind, feet for the lame, a father to the needy, defender of the stranger, and rescuer of the victims of the wicked. Although the term אָב, "father," always connoted authority, it also suggested protection and security, even when אָב was used in a metaphorical sense. Cf. Judg 17:10 and 18:19, according to which the unnamed Levitical priest was engaged as priest and "father," first by Micah, then by the Danites. He was not expected to govern either the household or the tribe, but to guarantee its security before God. When Naaman's servants addressed Elijah as אָב they expressed both their respect and their dependence upon him (2 Kgs 5:13). At the ascension of Elijah, Elisha's exclamation, "My father! My father!" reflected not so much his subjection to his mentor, but the warmth of the relationship between the two men, comparable to Isaac's similar utterance to his literal father in Gen 22:7. The same applies when YHWH is portrayed as divine Father of Israel (Deut 1:31; 14:1; 32:6; Isa 63:16; 64:7[Eng 8]; Jer 31:9; Mal 1:6), of the members of the community of faith (Mal 2:10), of orphans (Ps 68:7[Eng 6]), of the king of Israel (2 Sam 7:14; Ps 89:28[Eng 27]), or when an idol is addressed as the father of the devotee (Jer 2:27).

on the responsibilities associated with headship over the household (as opposed to its privileges and power) is consistent with the overall tenor of the Old Testament, which views leadership in general to be a privilege granted to an individual in order to serve the interests of those who were led.[14]

This perspective is reflected particularly in the Deuteronomic version of the Decalogue, to which we now turn for closer analysis. Few texts in the Old Testament have been studied as intensively and extensively as the Decalogue.[15] Given our limitations of space, there is no need to survey the history of interpretation, or even to summarize the wide range of approaches to this document that are reflected in the scholarly literature.[16] Instead, I offer a synoptic comparison of the versions of the Decalogue preserved in Exodus 20 and Deuteronomy 5, and reflect on the sociological and theological significance of some of the shifts that occur when we move from one to the other.

The Form and Function of the Decalogue

Many scholars look upon the Decalogue as a relatively late composition created by Deuteronomistic theologians as a ten-article compendium of covenantal expectations resembling a catechism and used in lay instruction. As such, it supposedly represents the most mature example of religious lay instruction. By casting the commands in the form of second person singular verbs of direct address, the Decalogue calls upon every individual Israelite to acknowledge YHWH, the Redeemer of Israel from Egypt, as one's personal God, and to celebrate one's freedom and YHWH's salvation through

14. In addition to Deut 17:14–20, see also the oracle on righteous rule by Lemuel's mother in Prov 31:2–9, as well as Ps 72:1–14 and Isa 32:1–8. These idealistic statements contrast with Samuel's warning of the oppressive nature of kingship in 1 Sam 8:11–18 and the preaching of the prophets which frequently denounced abuse of power by kings and other government officials (e.g., Ezek 34:1–19).

15. For a helpful and thorough recent study, see Miller, *The Ten Commandments*.

16. See also Block, "Reading the Decalogue Right to Left," 21–55. The most thorough recent study of the document is provided by Himbaza, *Le Décalogue et l'histoire du texte*. Hossfeld, *Der Dekalog*. For helpful collections of essays on the Decalogue see Brown, ed., *The Ten Commandments*; Segal and Levi, eds., *The Ten Commandments in History and Tradition*. For discussion of how the Decalogue has been handled through the centuries see Kuntz, *The Ten Commandments in History*. For further bibliographies on the Decalogue, see the commentaries, especially Durham, *Exodus*, 274–76; Childs, *The Book of Exodus*, 386.

obedience to him.[17] But this is precisely the opposite of the way the Decalogue presents itself in Exodus 19–20 and Deuteronomy 5. Both texts declare that the Decalogue was presented directly to Israel as oral revelation by YHWH on Mount Sinai as a fundamental part of the covenant-making event described in Exodus 20–24. Rather than viewing this document as a late summary or distillation of YHWH's will for his people, the texts consistently invite us to see it as the fountainhead from which later revelation springs and upon which it will expound.[18] The narratorial relationship of these documents may be portrayed diagrammatically as in Figure 1.

FIGURE 1: The Evolution of Israel's Constitutional Tradition

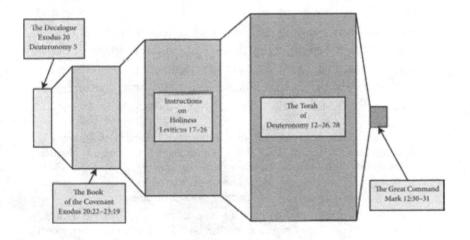

The Decalogue
Exodus 20
Deuteronomy 5

Instructions
on
Holiness
Leviticus 17–26

The Torah
of
Deuteronomy 12–26, 28

The Book
of the Covenant
Exodus 20:22–23:19

The Great Command
Mark 12:30–31

---

17. Albertz, *A History of Israelite Religion in the Old Testament Period*, 214–16.

18. Some even argue that the structure of the so-called Deuteronomic Law Code in Deuteronomy 12–26 derives from the structure of the Decalogue. See Braulik, *Die deuteronomischen Gesetze und der Dekalog*; idem, "Die Abfolge der Gesetze in Deuteronomium 12–26 und der Dekalog," 252–72; published in English as "The Sequence of the Laws in Deuteronomy 12–26," 313–35. See also Kaufman, "The Structure of the Deuteronomic Law," 105–58. While the influence of the Decalogue on the Deuteronomic Code seems indubitable, to argue for structural dependence is forced. It is an unlikely stretch, for example, to interpret Moses' instructions regarding administrative institutions in 16:18—18:22 as an exposition of the command to honor father and mother in 5:16. This approach is also rejected by Tigay, *Deuteronomy*, 446–49, and Otto, *Das Deuteronomium*, 226.

Regarding the nature of the document itself, we note first, that the Decalogue is cast as a complete entity. Resembling ancient Near Eastern treaties, the document includes its own formal introduction (the historical prologue, Exod 20:2; Deut 5:6), its own discreet number of terms (ten; Exod 20:3–17; 34:28; Deut 4:13; 5:7–21; 10:4), and later we read of a transcriptional epilogue (Exod 24:12–18; Deut 5:22). The surrounding narrative (cf. Exod 19:4–6), the form of the Decalogue, and the nature of the ten terms themselves demonstrate that this document is to be interpreted, not as a legal code, but as a statement of covenantal policy. Unlike other constitutional documents within the Pentateuch—the Book of the Covenant (Exod 21:1—23:19), the Instructions on Holiness (Lev 16–27), and the Deuteronomic Torah (Deut 12–26, 28),[19] the ten terms are cast in apodictic rather than casuistic form. They appear as second person commands (mostly negative), and occur without qualification and without sanctions or promised rewards.[20] Indeed they are so general as to be virtually unenforceable through the judicial system. The covenantal (rather than legal) nature of the document is also reflected in the designations by which it is identified: לֻחֹת הָעֵדֻת, "the tablets of the Pact" (Exod 31:18; 32:15; 34:29);[21] לוּחֹת הַבְּרִית, "the tablets of the

---

19. Although scholars commonly draw a sharp line between Deuteronomy 11 and 12, and refer to chapters 12–26 as the Deuteronomic Law Code, this obscures the overall unity of Moses' second address, underestimates the role of chapters 6–11 as an exposition of the preamble and the first command of the Decalogue, and misreads the genre of chapters 12–26. See further Block, *Deuteronomy*.

20. These categories, used here for the sake of convenience, derive from the seminal work of Alt, "The Origins of Israelite Law," 79–132. However, we do not accept Alt's hypothesis of the origins of these forms, which was rightly refuted long ago. See especially Gerstenberger, *Wesen und Herkunft des "Apodiktischen Rechts."*

21. The rendering of the expression in NJPSV. Based on the assumption of a derivation from the same root as עֵד, "testimony," most English translations render the expression "tablets of the testimony" (so also LXX, the Vulgate, and the Targums). S. T. Hague (*NIDOTTE* 1:502) comments, "[T]he translation of עֵדוּת as 'testimony' is reasonable, so long as we understand the testimony as *the law* that is the seal of the Lord's covenant with Israel." However, since today we usually think of a testimony as the utterances of a witness in a court of law or some less formal context in which a particular event is being debated/discussed, this rendering is actually misleading. In Deut 4:45 הָעֵדֹת clearly refers to the stipulations of the covenant (alongside הַחֻקִּים וְהַמִּשְׁפָּטִים, "the decrees and rulings"), suggesting that הָעֵדֹת should be interpreted equivalent to "the covenant." This interpretation is reinforced by the use of the Aramaic cognate, עֵדי, for "covenant," equivalent to Hebrew בְּרִית (Sefire 1A:1ff.) and Akkadian *adû/adê*, for "covenant/treaty" and "loyalty oath."

covenant" (Deut 9:9, 11, 15); עֲשֶׂרֶת הַדְּבָרִים, "the ten words" (Exod 34:28; Deut 4:13; 10:4). The meaning of the last expression is grasped by the Septuagint, which renders the expression οἱ δέκα λόγοι, from which we get *Decalogue*. This covenantal (rather than legal) interpretation of the document is confirmed by the designations for the receptacle in which the tablets were stored: אֲרֹן הָעֵדֻת, "Ark of the Pact" (Exod 25:22; 30:6; 39:35; Num 4:5; 7:89); אֲרֹן בְּרִית־יְהוָה, "the Ark of the Covenant of YHWH";[22] אֲרֹן בְּרִית הָאֱלֹהִים, "the Ark of the Covenant of God" (Judg 20:27; 1 Sam 4:4; 2 Sam 15:24; 1 Chr 16:6); or simply אֲרֹן הַבְּרִית, "the Ark of the Covenant" (Josh 3:6, 8, 11; 4:9; 6:6).

Second, by opening with a summary of the gospel of Israel's salvation the commands that follow are presented not as prerequisites to deliverance, but as divinely revealed ways of responding to deliverance already experienced. Far from calling for obedience as a matter of mere duty to an overlord, obedience to the terms of the Decalogue is to be motivated by gratitude for the grace the Israelites had experienced through YHWH's saving actions. This is a document for the redeemed.[23]

Third, instead of serving as a mere listing of commands, the Decalogue served as an Israelite version of a bill of rights.[24] By casting each of the terms in the second person of direct address, the document is addressed, not to potential victims of crime, but to a would-be perpetrator of a crime against God or the community. Unlike modern Western bills of rights, these terms do not seek to protect one's own rights, but the rights of the next person. The addressee is perceived as a threat to the community. Indeed, each of the

---

For the Aramaic, see Gibson, *Textbook of Syrian Semitic Inscriptions*, 2:34. On the meaning and significance of *adê*, see Parpola and Watanabe, *Neo-Assyrian Treaties and Loyalty Oaths*, xv–xxv.

22. E.g., Deut 10:8; 31:9, 25–26; Josh 3:3; 4:7, 18; 8:33; 1 Sam 4:3–5; Jer 3:16.

23. Which exposes the impropriety of the pressure in some circles to have the document (usually minus the preamble) displayed in courthouses and public schools. For a discussion of the issue see Duff, "Should the Ten Commandments Be Posted in the Public Realm?" 159–70.

24. Though we agree in general with those who treat this document as a "charter of human freedom" (Harrelson, *Ten Commandments*, 186–93; Stamm, *The Ten Commandments in Recent Research*, 114), here we are looking at the document from another angle, specifically with the view to seeing how the next person's freedom is protected.

terms may be recast as a statement of the other person's rights and the addressee's responsibility to guard the rights of others—first, of the divine Redeemer and covenant Lord, and second, of one's fellow Israelite. According to the Deuteronomic version of the Decalogue, these rights may be summarized as follows:[25]

The Divine Rights:

(1)   The Supreme Command: in view of his gracious saving action YHWH has the right to Israelites' exclusive allegiance.

(2)   YHWH has the right to proper representation (Israel bears his name).[26]

The Human Rights:

(3)   The members of the household have the right to humane treatment from the head (Deut 5:12–15).[27]

(4)   Parents have the right to respect from children.

(5)   The next person has the right to life.

(6)   The next person has the right to sexual purity.

(7)   The next person has the right to property.

(8)   The next person has the right to honest and truthful testimony in court.

(9)   The next person has the right to a secure marriage.

(10)   The next person has the right to enjoy property without fear that a neighbor may want it for himself.

Fourth, the Decalogue is a comprehensive document with a twofold purpose: (1) to provide the Israelites with a clear understanding of YHWH's view of the appropriate response to salvation; and (2) to instill in the redeemed a respect for God and other members of the community. And herein we discover the Mosaic understand-

---

25. Our numbering of the terms of the Decalogue accords with the enumeration in Roman Catholic and Lutheran tradition, and is supported by the discourse syntax of the document both in Exodus and Deuteronomy. See Excursus C.

26. On the meaning of this command, see Block, "Bearing the Name of the LORD with Honor," 61–72.

27. The Exodus version of the Decalogue treats the Sabbath ordinance as a divine right to the Israelites' time/life (cf. Exod 20:8–11).

ing of "love": total commitment to the well-being of others, whether God or one's fellow human being, demonstrated in acts that seek the well-being of the next person—rather than self-interest. The grouping of the commands is deliberate, beginning with the call to honor YHWH's rights (#1–2), and then calling on Israelites to honor the rights of others, who are created as God's image (#3–10).[28]

FIGURE 2: The Vertical and Horizontal Dimensions of Covenant Love

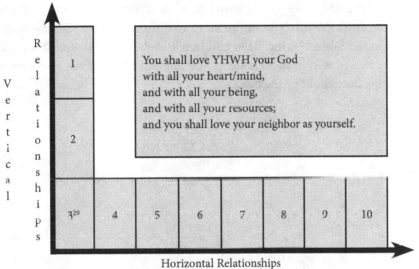

Horizontal Relationships

A recognition of the vertical and horizontal dimensions of covenantal actions, specifically this understanding of the Decalogue as a bill intended to protect others' rights, underlies Jesus' distillation of all the commands to two simple statements: "You shall demonstrate love for the Lord your God with all your heart and soul and mind and strength, and you shall demonstrate love for your neighbor as [you do for] yourself" (Mark 12:30–31; cf. Matt 22:37–39; Luke 10:27–28; Rom 13:9).

28. Though the perception is as old as Josephus (*Ant.* 3.5.8; 3.6.5) and Philo (*On the Decalogue* [*De Decalogo*] 12.50), and pervasive among theologians and New Testament scholars, identifying the two tablets of the Law with the vertical and horizontal commands, respectively, is based on a false understanding of the purposes of the two tablets. So also Kline, "The Two Tablets of the Covenant," 138–46.

29. On the transitional nature of the Sabbath command, see above.

Fifth, although the principles of the Decalogue were declared in the hearing of all the people and ultimately applied to every member of the covenant community, the document clearly reflects the patri-centric nature of Israelite society. The Decalogue is not addressed to priests or rulers, or to the population in general, but to "every *man*," specifically adult males who are heads of households with wives and children, and who possess property. Accordingly, the first command warns the head of the household to be scrupulous in his devotion to YHWH, not only for his own sake, but for the well-being of the household, for the consequences of crimes committed against YHWH extend to the entire family.[30] Similarly, the explicit extension of the Sabbath principle to children and slaves and domestic animals seeks to rein in potential exploitation and abuse of the members of the household by the head.

---

30. The idiom, "to visit (פָּקַד) the guilt of the fathers on the children to the third and fourth generation of those who reject (שָׂנֵא, usually rendered "hate") me," is commonly interpreted vertically, as if the effects of the father's sins carry on long after he is dead, even to his great grandchildren. However, it is preferable to inter-pret the idiom horizontally, that is, the effects of the sins of the head of a household extend to the entire בֵּית־אָב, "household of the father." In ancient Israel, up to four generations could live at one time in the household of a patriarch. Fundamental to this principle are notions of corporate solidarity and the responsibility of the male head of a household for the welfare of the family. Achan and his clan provide a clas-sic illustration of the principle (Josh 7:16–26).

TABLE 4: Synopsis of the Versions of the Decalogue in Exodus and Deuteronomy

Bold font = variation in reading; ***Italic font*** = addition

	Exodus 20:2–17	Deuteronomy 5:6–21	
2	I am YHWH your God, who brought you out of the land of Egypt, out of the house of slavery.	I am YHWH your God, who brought you out of the land of Egypt, out of the house of slavery.	6
3 – 6	You shall have no other gods before me. You shall not make for yourself a carved image, or any likeness of anything that is in heaven above, *or* that is in the earth beneath, or that is in the water under the earth. You shall not bow down to them or serve them, for I YHWH your God am a jealous God, visiting the iniquity of the fathers on the children to the third and the fourth generation of those who hate me, but showing steadfast love to thousands of those who love me and keep my commandments.	You shall have no other gods before me. You shall not make for yourself a carved image, any likeness of anything that is in heaven above, or that is on the earth beneath, or that is in the water under the earth. You shall not bow down to them or serve them; for I YHWH your God am a jealous God, visiting the iniquity of the fathers on the children to the third and fourth generation of those who hate me, but showing steadfast love to thousands of those who love me and keep my commandments.	7 - 10
7	You shall not carry in vain the name of YHWH your God, for YHWH will not hold him guiltless who bears his name in vain.	You shall not carry in vain the name of YHWH your God, for YHWH will not hold him guiltless who bears his name in vain.	11

8 – 11	**Remember** the Sabbath day, to keep it holy. Six days you shall labor, and do all your work, but the seventh day is a Sabbath to YHWH your God. On it you shall not do any work, you, or your son, or your daughter, your male servant, or your female servant, or your livestock, or the sojourner who is within your gates. **For in six days YHWH made heaven and earth,** **the sea, and all that is in them,** **and rested the seventh day.** Therefore YHWH **blessed the Sabbath day** **and made it holy.**	**Observe** the Sabbath day, to keep it holy, *as YHWH your God commanded you.* Six days you shall labor and do all your work, but the seventh day is a Sabbath to YHWH your God. On it you shall not do any work, you, or your son, or your daughter *or* your male servant, or your female servant, *or your ox or your donkey* or *any of* your livestock, or the sojourner who is within your gates, **that your male servant and your female servant** **may rest as well as you.** **You shall remember that you were a slave** **in the land of Egypt,** **and YHWH your God brought you out from there** **with a mighty hand and an outstretched arm.** Therefore YHWH **your God commanded you** **to keep the Sabbath day.**	12 – 15
12	Honor your father and your mother, that your days may be long in the land that YHWH your God is giving you.	Honor your father and your mother, *as YHWH your God commanded you,* that your days may be long, *and that it may go well with you* in the land that YHWH your God is giving you.	16
13	You shall not murder.	You shall not murder.	17
14	You shall not commit adultery.	*And* you shall not commit adultery.	18
15	You shall not steal.	*And* you shall not steal.	19

16	You shall not bear **false** witness against your neighbor.	*And* you shall not bear **useless** witness against your neighbor.	20
	You shall not covet your neighbor's **house;**	*And* you shall not covet your neighbor's **wife.**	
17	you shall not **covet** your neighbor's **wife,** or his male servant, or his female servant, *or* his ox, or his donkey, or anything that belongs to your neighbor.	*And* you shall not **desire** your neighbor's **house,** *his field,* or his male servant, or his female servant, his ox, or his donkey, or anything that belongs to your neighbor.	21

Adjustments to the Decalogue as a Whole in Deuteronomy[31]

When we juxtapose English translations of the two versions of the Decalogue found in Exodus 20 and Deuteronomy 5 it is evident that they differ in significant points, especially after the first two commands (Table 4). First, Deuteronomy makes several additions to the version found in Exodus: (1) "As YHWH your God commanded you" (twice, vv. 12, 16); (2) "or your ox or your donkey" to the Sabbath command (v. 12); (3) a motive clause, "that your male and female servant may rest as well as you," to the Sabbath ordinance (v. 14); (4) a second motive clause, "and that it may go well with you," in the command to honor parents (v. 16); (5) "his field" (שָׂדֵהוּ) in the prohibition on coveting (v. 21).

Second, Deuteronomy makes several striking modifications to the Exodus version: (1) the Sabbath is presented as a day to be "kept" (שָׁמַר), rather than "remembered" (זָכַר, v. 12); (2) instead of basing the Sabbath command on the pattern of divine work in creation, the command is grounded on Israel's experience of slavery in Egypt, and YHWH's mighty acts of deliverance (v. 15); (3) the forbidden testimony in a court of law is characterized as "useless, empty" (שָׁוְא), instead of "false" (שֶׁקֶר, v. 20); (4) "house" and "wife" are transposed

---

31. Our interpretation is based on the assumption that the Exodus version antedates the Deuteronomic version. Not all agree. See Lang, "The Number Ten and the Antiquity of the Fathers," 218, following Hossfeld, *Der Dekalog.* For a defense of the priority of Exodus see Weinfeld, *Deuteronomy 1–11,* 243 *et passim.*

in the last two commands (v. 21); (5) Instead of repeating the word "covet" (חָמַד) the last command uses "desire" (הִתְאַוָּה, v. 21).

Obviously, in Deuteronomy 5 Moses was not reading the Decalogue from the original tablets of stone.[32] He was apparently reciting the foundational covenant document from memory, which may account for the alterations, especially in the variations in individual words: "keep" instead of "remember" the Sabbath; "useless" instead of "false" testimony; "desire" instead of "covet" your neighbor's house. It may also account for the addition of "your ox or your donkey" in the Sabbath ordinance, the insertion having been influenced by Moses' familiarity with the last command, which also lists these as standard elements in an economic unit known as the household, as well as the added motive clause in verse 16, since Moses had used variations of these two motive clauses at the ending of his first address (4:40). However, a lapse in memory will scarcely account for the addition of "as YHWH your God has commanded you," the addition of the motive clause to the Sabbath command, the change in the basis for the Sabbath, and the reversal of "wife" and house" in the last command. These appear to have been deliberate rhetorical modifications by Moses the pastor to heighten the people's awareness of the gravity of the document ("as YHWH has commanded you") and to nuance the ordinances regarding the Sabbath and coveting.

But what is the significance of these modifications in the Decalogue? Scholars have long observed the moral and humanistic trajectory of Deuteronomy as a whole, especially when compared with corresponding regulations in the Book of the Covenant and the Instructions on Holiness.[33] But this trajectory is evident already in the Deuteronomic version of the Decalogue, particularly the Sabbath ordinance. First, in keeping with (or preparatory to) later expressions of concern for the well-being of animals,[34] Moses specifies the ox and the donkey, draft and pack animals respectively, as deserving of the Sabbath rest. While this insertion may reflect the influence of the last command, it may also have been inspired by the ruling in the Book of the Covenant: "Six days you shall do your

32. To which he would not have had access, since they were housed in the Ark of the Covenant in the Holy of Holies.

33. See Weinfeld, *Deuteronomy and the Deuteronomic School*, 282–97; Driver, *Deuteronomy*, 85.

34. Cf. 22:4, 6; 25:4.

work, but on the seventh day you shall rest; that your ox and your donkey may have rest, and the son of your servant woman, and the alien, may be refreshed" (Exod 23:12). Second, Moses acknowledges that beyond patterning human creative work after that of God the Creator of heaven and earth, the Sabbath is a gift, offering all who toil an opportunity to refresh themselves. Third, instead of calling on Israelites to remember the Sabbath, Moses calls on them to treasure the Sabbath by recalling their time in Egypt, when they labored for brutal taskmasters, without Sabbath or relief.[35] In addition to observing the seventh-day Sabbath by celebrating God's work in the creation of the cosmos, the Israelites were to use it to celebrate YHWH's special creative work in rescuing them from bondage with his strong hand and outstretched arm.[36]

When we read this document and the Sabbath ordinance in particular, we need to remember that the primary addressee is the head of the household. It is not difficult to imagine that in ancient Israel the male householder might be tempted to have his animals and hired hands continue working on the Sabbath even as he and his immediate family personally and smugly observed this ordinance. But this philanthropic sensitivity is not to be restricted to one's family or even fellow Israelites. All who live within the towns and villages of Israel—animal and human—are to be granted one day in seven as a day for rest and recuperation.

Adjustments to the Last Command[s] in Deuteronomy

Scholars have spent a great deal of time and energy exploring the significance of the shifts in the last command. Usually these explorations revolve around the meaning of the word חָמַד, "to covet," and הִתְאַוָּה, "to desire," specifically whether the former forbids envious desire for what belongs to another person or prohibits taking specific actions to satisfy those desires.[37] My own sense is that Deuteronomy's

35. In his second address Moses will repeatedly buttress his ethical and spiritual appeals with reminders of the Israelites' experience as slaves in Egypt. Cf. Deut 15:15; 16:12; 24:18, 22.

36. For the combination of the motifs of YHWH's deliverance of Israel as a special creative act and his cosmic creative actions, see, e.g., Psalms 95 and 136.

37. Thus most recently, Miller, *Ten Commandments*, 389–92. For earlier reviews of these discussions see Chaney, "'Coveting Your Neighbor's House' in Social

substitution of the second occurrence of חָמַד in Exod 20:17 with
הִתְאַוָּה argues for the former.[38] However one answers the issue, this
preoccupation with lexical and semantic matters may actually over-
whelm the ideological implications of the simple fact of the change
and other modifications Deut 5:21 makes to the command(s) on
coveting. Indeed, the substitution of one verb with another does not
appear to be nearly as monumental as the transposition of "house"
and "wife."

The Exodus version of the command concerning coveting consists of two statements, each involving the identical negative command, לֹא תַחְמֹד, "You shall not covet," followed by a direct object.
In the first statement the object consists of a single phrase, בֵּית רֵעֶךָ,
"the house of your neighbor." In the second command the object is
complex, consisting of a catalogue of items claimed by one's neighbor: his wife, his male servant, his female servant, his ox, and his
donkey, and then ending with a catch-all expression, "anything that
belongs to your neighbor."[39] The traditional numbering of the terms
of the Decalogue treats the first statement as titular and the second
as expositional: the listing in part 2 clarifies what is meant by בַּיִת in
part 1.[40] This is the בֵּית־אָב, "the household of the father," the entire
realm over which he exercises leadership. Although grammatically
these are two independent commands, by this interpretation they are
in essence only one, lending some support to the enumeration of the
ten terms of the Decalogue proposed by those in the Reformed and
Orthodox Christian traditions.[41]

However, if these are indeed to be interpreted as two separate
commands, which the syntax of the Decalogue as a whole and the

---

Context," 302–8; A. Rofé, "The Tenth Command in the Light of Four Deuteronomic
Laws," 45–54.

38. Acknowledging that the two verbs obviously overlap, Miller (*Ten Commandments*, 391–92) opines that הִתְאַוָּה highlights the sense of inner craving,
whether or not one acts on those cravings.

39. The list is intended to be inclusive, though not exhaustive. It does not specify
"your sons and daughters" or "the alien who is in your gates," referred to in the
Sabbath ordinance.

40. It includes anything and everything associated with the family as an economic unit. Cf. similar listings in Gen 12:5, 16; 26:14; Num 16:30, 32; Deut 11:6.

41. For a full discussion of the enumeration in Jewish tradition, see Breuer,
"Dividing the Decalogue into Verses and Commands," 291–330, esp. 314–18. See
also Himbaza, *Le Décalogue*, 92–116.

grammar of these two statements in particular[42] suggest, they distinguish coveting the neighbor's real property (the house) from coveting
the human beings who make up the economic unit, the household.[43]
This distinction is rendered even more explicit through the four
significant modifications that Moses makes in Deut 5:21. First, and
probably least significant, he changes the verb in the second command from חָמַד to הִתְאַוָּה. Second, Moses adds "his field" to the list
of prohibited entities.[44] Third, Moses isolates "your neighbor's wife"
from the rest of the human components of the household. Fourth,
he transposes "your neighbor's house" and "your neighbor's wife,"
and creates a separate line item protecting the neighbor's relationship
with his wife. "Your neighbor's house" is then dropped down to the
second command. This latter move highlights the ambiguity of the
term בַּיִת. On the one hand, coming at the beginning of a catalogue
of possessions, the word now seems to play a titular role: field, servants, and animals represent parts of the whole. On the other hand,
the addition of "his field" to "his house" creates a pair of elements[45]
clarifying the ambiguity in Exodus—"house" refers to the domicile/
home compound rather than to the "household"—and to match the
following pairs: his male and female servants; his ox and donkey. At
the same time this addition compensates for the loss of a member
from the catalogue and restores the full complement of seven items.[46]
Whether or not Moses was aware of it, this move brings the prohibition on coveting remarkably close to the form of a similar prohibition
in a recently published Old Assyrian Treaty text (1920–1840 BCE)
from Kültepe (*Kaneš*) in Anatolia:

---

42. See Exursus C below. For a discourse analysis of the Decalogue yielding
similar results, see DeRouchie, *A Call to Covenant Love*, 115–17, 127–32.

43. Hebrew בַּיִת bears both senses.

44. The Nash Papyrus and the Septuagint of Exod 20:17 add this element, perhaps under the influence of Deuteronomy.

45. These expressions appear together in Gen 39:5; Lev 25:31; Neh 5:3, 11; Isa
5:8; Jer 6:12; 32:15; Mic 2:2.

46. Like the list of those who are to benefit from the Sabbath rest in Exod 20:10.
Cf. Cassuto, *Exodus*, 249. By adding "your ox and your donkey," Deut 5:14 increases
the number to nine.

You shall not covet a fine house, a fine slave, a fine slave woman, a fine field, or a fine orchard belonging to any citizen of
Assur, and you will not take (any of these) by force and hand
them over to your own subjects/servants.[47]

In the absence of information in the text of Deuteronomy, we
are left to speculate what might have motivated this move. It seems
best to interpret this as a deliberate effort to ensure the elevated status of the wife in a family unit and to foreclose any temptation to
use the Exodus version of the command to justify men's treatment of
their wives as if they were mere property, along with the rest of the
household possessions. It may not be coincidental that the Decalogue
is framed by references to the בַּיִת as designations for domains. The
opening preamble portrays the land of Egypt as "house of slavery"
(בֵּית עֲבָדִים) from which YHWH had rescued Israel. The last command refers to the home by the same term; this is the male head
of the household's domain, in which his style of leadership may be
just as oppressive as the bondage under Pharaoh.[48] Indeed the Old
Testament narratives are rife with accounts of abusive men who treat
women as property that may be disposed of at will for the sake of
male honor and male ego.[49]

Some interpret the transposition of "wife" and "house" in the
last commands of the Decalogue as symbolic of "the interchangeabil-
ity of woman with other items of property."[50] However, Moses' adaptation of the command suggests the very opposite. Aware of men's
propensity to abuse women, Moses seems to have recognized that
men might marshal the ambiguous wording of the Exodus version of
the Decalogue to justify treating their wives the way one treats a slave

47. Kt 00/k6:62–66, as translated by Donbaz, "An Old Assyrian Treaty from
Kültepe," 65. Notice "house" is at the head of the list followed by two natural word
pairs. I am grateful to my colleague John Walton for drawing this text to my attention.

48. Cf. Sivan, *Between Woman, Man, and God*, 208.

49. See Trible, *Texts of Terror*.

50. Thus Sivan, *Between Woman, Man, and God*, 220. Regarding the menial status of women in ancient Israel, Anthony Phillips speaks for many: "They [women]
had no legal status, being the personal property first of their fathers, and then of
their husbands" (*Ancient Israel's Criminal Law*, 70). For discussion and critical responses to this notion see Block, "Marriage and Family in Ancient Israel," 61–72;
Wright, *God's People in God's Land*, 291–316.

or an ox. By isolating the neighbor's wife from the household and giving her priority over the property associated with the household, ever the pastor, Moses highlights the special nature of the relationship between a man and his wife. He reinforces this distinction by reserving the verb חָמַד for the illicit lust of a man toward another man's wife[51] and substituting it with הִתְאַוָּה when speaking of the desire a man might have for another man's household property. Sivan rightly recognizes that these modifications to the commands reflect "scales of desires." In Sivan's words, the Deuteronomic version "elevates women as the most desirable objects of coveting. It also implies that covert coveting of other men's wives is more pervasive and more complex than the rest of the listed inventory."[52]

The reasons for desiring a neighbor's wife obviously go beyond her utilitarian value as a part of the economic unit; she could also be coveted as an instrument of sexual pleasure, as well as tool to demonstrate superiority over one's neighbor, which would be implied by taking his wife. However, contrary to Sivan, the intent of the Deuteronomic version is not so much to secure the welfare of men, as if another man's wife is his enemy,[53] but to curb a fundamental weakness in men and to secure the rights of one's neighbor to a healthy and secure marital relationship. This goal is achieved by elevating wives above the status of household property and treating the marital covenant relationship as sacrosanct. Coveting one's neighbor's wife is a particularly heinous moral and social malady, and the general good of the community can only be preserved by "fencing off the home."[54] And this is best achieved by disciplining the passions of the heart, which is precisely Jesus' point in Matt 15:16, "For out of the heart come evil intentions, murder, adultery, fornication, theft, false witness, slander" (NRSV). This notion is expressed even more explicitly in Matt 5:27–28, where Jesus seems to have combined the prohibition against adultery (command #6 in Deuteronomy) with the present command: "You have heard that it was said, 'You shall not commit

---

51. The root may be employed with reference to licit desire for a woman—as in Ezekiel's reference to his wife as מַחְמַד עֵינֶיךָ, "the desire/delight of your eyes" (Ezek 24:16), or for objects that are aesthetically pleasing or delightful to eat (Gen 2:9).

52. Sivan, *Between Woman, Man, and God.* 215.

53. Ibid., 216–17.

54. Ibid., 217.

adultery.' But I say to you that everyone who looks at a woman with lust has already committed adultery with her in his heart" (NRSV).[55]

The Last Command as a Window into the Deuteronomic Domestic Ideology

One can imagine that the modifications Moses made to the Decalogue as he recited it at the beginning of his second farewell address on the Plains of Moab caught many in his audience by surprise. After all, had he not ended his first address by warning his hearers (and future readers) not to add or delete anything from the instruction on the divine ordinances and regulations he was presenting to them?[56] And now he has exhibited the *ḥuṣpâ* to tamper with the Decalogue, the document that came from the very mouth of God, and was written down by the very finger of God (Exod 31:18; 32:15–16; 34:1; Deut 9:10)! However, we must remember that the Israelites are now almost forty years removed from the original revelation at Sinai, and they are on the verge of a brand new phase in their history—life in the Promised Land. Having lived with this people for forty years, here Moses functions not only as the divinely authorized conduit and interpreter of the divine revelation, but as the people's pastor preparing them for the new circumstances that await them beyond the Jordan.

We have argued here that the Decalogue functioned as a bill of rights, seeking to protect my neighbor from my potential violation of his or her rights as a human being created as an image of God, and as a member of the redeemed community in covenant relation with God and with others. While the principles summarized in the Decalogue were to be determinative for the entire community, technically this document addressed the heads of the households, perceiving them as the greatest threats to the well-being of society. It recognizes that those at the head of this most basic human institution, the home, are particularly susceptible to the temptation to view their roles primarily as positions of power rather than as a divinely ordained stewardship of an office that exists for the good of those in

---

55. The Greek word for "lustful intent" (ἐπιθυμία/ἐπιθυμέω) involves the same root as that used by LXX to translate חָמַד in the present command.

56. "You shall not add to the word that I command you, nor delete from it, but you are to keep the commands of YHWH your God that I command you" (Deut 4:2).

one's care. Instead of accepting the model of Christ, who loves the church "and gave himself up for her that he might sanctify her . . . so that he might present the church to himself in splendor, without spot or wrinkle or any such thing, that she might be holy and without blemish" (Eph 5:25–27), male heads of households are prone to exercise their authority in the interests of their own honor and status. One of the primary functions of the Decalogue is to restrain the potential abuse of power by the heads of households.[57] If this was true of the original version, revealed at Sinai, it was even more so of the version we find in Deuteronomy. The modifications introduced by Moses in his recitation of Israel's basic constitutional document[58] reinforce this goal and signal the trajectory of the Torah's vision of the role of the head of the household in the remainder of the second address.

Earlier we had noted that one of Moses' aims in his second pastoral address was to prevent the abuse of power by those who sit in seats of authority: kings, judges, elders, and even priests. Once our eyes have learned to recognize this, they begin to see that this is even more emphatically so in those contexts that concern the relationship of a man with his family, particularly the women of the household.[59] Scholars have long recognized that Deuteronomy pays special attention to women's rights.[60] By reading the address serially we begin to recognize the pervasiveness of this perspective throughout the second address.[61]

57. Our approach differs fundamentally from that of David Clines, who argues that the document was drafted to secure the interests of elites and those who wield power. See Clines, "The Ten Commandments, Reading from Left to Right," 97–112.

58. M. Weinfeld rightly observes, "At the dawn of Israelite history the Ten Commands were received in their original short form as the basic constitution, so to speak, of the Community of Israel. The words were chiseled or written on two stone tablets that came to be known as 'the Tablets of the Covenant (*berith*)' or 'The Tablets of the Testimony (*'eduth*)' [*sic*, read 'the Pact']" ("The Uniqueness of the Decalogue and Its Place in Jewish Tradition," 27–28). Weinfeld reiterates these sentiments in another essay published the same year, "The Decalogue," 32, 37. These comments are repeated in his commentary, *Deuteronomy 1–11*, 262–63 and 267, respectively.

59. For a detailed analysis of the relevant texts in Deuteronomy, see Josberger, "Between Rule and Responsibility."

60. Thus Weinfeld, *Deuteronomy 1–11*, 318; idem, *Deuteronomy and the Deuteronomic School*, 282–92.

61. For further discussion of all of these, see Block, *Deuteronomy*, s.v.

1. The concern for widows (10:17–18 et passim). One of the striking features of the book of Deuteronomy is its concern for the members of the community who are marginalized and economically vulnerable because they do not have access to the security provided by a normal household led by a male figure, either a father or husband. Beginning in 10:18 and on nine additional occasions the book declares the responsibility of the Israelites, particularly the heads of household, for seeing to the well-being of the widow, the fatherless, and the alien.[62]

2. Invitations to participate in worship (12:12 et passim). Like the Book of the Covenant, the Deuteronomic Torah requires all males to gather at the central sanctuary three times a year for the Festivals of Passover (Unleavened Bread), Shabuoth (Weeks), and Sukkoth (Booths) (16:16; cf. Exod 23:14–17; 34:23). However, in contrast to the segregation that would characterize worship in Herodian times, Deuteronomy invites women, both free and slave, to worship freely in the presence of YHWH at the central sanctuary (12:12, 18; 16:11, 14; 31:12).

3. The manumission of female slaves (15:12). Whereas the regulations concerning the manumission of indentured slaves in the Book of the Covenant had spoken only of male slaves (Exod 21:2–11), the corresponding instructions in Deuteronomy 15 expressly stipulate that the law applies to both male and female slaves (v. 12).[63]

4. Military exemption for new husbands (20:7). Like the cases involving a newly constructed house (v. 5) and a newly planted vineyard (v. 6), on the surface the exemption of a man newly betrothed from military service for a year appears to be interested primarily in the man: it would be unfortunate for him if he could not enjoy the benefits of his own labor/commitment. However, in light of the fourth case involving the demoralizing effect of a fearful man on the broader community (v. 8), this ordinance also has the interests of his bride in mind. Surely she would be as eager as he to enjoy the fruits of their betrothal; she might even hope that before he leaves for his tour of

---

62. Deut 10:18; 14:29; 16:11, 14; 24:19–21; 26:12–13; 27:19.

63. The potential for abusive power that the heads of households may wield over children, both male and female, is also reined in by prohibitions on offering one's children as sacrifices to the gods (12:31; 18:10).

duty she will have conceived a child by him. From the construction of the last clauses, "lest he die and another man take her," it seems that a part of the issue is protecting her from another man. This interpretation is reinforced by 24:5, which speaks expressly of the man tending to his new wife's happiness (שִׂמַּח) for the year.

5. *The captive bride (21:10–14).* For women, few circumstances are more fearful than the conquest of their towns by a foreign army. It is clear from the concluding motive clause of 21:14, תַּחַת אֲשֶׁר עִנִּיתָהּ, "because you have degraded her,"[64] that the concern here is to rein in the potential for male abuse of women in such contexts. By this interpretation this paragraph serves not as a legal provision for a soldier to marry a woman in circumstances where contractual arrangements with the bride's family are impossible,[65] nor as an authorization of divorce from a foreign bride—both practices are assumed—but as an appeal to Israelites to be charitable in their treatment of foreign women, who, through no decision or fault of their own, are forced to become a part of the Israelite community. Verses 10–13 call for the charitable treatment of foreign brides when they are first taken; verse 14 for their charitable treatment in divorce.

6. *The second-ranked wife (21:15–17).* Bigamous and polygamous marriages provide fertile soil for the mistreatment of women. This text seems to assume, perhaps inevitably, that one of the wives will became a favored wife for the man, which would lead naturally to favored treatment of her son when the property of the head of the household is divided. This provision seeks to secure the well-being of the son of a rejected wife who happens to be the firstborn. Inasmuch as children were responsible for the care of their parents in old age, in so doing it also protects the interests and rights of the second-ranked wife.

64. Contrary to common understanding (e.g., Nelson, *Deuteronomy*, 254; McConville, *Deuteronomy*, 330) the piel verb עִנָּה, does not refer to "rape" or "sexual abuse." Ellen van Wolde ("Does *'innâ* Denote Rape?" 528–44) has demonstrated that in juridical contexts the word serves an evaluative function, expressing downward social movement, and should be translated "debased."

65. Contra Pressler, *The View of Women Found in the Deuteronomic Family Laws*, 11.

7. The mother of a rebellious child (21:18–21). The subject of the open-ing clause—"If a *man* has a stubborn and rebellious son"—and the focus of the paragraph on the son (rather than a child in general) reflect the patricentrism of ancient Israel. However, the instructions on how to deal with such a child modify this patricentrism by explic-itly including the child's mother *with* his father as the aggrieved party, and by involving her in every phase of the legal process: though *they* chastise him he will not listen to *them*; *they* seize him; *they* bring him before the elders; *they* address the elders; *they* speak of the child's insubordination to *them*. These instructions prevent the male head of the household from operating only in self-interest and force him to protect his wife from the abuse of the son.

8. The wife falsely accused of lying about her virginity (22:13–21). This paragraph divides into two parts, a primary case involving a false ac-cusation (vv. 13–19) and a counter-case in which the charges prove to be true (vv. 20–21). Whereas the latter makes no attempt to defend a woman who is actually guilty of lying to her husband about her pre-marital virginity, the former goes to great lengths to protect a woman from false accusations by an abusive husband who first turns against her and then trumps up and publicizes charges of immorality against her. (a) It invites the accused's parents (both father and mother) to come to her defense—a remarkable provision in a patrilocal society. (b) It calls for a public hearing of the case before the elders at the gate—commensurate with the public nature of the slander. (c) It in-vites the presentation of objective evidence to counter the false accu-sations. (d) It provides for the turning of the tables so that the accused becomes a plaintiff in court and the plaintiff becomes the accused. (e) It calls for the public disciplining of the man. (f) It secures the honor of the woman's parents by forcing the man to pay compen-sation for having charged them with providing him with "damaged goods." (g) By prohibiting the man from divorcing the woman, it forces him to guarantee her economic well-being for life.

Many modern readers will find the last prescription unpalat-able. Surely divorce is better than living with a man who has publicly defamed his wife. However, ancient texts should be read in the light of their own intention, rather than in the light of modern conventions. From the perspective of the husband, this order assumes the punishment will have a rehabilitative effect. Ideally, having been publicly shamed, he will return to his wife and assume his responsible role in caring for her and seeking to build a normal household. From the perspective of the woman, this order guarantees her security; she will be cared for all her days. From the perspective of her parents, they may keep the bride price (plus the fine), but more importantly, they can relax because their daughter is restored to a protective environment. These desired outcomes highlight the importance of the issue being resolved in a public court of law. The elders and the community who witnessed the proceedings become guarantors of the man's good behavior.

9. *The victims of rape (22:23–29).* Here Moses provides instructions for two scenarios involving rape: the rape of a virgin engaged to be married (vv. 23–27) and the rape of a virgin who is not engaged to be married (vv. 28–29). The first provision is interesting for the distinction it draws between the sexual violation of a virgin betrothed to another man in a town (vv. 23–24) and out in the country (vv. 25–27).[66] It assumes that if the act occurs in town an innocent woman will cry for help and either the man to whom she is betrothed or her townspeople will rescue her. However, since there is no one in the country to hear her cries when she is violated by a man, it gives her the benefit of the doubt and assumes her innocence. Meanwhile the man must be executed.

The second case involves a virgin who has not been engaged to a man. This case represents an adaptation of Exod 22:15–16[Eng 16–17]. Whereas Exod 22:16[Eng 17] considers the man's actions to be seductive (פָּתָה, piel), here Moses speaks of the man seizing (תָּפַשׂ)[67] the woman and "lying" with her, and being caught *in flagrante delicto*. In the prescribed response to this adulterous act the attention is focused entirely on the man. Because he has deflowered and degraded (עִנָּה) the woman by engaging in sexual intercourse with her, he must pay the father of the woman fifty shekels. Unlike verse 19, this payment is not a fine but the bride price, since upon its payment she be-

---

66. This compares with ancient Hittite Laws that distinguish rape cases occurring in the mountains and those in a woman's house, the latter being deemed a capital offense. See HL §§197–98.

67. Cf. הֶחֱזִיק, "to overpower," in verse 25.

comes his wife in a marriage from which there is to be no divorce as long as they live (cf. v. 19). On the surface it looks like Deuteronomy has tightened the law recorded in Exod 22:15–16[Eng 16–17]. Unlike the tendency toward a more humanitarian approach that we have witnessed in Deuteronomy's presentation of other laws found earlier in the Pentateuch, it appears Moses has eliminated any other options for the poor woman but to watch the man pay her father the bride gift and then accede to becoming his wife—hardly a pleasant prospect for someone who has been forcibly violated. However, the issue is probably not that simple. As in verse 22, the present text concerns the righteous response to forced sex involving a virgin. The regulation seems to assume the father's and daughter's rights of first refusal provided for in the earlier text. The point here is that if the man pays the bride gift and if the father agrees to accept him as a son-in-law, the man must fulfill all the marital duties that come with the rights to sexual intercourse, and in so doing guarantee the security of the woman.

10. The divorced woman (24:1–4). This text has been the subject of more attention than most of the above. Interpretations vary, but the key is found in properly identifying the protases and apodoses. The syntax is admittedly ambiguous, but the following represents the most likely flow of the text.

> *When* a man takes a woman and becomes her husband,
> *if*   she finds no favor in his eyes because he has found some defect in her,[68]
>   and he writes her a certificate of divorce and puts it in her hand
>   and lets her go out of his house;
>   and she departs out of his house,
>   and she goes and she becomes another man's wife,
>   and the latter man hates her
>   and he writes her a certificate of divorce
>   and he puts it in her hand
>   and sends her out of his house,
> *or if*   the latter man dies, who took her to be his wife,
> *then*   her former husband, who sent her away,

68. John Walton is correct in suggesting that עֶרְוַת דָּבָר refers, not to a voluntary sinful action, but an involuntary physical issue, perhaps some menstrual irregularity, like that of the woman who came to Jesus for healing in Mark 5:25–34. See Walton, "The Place of the *hutqaṭṭēl* within the D–Stem Group and Its Implications in Deuteronomy 24:4," 14–15.

may not take her again to be his wife,
after she has been declared defiled,
for that is an abomination before YHWH,
and you shall not bring sin upon the land
   that YHWH your God is giving you as a grant.

The text may be analyzed according to common diagnostic procedures:

TABLE 5: A Structural Portrayal of Deuteronomy 24:1–4

The Problem	When a man takes a woman and marries her, if she finds no favor in his eyes because he has found some defect in her,
The Prevailing Practice	and he writes her a certificate of divorce, and he puts it in her hand, and sends her out of his house,
The Complication	if she departs from his house, and goes and becomes another man's wife, and if the latter man hates her, and he writes her a certificate of divorce, and puts it in her hand, and he sends her out of his house, if the latter man dies, who took her to be his wife,
The Proscription	then her former husband, who sent her away, may not take her again to be his wife, after she has been declared defiled,
The Rationale	for that is an abomination before YHWH, and you shall not bring sin upon the land that YHWH your God is giving you as a grant.

Contrary to common opinion, the purpose of this text is not to authorize or even regulate divorce *per se*—the practice is assumed—but to rein in potential abuse by a husband after he has divorced his wife. Technically the primary issue is not divorce, but palingamy, remarriage to a former spouse.[69] As in 21:10–14, here Moses' concern is to protect the wife from abuse by men, specifically her first husband. He does so by reiterating the procedures already in existence for releasing wives from the bonds of marriage. Furthermore, he insists that when a husband divorces his wife he relinquishes his authority

69. Cf. Westbrook, "Prohibition on Restoration of Marriage in Deuteronomy 24:1–4," 388; Pressler, *View of Women*, 46–47. For defenses of the traditional interpretation, see Hugenberger, *Marriage as a Covenant*, 76–81.

over her. Having humiliated his wife by forcing her to declare herself unclean, he may not reclaim her if she has remarried and then loses her husband through divorce or death. The legislation seeks to protect the woman by requiring the husband to produce a severance document as legal proof for the dissolution of the marriage. Without this document the husband could demand to have her back at any time, and if she were to remarry, he could accuse her of adultery.[70]

11. Levirate marriage (25:5–10). The primary purpose of the institution known as levirate marriage was to secure the integrity of families and inherited estates, which were threatened when a married man died without having fathered an heir. This could be achieved by having the widow marry the deceased's nearest unmarried male relative. The first child born of this union would be legally considered the child of the deceased and would carry on his name and retain the property in his name. Verses 7–10 contemplate the case in which the nearest relative refuses to perform this duty on behalf of his departed relative. As in the case of divorce in 24:1–4, Moses prescribes a precise legal process whereby the יָבָם (levir) may be released from his obligations to his deceased brother.

While the details of the case are interesting in and of themselves, our concern here is the way in which the widow is to be treated. The policies laid down afford the widow remarkable freedom of movement and influence in prosecuting the case. Her authorized involvement may be summarized as follows. She is authorized to appear before the elders at the gate of the community and to present her complaint (v. 7b). The elders of the town shall summon the יָבָם and speak to him (v. 8a). The יָבָם is given an opportunity to speak for himself (v. 8b), and if he declares publicly his refusal to perform the duty of a יָבָם, the widow is invited to perform a ritual of public humiliation of the יָבָם—removing the sandal from his foot (v. 9). Thereafter, in a rude gesture of shame and humiliation,[71] she may spit in the face of the יָבָם, and is invited to interpret her actions before the elders. By announcing, "This is what shall be done to the man who will not build his brother's house," the widow declares that this response to being

---

70. So also Wright, *God's People in God's Land*, 217.

71. Cf. Num 12:14; Job 17:6; 30:10; Matt 26:67; 27:30; Mark 10:34; 14:65; Luke 18:32.

rejected by her brother-in-law is neither impulsive nor idiosyncratic, but accords with established legal procedure. Although the woman expressly acts in the interests of her deceased husband, in seeking to honor him she is also invited to defend her own honor. This text prevents a person on whose shoulders levirate responsibilities fall from simply disregarding those obligations and discarding his widowed sister-in-law. The elders of the city are to stand by the woman against a potentially abusive male.

Conclusion

In the past three decades feminist scholars have rightly alerted readers of the Scriptures to misogynistic elements in the biblical texts. It is clear that the documents were all written from a patricentric perspective. It is also clear that just as other leaders in the community were prone to twist positions of responsibility into positions of power and to exercise that power in brutal self-interest, so the narratives often paint pictures of the grossly abusive exercise of power by male heads of households. In our attention to these narratives it is tempting to assume that they reflect normal patricentrism; that the system itself is fundamentally flawed and needs to be overturned. The stories do indeed prove the fulfillment of the prediction made by God at the fountainhead of human history: "I will greatly increase your pangs in childbearing; in pain you shall bring forth children, You shall crave the power of your husband, but he will *rule* over you" (Gen 3:16). Because of sin, a woman's role becomes not only painful but also frustrating, and men respond by treating women as subjects rather than as co-regents in their exercise of dominion over the earth. It is easy to forget that while pervasive in the narratives, this represents neither the biblical ideal nor the covenantal norm. According to the covenantal standards signaled by the Decalogue but developed in greater detail in the Deuteronomic Torah, the role of the אָב, "father," in the בֵּית־אָב, "the house of the father," involved primarily care and protection of all those under his charge. However, because of sheer superior physical power, this care and protection often degenerates to exploitation and abuse of women as if they were nothing more than household property, as disposable as sheep or oxen. Contemporary efforts to determine and reestablish biblical ethical norms must pay attention not only to accounts of the way it was, but also to texts that seek to outline the way it should have been. In this and many other respects the book of Deuteronomy offers a glorious gospel, setting a trajectory of male-female relations that leads ultimately to Paul's statements in Eph 5:25–33.

> Husbands, love your wives, as Christ loved the church and gave himself up for her, that he might sanctify her, having cleansed her by the washing of water with the word, so that he might present the church to himself in splendor, without spot or wrinkle or any such thing, that she might be holy and without blemish. In the same way husbands should love their wives as their own bodies. He who loves his wife loves himself. For no one ever hated his own flesh, but nourishes and cherishes it, just as Christ does the church, because we are members of his body. "Therefore a man shall leave his father and mother and hold fast to his wife, and the two shall become one flesh." This mystery is profound, and I am saying that it refers to Christ and the church. However, let each one of you love his wife as himself. (ESV)

The seeds of this perspective were planted long ago in God's covenant with Israel. May they sprout and may this plant flourish anew among God's people today.[72]

72. An earlier draft of this paper was presented to the Evangelical Theological Society in 2006. It was modified significantly and presented as the installation address on the occasion of my appointment as Gunther H. Knoedler Professor of Old Testament at Wheaton College, October 18, 2007. I am extremely grateful for the support I receive from the Knoedlers (Gunther and Betty) and the Wheaton College community. I am also grateful for the invaluable help my research assistants (Chris Ansberry, Jerry Hwang, Charlie Trimm) have provided in refining the paper. Of course, any flaws in argument and presentation are my own.

Excursus C

How Shall We Number the Ten Commands?

The Deuteronomy Version (5:1–21)

Table 6: Two Approaches to Numbering the Decalogue

The Reformed Tradition	The Catholic and Lutheran Tradition
[6]I am YHWH your God, who brought you out of the land of Egypt, out of the house of slavery.	[6]I am YHWH your God, who brought you out of the land of Egypt, out of the house of slavery.
[7]You shall have no other gods before me.	[7]You shall have no other gods before me. [8]You shall not make for yourself a carved image, or any likeness of anything that is in heaven above, or that is on the earth beneath, or that is in the water under the earth. [9]You shall not bow down to them or serve them; for I YHWH your God am a jealous God, visiting the iniquity of the fathers on the children to the third and fourth generation of those who hate me, [10]but showing חֶסֶד to thousands of those who love me and keep my commands.
[8]You shall not make for yourself a carved image, or any likeness of anything that is in heaven above, or that is on the earth beneath, or that is in the water under the earth. [9]You shall not bow down to them or serve them; for I YHWH your God am a jealous God, visiting the iniquity of the fathers on the children to the third and fourth generation of those who hate me, [10]but showing חֶסֶד to thousands of those who love me and keep my commands.	
[11]You shall not bear the name of YHWH your God in vain, for YHWH will not hold him guiltless who takes his name in vain.	[11]You shall not bear the name of YHWH your God in vain, for YHWH will not hold him guiltless who takes his name in vain.

The Reformed Tradition	The Catholic and Lutheran Tradition
[12]Observe the Sabbath day, by keeping it holy, as YHWH your God commanded you. [13]Six days you shall labor and do all your work, [14]but the seventh day is a Sabbath to YHWH your God. On it you shall not do any work, you or your son or your daughter or your male servant or your female servant, or your ox or your donkey or any of your livestock, or the sojourner who is within your gates, that your male servant and your female servant may rest as well as you. [15]You shall remember that you were a slave in the land of Egypt, and YHWH your God brought you out from there with a mighty hand and an outstretched arm. Therefore YHWH your God commanded you to keep the Sabbath day.	[12]Observe the Sabbath day, by keeping it holy, as YHWH your God commanded you. [13]Six days you shall labor and do all your work, [14]but the seventh day is a Sabbath to YHWH your God. On it you shall not do any work, you or your son or your daughter or your male servant or your female servant, or your ox or your donkey or any of your livestock, or the sojourner who is within your gates, that your male servant and your female servant may rest as well as you. [15]You shall remember that you were a slave in the land of Egypt, and YHWH your God brought you out from there with a mighty hand and an outstretched arm. Therefore YHWH your God commanded you to keep the Sabbath day.
[16]Honor your father and your mother, as YHWH your God commanded you, that your days may be long, and that it may go well with you in the land that YHWH your God is giving you.	[16]Honor your father and your mother, as YHWH your God commanded you, that your days may be long, and that it may go well with you in the land that YHWH your God is giving you.
[17]You shall not murder.	[17]You shall not murder.
[18]And you shall not commit adultery.	[18]And you shall not commit adultery.
[19]And you shall not steal.	[19]And you shall not steal.
[20]And you shall not bear false witness against your neighbor.	[20]And you shall not bear false witness against your neighbor.
[21]And you shall not covet (חָמַד) your neighbor's wife. And you shall not desire (הִתְאַוָּה) your neighbor's house, his field, or his male servant, or his female servant, his ox, or his donkey, or anything that is your neighbor's.	[21]And you shall not covet (חָמַד) your neighbor's wife.
	And you shall not desire (הִתְאַוָּה) your neighbor's house, his field, or his male servant, or his female servant, his ox, or his donkey, or anything that is your neighbor's.

Considerations in Enumerating the Terms of the Decalogue[1]

1. The ambiguity of Exodus 20:17 in MT. The text is obviously cast as two independent clause commands. However, whereas the previous commands are marked as separate paragraphs by *sĕtûmôt* (סְתוּמוֹת, nine spaces), in the Leningrad Codex these two clauses are separated by only two spaces. The repetition of the verb חָמַד, "to covet," and the meaning of בַּיִת as "household," may suggest that the second command is intended to be interpreted as an expansion/clarification of the first. Nevertheless, the way the second clause opens (לֹא + imperfect) is identical to the previous four commands which scribes and scholars unanimously separate as discrete commands.

2. The modifications to these commands in Deuteronomy. Deuteronomy 5:17 removes the potential ambiguity by:

> (a) adding a *waw* conjunction to the second command exactly as it had done with the preceding four commands;

> (b) changing the verb of the second command from חָמַד, "to covet," to אוה (hithpael), "to crave for";

> (c) transposing בַּיִת, "house, household," and אֵשֶׁת רֵעֶךָ, "wife of your neighbor," thereby forestalling the treatment of one's wife merely as property like the rest of the household;

> (d) isolating the command not to covet one's neighbor's wife and treating it as a separate "line item";

> (e) adding "his field" as a complement to "his house," and creating a third pair of entities.

3. The grammar, syntax, and content of Exod 20:3–6, which is identical to Deut 5:7–10 (except for the addition of two *waw* conjunctions):

---

1. Discussions of the issue in Jewish tradition tend to focus on the relationship between the narrative opening statement and the commands. See Breuer, "Dividing the Decalogue into Verses and Commands," 291–330. Breuer also recognizes the syntactical and substantive differences between the Exodus and Deuteronomy versions of the Decalogue (ibid., 313–14). For a discourse analysis of the Decalogue yielding similar results, see DeRouchie, *A Call to Covenant Love*, 115–17, 127–32.

Figure 3: A Comparison of Exodus 20:3–6 and Deuteronomy 5:7–10

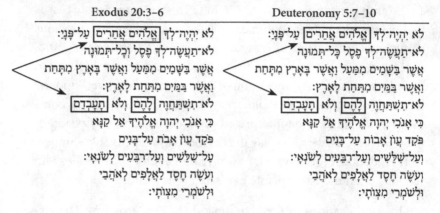

Exodus 20:3–6	Deuteronomy 5:7–10
לֹא יִהְיֶה־לְךָ אֱלֹהִים אֲחֵרִים עַל־פָּנָי׃	לֹא יִהְיֶה־לְךָ אֱלֹהִים אֲחֵרִים עַל־פָּנָי׃
לֹא־תַעֲשֶׂה־לְךָ פֶסֶל וְכָל־תְּמוּנָה	לֹא־תַעֲשֶׂה־לְךָ פֶסֶל כָּל־תְּמוּנָה
אֲשֶׁר בַּשָּׁמַיִם מִמַּעַל וַאֲשֶׁר בָּאָרֶץ מִתָּחַת	אֲשֶׁר בַּשָּׁמַיִם מִמַּעַל וַאֲשֶׁר בָּאָרֶץ מִתָּחַת
וַאֲשֶׁר בַּמַּיִם מִתַּחַת לָאָרֶץ׃	וַאֲשֶׁר בַּמַּיִם מִתַּחַת לָאָרֶץ׃
לֹא־תִשְׁתַּחֲוֶה לָהֶם וְלֹא תָעָבְדֵם	לֹא־תִשְׁתַּחֲוֶה לָהֶם וְלֹא תָעָבְדֵם
כִּי אָנֹכִי יְהוָה אֱלֹהֶיךָ אֵל קַנָּא	כִּי אָנֹכִי יְהוָה אֱלֹהֶיךָ אֵל קַנָּא
פֹּקֵד עֲוֹן אָבֹת עַל־בָּנִים	פֹּקֵד עֲוֹן אָבוֹת עַל־בָּנִים
עַל־שִׁלֵּשִׁים וְעַל־רִבֵּעִים לְשֹׂנְאָי׃	וְעַל־שִׁלֵּשִׁים וְעַל־רִבֵּעִים לְשֹׂנְאָי׃
וְעֹשֶׂה חֶסֶד לַאֲלָפִים לְאֹהֲבַי	וְעֹשֶׂה חֶסֶד לַאֲלָפִים לְאֹהֲבַי
וּלְשֹׁמְרֵי מִצְוֹתָי׃	וּלְשֹׁמְרֵי מִצְוֹתָי׃

(a) The commands regarding exclusive devotion to YHWH and the manufacture of images are held together by references to YHWH in the first person (like the preamble). Thereafter he is referred to in the third person.

(b) The first imperative statement concerns the prohibition of rivals to YHWH. The second is best interpreted as a clarification of the first, that is, a prohibition of the manufacture of images that may be treated as rivals to YHWH and erected next to the Ark of the Covenant in the Tabernacle/Temple (cf. 1 Samuel 5).

(c) Following the presentation of YHWH as formless in 4:12–14, in 4:15–19 the issue is clearly not the reduction of YHWH to plastic image, but the manufacture of images which, alongside the heavenly objects, might vie for Israel's allegiance.

(d) The identification/characterization of YHWH in these statements as אֵל קַנָּא, "impassioned El," points to the manufacture of rival deities, not the manufacture of physical representations of YHWH. Elsewhere this expression occurs only in contexts involving the worship of idols, never in contexts involving the portrayal of YHWH in physical form.

(e) If these two imperatives are separated and treated as two different commands, then the plural suffixes on לָהֶם, "to *them*," and תַעָבְדֵם לֹא, "you shall not serve *them*," in Deut 5:9 lack an antecedent. Since all the nouns preceding these forms in verse 8 are singular, the nearest antecedent is אֱלֹהִים אֲחֵרִים, "other gods," in the first command.

(f) The Massoretes treated these as a single entity, running the prohibition on images immediately after the prohibition on other gods. In fact, in both Exodus and Deuteronomy MT treats the declarative statement that functions as the preamble to this document as a part of this long paragraph.

6

All Creatures Great and Small

Recovering a Deuteronomic Theology of Animals [1]

O N JANUARY 17, 2007, a group of leading evangelicals announced the establishment of the Evangelical Climate Initiative and issued a manifesto called "Climate Change: An Evangelical Call to Action."[2] In recent years, several significant publications written by philosophers and ethicists have appeared, appealing for a distinctly Christian response to critical environmental issues.[3] Although biblical scholars are beginning to work out an authentic biblical theology addressing these matters,[4] there are reasons why evangelicals

---

1. This essay was previously published in *The Old Testament in the Life of God's People: Essays in Honor of Elmer A. Martens*. Edited by Jon Isaak, 283–305. Winona Lake, IN: Eisenbrauns, 2009. Combining a remarkable skill in extracting the theology of biblical texts with a passion not only to integrate that theology into one's belief system but also to translate it into everyday life, Prof. Elmer Martens has modeled God's design for a Christian scholar. See Martens, "Accessing Theological Readings of a Biblical Book," 223–37. The goal of this investigation is to expand his legacy into an area where few evangelicals have ventured.

2. The document may be accessed online at http://www.npr.org/documents/2006/feb/evangelical/calltoaction.pdf.

3. Toly and Block, eds., *Keeping God's Earth*; see especially Wilkinson, ed., *Earthkeeping in the Nineties*; Van Dyke, ed., *Redeeming Creation*; Berry, *The Care of Creation*; Berry, ed., *Environmental Stewardship*; Bouma-Prediger, *For the Beauty of the Earth*.

4. Under the leadership of Norman C. Habel of Flinders University, the number

are hesitant to join these discussions; the philosophers and ethicists tend to be broadly ecumenical, often considering Buddhist, Hindu, Daoist, and other perspectives on par with those derived from the Hebrew Bible or the New Testament.[5] However, this is scarcely an excuse for silence on the wasteful, oppressive, and exploitative ways we treat God's good earth.

Douglas Moo's recent appeal, in a mainstream evangelical journal, for a more thoughtful response[6] offers hope for a long overdue shift in thinking about the environment. With his massive bibliography and his erudite discussion of the theological issues involved in an evangelical ecotheology, Moo has established a firm basis for us all to be engaged in environmental issues from the perspective of New Testament theology.

For cultural and theological reasons,[7] the Old Testament often plays only a minimal role in the theological and ethical commitments of evangelicals. In ecotheological discussions, when appeal is made to the Old Testament, it is natural to refer to the Genesis account of creation and affirm our obligations for the welfare of the world by virtue of our status as images of God. But having done so, the search for a biblical understanding leapfrogs over the rest of the Torah to Psalm 8, and then over the poetic and prophetic writings to Romans 8 and New Testament portrayals of new creation. I do not wish to denigrate these efforts—any serious exploration of Scripture for the purpose of establishing theological truth and practical sanctified living is to be welcomed. I simply lament the fact that with this hop-skip-and-jump approach we have overlooked many rich seams of ore to be mined in the constitutional, historical, cultic, wisdom, and prophetic writings

---

of scholars concerned with the ecological and ecotheological messages of the Old Testament is growing. Many of the articles in the journal, *Ecotheology: The Journal of Religion, Nature and the Environment*, established in 1996 are devoted to Old Testament texts and themes. The same is true of the papers presented at the annual meeting of the SBL, which recently established a special Ecological Hermeneutics Consultation.

5. For an eloquent call for responsible treatment of environmental issues from a more general religious perspective, see Gottlieb, *A Greener Faith*.

6. Moo, "Nature in the New Creation," 449–88.

7. Though they do so for different reasons, the emphasis on the discontinuities between the testaments among Lutherans, Anabaptists, and dispensationalists has resulted in a widespread and persistent denigration of the Hebrew Bible (Old Testament) as a source and guide for Christian behavior.

of the Old Testament. The time has come for a detailed and systematic analysis of the data provided by each of the books of the Old Testament. Only when we have done this will we be able to develop a full-blown biblical zootheology.

The goal of this essay is to consider the theology of animals as it is presented in the book of Deuteronomy.[8] Analogous to the book of Romans in the New Testament, the book of Deuteronomy provides the most systematic presentation of theology that is found in the entire Old Testament. Contrary to prevailing opinion, this book comes to us not as legislation, but as a collection of final pastoral addresses by Moses to his people before he passes on and before they cross over the Jordan into the Promised Land. In reflecting on the theological and ethical implications of the glorious gospel embodied in YHWH's love for the ancestors, his gracious election of Israel as his chosen people, his deliverance from the slavery of Egypt, his covenantal relationship established with his people, and his gracious revelation of his will, Moses, the pastor, touches on a wide range of subjects, from the conduct of Israel's rulers to the way in which ordinary citizens present their offerings to YHWH.[9]

As biblical theologians have done with a wide range of topics, our investigation of the theology of animals in Deuteronomy involves collecting, studying, and applying those passages in the book that relate to this theme.[10] I propose to address the subject under two main headings: (1) The Deuteronomic ontology of animals: what is an animal, and what dimensions of animal life does the book recognize? (2) The Deuteronomic view of humankind's relationship to animals. The latter will be broken down into several subcategories. The primary goal of this paper is to collect and organize the evidence. Limitations of space will prevent full discussion of the theological

8. In so doing, this paper seeks to buttress the discussion of the philosopher Wennberg in his book, *God, Humans, and Animals*, 289–95.

9. The role of Moses in the composition is hotly disputed. Critical scholarship generally treats the book as a pseudepigraph, derived from a much later time, with Moses' name being attached to lend authority to the composition. For an alternative interpretation, see Block, "Recovering the Voice of Moses," 21–51. Whether Deuteronomy is historical or pseudepigraphic, because most of the book is presented as quoted speech, I will identify citations according to the purported speaker, rather than the final author/editor of the book.

10. For a methodological summary of biblical theology, see Zevit, "Jewish Biblical Theology: Whence? Why?" 305–6.

Figure 4: Clean and Unclean Animals according to Leviticus 11 and Deuteronomy 14

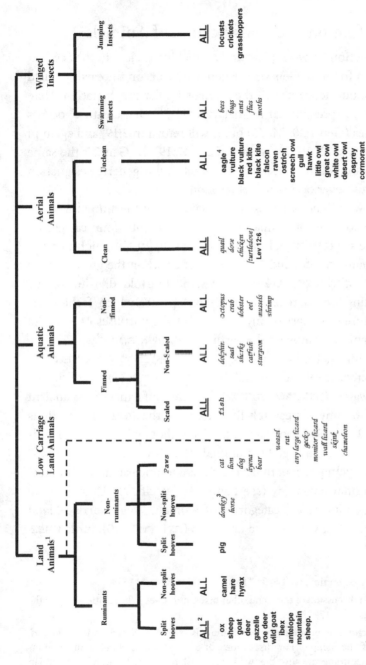

[1] Deuteronomy 14 mentions only high carriage land animals. Lev 11:29-31 adds the class of low carriage land animals that "swarm on the ground." Lev. 11:10-11 refers to corresponding aquatic "swarmers."

[2] Underlined: permitted as food.

[3] Italic font examples, not named in Leviticus 11 or Deuteronomy 14.

[4] The identity of some of these birds is uncertain.

and practical implications of our findings, a matter to which we will return in the future.[11]

The Definition and Classification of Animals

The distinction between plant and animal life is clear in the account of creation found in Genesis 1, where God calls on the earth to yield its plants, but he creates all the animals by fiat proclamation. Here the general expression for animal, נֶפֶשׁ חַיָּה, "living creature" occurs three times (Gen 1:20, 24; 30) but it will return in 2:19, and again in chapter 9 (vv. 12, 15, 16; see also Ezek 47:19). In Gen 2:7 the same phrase is used of the first man. Remarkably, this generic designation for animals never occurs in Deuteronomy.

The way Genesis 1 presents the creation of the animals reflects a clear taxonomy of animal species divided into four categories: fish of the sea (דְּגַת הַיָּם), birds of the sky (עוֹף הַשָּׁמַיִם), high carriage land animals (בְּהֵמָה), and "crawlies" that crawl on the ground (here רֶמֶשׂ הָרֹמֵשׂ עַל־הָאָרֶץ, v. 26).[12] The same fourfold division of the animal kingdom is reflected in Deut 4:17–18, which forbids the manufacture of images of any creature for the purposes of worship: (1) "any animal that is on the earth" (כָּל־בְּהֵמָה אֲשֶׁר בָּאָרֶץ); (2) "any bird of wing that flies in the sky" (כָּל־צִפּוֹר כָּנָף אֲשֶׁר תָּעוּף בַּשָּׁמָיִם); (3) "any creeper on the ground" (כָּל־רֹמֵשׂ בָּאֲדָמָה); (4) "any fish that is in the water" (כָּל־דָּגָה אֲשֶׁר־בַּמָּיִם).[13] Further information on ancient Israel's taxonomy of creaturely life is found in the dietary instructions of Lev 11:2–23, 29–31 and Deut 14:4–20. Although Lev 11:29–31 adds the class of low-carriage land animals that "swarm on the ground" (שֶׁרֶץ הַשֹּׁרֵץ עַל־הָאָרֶץ), both lists of clean and unclean animals follow the traditional taxonomy (see Figure 4). Specifically Deut 14:4–20 recognizes four broad categories of animals: "high carriage land animals" (בְּהֵמָה, vv. 4–8), sea creatures (דָּגָה, vv. 9–10), birds (צִפּוֹר,

---

11. For a beginning, see Block, "To Serve and to Keep," 116–40.

12. For a discussion of these and other taxonomies, see Whitekettle, "Where the Wild Things Are," 17–37.

13. Akkadian expressions for wild animals include *būl ṣēri* and *umām ṣēri*, "animals of the steppe." For discussions of ancient Mesopotamian distinctions between the domestic and the wild, see Foster, "Animals in Mesopotamian Literature," 272–74; Watanabe, *Animal Symbolism in Mesopotamia*, 147–50.

vv. 11–18),[14] and insects, which are divided into "unclean insects" (שֶׁרֶץ הָעוֹף, "swarmers of fliers," v. 19)[15] and "edible [clean] insects" (עוֹף טָהוֹר, v. 20).[16] The relationship between the categories in Deuteronomy 14 and modern designations may be compared by isolating the gazelle and juxtaposing the classifications as follows in Table 7.

TABLE 7: A Comparison of Modern and Ancient Hebrew Animal Categories

Category	Scientific Name	Hebrew Designation
Kingdom	*Animalia*	חַיָּה "animal"
Phylum	*Chordata*	
Class	*Mammalia*	בְּהֵמָה "land animal"
Order	*Artiodactyla*	מַפְרֶסֶת פַּרְסָה וְשֹׁסַעַת שֶׁסַע שְׁתֵּי פְרָסוֹת "divided and cleft of hoof"
Family	*Bovidae*	מַעֲלַת גֵּרָה "chews the cud, ruminant"
Subfamily	*Antilopinae*	
Genus	*Gazella*	
Species	*G. arabica*[17]	צְבִי "gazelle"

14. See 4:17, where the expression is expanded to צִפּוֹר כָּנָף, "bird of wing." Lev 11:13 introduces the birds with עוֹף, on which see further below.

15. Though the expressions exhibit some overlap, elsewhere שֶׁרֶץ, "swarmer," identifies primarily swarming insects and aquatic creatures, while רֶמֶשׂ, "creeping thing," identifies low carriage mammals and small reptiles. See Hill, "רֶמֶשׂ," 1127–28.

16. Hebrew עוֹף derives from עוּף, "to fly." In 28:26, the full expression, עוֹף הַשָּׁמַיִם, refers to "birds of the sky," which occurs frequently elsewhere in the Old Testament (Gen 1:30 + 17x; Gen 1:21 reads refers to birds as עוֹף כָּנָף, "bird of wing"). That 14:20 intends עוֹף to be interpreted as flying insects rather than birds is confirmed by Lev 11:20–23, where the general designation שֶׁרֶץ הָעוֹף, "swarmers of fliers," is followed by a list of edible locusts.

17. The exact identity of צְבִי is uncertain. *G. Arabica* is a good guess, but other possibilities include *G. gazelle*, *G. dorcas*, and *G. subgutterosa*. See Borowski, *Every Living Thing*, 187. *G. arabica* is extinct, the only surviving specimen being on display in the Berlin Museum. For further information, see http://www.iucnredlist .org/search/details.php/8981/al.

Whereas high carriage animals are divided on the basis of their hooves and ruminant stomachs, the two primary classes of sea creatures are those that have fins and scales and those that do not. Apparently, the unclean animals would include sea mammals like dolphins and whales, as well as octopus, catfish and shrimp. Birds ("sky fliers") seem to be divided on the basis of their eating habits: carnivorous birds (whether they kill their own prey or eat carrion, including bats) on the one hand, and those that eat grains on the other. This text seems to exclude all winged insects (שֶׁרֶץ הָעוֹף, "swarmers that fly"), though a comparison with Lev 11:20–23 distinguishes between winged insects with four feet (despite the fact that insects have six!) and winged, hopping insects with jointed legs, which are edible—insects such as crickets, locusts and grasshoppers.

Modern scientific approaches to biological taxonomies base their classifications on careful analysis and comparison of anatomical features, and breeding patterns, not to mention DNA testing.[18] These biblical classifications are obviously not based on scientific analysis, but on phenomenological observations. To the ancient Hebrews creaturely spheres of existence and the animals' diet were more significant markers than the boundaries we recognize between cold and warm-blooded animals or feathered and furry coverings. We will return to a consideration of the dietary significance of this taxonomy for Israel later.

The Relationship between Human Beings and Animals

Based on Genesis 1–2, the renewal of the Adamic mandate to Noah in Genesis 9, and the portrayal of humankind in Psalm 8 as the image of God, humans were assigned the honorific but responsible role of governing the world on God's behalf. The role of human beings in the maintenance of the relationship among Creator, the earth, and its animal population may be portrayed diagrammatically as in Figure 5.

18. DNA testing occurs regularly in our classifications, especially in the Latin names ascribed to creatures. For example, the scientific name of the giant panda, *Ailuropoda melanoleuca*, "black and white bear," is the scientific name of the giant panda, even though some biologists have wondered whether the creature belonged to the raccoon or the bear family. Recent DNA tests have confirmed that, despite its exclusively herbivorous habits, the giant panda is indeed a bear, whereas the red panda belongs to the family that includes raccoons and skunks.

FIGURE 5: Diagram of Relationships among Creator, the Earth, and Its Animal Population

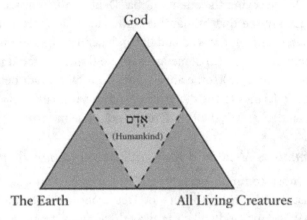

The earth is the realm that human beings are charged to govern on God's behalf, and all living creatures are the subjects to be governed as God would, were he physically present. Proverbs 12:10 characterizes persons who show regard for the life of their animals as "righteous" (צַדִּיק), that is, individuals who live according to covenantal standards. This accords not only with the Deuteronomic paradigm of kingship in Deut 17:14–20,[19] but also with the trajectory of the Deuteronomic instructions on the Israelites' treatment of creatures, both domestic and wild. The fundamental principle governing all of life is declared in 16:20: "Righteousness, righteousness you shall pursue, that you may live and possess the land that YHWH your God is giving you."[20] Every sub-unit in the second half of the second address (Deut 12:1—26:19)[21] should be interpreted as contributing to this agenda. Whereas Genesis 1–2 bases human responsibility toward all living things on humanity's status as bearing the image of God—that is, as God's representative and deputy—according to Deuteronomy,

---

19. On which, see Block, "The Burden of Leadership," 118–39.

20. Most translations render צֶדֶק צֶדֶק something like "justice, and justice alone," but then the Hebrew should read מִשְׁפָּט מִשְׁפָּט. Furthermore, the issues dealt with in the following chapters are not limited to social justice issues but involve the full range of human behaviors, including dietary regulations, prohibitions on idolatry, and so on.

21. The second address concludes with the blessings and curses of Deuteronomy 28. Chapter 27 seems to have been secondarily inserted.

the human disposition toward and treatment of animals is a matter of covenant righteousness.

In surveying the attention that Deuteronomy gives to animals, we quickly see that human beings relate to animals at four levels: (1) some animals are wild and live independent of and in opposition to human beings; (2) some animals are domesticated and work for human beings; (3) some animals are used by human beings as sacrificial offerings to the deity; and (4) some animals provide food for human beings. We shall explore each of these in turn.

Animals as Wild and Independent of Human Beings[22]

The most common generic epithet for wild animals, חַיַּת הַשָּׂדֶה, "beasts of the field," occurs in Deuteronomy only in Deut 7:22: "YHWH your God will clear away these nations before you little by little. You may not make an end of them at once, lest the wild beasts multiply against you." As in Exod 23:29, the idiom רַבָּה עָלֶיךָ, "to multiply against," portrays wild animals as antagonists and a threat to human well-being. This threat is expressed explicitly in the covenant curse of Lev 26:22, where YHWH warns that he will dispatch wild animals against his own people as agents of punishment for persistent rebellion against him. This threat finds no counterpart in the Deuteronomic version of the curses (Deut 28), though earlier Moses had spoken of YHWH sending hornets (צִרְעָה) ahead of the Israelites to clear away the enemy,[23] and later in 28:26, he refers to בֶּהֱמַת הָאָרֶץ, "the animals of the land," eating the carcasses of human victims of war.[24] In Moses' final benediction of the tribes, several times he alludes metaphorically to the threat that wild animals pose to human beings: "his [Joseph's] horns are the horns of a wild ox;[25] with them

---

22. For discussion of wild animals in the Old Testament and in the ancient Near East, see Borowski, *Every Living Thing*, 185–209.

23. The meaning of the term is uncertain. Many translate "pestilence." See NJPSV, NRSV.

24. See Jer 15:3: "I will appoint over them four kinds of destroyers—the declaration of YHWH—the sword to kill, the dogs to tear, and the birds of the air and the beasts of the earth (בֶּהֱמַת הָאָרֶץ) to devour and destroy." This expression occurs elsewhere in 1 Sam 17:44; Isa 18:6; Jer 7:33; 16:4; 19:7; 34:20.

25. The expression רְאֵם occurs elsewhere only in the poetry of Balaam's oracles (Num 23:22 and 24:8); Psalm 22:22[Eng 21]; 29:6; 92:11 [Eng 10]; Job 39:9, 10.

he shall gore the peoples, all of them, to the ends of the earth" (Deut 33:17).

Because wild animals are sanctioned for human consumption as food (Deut 12:15, 22; 14:5–6; 15:22), human beings obviously pose a threat to wild animals as well. Although Deuteronomy intentionally reins in the abuse of power at every level, the book has remarkably little to say on the potential abuse of wild animals by human beings.[26] In fact, the Deuteronomic policy on the sabbatical year of release (15:1–18) drops any hint of the concern for wild animals found in the Book of the Covenant: "The seventh year you shall let it [the land] rest and lie fallow, that the poor of your people may eat; and what they leave the beasts of the field (חַיַּת הַשָּׂדֶה) may eat. You shall do likewise with your vineyard, and with your olive orchard" (Exod 23:11). This does not mean that the concern for wild animals is lacking. On the contrary, in Deut 22:6–7 Moses encourages a tender and sympathetic disposition toward wild birds: "If you come across a bird's nest, in any tree or on the ground, with fledglings or eggs, with the mother sitting on the fledglings or on the eggs, you shall not take the mother with the young. Let the mother go; take only the young for yourself, that it may go well with you and you may live long." In many respects this injunction is a riddle. What use is to be made of the young,[27] which finders may take for themselves? The eggs of poultry and game fowl were valued as food, but what about the eggs of other birds, and even more seriously, the fledglings? Unless these have some use, this text seems to authorize their wanton slaughter. At the same time, if the passage had allowed the mother to be taken but the young spared, the effect would be the same as if the life of both were taken, for un-hatched eggs and fledgling birds are dependent on the continued care of the mother. But if the mother is released, she may nest again, incubate another batch of eggs, and see the new brood to maturity. The Israelites were neither to kill for killing's sake, nor to exploit natural resources without concern for conservation.[28]

---

26. Though Deut 20:19–20 expressly prohibits the Israelites from denuding the landscape of its trees when engaging enemy cities in battle.

27. Hebrew בָּנִים functions as shorthand for אֶפְרֹחִים, "fledglings," and בֵּיצִים, "eggs."

28. See Borowski, *Every Living Thing*, 152.

But this reasoning is speculative. In fact, the text expresses no explicit concern for the birds. Instead, it appears to ground the instructions in human self-interest: if the Israelites will treat birds' nests this way, it will go well with them and they will enjoy long life on the land. The addition of the motive clause promising well-being and long life for human beings not only highlights the covenantal significance of this injunction, but also places it in the same class of weighty commandments as the general commands to obey the statutes and commandments that Moses has given the Israelites elsewhere in his three addresses (4:40; 5:29; 6:18; 12:28). Furthermore, it links them with other weighty preconditions to longevity (4:40; 5:33; 11:9; see also 30:18).[29]

This motive clause is grounded on an assumption of the triangular relationship that exists among God, the earth, and its animal inhabitants, and of humankind's responsibility as the divine image not only to subdue the earth and restrain evil, but also to manage it in the interests of all the parties to this covenant. In the end, the Israelites' well-being was dependent on their righteousness, demonstrated in respect for the life of helpless creatures.

Animals as Domestic and Dependent on Human Beings

The counterpart to the designation for wild animals, חַיַּת הַשָּׂדֶה, "beast of the field," should be חַיַּת הַבַּיִת, "beast of the house/household." However, this expression never occurs in the Old Testament. Instead בְּהֵמָה, which serves as a designation for high carriage animals in general in Genesis 1 and Deut 4:17, functions as the most common general designation for household animals that included sheep, goats, cattle, and donkeys.[30] The first two were valued primarily for their meat, their milk, and their wool and hair, respectively, for the

---

29. Johnson ("The Least of the Commandments," 205–15) argues that the present instructions are included in "the least of these commandments" in Matt 5:19. According to Johnson, based on the hermeneutical principle of *qal wĕḥōmer*, "light and heavy," in rabbinic tradition this commandment was interpreted to mean that if God was so concerned about birds and their nests, how much more important to him are human beings! For a helpful study of the interpretation of verses 6–7 in Rabbinic Judaism, see Segal, "Justice, Mercy and a Bird's Nest," 176–95.

30. For a detailed study, see Borowski, *Every Living Thing*. See also King and Stager, *Life in Biblical Israel*, 112–22. Because horses were used primarily in military contexts, they are excluded from this list.

manufacture of cloth and clothing. Cattle were valued for their milk and their meat, but especially for their strength as draft animals, to transport goods and pull agricultural implements. Donkeys served primarily as pack animals, though they were also harnessed to pull carts and small plows.

Deuteronomy 22:1–4 seeks to secure the well-being of oxen, sheep, and donkeys by charging the Israelites to care for straying animals. The first response to finding a stray was to return it to its owner. However, if the owner lived some distance away or the identity of the owner is unknown, the finder was to bring[31] it home to his own house for safekeeping. When the owner came to claim the animal it had to be returned to him. The declaration, "You are not allowed to hide yourself from them" (הִתְעַלֵּם, "ignore"), places the plight of the straying animals in the same category as the man who was attacked by thieves, ignored by the priest and the Levite, but was ultimately rescued by the Samaritan (Luke 10:30–35).

However, Deuteronomy seems to assume that the threat of abusive masters was greater than the dangers of going astray. This issue is addressed by deliberately modifying the Sabbath command in a direction that establishes the profoundly humanitarian trajectory of the whole book (Deut 5:6–21).[32] By basing the observance of the seventh day as a day of rest on Israel's experience of slavery in Egypt, rather than the pattern of divine activity in the creation of the cosmos (5:12–15), this command provides the Israelites with a constant reminder of their own abuse at the hands of brutal taskmasters.[33] Moses hereby acknowledges that beyond patterning human creative work after that of God, the Creator of heaven and earth, on the Sabbath heads of households are to allow all who work in the domestic economic unit, including the animals, to refresh themselves. In so doing, this command reins in potential abuse of power over livestock by the head of the household.

---

31. The verb אָסַף, "to collect," may suggest a collective sense for the three types of animals referred to by singular nouns.

32. See Block, "You shall not covet your neighbor's wife," chapter 5 in this book.

33. In his second address Moses will repeatedly buttress his ethical and spiritual appeals with reminders of the Israelites' experience as slaves in Egypt. See Deut 15:15; 16:12; 24:18, 22.

The problem of abuse of power is highlighted even more dramatically in 22:4: "You shall not see your brother's donkey or his ox fallen down by the way and ignore them. You shall help him to lift them up again." Here the attention shifts from an animal that has strayed (22:1–3) to an animal that is abused. Although the entire passage assumes the treatment of the animals will be motivated by a sense of community with their owners, it also calls for sensitivity/compassion toward their livestock. Domestic animals played a vital role in securing the economic well-being of the people, but ownership and control could easily degenerate into harsh and abusive treatment.

The instruction in 25:4 is even more concrete: "You shall not muzzle an ox when it is treading out the grain." On the surface this fragment of apodictic instruction seems unrelated to the preceding. However, because draft animals were often prodded with switches and rods, some suggest the references to flogging in verses 2–3 may have triggered this insertion.[34] But if this had been the case, we would expect the present statement to curb excessive beating of one's animal. Instead, it displays a remarkable humanitarianism in a completely different form: oxen used for threshing grain were not to be muzzled.[35] The ordinance derives from the ancient practice of threshing grain by having oxen or donkeys trample the stalks or pull rock-studded sledges over the stalks spread out on the threshing floor.[36] It so happens that what is a staple of life for human beings is also food for animals. Out of greed a farmer might muzzle his ox or donkey to prevent it from slowing down and eating instead of working or simply to prevent it from eating what he hoped to harvest for his own consumption (see Prov 14:4). This text forbids Israelites from treating their animals this way.

The concern expressed here coheres with Deuteronomy's general concern to protect those vulnerable to exploitation, including

34. Thus Tigay, *Deuteronomy*, 458.

35. On this passage, see Noonan, Jr., "The Muzzled Ox," 172–75.

36. The Temple Scroll of Qumran (11Q19, 52:12) modifies the consonantal reading of the last word of MT, בדישו (which most interpret as a qal infinitive: "while it is treading"), to על דישו (which involves a noun: "on its threshing floor"). This reading suggests that a prohibition against muzzling an animal whenever food is present. For discussion, see Qimron, "The Biblical Lexicon in Light of the Dead Sea Scrolls," 296–98; Schiffman, "Some Laws Pertaining to Animals in Temple Scroll Column 52," 173–74.

widows, orphans, aliens, Levites, and now domestic animals. The heads of households are to safeguard the right to humane treatment of all under their roof. In this way they are to show the same regard for the life of the creatures as God himself does, as is reflected in several nature psalms (Pss 104:10–14; 145:16; 147:9). In 1 Cor 9:9 and 1 Tim 5:18, Paul applies the present ordinance to the right of apostles to derive their living from the work they do in spreading the gospel. Some would argue that his rhetorical question, "God is not concerned about oxen, is he?" which assumes a negative answer, is possible only if שׁוֹר, "ox," is interpreted as being figurative for human beings.[37] However, this is not necessary, if one interprets Deut 25:4 within the context of the entire chapter. Like Paul's statement, these instructions are addressed to human beings, not to animals. Throughout Deuteronomy 24 the concern has been to develop in the Israelites, the people of God, a sensitive and considerate disposition, especially toward the vulnerable. Moses' statement concerning the ox fits this agenda perfectly, extending even to animals the theological principle that in God's economy all workers, be they human or animal, deserve humane treatment and reward for their labor.[38]

The present ordinance may help explain the enigmatic prohibition of boiling a kid in its mother's milk in 14:21. It is difficult to know whether this command is primarily about dietary issues (meat cooked in milk) or a humanitarian concern for creatures.[39] Whatever its original intent, the prohibition underlies the orthodox Jewish dietary law of *kashrut* that prohibits mixing milk and meat in a meal. This strange ordinance occurs in identical form in two other contexts, the Book of the Covenant (Exod 23:19) and the so-called Dodecalogue (Exod 34:26). In both of these instances, this command is linked with the annual pilgrimage festivals, which may suggest a

37. See Grosheide, *First Epistle to the Corinthians*, 205.

38. For a helpful discussion of the hermeneutical issues involved, see Kaiser, "The Current Crisis in Exegesis," 3–18, esp. 11–16. For a discussion of the ethical implications of Paul's adaptation of this command for an entirely new situation, see Wennberg, *God, Humans, and Animals*, 297–98.

39. The literature on this enigmatic proscription is vast. See Keel, *Das Böcklein in der Milch seiner Mutter und Verwandtes im Lichte eines altorientalischen Bildmotifs*; Ratner and Zuckerman, "A Kid in Milk'?" 15–60; Haran, "Seething a Kid in Its Mother's Milk," 23–35; Labuschagne, "'You Shall not Boil a Kid in its Mother's Milk,'" 6–17; Propp, *Exodus 19–40*, 286; and Stuart, *Exodus*, 539–40.

cultic concern. If this interpretation is correct, the location of the command at the end of dietary instructions in Deuteronomy 14 would reinforce our linkage of the foods permitted on the Israelites' table with the sacrifices offered to YHWH.

Animals as "Food" for YHWH

According to the biblical narratives the use of animals for sacrificial purposes is almost as old as the human race. Genesis 4:4 reports Abel presenting a firstling of the flock as an offering (מִנְחָה) to YHWH. This picture was developed in great detail in the priestly legislation of Exodus and Leviticus. The slaughter of bulls, goats, and lambs for sacrificial meals was a critical part of Israelite worship (Deut 12:5–7, 11–14), but the psalmist recognizes that the meat of these animals was not perceived as food to be eaten by YHWH: "I will not accept a bull from your house or goats from your folds . . . If I were hungry, I would not tell you, for the world and its fullness are mine. Do I eat the flesh of bulls or drink the blood of goats? Offer to God a sacrifice of thanksgiving, and perform your vows to the Most High" (Ps 50:9–14).

In contrast to the cultures around, where through ritual offerings people perceived themselves and their priests to be caring for and feeding the gods, in Israel this notion is thoroughly demythologized. Even though many sacrifices involved animals,[40] in many instances the meat was actually consumed by the worshiper in the presence of YHWH. Deuteronomy 15:19–23 specifies that the unblemished first-born of the herds and flocks that the Israelites consecrate to YHWH they may eat in his presence in the central sanctuary. Similarly the Passover was to be eaten in the presence of YHWH (Deut 16:1–8). Neither in Deuteronomy nor elsewhere in the Old Testament does YHWH ever eat of the sacrifices presented to him. The closest we

---

40. The Passover (פֶּסַח; a one year old lamb or kid without blemish; Exod 12:5); the whole burnt offering (עֹלָה; a bull or sheep or goat; Lev 1:1–17); the sacrificial meal and the peace offering (זֶבַח and שְׁלָמִים; a bull or lamb or goat; Lev 3:1–17); the reparation offerings (אָשָׁם; a ram without blemish; Lev 6:1–6); the purification offering (חַטָּאת; bulls, male or female goats, lambs, turtle-doves; Lev 4:1–21). On ancient Mesopotamian sacrifices as food for the gods, see Scurlock, "Animal Sacrifice in Ancient Mesopotamian Religion," 389–97. On ancient Israelite use of animals as sacrifices, see Borowski, Every Living Thing, 214–18.

get is metaphorical statements suggesting that the sacrifices of God's people are a pleasing/soothing aroma to him.[41]

If YHWH does not eat the animal sacrifices presented to him, then who does? With reference to the עֹלָה, the answer is no one—this offering is burned up entirely on the altar.[42] As for the rest, Deut 18:1–8 provides a partial answer. The Levitical priests, indeed any from the entire tribe of Levi—whether they reside at the place of the central sanctuary or in the towns scattered throughout the land, those who are called to serve the nation spiritually in the name of YHWH—are entitled to portions of the animals offered as sacrifices by the people, specifically the shoulder, the jowls, and the stomach. However, a fuller answer is provided by a half dozen verses scattered throughout the second half of Moses' second address: "And you shall sacrifice peace offerings and shall eat there, and you shall rejoice before YHWH your God" (Deut 27:7; see also 12:7, 18; 14:23, 26; 15:20).

These texts portray YHWH as a divine host, receiving the offerings of his people and then turning around and spreading the meat of the offerings before them, inviting them thereby to celebrate the privilege of relationship with them. As sacrifices, the animals provided not only food for the people, but also a means whereby their relationship with YHWH may be celebrated and cemented. A more noble role for the creatures may scarcely be imagined.

Animals as Food for Human Beings in Everyday Life

The use of animals as food in cultic contexts leads naturally to a final issue: the use of animals as food in everyday life. Our discussion must consider two issues: (1) What kinds of animals were permitted as food for Israel? (2) How was the flesh of the animal to be prepared?

Although the descendants of Adam undoubtedly ate the flesh of animals, divine authorization for this custom is recorded for the first time in Gen 9:3, where Noah and his descendants are

---

41. The Hebrew expression רֵיחַ הַנִּיחֹחַ, "the soothing aroma," occurs only in Gen 8:21, but the idiom without the article occurs frequently: Exod 29:18; Lev 1:9, 13, 17; 2:2, 9; 3:5; 6:8, 14; 23:13, 18; Num 15:3, 7, 10, 13, 14; 28:8, 13, 24; 29:8, 13, 36; Ezek 6:13. Although the Old Testament never includes wild ungulates in lists of sacrifices, the remains of wild ruminants have been found in cult places (Borowski, *Every Living Thing*, 218). It is difficult to imagine how a wild animal could be caught without causing some blemish, which would disqualify it from cultic use.

42. See Averbeck, "עֹלָה," 407.

granted permission to eat the flesh of every moving thing that lives
(כָּל־רֶמֶשׂ אֲשֶׁר הוּא־חַי). Leviticus 11 and Deuteronomy 14 rein in this
comprehensive authorization for the Israelites by establishing boundaries between clean and unclean food, with only the former being
permitted in their diet.[43] Deuteronomy 14:1–21 is generally characterized as a collection of dietary laws. However, both the framework
and the tone of the text suggest this passage should rather be interpreted as an invitation to a family feast hosted by YHWH himself.

The opening verses (vv. 1–2) and the concluding statement
(v. 21) highlight Israel's special status before YHWH and in the
midst of all the nations of the earth. In the former, the people that
make up this nation are identified as "the sons of YHWH your God"
(בָּנִים אַתֶּם לַיהוָה אֱלֹהֵיכֶם), "a holy people belonging to YHWH your
God" (עַם קָדוֹשׁ אַתָּה לַיהוָה אֱלֹהֶיךָ), and YHWH's "treasure people"
(עַם סְגֻלָּה), chosen out of all the nations of the earth. Verse 21 distinguishes the Israelites from resident aliens (גֵּר) and strangers (נָכְרִי).
The significance of the instructions for Israel as YHWH's covenantal
people is reinforced by the fourfold repetition of "It is unclean for
you" (vv. 7, 8, 10, 19).

According to Gen 9:3, after the great flood, God authorized Noah
and his descendants to eat the meat of all living animals indiscrimi-
nately—though with the proviso that the blood, representing the life,
be drained from the carcass. Based upon the legislation in Leviticus
11, now Deuteronomy reins in that freedom for Israel. Because they
are the holy people of YHWH, the meat in their diet, whether from
domesticated animals raised at home or animals that they hunt, must
be like the food that God "eats" (in the sacrifices offered to him).[44]
Indeed, if Deut 12:1–14 represented an invitation to worship YHWH
at the place he would choose, and 12:15–28 the authorization to eat
meat away from the central sanctuary, then the dietary instructions
in chapter 14 suggest that every meal is a sacred moment, and every

---

43. For a detailed study of these texts, see Moskala, *The Laws of Clean and
Unclean Animals in Leviticus 11*.

44. This is the reverse of the ancient Mesopotamian practice, because "draft
animals were not generally eaten by ancient Mesopotamians and, since gods usually
share the tastes of their worshipers, horses or donkeys were not offered as food for
the divine table" (Scurlock, "Animal Sacrifice," 392). Pigs represented an exception;
they were generally eaten, but evidence for their use as offerings to divinities is
scarce.

animal slaughtered for consumption a sacrifice. Through their diet
the Israelites were to declare to one another and to outsiders their unprecedented and unparalleled proximity to their God.[45] These dietary
boundaries did not apply to people outside the covenant, as verse 21
will reiterate (the flesh of an animal that has died of natural causes
may be given or sold to an outsider). Adapting a comment of Mary
Douglas, we conclude that by rules of avoidance (Israel's) sanctified
status as the covenant people of YHWH "was given a physical expression in every encounter with the animal kingdom and at every meal."[46]
Accordingly, the dietary instructions inserted between these frames
(vv. 1–2 and 21) are best considered an invitation to feast at the table
of YHWH, a conclusion reinforced by the singular designation in the
book of the guests as the "sons of YHWH your God" in 14:1.[47]

The apodictic command in verse 3 functions as a thematic introduction to the material between the two frames, with verses 4–20
fleshing out what is meant by the prohibited "abominable food"
(תּוֹעֵבָה). These seventeen verses have the appearance of a self-con-
tained literary unit, stylistically distinguished from the surrounding
frame, not only by its lists of various kinds of land animals (ten kosher species, vv. 4–6; four prohibited species, vv. 7–8) and species of
inedible fowl (twenty-one species, vv. 12–18), but also by its relative
secularity. Verses 4–20 represent the second-longest continuous text
in Deuteronomy without any reference to the name of YHWH.[48] Not
that this material is lacking in theological significance; the fourfold
reference to uncleanness (טמא, vv. 7, 8, 10, 19) confirms that the concern here goes far beyond the mere listing of clean and unclean foods
and diet.

A detailed comparison of the links between this passage and
Leviticus 11 is beyond the scope of this study. But the net effect of
the adaptations of material from Leviticus 11 in Deuteronomy 14 is
to transform a legal document (concerned with precise definitions
of the boundaries between clean and unclean and revolving around
the technical understanding of defilement) into a moral document
seeking to declare how Israel's status as YHWH's "holy people"

---

45. Similarly Firmage, "Biblical Dietary Laws," 196–97.

46. Douglas, *Purity and Danger*, 57.

47. Compare the fatherly similes in 1:31 and 8:5.

48. Only 21:11–22 is longer by word count.

(עַם קָדוֹשׁ לַיהוָה) is to be demonstrated in all of life. In keeping with the pastoral concern of the present text, the tone of Deut 14:4–20 is much more positive than Lev 11:3–21; it seems more interested in affirming what the Israelites may do than in prohibiting what they may not do. This would account for the affirmations brought forward in the present context: the listing of the names of ten edible animals in verses 4–5, as well as the direct confirmation that the Israelites may eat all clean fowl (v. 11) and all clean insects (v. 20).

But it would also account for some absences: the deletion of re-petitive explanations as to why the camel and the hare are excluded (v. 7), the reduction of the extended presentation of clean and un-clean aquatic creatures (as in Lev 11:9–12) to two simple statements affirming finned and scaled creatures as kosher food and excluding non-finned and non-scaled creatures (vv. 9–10),[49] and the elimina-tion of the descriptions of edible insects (as in Lev 11:21–22). The net effect is one of psychologically "opening the door," rather than closing it. This impression is reinforced by opening the entire unit with "You are the sons of YHWH your God" (v. 1a) and framing verses 2–20 with statements that are profoundly ethical. Both verse 1b–3 and verse 21 highlight the distinction between Israelites and outsiders, and both refer to Israel's status as YHWH's holy people.

Having appealed to Israel to avoid food considered by YHWH to be abominable, it was natural for Moses to remind the present generation of the established boundaries between kosher[50] and pro-hibited food. While all cultures appear to have their own sets of rules defining boundaries between the clean and unclean, especially in relationship to food, the rationale for the boundaries is not clearly understood. The same applies to Israel's understanding of dietary cleanness and uncleanness. Scholars have proposed a variety of theories for the prohibition on certain kinds of food as outlined in Leviticus 11 and Deuteronomy 14: cultic (because they are associated with Canaanite religious practices), aesthetic (because they are loath-some or repulsive), hygienic (because they cause illness), sociological

---

49. Where Lev 11:9–12 has fifty-three words, Deut 14:9–10 has only twenty-two.

50. The Yiddish term *kosher* derives from an apparently common west Semitic root *kāšar*, "to be appropriate, deemed fit." For the Hebrew, see *HALOT* 503; for Aramaic and Palmyrene, see *DNWSI* 539–40. For the Mishnaic Hebrew usage, see Jastrow, *Dictionary of the Targumim*, 677–78.

(because they have an ambiguous form and lack physical integrity), didactic (because they illustrate/teach wrongful behavior).[51] Both Leviticus 11 and Deuteronomy 14 link Israel's dietary laws with her status as a holy people. Deuteronomy in particular is concerned to celebrate Israel's status as a single people under the one God, YHWH. Even as the dietary instructions serve to unite the people around the table, they also function as boundary markers between Israel and all other nations.[52]

Although both texts link the lists of clean and unclean animals with Israel's holiness, neither spells out what it is about the clean animals that coheres with the biblical notion of holiness or explains the features of unclean animals that violate those notions.[53] However, given the emphasis on the defiling effect of contact with the carcasses of dead animals in Lev 11:24–40[54] and the framing of the dietary regulations in Deuteronomy 14 with references to ritual practices related to the cult of the dead (v. 1), on the one hand, and brief regulations on the treatment of animals that have died a natural death, on the other (v. 21), the most likely hypothesis suggests that the forbidden animals are rejected because of their association with death.[55] Most are carnivores and/or scavengers that feed on carrion. Many of the rest are ground creatures that constantly come in contact with unclean matter.[56]

51. For discussion of each of these and other explanations, see Houston, *Purity and Monotheism*, 68–123. For an Asian perspective on the dietary laws, see Chan, "You Shall Not Eat These Abominable Things," 95–104.

52. See Houston, *Purity and Monotheism*, 225–28.

53. See the discussion by Moskala, *The Laws of Clean and Unclean Animals*, 315–48.

54. This section interrupts the catalogue of clean and unclean animals that runs from Lev 11:2b–23 and is later resumed in vv. 41–43.

55. See Isa 65:2–7, which associates nocturnal and necromantic activity with eating swine's flesh (see also 66:17). Bulmer follows Douglas in arguing that animals are prohibited because they deviate from the norm applying to their respective species ("The Uncleanness of the Birds of Leviticus and Deuteronomy," 304–21).

56. Leviticus 11:21–22 forbids winged insects that walk on all fours, but permits locusts and grasshoppers that jump. It is probably not coincidental that these creatures are obvious vegetarians as well. Some of the animals are associated with ruins and the barren desert, considered by many to be the abode of demons (Kornfeld, "Reine und unreine Tiere im Alten Testament," 134–47, esp. 146–47). For further discussion, see Hartley, *Leviticus* 141–47; and Hartley, "Clean and Unclean," 718–23.

While this explanation is the most attractive, in the end we must admit that the Old Testament fails to spell out the reasons for the boundaries it defines, and ultimately the only certain conclusion is that the boundaries are as they are because YHWH, the God of Israel, declared them to be so. To modern readers they may seem arbitrary, but YHWH's covenant with Israel is a suzerainty covenant—the terms are not negotiated and need not even make sense to the vassal. They are to be accepted simply because they represent the will of the divine suzerain. But this does not mean that they represented burdensome demands. On the contrary, both texts provide the Israelites with ample incentive to accept these dietary boundaries. In Lev 11:45, YHWH reminds the Israelites that they are the objects of his gracious redemption; Deuteronomy 14 reminds them that they are the objects of his election and his exceptional favor. Accordingly, obedience to these regulations should have been a delight—a thankful response for unmerited kindness.

Furthermore, this chapter should be interpreted against the backdrop of the broader ancient Near Eastern cultural and religious climate out of which it derives and to which it responds. As already noted, it is generally recognized that all cultures have their own taboos, particularly relating to edible and inedible food.[57] This was true also of the ancient Near Easterners in general.[58]

With all this attention to the boundaries between edible and inedible food, it is easy to overlook another vital element in the dietary implications of Israel's status as a holy people—the manner in which meat is prepared. Deuteronomy does not actually have much to say on the matter. The verb בִּשֵּׁל occurs in 14:21 and 16:7. In the former בַּחֲלֵב אִמּוֹ, "in its mother's milk," suggests boiling, though חָלָב may admittedly be used of other milk products like yoghurt as well.[59] However, elsewhere the verb בִּשֵּׁל is used of baking cakes

---

57. See the discussion by Douglas, *Purity and Danger*, 41–57.

58. This passage should be interpreted in the light of texts like the Sumerian "Prayer to Every God," that was discovered among the thousands of texts in the library of Ashurbanipal (668–633 BCE). With telling frankness the petitioner complains before the god/goddess about his ignorance of some the dietary taboo (*ANET*, 391). For the translation of this text, see above, pp. 126–28, and below pp. 234–36.

59. As reflected in the Jewish prohibition not to eat meat and dairy products together.

(2 Sam 13:8), preparing manna (Num 11:8), and cooking meat for offerings (Ezek 46:20). Neither Deut 14:21 nor 16:7 is concerned with the process by which food is prepared. For the people of YHWH, the way an animal is slaughtered is of much greater consequence than the manner in which it is cooked. After freely permitting the consumption of meat, including that of domestic and wild animals, within the Israelites' own towns away from the central sanctuary, Deut 12:16 and 23–25 provide some explicit guidelines for the slaughter of animals:

> However, you may not eat the blood; you must pour it out on the earth like water. (v. 16)

> Only be sure that you do not eat the blood, for the blood is the life, and you shall not eat the life with the flesh. You may not eat it; you shall pour it out on the earth like water. You shall not eat it, that all may go well with you and with your children after you, when you do what is right in the sight of YHWH. (vv. 23–25)

This identification of the blood with life[60] derives from the common observance of the life of an animal or person ebbing away with the loss of blood.[61] Because the blood is identified with the life, the consumption of blood was viewed as the consumption of life itself, which explains the added comment in verse 23: "You may not eat the life with the meat." Although the blood of an animal slaughtered for its meat did not require satisfaction, in a sense all slaughter is sacrificial and substitutionary: a life for a life. Accordingly, the slaughter of animals may be profane (dissociated from the cult), but it is never secular.[62] The taboo on the consumption of blood provides a perpetual reminder that life is sacred, and life itself is a gift of God.

The prohibition on eating the meat of any animal that had died a natural death in 14:21 appears on the surface to arise out of a concern to protect Israel's status as the holy people of YHWH. Here Moses authorizes the Israelites to sell this meat to a foreigner or give it to an

---

60. Whereas in vv. 15 and 20–22 נֶפֶשׁ had referred to the seat of desire, now the word denotes "life, the vital self." See *DCH* 5:728.

61. See Homer's reference to "life running out." *Iliad*, 14.518.

62. Contra Weinfeld (*Deuteronomy and the Deuteronomic School*, 214), who, in defense of a secularizing tendency in Deuteronomy, argues that "pouring the blood out like water" means "the blood has no more a sacral value than water has." The comparison with water relates to its liquid constitution rather than its religious significance.

alien living among them, but the members of the covenant community may not eat it. The present taboo may suggest that only Israelites are to guard the sanctity of life this way. However, the reason for the taboo probably lies elsewhere, presumably in the defiling effects that contact with this carcass had on the Israelites. In any case, this taboo on eating the blood goes back to the fountainhead of humanity (Gen 9:4), in which God forbids the consumption of blood by any of Noah's descendants. The permanence and supra-Israelite validity of the ban on blood was recognized in the decision of the Council of Jerusalem to bind Gentile Christians to this ordinance in Acts 15:20.[63] The principle of the sanctity of all life transcends the Torah of Deuteronomy.

In the original ordinance (Lev 17:10–14) YHWH had emphasized the importance of the taboo on the blood of slaughtered animals by threatening those who refused to comply with personal hostility and cutting them off from their people. In the present context (14:25), when Moses seeks to impress upon his audience the importance of this principle, he takes a more positive and pastoral approach: this is the precondition to well-being for them and their children, and it is guaranteed to win the approval of YHWH. After all, according to Deut 12:15, then "you will do what is right in the eyes of YHWH" (תַּעֲשֶׂה הַיָּשָׁר בְּעֵינֵי יְהוָה). This clause answers directly to 12:8, where he had called upon the people to stop doing "all that is right in their own eyes" (כָּל־הַיָּשָׁר בְּעֵינָיו). When people eat meat in their own towns they may not be "before YHWH" in the same sense as when they were at the central sanctuary, but they were still under his watchful care and supervision.

Conclusion

With this observation we have reached the end of the presentation of the data. But this raises the question of the significance of this biblical information for us. The following represent preliminary conclusions on the relevance of Deuteronomy's theology of animals for evangelical Christians at the beginning of the twenty-first century.

First, if the heavens declare the glory of God and gazing at the sky inspires awe, this is no less true of the earth and its creatures,

---

63. For an excellent discussion of the relationship of these apostolic injunctions to and their grounding in Leviticus 17–18, see Davidson, "Which Torah Laws Should Gentile Christians Obey?"

which are also the works of his hands. The creatures are all special to God simply because they are the work of his hands (Jonah 4:11). Furthermore, with all its variety and with its consistency, the animal world testifies both to the divine imagination and to the beauty of order. Like Genesis 1, the zoological diversity recognized by Deuteronomy invites the reader to acknowledge in the animals the handiwork of God.

Second, the divine mission of Israel was to embody in microcosm the design of God for the cosmos. Just as humanity was created in the image of God and endowed with glory and majesty to govern the world for him (Psalm 8), so Israel's mission within the context of a fallen world was to declare to the world YHWH's glory and grace by being redeemed, entering into the land, and prospering in it (Deut 26:16–19). But this prosperity depended upon their fulfillment of covenant righteousness, the scope of which involved not only exclusive devotion to YHWH and compassionate concern for the welfare of one's fellow Israelites and the marginalized,[64] but also of the creaturely world. Humane treatment of animals is fundamental to covenant righteousness.

Third, while Christians are no longer bound by the dietary boundaries that marked the Israelites as the people of God (Acts 15:29; cf. v. 20),[65] the early disciples at the Council of Jerusalem reaffirmed the prohibitions on idolatry (εἰδωλόθυτος) and sexual immorality (πορνεία), as well as the prohibitions on the consumption of blood (αἷμα) and the meat of animals that had not been properly slaughtered (πνικτός).[66] The latter proscriptions recognize the sanc-

---

64. Note the emphasis on securing the well-being of the fatherless, widow, and sojourner in Deut 10:18; 14:29; 16:11, 14; 24:19–21; 26:12–13; 27:19.

65. In the end, the significance of these dietary prescriptions may be linked to the sacrificial system of the old covenant. If indeed Deuteronomy 14 involves YHWH's invitation to eat of the food in which he himself takes delight in the form of sacrifices, then with the termination of all sacrifices in Christ, these food regulations also become *passé*. Because we no longer provide God with these offerings, but celebrate the sacrificial work of Jesus Christ, then whenever we partake of the Lord's table, that is, the bread and the wine of Communion, we participate in the feast to which the Lord has graciously invited us.

66. Note that the prohibitions are the same as those applied to native Israelites (אֶזְרָח) and aliens (גֵּר), who by faith had attached themselves to Israel as the holy community of faith (Davidson, "Which Torah Laws Should Gentiles Obey?"). The term נָכְרִי, "stranger," in Deut 14:21 represents an ethic and spiritual outsider to the covenant, and is to be distinguished from the גֵּר of Leviticus 17–18.

tity of all life. In a sense, every meal, especially those involving the meat of animals, is a sacrifice—an animal has given its life for our sakes. Neither the Old Testament nor the New Testament calls for a vegetarian diet; on the contrary they freely authorize the consumption of animals, provided the consumer continues to respect the sanctity of the life of the animal. Rightly understood, "humans do not live to eat, but they eat to live."[67] According to the Talmud, "A man's table is like an altar."[68] Moskala rightly declares that "both sacrifice and food should be taken with or as an expression of gratitude and thankfulness."[69] But this thankfulness is not only expressed in explicit declarations to God for his gracious provision of food, but is also felt toward the animal world that has provided both pleasure and nourishment to God's vice-regent.

Fourth, Deut 22:6–7 reminded ancient Israelites and continues to remind modern readers of humanity's responsibility for the care of creation, even of the wild creatures. This notion is reflected in Gen 2:15, which explicitly declares humanity's mandate to be "serving" (עָבַד) and "preserving" (שָׁמַר) the garden of Eden. The common translation of the former expression as "to till" assumes an inordinate focus on the ground. Adam is commanded to care for the garden. But gardens are more than soil. This is the original *Tierpark*,[70] made up of soil, vegetation, and animals, the service of which involves much more than cultivating the soil. Like YHWH himself in Jonah 4:11, God's vice-regents are to display compassion to all creatures. In securing the well-being of individual creatures and individual species, people secure the well-being of humanity and open themselves and the cosmos to the blessing of God.

Underlying Deuteronomy's portrayal of the Israelites' relationship to animals is a profound theology of privilege and holiness whose relevance transcends the old covenantal order. Like the Israelites, the people of God in every age should treasure the special status that has been afforded them by virtue of YHWH's gracious election, and his claims upon them as his holy people. Living as the holy people of God

---

67. Moskala, *Laws of Clean and Unclean Animals*, 106.

68. *B. Hagigah* 27a.

69. Moskala, *Laws of Clean and Unclean Animals*, 106.

70. For a comparison of the garden of Eden with neo-Assyrian royal parks, see Hutter, "Adam als Gärtner und König," 258–62.

is not to be relegated to the days or contexts of formal cultic service, but is to be expressed in all areas of life. Like the ancient Israelites, we need to realize that everything about us, even the food we eat, should be governed by order, a respect for life, and a concern to represent YHWH well before a watching world.[71]

71. I am grateful to my colleague Richard Schultz for his helpful responses to an earlier draft of this paper. Of course, any deficiencies in interpretation and style are my own.

7

Other Religions in Old Testament Theology[1]

O NOMASTIC EVIDENCE AVAILABLE FROM both the Old Testament and extra-biblical inscriptions suggests that throughout Israel's history as a nation, Yahwism was the predominant religion in every stratum and region of the nation.[2] However, the Old Testament presents a rather different picture. From the nation's founding at Sinai (Exod 32) to her final demise in 586 BCE, the religion practiced by the Israelites apparently followed a variety of forms, some syncretistic, others thoroughly pagan. How the course of Israel's history—and indeed the shape of the Old Testament itself—would have turned out had the people as a whole lived according to the ideals championed by the authors of the Old Testament can only be imagined. As attested to in the Old Testament and in the archaeological record, Israelite faith varied textually, iconographically, and monumentally. The writers of

1. An earlier version of this paper was presented to the Evangelical Theological Society in November, 2002, in Toronto, Canada.

2. For brief discussion and bibliography, see Block, *The Gods of the Nations*, 40–41. Tigay (*You Shall Have No Other Gods*, 7–8) estimates that approximately eleven percent of the names in the Old Testament were probably pagan, bearing elements like "Baal" (Ishbaal) and "Haddu" (Hadoram). The epigraphic evidence is even more one-sided. Based on the evidence available in 1986, Tigay noted that only 35 names bear pagan theophores (5.9 percent), while 592 are Yahwistic (94.1 percent). His calculation excludes names containing אֵל, "God," or אֵלִי, "My God" (ibid., 15).

the Old Testament represent only one form of ancient Israelite faith, that of monotheistic and ethical Yahwism, which we refer to hereafter as "orthodox Yahwism."

Of course, the question of predominant religion involves not just those Old Testament texts that explicitly refer to deviant expressions of faith (from the Yahwistic authors' points of view)—that is, texts that proscribe the worship of other deities, that describe Israel's participation in the worship of other deities, or that denounce Israel for worshiping other deities. The book of Judges illustrates dramatically and graphically the link between spiritual recidivism and ethical degeneration. Many, if not most, of the social ills that afflicted the nation relate directly to the abandonment of the ethical monotheism of orthodox Yahwism in favor of syncretistic henotheism or overtly pagan idolatry. But by its very nature the current subject of biblical faith and other religions in the Old Testament theology privileges orthodox Yahwism, for the Old Testament represents the perspective of the winners in the centuries-long conflict between Yahwism and other forms of religion. Not only does the Old Testament from beginning to end deride and denounce other expressions of faith and devotion, but the authors persistently and consistently suppress the voices of those more sympathetic to other forms.

The question is complicated, however, in that the Old Testament knows nothing of faith in the abstract—that is, faith as "a doctrine or system of doctrines, propositions, etc., held to be true,"[3] or faith as "belief in the truths of religion."[4] Indeed biblical Hebrew lacks a word for "faith" in this sense. The nearest counterpart is יָרֵא, "fear," but as an abstract notion it generally means "fright, awe." When used as an approximate designation for faith it is regularly followed by a divine direct object, that is, "to fear YHWH," or "to fear another god/other gods." Biblical Hebrew also lacks a word for "religion."[5] Religious devotion is concretized with specific expressions like הִשְׁתַּחֲוָה לְ, "to prostrate oneself before [a deity]"; הִתְהַלֵּךְ לִפְנֵי/הָלַךְ לִפְנֵי, "to walk

---

3. *New International Webster's Comprehensive Dictionary*, 455.

4. *Oxford English Dictionary*, 952.

5. The word is lacking in all the modern translations of the Old Testament: AV, ASV, RSV, NASB, NIV, NRSV, ESV. Related to this point James Barr observes, "But the Bible is not about religion; it is about God and his action, his revelation, and so on." *The Concept of Biblical Theology*, 107.

before [a deity]"; הָלַךְ אַחֲרֵי, "to walk after, that is follow [a deity]"; עָבַד, "to serve, work for [a deity]"; and in Aramaic פלח, "to serve, worship, revere, minister to [a deity]." Accordingly, an essay that addresses biblical faith and other religions in the Old Testament would be extremely short. But when contemplating this topic, what is really meant is the disposition of biblical Yahwism toward devotion to and/ or the service of other gods in the Old Testament. And on this matter the Old Testament has a great deal to say. This subject, then, will be examined under three headings:

A.   Yahwistic parallels to pagan religious ideas and practices;

B.   Yahwistic exploitation of pagan religious ideas and practices;

C.   Yahwistic repudiation of pagan religious ideas and practices.

It should be noted at the outset that this discussion will not be balanced, and each of these topics will not be given equal treatment. Most readers will recognize immediately that the last of these three issues is much more overt in the Old Testament than the first two.

A.   Yahwistic Parallels to Pagan Religious Ideas and Practices

One need not look far to discover fundamental common denominators between Yahwistic faith and extrabiblical religious perceptions. Shared notions include customs, rituals, sacred objects, architecture, iconography, religious personnel, but the current discussion will be limited to two areas: shared *belief* and shared *religious practices*.

1. Shared Beliefs

Most ancient Near Easterners believed in a three-tiered universe structured something like this:

FIGURE 6: The Three-Tiered Universe

Heaven:
The Realm of Deity

Earth:
The Realm of the Living

Sheol:
The Realm of the Dead

Most ancient Near Easterners would have assumed that the occupants of the heavenly realm antedated the universe—in fact they created the world. It was also assumed that human beings were subservient to the gods. Most ancient Near Easterners were also keenly aware that their behavior, whether ethical or cultic, had angered the gods and that the gods expected some sort of penitential ritual to placate their wrath. All ancient Near Easterners assumed that the gods determined the fates of human beings, this applying not only to the course of historical events in particular but also to people's prosperity in general. Yahwists also shared with their neighbors the conviction that in death people departed to the netherworld, where they continued to exist as "living corpses."

Obvious parallels are also evident in the manner in which gods relate to their subjects. Specifically, in the ancient Near East there was the widespread recognition of the tripartite symbiotic relationship involving a patron deity, the land over which the god exercised authority/care, and the human occupants of that land. Just as the god's disposition toward his or her land was influenced by the ethical and cultic conduct of the human subjects, so YHWH's disposition toward his land and toward his people was determined by the response of the Israelites to him. Persistent human misconduct, in fact, resulted in the deities' abandonment of their respective lands, leaving the people at the mercy of invaders. In Yahwism this perspective is evident especially in the covenant curses of Leviticus 26 and Deuteronomy 28, and represents the heart of the judgment oracles of later prophets. At the same time, the Israelites shared with some of their neighbors the view that their God would not be angry with them forever. In due course, he would have a change of heart, restore the exiled population to their native land, install a king over the land and return to the land himself. In this respect Israel's later messianic hope, as expressed for example in Ezekiel, is perfectly at home in the ancient Near Eastern religious world.[6]

Although a previous generation of critical scholars tended to interpret these links in ideology, custom, and design as evidence for Israelite borrowing from other cultures, now we are more prepared to recognize parallel developments and/or Yahwists' adoption of familiar symbols to communicate divine truth. An evangelical perspective proposes that these common features originate in some pristine revelation that, in the hands of pagans, was garbled almost beyond recognition, but whose purity was secured in Israel through the inspirational work of the Holy Spirit.

2. Shared Religious Practices

In addition to these shared beliefs, orthodox Yahwists shared many religious practices with their neighbors. For example, they communed with the deity through prayer and sacrifice. The need for both arose not only from a sense of dependence upon the deity, but also from the deep conviction that the god/gods were angered through human sin. Accordingly certain offerings were presented to "smooth the face" of the deity;[7] others were presented as food/gifts for the deity and/or eaten in his or her presence as an act of fellowship; still others simply involved purification rites. Most of the categories of sacrifice found in Leviticus 1–5 are attested outside Israel, most notably זֶבַח, "sacrifice, sacrificial meal"; שְׁלָמִים, "peace/well-being offering"; עֹלָה, "whole burnt offering"; מִנְחָה, "gift, grain/cereal offering."[8]

---

6. I have developed this theme in several places. In addition to my commentary on Ezekiel, see Block, *Gods of the Nations,* 113–47, as well as Block, "Divine Abandonment: Ezekiel's Adaptation of an Ancient Near Eastern Motif," 15–42.

7. See Mal 1:9, חַלָּה פְנֵי־אֵל, "to smooth the face of God."

8. Cognates of זֶבַח, are attested in Ugaritic (*dbh*, *UT* #637), Phoenician/Punic ("*zbh*," in *DNWSI* 1:301–2), Aramaic (*zbh*), Akkadian (von Soden, "*zību*," in *AHw*

It has long been recognized that, although the blueprint for the Temple was revealed by YHWH to David in writing (1 Chr 28:11–19), in the actual construction Solomon decorated it with many well-known Phoenician motifs: cherubim, palm trees, open flowers (1 Kgs 8:29–36).[9] Perhaps even more remarkable is the basic structure of both the Tabernacle and the Temple. Like other ancient Near Eastern temples, both structures were perceived primarily as the residence of God and consisted of two main rooms: the large front hall (Holy Place), and the most sacred room at the back, the דְּבִיר (Holy of Holies). In pagan temples this room housed the statue of the deity. Although Yahwism was aniconic,[10] conceptually the room served a similar function, housing the Ark of the Covenant and the כְּבוֹד־יְהוָה, "glory of YHWH," both symbols of the divine presence. The parallels between the Israelite Temple and extra-biblical patterns have been dramatically illustrated by John Monson's recent analysis of the Syrian Temple at Ain Dara.[11]

3:1525; cf. Averbeck, "זבח," *NIDOTTE* 1:1066–68). Cognates of שְׁלָמִים, "peace/well-being offering," are attested in Ugaritic (*šlm/ šlmm, UT* #2424), Punic ("*šlm*," *DNWSI* 2:1152); in Akkadian this offering is represented by *keldi*; in Hittite by *keldiya* or *talešulaš* (cf. Averbeck, "שֶׁלֶם," *NIDOTTE* 4:135–36). Cognates of עֹלָה, "whole burnt offering," are apparently attested in Neo-Punic ('*lt*) and perhaps in the Proto-Sinaitic inscriptions (see Kellermann, *TDOT* 11:97–98), but corresponding designations for this offering elsewhere include *kll* (cf. Hebrew כָּלִיל, "whole, complete") in Punic, *šrp* (cf. Hebrew שָׂרַף, "to burn") in Ugaritic (*UT* #2489), and *ambassi* in Hittite (cf. Averbeck, "עֹלָה," *NIDOTTE* 3:405–7). Cognates of מִנְחָה, "gift, grain/cereal offering," are attested in Ugaritic (*mnh, UT* #1500), Phoenician and Punic (*mnh*) and Official Aramaic ("*mnhh*," in *DNWSI* 2:659; cf. "מִנְחָה," *NIDOTTE* 2:978–79). For a discussion of these and other sacrificial expressions within their ancient Near Eastern context, see Weinfeld, "Social and Cultic Institutions in the Priestly Source," 105–11.

9. Cf. Keel, *The Symbolism of the Biblical World*, 141–44. For a detailed discussion of the Israelite Temple within its ancient Near Eastern context, see Hurowitz, *I Have Built You an Exalted House*; for a more popular treatment, see Fritz, "Temple Architecture," 38–49.

10. For a study of the nature and history of aniconism in Israel against its ancient Near Eastern cultural background, see Mettinger, *No Graven Image?*

11. Monson, "The New 'Ain Dara Temple, 20–35, 67.

B.   Yahwistic Exploitation of Pagan Religious Ideas and Practices

One does not need to read far in the biblical text before one encounters pagan notions that have been picked up and exploited for Yahwistic purposes, though without the process giving assent to the veracity of those notions.

1. YHWH's Exploitation of Pagan Practices

Included in this category would be Ezekiel's reference to YHWH guiding Nebuchadnezzar to attack Jerusalem rather than the Ammonites through the Babylonian king's resorting to divination, specifically by manipulating (קָסַם) arrows (rhabdomancy), consulting (שָׁאַל) the *teraphim*, and examining (רָאָה) a sheep liver (hepatoscopy; Ezek 21:26[Eng 21]). Although the Mosaic Torah expressly condemns these kinds of activities as detestable practices of the nations (תּוֹעֲבֹת הַגּוֹיִם, Deut 18:9–14), in this case they worked. A pagan king employed strictly forbidden techniques of divination and thereby discovered the will of YHWH.[12]

Closer to Israel's home we may also cite Saul's consultation of the medium (אוֹב) at Endor on the day before his death (1 Sam 28:3–25). With his alienation from Samuel, Saul—this most tragic figure in Israel's history—had also lost contact with God. In Saul, a descendant of the wretched Benjamites who had stood up to defend sodomites among them (the people of Gibeah, Judg 19–21), YHWH had given the Israelites exactly what they had demanded—"a king like the nations [had]" (1 Sam 8:5, 19–20). Despite Saul's earlier efforts to eradicate all mediums (אֹבוֹת and יִדְּעֹנִים), he thoroughly compromised himself spiritually. And when YHWH refused to respond to his pleas for guidance, either through dreams or the Urim or his prophets (28:6), Saul sought out the medium at Endor to bring Samuel back from the netherworld. Again, even though YHWH was absolutely opposed to such practices, remarkably it worked! From the ground emerged a figure, whom the medium perceived as a divine being (אֱלֹהִים, v. 13). But there was no doubt in the writer's mind about the identity of this shrouded figure (vv. 15–16). That this was indeed Samuel is confirmed both by the figure's recollection of his

---

12. On this text, see Block, *Book of Ezekiel Chapters 1–24*, 681–89.

past relationship with Saul (vv. 16b–18), and by the precise fulfillment of his prediction on the following day.[13]

How could this happen? As puzzling as YHWH's communicat-
ing with a pagan in the first instance and a syncretistic Israelite in the
second is the fact that he would do so through absolutely forbidden
pagan forms. YHWH obviously retains complete freedom with respect to the means he uses to relate to human beings. When communicating with pagans or paganized Israelites, he speaks in a language
they understand. But this is more than mere accommodation; in so
doing he also exposes the folly of their perceptions.

2. YHWH's Exploitation of Pagan Perceptions

Similar phenomena occur elsewhere. Although Ezekiel's inaugu-
ral vision is a complete riddle to most modern readers, within the
context of ancient Near Eastern religious iconography all of the elements—the multiheaded creatures, the cherubim, the chariot, the
platform bearing a throne which in turn bears a divine figure—make
perfect sense.[14] What Ezekiel sees is not an actual representation,
but a reflection of deity. Nevertheless, the redundancy of "a likeness
like the appearance of a man" guards the prophet from even contemplating any idolatrous notions. While extra-Israelite motifs have
been incorporated into the vision, this strategy does not represent
capitulation to pagan thought. On the contrary, with powerful visual
rhetoric this vision challenges pagan conceptions at every turn. The
glory of YHWH cannot be reduced to human definition or plastic
art. Everything about the vision is in the superlative mode. God is
alone above the platform, removed from all creatures, and stunning
in his radiance. There is none other beside(s) him. But this does not
prevent him from communicating with mortals. Whereas YHWH
had chosen "the lip of Canaan" (Isa 19:18) as the vehicle of verbal
intercourse in an earlier revelatory moment, now he adopts the art
of Mesopotamia as his method of ocular communication. And in so
doing he beats the pagans and their gods at their own games.

13. Compare 1 Sam 28:19 and 31:1–13.

14. For an extremely helpful study of the correlation between Ezekiel's vision
and ancient Near Eastern art, see Keel, *Jahwe-Visionen und Siegelkunst*, 125–273.
For additional discussion, see Block, *Ezekiel 1–24*, 95–104.

3. YHWH's Exploitation of Roles Attributed to Pagan Gods

Under the rubric of exploited pagan ideas should also be included those numerous texts that apply to YHWH roles that non-Yahwists normally associated with pagan gods. In the Old Testament these roles are especially evident in pronouncements of blessing and judgment. With respect to the former, Deut 7:13–14 provides a striking example of YHWH assuming fertility functions that Canaanites generally attributed to Baal/Hadad—the storm god—and other lesser divinities responsible for specific crops. The blessings Moses lists here represent tangible rewards that YHWH promises those who pass the test of love through their obedience. Moses begins by cataloguing on the one hand those areas of life upon which people are most dependent for their security, and on the other those areas where the fertility gods of Canaan were thought to be active (v. 13). "The fruit of your womb and the fruit of your soil" serves as a thesis statement covering all areas of agriculture on which humans are dependent.[15] Reversing the order, Moses specifies three products that derive directly from the soil (grain, wine, and oil), and a pair that derive from domesticated livestock (calves and lambs).

Inasmuch as each of the terms Moses uses for these products is linked with the pantheon of Canaanite deities, here an informed reader recognizes a subtle polemic against the idolatry of the land. Hebrew דָּגָן, "grain," is cognate to the name for the god of grain, Dagon, known in the Ugaritic texts as the father of Baal (cf. Judg 16:23; 1 Sam 8:1–12) and from the Emar and Mari texts as the head of the pantheon in the region of Syria around the great bend of the Euphrates.[16] The rare word תִּירשׁ, which Moses uses instead of the more common יַיִן (cf. 14:26), is cognate to the name of the god Tirshu/Tirash, attested in the El-Amarna letters and in Ugaritic (as *trt*).[17] Another rare word, יִצְהָר, employed in place of the more common שֶׁמֶן (cf. 8:8), for olive oil, may be cognate to the name of the

---

15. Though, as we shall learn from verse 14, "fruit of the womb" also includes children.

16. On *Dāgān*/Dagon, see Healey, "Dagon," 216–19; Fleming, *The Installation of Baal's High Priestess at Emar*, 240–48.

17. On which, see Healey, "Tirash תירש תירוש," 871–72.

old god of olive oil.[18] The unusual expression, שְׁגַר־אֲלָפֶיךָ,[19] literally, "increase of your herds," rather than עֵגֶל, for calf, is linked to the god Shaggar/Sheger, whose veneration is attested in Ugaritic, Emar, Deir 'Allā, and Punic texts, and who in some instances apparently functions as the deity of the full moon.[20] However, the mythological connection is most obvious in the designation for lambs, עַשְׁתְּרֹת צֹאנֶךָ, which substitutes for the more common כֶּבֶשׂ (cf. Exod 29:39). The veneration of Ishtar/Astarte, the goddess of fertility, was among the most widespread of any divinity in the ancient Near East. Her role in fertility is reflected in an ancient text from Babylon: "Bow down to your city goddess [Ishtar] that she may grant you offspring, take thought for your livestock, remember the planting."[21] The extent to which the Israelites in Moses' audience caught the links between the words he chose to use and the religion of the Canaanites is uncertain. However, his preference for these rare expressions seems to represent a deliberate stab at the jugular of Canaanite religion. Not these pagan deities, but YHWH, the God of Israel, is Israel's only guarantee of security. In the land that he promised on oath to give to the descendants of their ancestors, the blessing of the crops and herds would be in his hands alone.[22]

Much later in the book, Moses concludes his blessing of the Israelite tribes on an exuberant note of praise to YHWH and congratulations to Israel, so privileged to have him as their God:

> There is none like God, O Jeshurun,
> who rides through the heavens to your help,
> majestic through the skies.
> He subdues the ancient gods,
> shatters the forces of old;

18. Cf. Wyatt, "Oil יצהר," 640.

19. Elsewhere only in Deut 28:4, 18, 51; Exod 13:12, substituting for the more common עֵגֶל (cf. 9:16, 21).

20. Cf.van der Toorn, "Sheger שגר," 760–62; Fleming, *Installation of Baal's High Priestess at Emar*, 205.

21. Cf. Lambert, *Babylonian Wisdom Literature*, 108–9. For further information on Astarte, see Wyatt, "Astarte," 109–14.

22. Weinfeld (*Deuteronomy 1–11*, 373) notes that the sequence grain, wine, cattle, and sheep, is identical to that found in the blessings recorded in a Phoenician inscription by Azitawada (early seventh century BCE). For the text, see *CIS* 2.148–49 (iii.2–11).

he drove out the enemy before you,
and said, "Destroy!"
So Israel lives in safety,
untroubled is Jacob's abode
in a land of grain and wine,
where the heavens drop down dew.
Happy are you, O Israel! Who is like you,
a people saved by YHWH,
the shield of your help,
and the sword of your triumph!
Your enemies shall come fawning to you,
and you shall tread on their backs.[23]
(Deut 33:26–29, NRSV, modified)

The image of YHWH riding the heavens/skies recalls Canaanite myths recorded in the tablets found at Ugarit, in which one of Baal's epithets is "Cloudrider" (*rkb ʿrpt*).[24]

The exploitation of Canaanite religious ideas occurs also in several of the Psalms, most notably Psalms 29 and 104, which some have argued represent Yahwistic makeovers of originally Egyptian or Canaanite hymns in praise of the storm god.[25] The storm god imagery is especially impressive in the opening stanza of the latter:

Bless YHWH, O my soul.
O YHWH my God, you are very great.
You are clothed with honor and majesty,
wrapped in light as with a garment.
You stretch out the heavens like a tent;
You set the beams of your chambers on the waters;
You make the clouds your chariot;
You ride on the wings of the wind;
You make the winds your messengers,
fire and flame your ministers.
(Ps 104:1b–4, NRSV, modified)

23. In general our scriptural citations represent adaptations of NRSV.

24. As translated by Smith in *Ugaritic Narrative Poetry*, 124, *passim*. For a study of the significance of the epithet, "Cloudrider," see Herrmann, "Rider Upon the Clouds," 703–5. On the mythical sea monster Leviathan, see Uehlinger, "Leviathan," 511–15.

25. For discussion of these and other psalms of this type, see Loretz, *Ugarit-Texte und Thronbesteigigungspsalmen*.

In 104:20–27 the psalmist celebrates YHWH's role in ensuring the fertility of the earth, and in verses 18–30 he praises YHWH for his care for the animals, noting specifically Leviathan, the mythical sea monster (Ugaritic *ltn*), whom YHWH has created to be his pet.[26] In regard to the Canaanite images found in the psalm, Craigie commented, "External influences on the psalm have undergone thorough adaptation and have been brought into harmony with the general tenor of Hebrew religious thought."[27]

Similar rhetorical exploitation of pagan motifs occurs in Old Testament pronouncements of judgment. Such is evident especially in the way biblical authors speak of the involvement of secondary forces of destruction. Deuteronomy 32:23–25 offers a striking illustration of the issue:

> I will heap disasters (רָעוֹת) upon them,
> spend my arrows (חִצַּי) against them:
> wasting hunger (רָעָב),
> burning consumption (רֶשֶׁף),
> bitter pestilence (קֶטֶב).
> The teeth of beasts (בְּהֵמוֹת) I will send against them,
> with venom of things crawling in the dust.
> In the street the sword (חֶרֶב) shall bereave,
> and in the chambers terror (אֵימָה),
> for young man and woman alike,
> nursing child and old gray head.

This text provides the background for Ezek 5:16–17. All three words in Ezekiel's חִצֵּי הָרָעָב הָרָעִים, "deadly arrows of famine," appear in the first three lines quoted above. But this raises the question, *How can Ezekiel associate arrows so directly with famine?* The answer may lie in this same Deuteronomy text, which juxtaposes רָעָב, "famine," with רֶשֶׁף, "plague," and קֶטֶב, "scourge." The mythological connotations of the latter two expressions surface elsewhere in the Old Testament. Note especially Hab 3:5, in which Pestilence (דֶּבֶר) and Plague (רֶשֶׁף) appear as attendants of God as he proceeds

---

26. For more detailed study of the possible foreign cultural roots of this psalm, see Craigie, "The Comparison of Hebrew Poetry," 10–21. For a general discussion of the issues and further bibliography, see Allen, *Psalms 101–150*, 28–32.

27. Craigie, "Comparison of Hebrew Poetry," 18. For a recent interpretation of the book of Job against the backdrop of ancient Near Eastern mythology, see Fyall, *Now My Eyes See You.*

from Teman.[28] Remarkably, several extra-biblical texts indicate that the symbol of Resheph was the arrow.[29] Resheph may also serve as background to the חֵץ יָעוּף, "flying arrow," which is conjoined with דֶּבֶר, "plague," and קֶטֶב, "scourge" in Ps 91:5–6. The origin of the expression "calamitous arrows of famine," should therefore probably be sought in pagan mythology.

Similar exploitation may be observed in regard to the figure of Mot, the god of the netherworld, in Canaanite mythology. The term מָוֶת/מוֹת usually refers to the experience of death. However, in some poetic texts with mythological backgrounds the word appears to be used as a proper name identifying the chthonic power behind death, Mot of the Ugaritic texts.[30] Especially striking is Hos 13:14, where Mawet, "Death," is personified as the ruler of the netherworld who sends out his plagues (Deber, pl.) as his agents:

> Shall I ransom them from the power of Sheol?
> Shall I redeem them from Death (מָוֶת)?
> O Death (מָוֶת), where are your plagues?
> O Sheol, where is your destruction?
> Compassion is hidden from my eyes.

Although critical scholars tend to interpret texts like this as tacit admissions of the existence of such divinities, neither psalmist nor prophet would have countenanced such an idea.[31] On the contrary,

---

28. See also Job 5:7, Pss 76:4, 78:48, and Song 8:6.

29. *UT* 1001:3, *b'l ḥz ršp*, "Resheph, lord of the arrow," and *UT* 128:II:6, *ršp zbl*, "Prince Resheph." His ventures are reflected in the legend of Kirta 19: *mḥmšt . yitsp . ršp*, "A fifth was gathered by Resheph." Cf. Smith, *Ugaritic Narrative Poetry*, 12. Note also the reference to *rsp ḥs*, "Resheph of the Arrow," mentioned on a fourth-century BCE Phoenician inscription (*KAI*, 32:3–4). On this figure, see Day, "New Light on the Mythological Background," 259–74; Yadin, "New Gleanings on Resheph), 259–74. Weinfeld ("Divine Intervention in War, 124–31) associates Resheph with the "shooting stars" in Judg 5:20–22. For a discussion of Resheph, see Xella, "Resheph," 700–703.

30. Hab 2:5; Job 18:13–14; 28:22; Hos 13:14; Isa 28:15,18; Ps 49:16 [Eng 15]; Song 8:6; cf. also Ps 141:7; Prov 1:12; 27:20; 30:15–16; Isa 5:14. In a few instances מָוֶת/מוֹת refers to the place of the dead (Job 38:17; Pss 6:6 [Eng 5]; 9:14 [Eng 13]; 107:18; Prov 7:27).

31. The comment of Gowan with respect to Jeremiah (*Theology of the Prophetic Books*, 104–5) is typical: "Like his predecessors since the time of Amos, he [Jeremiah] does not speak of a theoretical monotheism, but he is a 'practical monotheist'; that is, it matters not whether other gods may exist; for Israel, YHWH is the only God." Support for this interpretation is found in the first commandment, "You shall have

orthodox Yahwists thoroughly demythologized all these notions. YHWH himself assumed the role of Resheph and all other malevolent spirits that might have kept non-Israelites in constant fear. Furthermore, it is not Mot but YHWH alone who has the keys to the gates of death and the netherworld.[32] In Ezek 5:16–17 the arrows pointed at Jerusalem are YHWH's own. His intention is to intensify the famine in the city until the staff of bread is broken, in fulfillment of the covenant curses of Leviticus 26 and Deuteronomy 28. According to these texts, YHWH has a host of destructive agents at his disposal: pestilence, disease, foreign armies (the sword), drought, and wild animals. When disaster strikes, it is his work, not the effects of malevolent spirits dispatched by Mot, the supposed king of the netherworld.[33]

4. YHWH's Exploitation of Divine Epithets

Biblical authors exploit pagan mythological motifs for rhetorical purposes, either to expose the folly of Israelite syncretism or to declare the supremacy of YHWH. This is the function of epithetic expressions like "God of gods," which appears four times in the Old Testament: Deut 10:17; Ps 136:2; Dan 2:47; 11:36. Interpreted literally, this phrase suggests the existence of other gods. This is undoubtedly how Nebuchadnezzar, a non-Israelite, used the expression in Daniel 2:47, to which we will return in a moment.

Moses' use of the expression in Deut 10:17, however, should be interpreted in the light of earlier unequivocally monotheistic statements such as those found in 4:32–40.[34] In 10:17 Moses declares

no other gods before [or besides] me" (Exod 20:3).

32. On this image of Sheol, see Isa 38:10 ("the gates of Sheol") and Job 38:17; Ps 9:14[Eng 13]; 107:18 ("the gates of death"). Cf. also Rev 1:18.

33. In contrast to the peoples around Israel, who lived in constant dread of malevolent spirits, Old Testament Yahwism has no place for such divine or semi-divine beings. The nearest equivalent is the "evil spirit" that YHWH sends upon people to create disaster (cf. Judg 9:23; 1 Sam 16:14). The epilogue in Job expressly attributes to YHWH the calamities (רָעָה) with which Job's adversary (הַשָּׂטָן) had robbed this saint of all he possessed (42:11).

34. Whether they treat this chapter as a unity or a literary conglomerate, critical scholars are virtually unanimous in interpreting it as a late, if not the latest, insertion into the book of Deuteronomy, composed during the exile to give hope to a community that had lost its way spiritually and whose election as the people of YHWH seemed jeopardized. See Braulik, "Wisdom, Divine Presence and Law," 1–25; Rose, *5. Mose*, 2:488–503; Weinfeld, *Deuteronomy 1–11*, 229–30.

YHWH's supremacy through a single verbless clause with three predicates: "For YHWH your God, he is God of gods, Lord of lords, the El." Each epithet is loaded with meaning. Like "heaven of heavens" in verse 14, "God of gods" (אֱלֹהֵי הָאֱלֹהִים) and "Lord of lords" (אֲדֹנֵי הָאֲדֹנִים) express the superlative degree. Both epithets appear in hymnic liturgical formulas in later texts. Note especially Ps 136:2–3, the only place where these two epithets appear together:

> Give thanks to the God of gods,
> for his covenant love (חֶסֶד) endures forever.
>
> Give thanks to the Lord of lords,
> for his covenant love (חֶסֶד) endures forever.

The expression "God of gods," declares YHWH's superiority over all divine and semi-divine beings. It expresses a truth that became especially important as the collapse of Judah and Jerusalem approached in the sixth century BCE. In the ancient world it was generally assumed that the outcomes of military battles on earth were actually determined by the relative strengths of the patron deities of the respective nations at war. And even as Nebuchadnezzar's battering rams were being set up against the walls of Jerusalem, the inhabitants remained convinced that their God, who had entered into an irrevocable covenant with them, was superior to Marduk, the god of the Babylonians, and that he would protect his temple, his city, and his people. When Jerusalem finally fell, the faith of many of its citizens was devastated. Just as in an earlier era YHWH had demonstrated his superiority over the gods of Egypt in the plagues and the exodus (Exod 12:12; Num 33:4), so Marduk had apparently demonstrated his superiority over YHWH in this context.

It is scarcely coincidental that the only other occurrences of the expression, "God of gods," appears in the book of Daniel, one of whose major themes is the supremacy—despite all appearances to the contrary—of YHWH over all gods. In fact, in 2:47 we hear from the lips of the king of Babylon himself, "Truly, your God is God of gods and Lord of kings." The expression recurs in 11:36, where Daniel predicts the appearance of a hostile king who will "exalt and magnify himself above every god and will say unheard-of things against the God of gods." If Moses speaks of YHWH as "God of gods," he is not thereby assenting to the existence of other gods alongside YHWH (cf. Deut 4:35, 39); his statement is purely rhetorical.[35]

The third title Moses ascribes to YHWH, the God of Israel, is "the El" (הָאֵל; cf. also 7:9). Strictly speaking אֵל is a common noun meaning "god, divine being," a fact confirmed by the Old Testament usage of the singular,[36] as well as the plural אֵלִים, which may denote either gods in general,[37] or the heavenly angelic assembly in particular.[38] Moses' attachment of the article to "El" may bear a double significance. On the one hand, within the context of Deuteronomy he hereby declares that YHWH is *the* [one and only] God, and on the other hand, he declares that YHWH is "the [one and only] El" who presides over heavenly and earthly affairs. As is well known, in Canaanite mythology El was the name of the head of the pantheon, the husband of Asherah and father of seventy gods of second rank, including Baal, Mot, and Yamm. In the Ugaritic texts El's epithets include "Holy One" (*qdš*), "Father" (*ab*), "Father of Years" (*ab šnm*), "Father of Humanity" (*ab adm*), "Creator of Creatures" (the common understanding of *bny bnwt*), "the benevolent, good-natured El" (*ltpn*

35. If "God of gods" declares YHWH's supremacy over all spiritual and heavenly powers, then "Lord of lords" speaks to his supremacy over earthly rulers. This expression occurs in the Old Testament only here and in Psalm 136:3. Elsewhere supreme earthly rulers are referred to as "king of kings" (מֶלֶךְ מַלְכַיָּא, Ezra 7:12 and Dan 2:37; מֶלֶךְ מְלָכִים, Ezek 26:7) and "lord of kings" (מָרֵא מַלְכִין; Dan 2:47), which probably explains why the Aramaic Targums and the Syriac Peshitta translate מֶלֶךְ מְלָכִים as if it were מָרֵא מַלְכִין, "lord of kings." Similar epithets for supreme rulers occur also in extrabiblical texts: a Philistine king refers to Pharaoh in Aramaic as מרא מלכי, "lord of kings" (*KAI* 266:1, 6); Eshhmunazzar king of Sidon refers to his Persian overlord as מלכם אדן, "lord of kings" (ibid., 14:18); Akkadian equivalents include *bēl bēle*, "lord of lords;" *bēl šarrāni*, "lord of kings;" *šaršarrāni*, "king of kings." On the Akkadian epithets, see Seux, *Épithètes royales akkadiennes et sumériennes*, 55–56 and 318–19. In the New Testament the divine epithet "King of kings" always accompanies "God of gods" (1 Tim 6:15; Rev 17:14; 19:16).

36. Exod 34:6; Deut 3:24; 32:12, 21(//הֲבָלִים, "idols"); Ps 44:21[Eng 20]; 77:14[Eng 13]; 81:10[Eng 9]; Isa 31:3; 43:10; 44:10, 15, 17 (making images of a god); 45:20 (//פֶּסֶל, "image/idol"); 46:6; 8:2, 9; Mal 2:11.

37. Exodus 15:11 asks "Who is like you among the gods (בָּאֵלִם)?" Daniel 11:36 speaks of the monstrous king who will exalt himself above every God (כָּל-אֵל) and speak horrible things against "the God of gods." Here אֵל אֵלִים is best interpreted as equivalent to אֱלֹהֵי הָאֱלֹהִים. Cf. Goldingay, *Daniel*, 280.

38. Ps 29:1; 89:7 [Eng 6] (both בְּנֵי אֵלִים); Job 41:17. Cf. the similar use of the singular in Ps 82:1.

il dbid), and "the Bull El" (*ṭril*).[39] But the myths portray this El incon-
sistently: on the one hand, he is a lusty figure who brazenly boasts
of his sexual prowess,[40] and on the other hand, he is a gray-bearded
old man who presides rather ineptly over an extremely unruly and
dysfunctional pantheon.

In Moses' portrayal of YHWH as הָאֵל, "the El," we should probably recognize an intentional polemic against Canaanite perceptions
of El. In Deut 7:9–10 he challenges Israel: "Know therefore that
YHWH your God is God, the faithful El who maintains covenant
loyalty with those who love him and keep his commandments, to
a thousand generations, and who repays in their own person those
who reject him. He does not delay but repays in their own person
those who reject him."[41]

Moses is even more specific in 10:14–18, where he highlights
what is distinctive about YHWH, the God of Israel, alternating tran-
scendent (vv. 14, 17a) and immanent (vv. 15, 17b–18) qualities. With
respect to God's transcendence, first with the skillful use of parallelism, merismus ("heaven and earth"), and the superlative degree
("heaven of heavens"),[42] he declares that YHWH, the God of Israel,

39. For discussion of these epithets, see Herrmann, "El," 274–20.

40. See especially *CAT* 1.23, conveniently published in original text and translation by Lewis in *Ugaritic Narrative Poetry*, 208–14. Lewis' comments on this text
(ibid., 205–7) are very helpful. Translation and even more detailed commentary are
also provided by Pardee, "Dawn and Dusk," 274–83; and Wyatt, *Religious Texts from
Ugarit*, 324–35.

41. Hebrew:

וְיָדַעְתָּ כִּי־יְהוָה אֱלֹהֶיךָ הוּא הָאֱלֹהִים הָאֵל

הַנֶּאֱמָן שֹׁמֵר הַבְּרִית וְהַחֶסֶד לְאֹהֲבָיו וּלְשֹׁמְרֵי מִצְוֹתָו לְאֶלֶף דּוֹר׃

וּמְשַׁלֵּם לְשֹׂנְאָיו אֶל־פָּנָיו לְהַאֲבִידוֹ לֹא יְאַחֵר לְשֹׂנְאוֹ אֶל־פָּנָיו יְשַׁלֶּם־לוֹ׃

42. In general ancient Near Easterners, the Israelites included, perceived the
universe as a multi-tiered structure consisting of Sheol below (the realm of the
dead), earth (the realm of the living), and heaven (the realm of God/the gods and
semi-divine beings). However, some imagined these tiers to be sub-divided further.
Some Mesopotamian texts, for example, know of three heavens, occupied from top
to bottom by 300 Igigi, Bel/Marduk, and the stars/constellations, respectively. For
discussion, see Lambert, "The Cosmology of Sumer and Babylon," 58–59; Lambert,
"Himmel," *Reallexikon der Assyriologie* 4:411–12. A series of medical incantation
texts speak of "seven heavens, seven earths," or "earth seven, heaven seven." These
probably do not refer to the number of heavens, but like the Hebrew expression,
"heaven of heavens," refer to the totality of the cosmos. Thus Wright, *The Early
History of Heaven*, 40–41. Jewish tradition speaks of as many as seven heavens
(see Rabinowitz, "Cosmology," in *EncJud*, 5.982), and even in the New Testament

owns the entire cosmos: "To YHWH your God belong the heavens and the heavens of heavens: the earth and all that is in it" (v. 14).

As we have already observed, the ancient Israelites shared with their Near Eastern neighbors the perception of the universe as a three-tiered structure consisting of Sheol below (the realm of the dead), earth (the realm of the living), and heaven (the realm of God/ the gods and semi-divine beings). Here, Moses claims that all those realms that others ascribed to other gods were under the exclusive authority of YHWH, the God of Israel. Furthermore YHWH is the "great" (גְּדֹל), "strong" (גִּבֹּר),[43] and "awesome" (נוֹרָא) El.[44] If this triad of expressions does not express the superlative degree, it is certainly emphatic—YHWH is the supreme God.[45] This statement builds on Moses' earlier semi-catechetical declaration in 7:21, "For YHWH your God in your midst is El, great and glorious."[46]

---

we read of multiple heavens generally (Eph 4:11; Heb 4:14) and the third heaven specifically (1 Cor 12:2). For discussion, see Wright, *History of Heaven*, 145–50. These perceptions apparently derive from geocentric Pythagorean Greek models. According to Plato, each of the seven celestial bodies traveled alone in its orbital space around the earth. For full discussion, see Wright, *History of Heaven*, 98–104. In the present context this is obviously a figure of speech whereby Moses declares that whatever cosmic entity one may imagine to exist out there, or however far one may travel in space, it all belongs to YHWH, the God of Israel.

43. Cf. the title אֵל גִּבּוֹר "El Gibbor" in Isa 9:5[Eng 6]. In Deut 3:24 Moses had referred to YHWH's actions on behalf of Israel as גְבוּרֹת, "might acts."

44. Neh 9:32 picks up these expressions and employs them liturgically, adding, "who keeps his covenant and steadfast love (חֶסֶד)," from Deut 7:9 and 12.

45. Cf. Exod 34:7, according to which YHWH forgives iniquity (עָוֹן), rebellion (פֶּשַׁע) and sin (חַטָּאָה), that is, every kind of sin; and Deut 6:5, according to which Israelites are to love YHWH with all their hearts (כָּל־לֵב), their entire person (כָּל־נֶפֶשׁ) and all their substance (כָּל־מְאֹד), that is, without any reservation whatsoever.

46. Which in turn, builds on 6:15, but note the differences in the syntax of the three verses:

6:15	כִּי אֵל קַנָּא יְהוָה אֱלֹהֶיךָ בְּקִרְבֶּךָ	For YHWH your God in your midst is an impassioned God.
7:21	כִּי־יְהוָה אֱלֹהֶיךָ בְּקִרְבֶּךָ אֵל גָּדוֹל וְנוֹרָא	For YHWH your God in your midst is El, great and awesome.
10:17	כִּי יְהוָה אֱלֹהֵיכֶם הוּא . . . הָאֵל הַגָּדֹל הַגִּבֹּר וְהַנּוֹרָא	For YHWH your God is . . . the El, great, strong, and awesome.

With respect to YHWH's immanence, Moses declares in Deut 7:6–8 that YHWH has chosen (בָּחַר) Israel out of all the families on earth and hand-picked them as the object of his affection (חָשַׁק) and love (אָהֵב), and in so doing fulfilled his oath to the ancestors. This statement builds on Deut 4:32–34, where Moses affirms YHWH's absolute uniqueness vis-à-vis all other gods as demonstrated by his rescue of Israel from Egypt, an extraordinary act based upon his love for the ancestors. In Deut 10:17–18 Moses declares that YHWH governs his people fairly, executing justice for the marginalized and demonstrating his covenant commitment (אָהֵב) to aliens by providing them with food and clothing. This concern for human beings contrasts sharply with the personality of El in Canaanite myths, which portray him as preoccupied with pantheonic affairs.[47] It is Moses' custom to exploit pagan notions by alluding to pagan divinities and then ascribing many of their titles and functions/spheres of influence to YHWH.

C. Yahwistic Repudiation of Pagan Religious Ideas and Practices

The last, and probably most fascinating, part of this discussion concerns explicit Yahwistic rejection of pagan religious ideas. Hostility toward idols and the worship of other gods is expressed in four principal ways: (1) pejorative designations for idols and the gods they represent; (2) explicit prohibitions of idolatry; (3) hostile actions against idols; and (4) polemical portrayals of idols and idolaters. Each shall be examined in turn.

1. Pejorative Designations for Idols and the Gods They Represent

Even though, or perhaps precisely because, orthodox Yahwists denied the existence of other gods or the validity of their worship, the Old Testament attests to a remarkably extensive vocabulary referring to idols. The most common expression for an idol or the divinity behind the idol is, of course, אֱלֹהִים, "god." When referring to smaller household idols this word was occasionally interchanged with תְּרָפִים.

---

47. As in Psalm 8, where the psalmist's reflection on the cosmos as the handiwork of God leads to an expression of utter amazement at his interest in humankind, Moses' doxology of Deut 10:14 sets the stage for his election of Israel.

The etymology of this word remains uncertain, but a derivation from Hittite *tarpi/tarpiš*, which designates a spirit that can on some occasions be regarded as protective and on others as malevolent, seems most likely.[48]

Some designations for idols/divine images are actually neutral in value, but they reflect the view expressed by Moses in Deut 4:28, that these gods are no more and no less than the products of human efforts, mere objects of wood and stone. Accordingly, an idol/pagan deity is often referred to generally as "the work of human hands" (מַעֲשֵׂה יְדֵי אָדָם),[49] but more specifically as a צֶלֶם, "image, replica";[50] a פֶּסֶל, a divine image carved from wood, sculpted from stone, or cast in metal (Deut 4:16, 23, 25); a סֶמֶל, a sculpture of a divine image (Ezek 8:3, 5; 2 Chr 33:7, 12 (//פֶּסֶל); a תְּמוּנָה, a likeness, representation, form (Deut 4:16, 23, 25); a מַשְׂכִּית, a monument, image (Ezek 8:12); a תַּבְנִית, "construction, model, copy" (Ezek 8:10); a נֶסֶךְ, "molten image";[51] an עָצָב, "effigy."[52]

The occasional vocalization of the last word as עֹצֶב (Isa 48:5; Ps 139:24), in imitation of בֹּשֶׁת ("shame"), leads us into another vast category of designations, that is, derogatory expressions for idols/pagan gods: אֱלִילִים, nonentities, nothings;[53] אָוֶן, nothingness;[54] הַבְלֵי־שָׁוְא, empty trivialities, worthless things;[55] הֶבֶל, vanity, or as my

---

48. Cf. Lewis, "Teraphim תרפים," 844–50, for discussion. For references, see Gen 31:19, 34–35; Judg 17:5; 18:14, 17–18, 20; 1 Sam 15:23; 19:13, 16; 2 Kgs 23:24; Ezek 21:26[21]; Hos 3:4; Zech 10:2.

49. Deut 4:28; 27:15; 2 Kgs 19:18 = Isa 37:19 = 2 Chr 32:19; Pss 115:4; 135:15; Isa 2:8; Jer 1:16; 10:3, 9; 25:6–7; 44:8; Hos 14:4; Mic 5:12; 2 Chr 34:25.

50. Num 33:52; Ezek 7:20; Amos 5:26.

51. Isa 41:29; 48:5; Jer 10:14; 51:17. Cf. נְסִיךְ מַסֵּכָה, Dan 11:8; מַסֵּכָה Exod 32:4, 8; 34:17; Lev 19:4; Num 33:15; Deut 9:12, 16; 18:17–18; 27:15; Judg 17:3–4; 1 Kgs 14:9; 2 Chr 28:2; 34:3–4; 2 Kgs 17:16; Neh 9:18; Isa 30:22; 42:17; Hos 13:2; Nah 1:14; Hab 2:18; Ps 106:19.

52. 1 Sam 31:9; 2 Sam 5:21; Isa 46:21; 1 Chr 10:9; Hos 8:4; 13:2; 14:9; Isa 2:8; 10:11; Jer 50:2; Mic 1:7; Zech 13:2; Pss 106:36, 38; 115:4; 135:15.

53. Lev 19:4; 26:1; Isa 2:8, 18, 20; 10:10–11; 19:1, 3; 31:7 [Eng 6]; Hab 2:18; Pss 96:5; 97:7; 1 Chr 16:26.

54. Isa 66:3; cf. 41:29; 1 Sam 15:23; Zech 10:2; Hos 4:15; 10:8; 12:12 [Eng 11]; Isa 1:13; 66:3.

55. Jon 2:9 [Eng 8]; Ps 31:6[Eng 7]; cf. Ps 24:4; Jer 18:15.

teacher Thomas McComiskey used to say, "soap bubbles";[56] כְּזָבִים, lies;[57] רִיק, emptiness (Ps 4:2[Eng 3]; cf. Isa 30:7; 49:4); שֶׁקֶר, illusions, tricks, lies;[58] אֵימָה, frightful and horrifying objects (Jer 50:38); גִּלּוּלִים, dung pellets, round things, as in sheep droppings;[59] שִׁקּוּצִים, monstrosities, abhorrent/detestable objects;[60] תּוֹעֵבָה, abhorred/abominable object.[61] Ironically Yahwists dismissed that which can be seen as nothing, and that which cannot be seen they accepted as the ultimate reality. The nations worship gods of wood and stone that have eyes but see not, ears but hear not, and hands that can lend no aid at all (Deut 4:28; Ps 115:4–8).

2. Explicit Prohibitions of Idolatry and the Worship of Other Gods

The Old Testament frequently expresses the hostility of orthodox Yahwists toward the worship of other gods and explicitly prohibits the worship of any deities other than YHWH. Based on his exclusive claims to Israel's devotion (Deut 6:4–5), his covenantal passion (קִנְאָה; Exod 34:14; Deut 4:24; 5:9; 6:15), and his repudiation of the existence of any other gods (Deut 4:35, 39), reverential acts of submission and homage before beings or objects in the place of the one true God are absolutely forbidden in Israel's constitution. This prohibition is so fundamental that it is built into the covenant itself, involving the first principle of covenant relationship as expressed in the Decalogue:

> You shall have no other gods before me. You shall not make
> for yourself an idol, whether in the form of anything that is
> in heaven above, or that is on the earth beneath, or that is in
> the water under the earth. You shall not bow down to them
> or worship them; for I YHWH your God am an impassioned
> God, punishing children for the iniquity of parents, to the

56. Deut 32:21; 1 Kgs 16:13, 26; 2 Kgs 17:5; Jer 2:5; 8:19; Jer 10:8, 15; 14:22; 51:18; 14:22; Jon 2:9; Ps 31:7.

57. Amos 2:4; Pss 4:3 [Eng 3]; 40:5 [Eng 4].

58. Isa 44:20; Jer 10:14; 51:17; 16:19.

59. Lev 26:30; Deut 29:16 [Eng 17]; 1 Kgs 15:12; 21:26; 2 Kgs 17:12; 21:11, 21; Ezekiel (thirty-eight times!).

60. Deut 29:16 [Eng 17]; 2 Kgs 23:24; Isa 66:3; Jer 4:1; 7:30; 13:27; 16:18; 32:34; Ezek 5:11; 7:20; 11:18, 21; 20:7–8, 30; 37:23; 2 Chr 15:8.

61. Deut 32:16; Isa 44:19. Cf. Deut 13:15 [Eng 14]; 17:4 (the worship of foreign gods).

> third and the fourth generation of those who reject me, but
> showing steadfast love to the thousandth generation of those
> who love me and keep my commandments.
> (Exod 20:3–6; Deut 5:7–10)[62]

The exclusivity of Israel's devotion to YHWH is highlighted in the Shema', which Orthodox Jews recite twice a day to this day: שְׁמַע יִשְׂרָאֵל יְהוָה אֱלֹהֵינוּ יְהוָה אֶחָד. This declaration should be interpreted as "Hear O Israel, our God is YHWH, YHWH alone."[63] Admittedly this interpretation goes against the grain of longstanding tradition, but in context this is the correct interpretation, for as R. W. L. Moberly rightly affirms, "what 'YHWH is one' means must be something that makes appropriate the total and unreserved 'love' that is immediately specified" in Deut 6:5;[64] that is, covenant commitment with one's whole heart, person, and substance. Surely this involves having only YHWH as one's God. Indeed, in Deuteronomy Moses treats this as הַמִּצְוָה, "the commandment" *par excellence*, and he labels spiritual apostasy and/or the division of allegiance with other gods "the [supreme] evil" (הָרַע) in the eyes of YHWH (cf. 4:25; 13:6[Eng 5]).[65]

In Deut 4:24–27 and 11:16–18 Moses spells out the consequences of violating this prohibition in principle, and in his recitation of the covenant curses in chapter 28, he develops this theme in great detail. In short, if the Israelites will behave like the Canaanites and go after other gods, rejecting the one who had rescued them from Egypt, then YHWH will treat them like the Canaanites (7:25–26; 8:19–20). Whereas these texts all highlight YHWH's personal expression of fury in the face of Israelite idolatry, in Deuteronomy 13 Moses

---

62. The prohibition is reiterated repeatedly in the Sinaitic revelation and Mosaic preaching: Exod 20:23; 34:11–17; Lev 19:4; 26:1; Deut 4:15–24; 25–31; 6:14–15; 7:3–5; 13:1–19 [Eng 12:32—13:18]; 16:21–22; 27:15.

63. For detailed discussion of the Shema' and a defense of this translation, see my essay, "How Many is God?" 73–97.

64. "Toward an Interpretation of the Shema," 132–33, modifying the position taken in an earlier essay ("Yahweh is One," 209–15).

65. The article on רַע suggests a particular kind of evil, in this instance violation of the first principle of covenant relationship: no other gods and no physical representations of God. This formula will be picked up and repeated seven times in the book of Judges, "The sons of Israel did 'the evil' in the eyes of YHWH" (2:11; 3:7; 12; 4:1; 6:1; 10:6; 13:1).

places the responsibility squarely on the community for maintaining exclusive devotion to YHWH by all the members. If a prophet, or a member of one's own family, or any scoundrel (אֲנָשִׁים בְּנֵי־בְלִיַּעַל, v. 13) attempts to entice any Israelite to worship other gods, both leaders and followers in the crime shall be executed.

The prophets follow in the tradition of Deuteronomy, denouncing with the strongest language the veneration of deities other than YHWH. Idolatrous practices are treated as spiritual harlotry,[66] an abomination,[67] detestable,[68] foolishness,[69] and utterly disgusting.[70] According to the orthodox Yahwists, the God of Israel would brook no rivals.[71] In this respect the Old Testament's view of Israel's relationship to its patron deity differed fundamentally from the perceptions of all other surrounding nations.

The orthodox Yahwism of the Old Testament is unequivocal in its prohibition of Israelites worshiping any other gods besides, in addition to, or in place of YHWH. But what stance does the Old Testament take on the worship of other gods by outsiders? A related issue addresses the openness of YHWH to the acceptance of other gods for other nations. Does the Old Testament contemplate two ways to relationship with God, one way for the Israelites and another way for non-Israelites?

---

66. Judg 2:17; 8:27, 33, and many more. Cf. BDB 275–76.

67. תּוֹעֵבָה, Deut 13:15 [Eng 14], and many more. Cf. BDB 1072–73. On the expression, see Gerstenberger, "תועב *tʻb*, pi. to abhor," 1428–31 (English translation of *THAT* 2:1051–55).

68. שִׁקּוּץ, Deut 29:16 [Eng 17], etc. Cf. BDB 1054–55; Grisanti, "שקוץ," 243–46.

69. Note the satirical attacks of the prophets in Isa 40:18–20; 41:6–7; 44:9–20; 46:1–2; Jer 10:1–10. Cf. also Ps 115:1–8. See further below.

70. גִּלּוּלִים, Ezek 8:10 + 37 times in Ezekiel. Cf. BDB 165, "dungy things;" *HALOT* 1:192, "droppings." This seems to have been an artificially created word derived from the root גלל, "to roll," to which was added the vowels of שִׁקּוּצִים. Cf. Preuss, "גִּלּוּלִים *gillulim*," 1–5. Ezekiel's adoption of this expression for idolatry may have been prompted by the pellet like shape and size of sheep feces. One can hardly imagine a more caustic remark about idolatry. Cf. Block, *Book of Ezekiel Chapters 1–24*, 226.

71. On the issue of monotheism in Israel, see Albright, *YHWH and the Gods of Canaan*, 153–64; idem, *From Stone Age to Christianity*, 257–72; Baly, "The Geography of Monotheism," 253–78; Ringgren, "Monotheism," 602–4; Stolz, "Monotheismus in Israel," 163–74; Smith, *The Early History of God*, 147–57; Albertz, *A History of Israelite Religion* 1:82–91, 146–56.

There is no doubt that characters in the narratives of the Old Testament accepted a more open stance. While Jephthah may have gotten his facts wrong, according to his response to the Ammonites in Judg 11:24, he seems to have recognized the actual involvement of Chemosh (*sic*) in Ammonite affairs, as on par with YHWH's activity in Israel's: "Should you not possess what your god Chemosh gives you to possess? And should we not be the ones to possess everything that YHWH our God has conquered for our benefit?" It should be remembered, however, that Jephthah embodies all that is wrong with Israel at this time. With his self-interested perspective on his own office and in particular his sacrificing of his daughter in fulfillment of a stupid vow to secure the favor of YHWH, Jephthah's syncretism is typical of the recidivist Israelites in the dark days of the judges. Consider, too, David's response to Saul in 1 Sam 26:19, when he tells him to "Go, serve other gods." Surely David's faith and religious commitment at this point are impeccable. However, the problem evaporates when it is recognized that David is quoting cursed men who have been trying to drive him away from YHWH.

Aside from the way characters in the narratives treat other religious commitments, the Old Testament seems to reflect on this issue at several levels. At the literary level, prophets and poets refer freely to the Moabites as the people of Chemosh (Num 21:29; Jer 48:46), and the Ammonites as the people of Milkom (Jer 49:1), and of these and other gods as active participants in the affairs of their respective peoples.[72] However, these references are recognized as poetic and exploiting rhetorical license, for the same prophets who speak of other gods this way explicitly deny their objective reality, as in Jeremiah's sarcastic comment in 2:11: "Has a nation ever changed its gods (even though they are not gods)? But my people have exchanged my glory for 'The Useless One.'"[73] In fact, Jeremiah goes beyond sarcasm and

---

72. In Jer 49:1, YHWH himself asks, "Why has Milkom dispossessed Gad, and his people settled in its cities?" Cf. also 49:3, where Jeremiah predicts that "Milkom shall go into exile, along with his priests and his officials." In 48:7 he makes a similar comment about Chemosh. Elsewhere Jeremiah speaks of Bel being put to shame and Merodach (i.e., Marduk) being dismayed (50:2), and of YHWH punishing Bel in Babylon as if he were a real entity (51:44). In a similar vein Isaiah speaks of Bel bowing down and Nebo (i.e., Nabu) stooping, and their images being carried off (Isa 46:1).

73. Treating בְּלוֹא יוֹעִיל as a proper name, a play on the name *Baal*, with Thompson, *The Book of Jeremiah*, 166, 170. The reading "my glory" follows the note

speaks of idolatry as a crime for which the nations will experience the sword (50:35–40; cf. 12:14–17).

But how are we to understand Moses' declaration in Deut 4:19: "And when you look up to the heavens and see the sun, the moon, and the stars, all the host of heaven, do not be seduced and bow down to them and serve them, objects that YHWH your God has allotted to all the peoples everywhere under heaven." Most of this verse is clear and sensible in the present context. Having warned his people not to attempt to reduce YHWH to physical definition (after all, he had not revealed himself in any form, vv. 15–18), in verse 19a Moses cautions against a second kind of twisted religious thinking: turning to the sun and moon and stars as if they were representations of YHWH or divinities in their own right, thereby rejecting not only YHWH, their redeemer, but also YHWH's definition of himself (cf. Job 31:24–28). But the last clause is arguably the most difficult theologically in the entire book of Deuteronomy, especially in the light of Moses' later absolute rejection of the existence of any other gods besides YHWH (Deut 4:35, 39). How is his statement—the sun, the moon, the stars, and all the other heavenly objects that have been allotted to all the peoples under the whole heaven—to be understood? Did YHWH really allot (חָלַק) these to the other nations as objects of worship, while reserving himself for Israel's worship?[74]

Interpreting this verse within a henotheistic framework, most critical scholars answer the question in the affirmative. Moshe

---

in *BHS* indicating the third masculine suffix in place of the first common suffix as a case of *Tiqqun Sopherim*. On Isaiah's parodies on idolatry in 44:6–20, see below. Cf. Jer 2:9–13; 5:7; 16:20; also Hos 8:6; Ps 96:5 (= 1 Chr 16:26). Critical scholars generally dismiss these categorical rejections of the existence of other gods as late insertions deriving from a later stage in the evolution of Israelite monotheistic thinking. For a recent discussion of this issue, see Barr, *The Concept of Biblical Theology*, 85–99. However, this conclusion is possible only if one dates Deuteronomy as a whole to a late pre-exilic period and the hortatory sections of chapters 4 and 10 to the post-exilic period, a procedure that relies on suspiciously circular argumentation.

74. In 32:8–9 Moses sings of Elyon allocating (נחל in hiphil) the grants of land to the nations; at that time he divided the human population on the basis of the number of בְּנֵי אֱלִים available to function as intermediary patrons on his behalf (following LXX and a Qumran fragment (4QDeutʲ); see my discussion in *Gods of the Nations*, 25–32). But YHWH reserved Israel for a direct relationship with himself as his חֵלֶק, "allotment," and his נַחֲלָה, "reserved property." The verb חָלַק is used elsewhere of apportioning the land of Canaan among the tribes of Israel (Josh 14:1; 18:2) or distributing the spoils of their enemies (Josh 22:8).

Weinfeld's comment is typical of many: "The heavenly bodies as objects of worship were assigned to the nations by God himself. The stars were considered divine beings."[75] This interpretation may be questioned, however, on several counts. First, and most obvious, it is impossible to square with Moses' own unequivocal denial of the existence of any other gods (vv. 35, 39). Second, this interpretation flies in the face of the Old Testament's consistent antipathy toward idols of any kind. Third, this interpretation reads too much into this verse. The last clause translates simply, "and you serve what YHWH assigned to all the peoples under the whole heaven."[76] While Moses clearly affirms YHWH's role in allocating the hosts of heaven to all the peoples under the whole heaven, the assumed purpose, "as objects of worship," must be supplied from outside. The text is in fact silent on the purpose for the allotment. Fourth, this interpretation excludes Israel from "all the peoples under the whole heaven," and assumes this nation has no relationship to (let alone dependence upon) the heavenly bodies. Fifth, this interpretation misses the links between this passage and the account of creation in Genesis 1. Having borrowed the categories of creatures listed in vv. 17–18 from Gen 1:20–23—which are the products of days five and six of creation—with his references to the heavenly bodies Moses appears to be backing up to day four, which involved the creation of these objects. His comment that they were apportioned "to all the peoples under the whole heaven" represents a legitimate interpretation of Gen 1:14–19. These objects were created and placed in the sky not as objects to be worshiped but as instruments of divine providence, governing (מָשַׁל) the world, and guaranteeing the annual rhythm of

---

75. Weinfeld, *Deuteronomy 1–11*, 206. Tigay explains the issue as follows: "The view of polytheism reflects the assumption that if the rest of mankind does not worship the true God, that must be God's will. For this reason it is no sin for other nations to worship idols and the heavenly bodies; it is considered sinful only when done by Israel, to whom God revealed Himself and forbade the worship of these objects" (*Deuteronomy*, 435). This compares with Driver's comment: "The God of Israel is supreme: He assigns to every nation its objects of worship; and the veneration of the heavenly bodies by the nations (other than Israel) forms part of His providential order of the world. Natural religion, though it may become depraved (Rom 1:21ff.), is a witness to some of the deepest needs and instincts of humanity: in default of a purer and higher faith, the yearnings of mankind after a power higher than themselves find legitimate satisfaction in it" (*Deuteronomy*, 70–71).

76. So also Wright, *Deuteronomy*, 52.

life for the sake of its inhabitants. In other words, by means of these objects YHWH exercised general providential care over all the peoples. Sixth, this interpretation sidetracks the primary agenda of this passage, which is to highlight Israel's special covenant relationship with God. As the following verse indicates, and verses 32–40 will develop in detail, only Israel is the special object of YHWH's redemptive action. For Israel to cast YHWH in physical form is blasphemous because it inevitably underestimates the infinite nature of divinity and in any case rejects YHWH's own self-definition (vv. 15–18). For Israel to worship the sun, moon and stars in place of YHWH is blasphemous because it rejects his gracious actions on her behalf (v. 20). While God exercises his general providential care over all peoples through these intermediaries, only Israel has been singled out for a specific and special covenant relationship with himself. The first principle of covenant relationship calls for a direct response to the preamble of the covenant document: "I am YHWH your God who brought you out of the land of Egypt, out of the house of slavery" (Exod 20:2; Deut 5:6).

3. Hostile Actions against Idols and Idolaters

The historical narratives of the Old Testament include several accounts in which the preceding prohibitions were actually enforced. It is evident from these accounts that the danger of spiritual recidivism haunted the Israelites from their birth as a nation until their final demise in 586 BCE. Despite YHWH's dramatic revelation of his power and his person in the deliverance of Israel from Egypt, and his verbal revelation at Sinai, and despite their threefold declaration in Exodus 19 and 24 of fidelity to YHWH and his covenant, within a matter of days they apostatized, creating for themselves a golden calf and celebrating its role in their deliverance. Moses' response was decisive: "He took the calf that they had made, burned it with fire, ground it to powder, scattered it on the water, and made the Israelites drink it" (Exod 32:20). He then ordered those who had participated in the rebellion to be executed by sword, resulting in the deaths of about three thousand people (v. 28).

In Judg 6:25–27 we find a description of Gideon's demolition of the altar of Baal and the Asherah in his father's backyard. It is ironic that when the perpetrator of this act was exposed, the townsfolk demanded that he be killed, which was precisely the punishment the Torah had prescribed for those who might promote idolatry in Israel (Deut 13). This prescription undoubtedly underlies Elijah's treatment of the altar of Baal and its prophets at Mount Carmel. After YHWH's dramatic demonstration of his superiority over Baal, at Elijah's order the prophets of Baal were seized and dragged to the Wadi Kishon and killed (1 Kgs 18:40). Following his anointing by Elisha, Jehu engaged in a purge of Baalism in the northern kingdom of Israel, slaughtering all of Baal's followers, whom he had deceitfully invited to a celebration at a Baalistic shrine, burning the idolatrous images and turning the temple of Baal into a latrine (2 Kgs 10:18–28). More than a century later, as part of Hezekiah's reforms in Judah he demolished the pagan shrines, tearing down the מַצֵּבֹת (phallic symbols of Baal), and cutting down the Asherah (wooden symbols of the fertility goddess). Apparently because the people were treating the bronze serpent that Moses had made centuries earlier (Num 21:8–9) as an idolatrous relic, Hezekiah even had this reminder of YHWH's past grace destroyed (2 Kgs 18:1–5; cf. 2 Chr 31:1).

At the end of the seventh century BCE Josiah's religious reforms seem to have been even more thorough than those of Hezekiah almost a hundred years earlier (2 Kgs 23:1–25; cf. 2 Chr 34:33). Extending his purge into what had formerly been the northern kingdom, he eradicated the idolatrous priests, desecrated the pagan and syncretistic cult sites, and demolished the cult images and other appurtenances. His treatment of the latter recalls Moses' actions with respect to the golden calf: combustible items (like the Asherah) he burned outside the city near the garbage dump (the Kidron), and incombustible items (like the sacred pillars of Baal) he smashed. The remains of both he ground to dust and desecrated by carrying them off to Bethel (2 Kgs 23:4), scattering them over the graves of the common people (v. 6), or throwing them into the Kidron brook (v. 12). The sacred sites themselves he desecrated by replacing the cult images with the bones of the victims of his purge (v. 14). But it was too little and too late. YHWH had already sealed the fate of the city, and in 586 BCE his agents, the Babylonians, performed the ultimate purge by destroying the Temple, razing Jerusalem, and either slaughtering or deporting the population. The covenant curses for persistent rebellion expressed in going after other gods were fulfilled.

4. Polemical Portrayals of Idols and Idolaters

The narratives of the Old Testament contain many subtle attacks on pagan beliefs. Almost thirty years ago Gerhard Hasel argued convincingly that the account of creation in Gen 1:1—2:4a deliberately challenges pagan perceptions of God and the nature of the cosmos.[77] But this polemic is not restricted to the Genesis 1 account. The Old Testament understanding of creation generally makes a decisive break with typical ancient Near Eastern creation theology. Concerning this matter E. W. Nicholson asserts, "God is not continuous with his creation, does not permeate it, is not to be identified with, or represented by, anything within it, but stands outside his creation confronting it with his righteous will."[78]

Anti-pagan/idolatrous polemics are also recognized in Gen 31:30–35—the comical episode of Laban looking for his stolen gods/ household idols (אֱלֹהִים/תְּרָפִים). Here, the narrator spoofs not only Laban's powerlessness vis-à-vis Jacob, but also the gods' powerlessness to defend themselves against theft in the first instance and ritual contamination in the second; Rachel is sitting on them while having her menstrual period. The impotence of Baal is surely an important motif in the account of Gideon's destruction of Baal in Judg 6:25–32. Joash's comment in defense of his son, "If Baal is a god let him defend himself because someone has torn down his altar" (v. 31), represents a damning admission that the idolatrous cult he has been sponsoring in his own backyard is precisely what the designations for idols listed above had declared—a vain and empty lie.

Elijah's contest with the prophets of Baal on Mount Carmel as described in 1 Kings 18 represents the most striking and caustic attack on idolatry in all the historiographic writings. The point of Elijah's victory over the pagan prophets was to demonstrate YHWH's supremacy over the gods of Canaan. However, Elijah takes advantage of the occasion to mock the prophets of Baal and their futile confidence in their god. Many have recognized his taunt of the prophets in verse 27 to be laced with Canaanite mythological coloring, now familiar to all who have read the religious texts from Ugarit. In the face of Baal's silence the fearless prophet of YHWH challenges the

---

77. Hasel, "The Polemic Nature of the Genesis Cosmology," 81–102; cf. Heidel, *The Babylonian Genesis*, 91, *passim*.

78. Nicholson, *God and His People*, 207–8.

prophets of Baal to cry louder, for Baal is a god, and as such he does not respond to casual entreaties. His devotees must be serious in seeking his attention, for, like ordinary mortals, Baal is often preoccupied: either he is defecating/urinating (שִׂיחַ and שִׂיג לוֹ), or he is on a journey (דֶּרֶךְ לוֹ), or he is asleep (יָשֵׁן).[79] That Elijah's scurrilous derision of his opposition betrays thorough knowledge of Baal mythology has become evident from the mythological texts discovered at Ras Shamra/Ugarit. These and other examples suggest that biblical narrators took great delight in exposing the futility and stupidity of idolatry through satire and parody.[80]

In the latter prophets this strategy is employed with even greater force. The rhetorical tradition may be traced back to Moses, who dismisses foreign gods as "the work of human hands, objects of wood and stone that neither see nor eat nor smell" (Deut 4:28). Their unresponsiveness contrasts sharply with YHWH's personal unprecedented and unparalleled deliverance of Israel from Egypt, thereby demonstrating that he alone is God in heaven above and on earth below; there is no other (4:31–40). Later prophets display a particular penchant for satirizing the manufacture and care of idols. We witness this in Hosea (8:4–6; 13:2–3), Micah (5:12–13), Habakkuk (2:18–19), Jeremiah (10:1–6), and Zephaniah (2:10–11).[81] No one, however, satirizes idolatry more effectively than Isaiah, whose utterances become increasingly pointed in 40:19–20; 41:5–14; and 44:6–20.

In the light of recent research on the manufacture of cult images in Mesopotamia by Michael Dick and Christopher Walker these texts take on much greater significance than when they are interpreted in cultural isolation.[82] Because earthly and godly artisans produced the

---

79. שִׂיחַ and שִׂיג לוֹ apparently function as a hendiadys, that is, the use of two words to express a single idea. Our interpretation is supported by Rendsburg, "The Mock of Baal in 1 Kgs 18:27," 414–17. For another interpretation, see Preuss, *Die Verspottung fremder Religionen im Alten Testament*, 86.

80. See further Exod 32:1–6, 21–24; Judges 17–18; 1 Sam 5:1–5; 1 Kgs 12:25—13:6; 2 Kgs 5:15–19. Leah Bronner has argued convincingly that the entire Elijah-Elisha cycle of narratives is driven by an anti-Baalistic polemic. See *The Stories of Elijah and Elisha as Polemics against Baal Worship*.

81. Zephaniah 2:10–11 speaks of starving all the gods of the earth, on which, see Rudman, "When Gods Go Hungry," 37–39.

82. See Walker and Dick, "The Induction of the Cult Image in Ancient Mesopotamia," 55–121. For a more popular presentation, see Dick, "Worshiping Idols," 30–37.

cult statue, the creation of a god represented a supremely synergic act between heavenly and earthly "hands." The procedure whereby an ordinary piece of wood or stone was transformed into a legitimate object of worship animated by the spirit of the god whom it represented was complex and various, but the process in general may be summarized as follows:

1. The artisans who were to create the cult statue were carefully chosen and subjected to purification rituals that prepared them to enter the *bīt mummi*, the temple workshop, where statues and ornaments of the gods and other sacred objects used in temple worship were made and animated or restored and reanimated.

2. Using the materials available (wood, stone, clay), the artisans crafted the image.

3. Based upon the calendar and special rites of divination "a propitious day in a favorable month" was chosen for the "birth of the god."

4. By special incantations and a ritual known either as *pit pî* ("the opening of the mouth") or *mīs pî* ("the washing of the mouth") the god was "born," that is, transformed from a merely physical object into an animated representative of the deity. In one attested instance the statue was brought to an orchard next to a canal. It was purified with holy water from a sacred basin, and its mouth was opened/washed four times with honey, ghee (specially prepared soap), cedar, and cypress.[83] Without this ritual the statue remains the dead product of human hands, incapable of smelling incense, drinking water, or eating food (all provided by the devotees and priests), let alone hearing the pleas and praise of a supplicant or speaking a word of reassurance or hope.

83. This part of the ritual apparently alludes to the actions of a midwife who cleans and opens the breathing passage of a newborn at birth. This enables the spirit of the god, whom it represents to enter the statue and animate it. Therefore the cult image was ultimately not the product of a human craftsman but was "born of the gods." This interpretation is reinforced by the perceived role of the birth goddess, Belet-ili and her brick (a structure on which a woman lay/sat for her labor [cf. Exod 1:16]). By this process of "theogony" ("birth of a god") the new god becomes the child of the Mother Goddess.

5. Special rituals were performed to dissociate the cult images from the human hands that made them and reinforce the conviction that they were actually the products of divine creation. While they were swearing that not they but the craft-deities had made the image, the artisans' hands were cut off with a tamarisk sword. The tools used to make the image were wrapped in the carcass of a sheep that had been sacrificed and thrown into the river, thereby returning them to Nudimmud (Ea), the craft-god. Accordingly, despite being the work of human hands, the cult image was in fact perceived as "the work of the god."

6. The god could then be transported to and installed in the cella, the "holy of holies" of the temple constructed as its official residence.

7. Since the welfare of the people depended upon the happiness of the god, special priestly orders were appointed to take care of the material needs of the gods. Animal and vegetarian sacrifices were regarded as literal means of satisfying the gods' appetites and aromatic incense was waved in front of the statue's nose as a soothing aroma or narcotic. These were prepared in the temple kitchens and the food was eaten by the temple staff. The cult statue had to be constantly bathed, dressed in the finest garments, taken to bed in the god's ornately decorated bedchamber, and treated to festivities and entertainment, including music.

Although the specific customs involved in making gods will have varied from place to place, some such procedures lie behind Isaiah's scathing critique of idolatry. Following a powerful and poetic affirmation of YHWH's incomparability and unrivaled status as the only God, in 44:6–20 Isaiah provides his own colorful but realistic prose description of the process whereby idols are fabricated:

> All who make idols are nothing, and the things they delight in do not profit; their witnesses neither see nor know. And so they will be put to shame. Who would fashion a god or cast an image that can do no good? Look, all its devotees shall be put to shame; the artisans too are merely human. Let them all assemble, let them stand up; they shall be terrified, they shall all be put to shame.

The ironsmith fashions it and works it over the coals, shaping it with hammers, and forging it with his strong arm; he becomes hungry and his strength fails, he drinks no water and is faint. The carpenter stretches a line, marks it out with a stylus, fashions it with planes, and marks it with a compass; he makes it in human form, with human beauty, to be set up in a shrine. He cuts down cedars or chooses a holm tree or an oak and lets it grow strong among the trees of the forest. He plants a cedar and the rain nourishes it. Then it can be used as fuel. Part of it he takes and warms himself; he kindles a fire and bakes bread. Then he makes a god and worships it, makes it a carved image and bows down before it. Half of it he burns in the fire; over this half he roasts meat, eats it and is satisfied. He also warms himself and says, "Ah, I am warm, I can feel the fire!" The rest of it he makes into a god, his idol, bows down to it and worships it; he prays to it and says, "Save me, for you are my god!"

They do not know, nor do they comprehend; for their eyes are shut, so that they cannot see, and their minds as well, so that they cannot understand. No one considers, nor is there knowledge or discernment to say, "Half of it I burned in the fire; I also baked bread on its coals, I roasted meat and have eaten. Now shall I make the rest of it an abomination? Shall I fall down before a block of wood?" He feeds on ashes; a deluded mind has led him astray, and he cannot save himself or say, "Is not this thing in my right hand a fraud?"

But such critiques of idolatry were not distinctive to prophets and historians. Similar dispositions are expressed by psalmists in Pss 113:1–8 and 135, especially verses 15–18. Even Job, a non-Israelite, recognized the worship of the sun, moon, and stars as incompatible with true devotion to God (Job 31:24–28).

Conclusion

It is appropriate to conclude by considering briefly one final question: If this was how orthodox Yahwists viewed the worship of other gods, how did they perceive the place of their own religion within the broader cultural environment? Specifically, how did they think non-Israelites' perceived their religion? One's immediate response is to cite the familiar references to Israel as a light to the nations in Isaiah:

I am YHWH, I have called you in righteousness, I have taken you by the hand and kept you; I have given you as a covenant to the people, a light to the nations to open the eyes that are blind, to bring out the prisoners from the dungeon, from the prison those who sit in darkness. I am YHWH, that is my name; my glory I give to no other, nor my praise to idols. (Isa 42:6–8)

He [YHWH] says, "It is too light a thing that you should be my servant to raise up the tribes of Jacob and to restore the survivors of Israel; I will give you as a light to the nations, that my salvation may reach to the end of the earth." Thus says YHWH, the Redeemer of Israel and his Holy One, to one deeply despised, abhorred by the nations, the slave of rulers, "Kings shall see and stand up, princes, and they shall prostrate themselves, because of YHWH, who is faithful, the Holy One of Israel, who has chosen you." (Isa 49:6–7)

But Isaiah was not the first to recognize the privilege the Israelites enjoyed in view of YHWH's gracious redemption, his gracious call to covenant relationship with himself, and his gracious revelation to them of a pattern of religious expression that would actually solve the problem of human alienation from god/the gods and make them the envy of the whole world. In the previous millennium, Moses had already reflected on the significance of their experience with YHWH. In Deut 4:5–8 he declared:

See, just as YHWH my God has charged me, I now teach you statutes and ordinances for you to observe in the land that you are about to enter and occupy. You must observe them diligently, for this will show your wisdom and discernment to the peoples, who, when they hear all these statutes, will say, "Surely this great nation is a wise and discerning people!" For what other great nation has a god so near to it as YHWH our God is whenever we call to him? And what other great nation has statutes and ordinances as just as this entire law that I am setting before you today?

It is difficult for American evangelicals—whose disposition toward the Old Testament tends to be determined by critical statements by Paul concerning the law taken out of context—to grasp the significance of this statement. Perhaps appeal to an ancient text, written in Sumerian and discovered in the library of Ashurbanipal, will help.

A Prayer to Every God[84]

May the fury of my lord's heart be quieted toward me.[85]
May the god who is not known be quieted toward me;
May the goddess who is not known be quieted toward me.
May the god whom I know or do not know be quieted toward me;
May the goddess whom I know or do not know
be quieted toward me.
May the heart of my god be quieted toward me;
May the heart of my goddess be quieted toward me.
May my god and goddess be quieted toward me.
May the god [who has become angry with me][86]
be quieted toward me;
May the goddess [who has become angry with me]
be quieted toward me. (10) (lines 11–18 cannot be restored
with certainty)
In ignorance I have eaten that forbidden of my god;
In ignorance I have set foot on that prohibited by my goddess.

84. Adapted from *ANET*, 391–92. Bibliography is provided. In the preamble to his translation, F. J. Stephens wrote,

> This prayer is addressed to no particular god, but to all gods in general, even those who may be unknown. The purpose of the prayer is to claim relief from suffering, which the writer understands is the result of some infraction of divine law. He bases his claim on the fact that his transgressions have been committed unwittingly, and that he does not even know what god he may have offended. Moreover, he claims, the whole human race is by nature ignorant of the divine will, and consequently is constantly committing sin. He therefore ought not to be singled out for punishment. The text is written in the Emesal dialect of Sumerian, furnished with an interlinear Akkadian translation. The colophon of the tablet indicates that it was part of a series of prayers' the next tablet of which began with the line "By his word he has commanded my well–being." The tablet comes from the library of Ashurbanipal, 668–633 BCE, and was copied from an older original. There are, however, numerous features of the Sumerian text that are characteristic of the late period, and it is probable that the original composition of the text is not much older than Ashurbanipal.

85. According to Stephens, "Literally the Sumerian says, 'of my lord, may his angry heart return to its place for me.'" The phrase "return to its place" is figurative language meaning "to settle down;" the imagery may be that of a raging storm or of the contents of a boiling kettle. The scribe indicates that each of the next nine lines ends with the same phrase, though he actually writes only the first word of the phrase after having written it once fully.

86. Stephens restores the line on the basis of line 32, after Langdon.

O Lord, my transgressions are many; great are my sins.

O my god, (my) transgressions are many; great are (my) sins.

O my goddess, (my) transgressions are many; great are (my) sins.

O god whom I know or do not know,

(my) transgressions are many; great are (my) sins;

O goddess whom I know or do not know,

(my) transgressions are many; great are (my) sins.

The transgression which I have committed, indeed I do not know;

The sin which I have done, indeed I do not know.

The forbidden thing which I have eaten, indeed I do not know;

The prohibited (place) on which I have set foot,

indeed I do not know.

The lord in the anger of his heart looked at me;

The god in the rage of his heart confronted me;

When the goddess was angry with me, she made me become ill.

The god whom I know or do not know has oppressed me;

The goddess whom I know or do not know

has placed suffering upon me.

Although I am constantly looking for help,

no one takes me by the hand;

When I weep they do not come to my side.

I utter laments, but no one hears me;

I am troubled; I am overwhelmed; I can not see.

O my god, merciful one, I address to thee the prayer,

"Ever incline to me;"

I kiss the feet of my goddess; I crawl before thee.

(lines 41–49 are mostly broken and cannot be restored with

certainty)

How long, O my goddess, whom I know or do not know,

ere thy hostile heart will be quieted?

Man is dumb; he knows nothing;

Mankind, everyone that exists,—what does he know?

Whether he is committing sin or doing good,

he does not even know.

O my lord, do not cast thy servant down;

He is plunged into the waters of a swamp; take him by the hand.

The sin which I have done, turn into goodness;

The transgression which I have committed, let the wind carry away;

My many misdeeds strip off like a garment.

O my god, (my) transgressions are seven times seven;

remove my transgressions;

O my goddess, (my) transgressions are seven times seven;

remove my transgressions;

O god whom I know or do not know,

> (my) transgressions are seven times seven;
> remove my transgressions;
> O goddess whom I know or do not know,
> (my) transgressions are seven times seven;
> remove my transgressions.
> Remove my transgressions (and) I will sing thy praise.
> May thy heart, like the heart of a real mother,
> be quieted toward me;
> Like a real mother (and) a real father may it be quieted toward me.

Is this not a pathetic piece? And what an indictment this prayer is on the religious systems of the world around ancient Israel! To be sure, with his keen sense of sin and his awareness of ultimate accountability before deity, this person expresses greater enlightenment than many in our own day. However, he is faced with three insurmountable problems: first, he does not know which god he has offended; second, he does not know what the offense is; and third, he does not know what it will take to satisfy the god/gods. It is against this backdrop that we must interpret Moses' statements in Deut 4:5–8. With their clear knowledge of the will of YHWH, the faithful in Israel perceived themselves as incredibly privileged and the envy of the nations. Unlike other peoples, whose gods of wood and stone crafted by human hands neither saw nor heard nor smelled (Deut 4:28; cf. Ps 135:15–17), YHWH hears his people when they call upon him (Deut 4:7). And unlike the nations, whose idols have mouths but they do not speak (Ps 135:16), Israel's God has spoken. By his grace he has given his people statutes and judgments that are perfect in righteousness (Deut 4:8), because: (1) they reveal with perfect clarity who he is; (2) they reveal with perfect clarity what sin is; and (3) they reveal with perfect clarity how that sin may be removed and a relationship of peace and confidence with him established. Why would anyone give up this sparkling spring of water that leads to life for the broken cisterns of idolatry that can only yield death (cf. Jer 2:9–13)? This is a question that the people of God must answer in every age. May the Lord deliver us from our idolatries,[87] and may we, the twenty-first-century people of God, delight in the revelation and life that God offers in Jesus Christ. And may we radiate this light to all who still languish in the darkness of their futile idolatries.

87. For an insightful series of analyses of contemporary evangelical idolatry, see Guinness and Seel, eds., *No God but God.*

8

No Other Gods

Bearing the Name of YHWH
in a Polytheistic World[1]

Introduction

IN AN EARLIER ESSAY, "Bearing the Name of the LORD with Honor,"[2] I addressed the meaning and significance of the second command of the Decalogue, "You shall not bear the name of YHWH your God in vain."[3] The goal of this study is to expand the horizons of that paper and ask several more wide-ranging questions: "What did it mean to bear the name of YHWH in the polytheistic world in which the Israelites found themselves?" and "What dimensions of the notion were in play for ancient Israel?" Although I shall consider adjunctively other texts of Scripture, my primary analysis will be based on the book of Deuteronomy.

---

1. This is an expanded version of a paper read to the Evangelical Theological Society in San Francisco, November 17, 2011. I am grateful to Carmen Imes, who read earlier drafts of this paper and offered many helpful suggestions for its improvement. However, any infelicities in argumentation and conclusions are my own responsibility.

2. Published in Block, *How I Love Your Torah, O Lord!*, 61–72.

3. Based on the numbering required by the discourse grammar of the document. See further Block, "You Shall Not Covet Your Neighbor's Wife," 472–74.

What Does It Mean to Bear a Name?

The naming of a child represents a significant moment in that person's life. Names identify people; they distinguish individuals from others in the same class and they serve as identity markers.[4] In Western societies one's identity is tied up in a combination of family name and given names. In 1993 I was in Moscow to teach the first class of the newly founded Moscow Theological Seminary of Evangelical Christians—Baptists. After reading off the list of nineteen tongue-twister names, one of the young scholars asked me how the students should address me. I replied, "You may call me Daniel, or Brother Block, or Professor, or Dr. Block." It was obvious immediately that this answer did not satisfy him. So the translator leaned over and said, "They want to know your father's name." So I said, "My father's name is Isaac, which also happens to be my middle name, and the name of every one of my twelve brothers, including number three, whose first name is Isaac." Then they knew what to call me. Immigrants from Russia, my parents had brought with them the honorable and helpful custom of making the first name of the father the second name of sons. So now, when I write my friends in Russia, I sign my name as Daniel Isaakovitch, which identifies me as Daniel, from the Isaac branch of Blocks.

But names do more than identify a person. When one person's name is attached to another person (as in the common custom of women assuming the last names of their husbands), they also indicate status or relationship. This is illustrated in the opening chapters of Daniel, where Nebuchadnezzar replaces the Jewish names of Daniel and his three friends with Babylonian names (Daniel > Belteshazzar; Hananiah > Shadrach; Mishael > Meshach; Azariah > Abed-nego).[5] In the ancient Near Eastern world, personal names often expressed the faith of parents (e.g., Jaazaniah, "May YHWH hear"), or their disposition at the birth of a child (cf. Leah's comment when she named Asher ["Fortunate"], "What fortune!" meaning, "Women will deem me fortunate" [Gen 30:13, NJPSV]). Some names told a story: בֶּן־אוֹנִי, "son of my sorrow" (Gen 35:18); בֶּן־עַמִּי, "son of my male relative" (Gen 19:38); מוֹאָב, "from [my own] father" (Gen 19:37). Names also

---

4. The neo-logism, "identity theft," reflects the heightened significance of this notion in the electronic age of the microchip.

5. On which see Berger, "Der Kyros-Kylinder mit dem Zusatzfragment," 219–34; Millard, "Daniel 1–6 and History," 67–73.

connoted ownership—especially when inscribed on an object (e.g., לצדק, "belonging to Zadok")[6] or branded on a person[7]—or authority, as in stamped documents or documents sealed with stamped bullae.[8] For a biblical book the size of Deuteronomy, personal names are remarkably infrequent,[9] while Israelite clan/tribal names,[10] national names and gentilics derived from these,[11] and geographic names,[12] are very common, as are divine names and epithets.[13]

6. Arad #97 and #93, respectively. For these and many other examples, see Dobbs-Allsopp, et al, *Hebrew Inscriptions*.

7. See Dandamaev, *Slavery in Babylonia*, 229–35.

8. See, for example, the collection in Avigad, *Hebrew Bullae from the Time of Jeremiah*.

9. By simple name: Aaron (4x), Abiram (11:6), Abraham (7x), Anak (9:2), Dathan (11:6), Eliab (11:6), Esau (6x), Isaac (7x), Jacob (7x + an additional 4 used as a national name; see n. 11), Lot (2:9, 19), Miriam (24:9), Moses (38x), Og (10x), Reuben (11:6), Sihon (11x); by patronymic: Balaam ben Beor (23:5, 6 [Eng 4, 5]), Caleb [ben Jephunneh] (1:36), Eleazar son of Aaron (10:6), Jair ben Manasseh (3:14), Joshua [ben Nun] (10x).

10. Asher (3x), Benjamin (2x), Dan (4x), Ephraim (2x), Gad/Gadites (7x), Issachar (2x), Joseph (3x), Judah (4x), Levi/Levites (27x), Machir (3:15), Manasseh/ Manassites (5x), Naphtali (4x), Reuben/Reubenites (6x, excluding 11:6), Simeon (27:12), Zebulun (3x). Several of these also function as geographic names, identifying territories named after the tribe descended from an eponymous ancestor. See note 11.

11. Amalek (25:17, 19), Ammon/Ammonite (7x), Aramaean (26:5), Amorite/ Amorites (15x), Anakites (6x [twice in 9:2]), Avvim (2:23), Canaanites (3x), Caphtorim (2:23), Edom/Edomite (23:8[Eng 7]), Egypt/Egyptian/Egyptians (51x), Emim (2:10–11), Geshurites (3:14), Girgashites (7:1), Hittites (7:1; 20:17), Hivites (7:1; 20:17), Horites (2:12, 22), Jacob (32:9; 33:4, 10, 28), Israel/Israelites (72x + Jeshurun, 32:15; 33:5, 26), Jebusite (7:1; 20:17), Maacathites (3:14), Moab/Moabite (13x, Perizzite (7:1; 20:17), Rephaim (5x), Sidonians (3:9), Zamzummites (2:20). Some of these also appear to function as territorial designations.

12. Tribal territory (Dan, 34:1; Naphtali, 34:2; Ephraim, 34:2; Manasseh, 34:2; Judah, 34:2); Canaan (32:49). Mountains/mountain regions (Abarim, Ebal, Gerizim, Hermon, Hor, Horeb, Nebo, Paran, Pisgah, Seir, Sinai, Sion, Sirion), rivers/wadis (Arnon, Eshcol, Euphrates, Jabbok, Jordan, Zered, Euphrates, Jabbok), seas (Chinnereth, Red, Salt, Western), regions (Ar, Arabah, Argob, Bashan, Gilead, Hormah, Kedemoth, Lebanon, Mesopotamia [Aram Naharaim], Negeb, Suph, Zin), places (Admah, Aroer, Ashtaroth, Baal-peor/Beth Peor, Beeroth Bene-jakin, Bezer, Dizahab, Edrei, Elath, Ezion-geber, Gaza, Gilgal, Golan, Gomorrah, Gudgodah, Havvoth-jair, Hazeroth, Heshbon, Jahaz, Jericho, Jotbathah, Kadesh-barnea, Kibroth Hataavah, Laban, Massah, Meribah Kadesh, Moserah, Oaks of Moreh, Pethor, Rabbah, Ramoth, Salecah, Sodom, Taberah, Tophel, Zeboiim, Zoar).

13. YHWH (540+), Rock (Deut 32:4, 15, 18, 30, 31), [Hā] ʾēl (3:24; 4:24, 31; 5:9; 6:15; 7:9, 21; 10:17; 32:4, 18; 33:26); Baal (4:3); Asherah/Asherim (7:5; 12:3;

The Hebrew Scriptures express the process of naming with several different expressions. Often it involves the verb קָרָא, "to call, name," usually either קָרָא שֵׁם ("to call a name") + accusative (PN/GN),[14] or קָרָא לְ/אֶל ("to call [with reference to]") + PN,[15] though sometimes elliptically, without specifying שֵׁם, "name."[16] Occasionally it involves the verbs, שִׂים, "to set, place": שִׂים שֵׁם ("to set a name") + accusative (PN);[17] or שִׂים לְ שֵׁם ("to set [with reference to] a name") + accusative (PN),[18] or in the case of renaming, שִׂים לְ + PN + accusative (PN).[19] Entities may also be named simply by declarations involving

---

16:21, though here the name of the divinity is applied to a cult object representing the goddess). To this list we could add Elohim, which functions as a proper noun referring to YHWH ca. 360 times. "Lord" is not a name, either in Hebrew or English, but a title (3:24; 9:26).

14. E.g., Gen 3:20, וַיִּקְרָא הָאָדָם שֵׁם אִשְׁתּוֹ חַוָּה, "and the man called the name of his wife Eve." Cf. 4:25 (Seth); 17:5 (Abram). For a geographic name, see Gen 11:9 (Babel); Exod 15:23 (Marah). Cf. also the naming of the manna in Exod 16:31.

15. E.g., Deut 2:11, וְהָעֲמֹנִים יִקְרְאוּ לָהֶם אֵמִים, "but the Moabites call them Emim"; 2:20, וְהָעַמֹּנִים יִקְרְאוּ לָהֶם זַמְזֻמִּים, "but the Ammonites call them Zamzummim"; 3:9, וְהָאֱמֹרִי יִקְרְאוּ־לוֹ שְׂנִיר, "The Sidonians call Hermon Siryon, and the Amorites call it Senir." Cf. Gen 1:8, וַיִּקְרָא אֱלֹהִים לָרָקִיעַ שָׁמָיִם, "and God called the firmament sky/heaven."

16. E.g., Gen 26:33, וַיִּקְרָא אֹתָהּ שִׁבְעָה, "and he called it Shibah"; Deut 3:14, אֶת־הַבָּשָׁן חַוֹּת יָאִיר ... וַיִּקְרָא אֹתָם "And he called them—that is Bashan—Havvoth-Yair."

17. E.g., Judg 8:31, וַיָּשֶׂם אֶת־שְׁמוֹ אֲבִימֶלֶךְ, "and he set his name [as] Abimelech"; 2 Kgs 17:34, יַעֲקֹב אֲשֶׁר־שָׂם שְׁמוֹ יִשְׂרָאֵל, "Jacob, whose name he set [as] Israel"; Neh 9:7, וְשַׂמְתָּ שְׁמוֹ אַבְרָהָם, "and you set his name [as] Abraham."

18. E.g., Dan 1:7, וַיָּשֶׂם לָהֶם שַׂר הַסָּרִיסִים שֵׁמוֹת, "and the chief of the eunuchs set for them names."

19. E.g., Dan 1:7, וַיָּשֶׂם לְדָנִיֵּאל בֵּלְטְשַׁאצַּר וְלַחֲנַנְיָה שַׁדְרַךְ וּלְמִישָׁאֵל מֵישַׁךְ וְלַעֲזַרְיָה עֲבֵד נְגוֹ, "and he set for Daniel Belteshazzar, and for Hananiah Shadrach, and for Mishael Meshach, and for Azariah Abednego." Renaming is also described as "changing" (הֵסֵב) someone's name (2 Kgs 23:34; 2 Kgs 24:17). Although the names do not apply to individuals, Deuteronomy also knows of entities bearing more than one name. Among people groups that have more than one name, Deuteronomy notes that those whom Israelites call Anakim, Moabites call Emim (2:11), and those whom they call Rephaim, Ammonites call Zamzummim (2:20)—but neither case involves the name of a deity. They simply show that different people often have different names for the same entity. Deuteronomy also knows of renaming. In 25:10, Moses speaks of renaming the household of a man who refuses to perform the duties of a levir for a deceased brother: וְנִקְרָא שְׁמוֹ בְּיִשְׂרָאֵל בֵּית חֲלוּץ הַנָּעַל, "In Israel his name shall be called 'The house of him whose sandal was pulled off.'" This obviously has nothing to do bearing a divine name, unless, of course, we recognize that the man's behavior reflects badly on the name of YHWH whose name the Israelite bears (cf. 5:11).

הָיָה שֵׁם + PN, "a [person's] name shall be PN,"[20] or PN + שֵׁם ("name") + suffix.[21] However, our concern in this project is not the practice of naming generally, but cases where a person or place bears someone else's name—especially the name of a deity—and thereby reflects the namer's claim to that person or place that is named.[22]

Bearing the Divine Name: The Personal Dimension

Clear examples of persons identified by name with a deity are hard to find in the Hebrew Bible. To be sure, a high proportion of names involve deities' names, and thereby express faith in a deity. However, this is not the same as calling a person by the name of the deity. Outside ancient Israel's borders sentence or construct-phrase names involving the names of deities were often abbreviated by dropping the theophorous, nominal, or verbal elements. When nominal or verbal elements drop from theophoric names (names that include the name of a deity), what remains is a divine name used as a personal name, but this is not to say the person is identified as a god.[23]

Hypocoristic personal names like בַּעַל/בַּעֲלִי, *Ba'al/Ba'ali*, and אָדוֹן/אֲדֹנִי, *'Adon/'Adoni* and YHWH are missing in the Hebrew Bible,[24]

20. E.g., Gen 17:5, וְהָיָה שִׁמְךָ אַבְרָהָם, "And your name shall be Abraham" (which is equivalent to "I set your name [as] Abraham," cf. Neh 9:7).

21. E.g., Gen 17:15, שָׂרָה שְׁמָהּ, "Sarah is her name."

22. Our study excludes patronymic identifications (X בֶּן Y, "X son of Y"; note 8 above), or tribal or national names derived from eponymous ancestors. Naming another person in and of itself reflects the namer's authority over the named, whether it be a child named by parents, servants renamed by masters (e.g., the Babylonian renaming of Daniel and his compatriots, Dan. 1:7), or vassal kings renamed by their overlords (e.g., Eliakim renamed Jehoiakim by Necho of Egypt [2 Kgs 23:34]; Mattaniah renamed Zedekiah by Nebuchadnezzar [2 Kgs 24:17]).

23. Phoenician inscriptions refer to individuals named אדא ('Ada'? for 'Adad or 'Adon, cf. the full form אדנבעל ('Adanba'al) אשמן ('Eshmun, cf. the full form אשמנעזר, 'Eshmunazar, and אשמניתן, 'Eshmunyatan, בעלי (Ba'lay?, see *PNPPI*, 94; corresponding forms occur in Amorite (*bá-ah-li*, *APNM*, 174; cf. Hos 2:18[Eng 16]), Ugarit (*b'ly*, *ba'aliya*, *PTU* 116, 117), Amarna tablets (*bá-a-lu-ia*, Hess, *APN*, 49); מלקרת (Melqart, cf. the full forms בדמלקרת and עבדמלקרת, etc., on which, see *PNPPI*, 233–35. Note also Esarhaddon's treaty with Ba'lu, king of Tyre (*ANET*, 533–34), and Βααλ, a Tyrian king, in Josephus, *Ap*. 1.156. Examples of theophoric hyporisticons in Aramaic inscriptions include אדן ('Adon, *KAI* 266:1; cf. Hebrew אֲדֹנִיָּה, 'Adonijah); חור (Horus, *KAI* 267:1).

24. Cf. David's son (2 Sam 3:4; 1 Kgs 1:8-2:24), who bore the name, אֲדֹנִיָּה, Adonijah, "YHWH is Lord," and בְּעַלְיָה, Be'aliah, "YHWH is Lord," among his personal troops (1 Chr 12:6[ET 5]).

but בעלי (Ba'ali/Ba'alay) and בעלא (Ba'ala') have surfaced in inscriptional materials from Beth Shan and Samaria respectively.[25] Since these are dated to the waning decades of the northern kingdom of Israel (eighth century BCE), they probably reflect the spiritual recidivism of the time. In the Hebrew Bible the best candidate for a person bearing a divine name as his personal name is Samson. The name שִׁמְשׁוֹן consists of the Hebrew/Canaanite word for sun, שֶׁמֶשׁ + the diminutive ending וֹן-, hence, "Little Sun." Many features in the narratives of Judges 13–16,[26] as well as the geographic location of these events suggest a link with the solar cult. Born in Zorah and growing up in Mahaneh-Dan, between Zorah and Eshtaol, Samson lived up the Sorek valley within a few miles of Beth Shemesh, once the focal point of sun worship.[27]

While names like *Ba'ali* and *Ba'ala'* reflect the spiritual allegiances of those they identify, or more precisely the faith of their parents, they were probably abbreviations of sentence or construct-phrase names and did not rise to the level of names borne by a person as the mark of enslavement to a divine master, a custom widespread in the ancient world.[28] In this regard the marking of temple slaves in ancient Mesopotamia is especially interesting. Slaves of the Eanna temple in Uruk were branded on the wrist with the star of Ishtar; in Borsippa slaves belonging to Marduk and Nabu were branded on the wrists with images of the spade and reed stylus, the symbols of these gods respectively.[29] While ancient Mesopotamians may have taken slavery

---

25. On בעלי (Ba'lay?) at Beth Shan, see Dobbs-Allsopp, *Hebrew Inscriptions*, 145; on *b'l* in the Samaria Ostraca, see Ibid., 774 for references. To these we should add עם, "Paternal Uncle" on a vessel inscription from Khirbet el-Qom, Ibid., 417.

26. Cf. Block, *Judges, Ruth*, 417.

27. בֵּית־שֶׁמֶשׁ, "House of Shemesh"; cf. עִיר שֶׁמֶשׁ, "City of Shemesh," in Josh 19:41. On the archaeological record of Beth Shemesh, see Bunimovitz and Lederman, "Beth-Shemesh," 249–53. Beyond this, the closest onomastic hints of deities' claims on the lives of their devotees are found in epithetic expressions like A עֶבֶד B, "A servant of B" (e.g., 1 Sam 29:3; 1 Kgs 11:26; 2 Chr 13:6; though in no case does the servant assume the name of the superior), or names like Eshbaal (אֶשְׁבָּעַל, "Man of Baal," 1 Chr 8:33; 9:39), which so offended the Deuteronomistic historian that he consistently rendered it as Ishbosheth (אִישׁ־בֹּשֶׁת, "Man of Shame," 2 Sam 2:8, 10, 12, 15; 3:8, 14–15, 4:5, 8, 12).

28. The custom is attested in Egypt from the New Kingdom (sixteenth-eleventh century) to the fifth century BCE, as well as in Assyria and Babylonia. See Dandamaev, *Slavery in Babylonia*, 229–35.

29. Ibid., 488–89.

for granted generally, human beings who had been dedicated to a god were viewed as "belonging to the gods."[30]

The literal practice of branding humans is unattested in the Hebrew Bible, but ancient Israelites were familiar with the notion of inscriptions signifying objects as the property of an owner. Dozens of seals, bullae, and stamped pieces of pottery that contain *lamedh* + the personal name or title of the owner illustrate this function of the prefix.[31] It is also implied in several biblical texts. In Ezek 37:16 YHWH commands the prophetic priest to take two pieces of wood (sticks?) and inscribe (כָּתַב עַל) them respectively,

לִיהוּדָה	"Belonging to Judah
וְלִבְנֵי יִשְׂרָאֵל חֲבֵרוֹ	and to the sons of Israel associated with him."
לְיוֹסֵף עֵץ אֶפְרַיִם	"Belonging to Joseph the stick of Ephraim
וְכָל־בֵּית יִשְׂרָאֵל חֲבֵרוֹ	and the whole house of Israel associated with him"

Ancient Israelites will also have understood the notion of deities' claims to people being expressed by inscriptions of this kind. The exciting declaration of Israel's full spiritual renewal and the restoration of YHWH's covenant in Isa 44:5 consists of four parallel lines cast in an ABAB pattern:

זֶה יֹאמַר לַיהוָה אָנִי	This one will say, "I belong to YHWH,"
וְזֶה יִקְרָא בְשֵׁם־יַעֲקֹב	and this one will be called by the name of Jacob,
וְזֶה יִכְתֹּב יָדוֹ לַיהוָה	and this one will inscribe his hand, *lyhwh,*
וּבְשֵׁם יִשְׂרָאֵל יְכַנֶּה׃	and will claim the name "Israel."

At issue in this statement is YHWH's explicit claim to Israel as his covenant people, symbolized by the inscription of his name on their hands, like a brand on the hand of a slave.[32] An analogue to this practice is found in the official garments of Israel's high priest. On his body he bore (נָשָׂא) the names of the tribes of Israel, engraved on two black onyx stones and worn on his shoulder pieces (Exod 28:6–14), and apparently on twelve gemstones—representing the twelve tribes—fastened on his priestly pectoral (vv. 15–30), which

30. Black and Green, "Dedication," 62. That a deity's name tattooed on a body signifies consecration and ownership was argues long ago by Guillaume, "Is 44:5 in the Light of the Elephantine Papyri," 377–79.

31. See the lengthy list in Dobbs-Allsopp, *Hebrew Inscriptions*, 699–705.

32. See further, Block, "Bearing the Name of the LORD with Honor," 65.

he wore when he entered the presence of YHWH. The priest thereby identified with the tribes, representing them before YHWH and performing his duties on their behalf. However, on the front of the turban on his head he wore a pure gold medallion engraved like a seal (חֹתָם) with the inscription, קֹדֶשׁ לַיהוָה, which translates literally, "Holy. Belonging to YHWH" (vv. 36–38).[33] Deuteronomy adapts this phrase and uses it to mark Israel as YHWH's people: עַם קָדוֹשׁ אַתָּה לַיהוָה אֱלֹהֶיךָ, "You are a holy people, belonging to YHWH your God" (7:6; 14:1, 21; 26:18–19).[34] The linkage of Israel's status to that of the high priest is reinforced by the clarification that follows in almost identical style in 7:6 and 14:2 respectively:

בְּךָ בָּחַר יְהוָה אֱלֹהֶיךָ לִהְיוֹת לוֹ לְעַם סְגֻלָּה	You YHWH your God has chosen to become his own treasured people,
מִכֹּל הָעַמִּים אֲשֶׁר עַל־פְּנֵי הָאֲדָמָה	[chosen] from all the peoples who are on the surface of the earth.
וּבְךָ בָּחַר יְהוָה לִהְיוֹת לוֹ לְעַם סְגֻלָּה	And you YHWH has chosen to become his treasured people,
מִכֹּל הָעַמִּים אֲשֶׁר עַל־פְּנֵי הָאֲדָמָה	[chosen] from all the peoples who are on the surface of the earth.

Israel's status is declared in similar terms in 26:18–19:

וַיהוָה הֶאֱמִירְךָ הַיּוֹם	And you have had YHWH declare today
לִהְיוֹת לוֹ לְעַם סְגֻלָּה כַּאֲשֶׁר דִּבֶּר־לָךְ . . .	that you would be his treasured people, as he promised you . . .
וּלְתִתְּךָ עֶלְיוֹן עַל כָּל־הַגּוֹיִם אֲשֶׁר עָשָׂה	and that he would set you high over all the nations that he has made,
לִתְהִלָּה וּלְשֵׁם וּלְתִפְאָרֶת	for praise, for a name (שֵׁם), and for honor,
וְלִהְיֹתְךָ עַם־קָדֹשׁ	and that you would be a holy people,
לַיהוָה אֱלֹהֶיךָ כַּאֲשֶׁר דִּבֵּר	belonging to YHWH your God, as he has declared.[35]

---

33. On חֹתָם as a seal, marking ownership, authority, see Gen 38:18; 1 Kgs 21:8; Jer 22:24; Hag 2:23. The use of the *lamedh* of ownership is clear in Deut 10:14: "See, to YHWH your God belong the heavens and the highest heavens, the earth and everything in it" (הֵן לַיהוָה אֱלֹהֶיךָ הַשָּׁמַיִם וּשְׁמֵי הַשָּׁמָיִם הָאָרֶץ וְכָל־אֲשֶׁר־בָּהּ). On vowed/dedicated objects belonging to YHWH, see 15:19, and less explicitly 12:11 and 23:22 [Eng 21].

34. As in Isa 44:5, the *lamedh* before the divine name seems to function as a *lamedh inscriptionis*, which "introduces the exact wording of an inscription or title" (thus GKC §119u).

35. On this translation, see Block, *Deuteronomy*.

Several features of these statements deserve comment. First, the characterization of Israel as an עַם סְגֻלָּה, "a treasured people," involves a rare expression that occurs only eight times in the Hebrew Bible. Six of these employ the word סְגֻלָּה metaphorically of Israel (Exod 19:5; Deut 7:6; 14:2; 26:18; Mal 3:17; Ps 135:4). However, the key to its theological significance is found in the two texts where it bears its normal literal sense. In 1 Chr 29:3 and Eccl 2:8 סְגֻלָּה refers to valued possessions, especially the treasure of kings,[36] suggesting that to YHWH Israel was like a diamond, hand-picked and separated from ordinary rocks to be YHWH's crown jewel.[37] Second, the characterization of Israel as עַם קָדוֹשׁ, "a holy people," links these statements to Exod 19:5–6, where YHWH declared Israel to be his priestly kingdom (מַמְלֶכֶת כֹּהֲנִים) and a "holy nation" (גּוֹי קָדוֹשׁ). Through the rituals of covenant making at Sinai (Exod 19–24) and covenant renewal on the plains of Moab, Israel claimed YHWH as their God and they signed themselves over to him to be his vassal priests (cf. Deut 27:9; 29:9–12 [Eng 10–13]). Like the high priest, Israel was holy, consecrated to YHWH for divine service to the nations,[38] and like the high priest, Israel bore the stamp of his name. YHWH had placed them above the nations that his name might be proclaimed through-

36. The rendering of the Hebrew term as "peculiar" in the Authorized Version is not to be understood as "odd, weird," but in the sense of the underlying Latin, *peculium*, that is, "personal/private property." The Septuagint translates the expression, λαὸς περιούσιος, "a people of his special possession." Similarly Titus 2:14; Eph 1:14 and 1 Pet 2:9 read blandly περιποίησις/ιν, "possession, property."

37. This interpretation is reinforced by the usage of its Akkadian cognate, *sikiltum*, in extrabiblical inscriptions. A second millennium seal impression from Alalakh reads, "the servant of Adad, the beloved (*na ra am*) of Adad, the *sikiltum* of Adad." See Collon, *Seal Impressions from Tell Atchana/Alalakh*, 12–13. Cf. also the personal name, Sikilti-Adad, "Treasured one of Adad." For further discussion, see Greenberg, "Hebrew *segulla*: Akkadian *sikiltu*," 172–74. For additional attestation, see *CAD* S.244–45. The juxtaposing of "servant," "beloved," and *sikiltum* to describe the vassal relationship of the king to his god is especially telling. A similar usage is attested also in a thirteenth century BCE letter from the Hittite emperor to Ammurapi, the last king of Ugarit, in which the former reminds the latter that he is his servant and his *sglt*. See *KTU* 2.39:7, 12=*PRU* V.18:38:7, 12.

38. On Israel's mission as a priestly kingdom, see Davies, *Royal Priesthood*. The traditional etymology associates the root with "to be separate," but C. B. Costecalde has recently demonstrated that fundamentally the root communicates the notion of "holy," "holiness," "sacred," "to consecrate." The notion of separation depends upon the context (as in our text). See Costecalde, *Aux origins du sacré biblique*; also Kornfeld, *TDOT* 12.521–30; Gentry, "No One Holy, Like the Lord."

out the world, and that their ethical and cultic performance might bring praise to his name. Moses concretized this missional role of the covenant people in Deut 28:1–14, summarizing the consequences of representing him well in verses 9–10: "YHWH will establish you as his holy people, as he has sworn to you, if you keep the command of YHWH your God and walk in his ways. Then all the peoples of the earth shall see that you bear the name of YHWH, and they shall be in awe of you." Although the critical final statement, וְרָאוּ כָּל־עַמֵּי הָאָרֶץ כִּי שֵׁם יְהוָה נִקְרָא עָלֶיךָ, is generally rendered something like, "All the peoples of the earth will see that you are called by the name of YHWH,"[39] the construction involves a technical expression, נִקְרָא שֵׁם עַל, meaning someone's name is proclaimed over/read on someone else.[40] C. J. Labuschagne and others recognize that this "refers to the proclamation of the name of the new owner in the case of property transfer."[41] However, the idiom may be interpreted even more concretely as reading the name of YHWH branded on his people. The New Jerusalem Bible captures the preferred sense, "The peoples of the earth will see that you bear YHWH's name." Nowhere does the Hebrew Bible explain when Israel was branded with YHWH's name. X *ben* Y patronymics like "Jerubbaal/Gideon son of Joash" (Judg 6:29; 7:14; 8:13, 29) suggest that in a sense children bore the names of their fathers by virtue of biological descent. Despite Deut 32:6 and 18, which speak poetically of the people of Israel having their origins in YHWH, he was obviously not their biological father. Prose texts like Deut 14:2, which explicitly identify Israel as YHWH's sons, suggest that Israel received YHWH's name at the moment of their formal adoption at Sinai. Deuteronomy never speaks explicitly of Yahweh's entrance into covenant relationship with Israel with adoptive language, but this is how Jer 3:19–20 understands it: "I thought how I would set you among my children, and give you a pleasant land, the most beautiful heritage of all the nations. And I thought you would call me, 'My Father,' and would not turn from following me."[42]

---

39. NIV, NRS, NAS, ESV.

40. Cf. NJPSV, "And all the peoples of the earth shall see that the LORD's name is proclaimed over you."

41. "קָרָא *qr'* to call," *TLOT* 3:1162; for the original German, see *THAT* 2:67. See also *HALOT* 1130.

42. The present use of the metaphor derives from ancient Near Eastern political relationships in which the vassal could be called the "son" of the suzerain (cf.

Just as sports fans today advertize their favorite sports teams by wearing hats and shirts bearing their names or logos, so the Israelites were to advertise the name of the God whose name they bore. When the nations observed Israel, they should have witnessed YHWH's transforming power and responded with the same disposition (יָרֵא, "awed fear") the Israelites had exhibited when they witnessed YHWH's glory and heard his voice at Sinai (Exod 20:18–21; Deut 4:10–12, 36–39; 5:22–33). However, Israel's brand of devotion was to be different from that of the nations. Whereas other peoples often expressed allegiance to more than one god, the Deuteronomic vision of spiritual integrity prohibited those who were branded with the name of YHWH from bearing the brand of any other god. Deuteronomy calls them to uncompromising and unadulterated covenant commitment (אָהֵב) to him alone (Deut 6:4–5), demonstrated in wholehearted and full-bodied vassaldom (10:12). This ideal is expressed in the second command of the Decalogue, which is addressed to a people branded by the name of YHWH:

לֹא תִשָּׂא	You shall not bear
אֶת־שֵׁם־יְהוָה אֱלֹהֶיךָ לַשָּׁוְא	the name of YHWH your God in vain,
כִּי לֹא יְנַקֶּה יְהוָה אֵת	for YHWH will not treat as innocent anyone
אֲשֶׁר־יִשָּׂא אֶת־שְׁמוֹ לַשָּׁוְא	who bears his name in vain.[43]

Bearing the Divine Name: The Geographic Dimension

Since Deuteronomy's vision of the covenant also involved the land that YHWH granted to Israel, we should not be surprised to find that the book's vision of monotheistic spiritual integrity extends to the land. If the people were not to tolerate any brands other than the name of YHWH, they were also to recognize that he had exclusive claim to the land, which was to bear only his name.

---

2 Kgs 16:7). Accordingly, within this relationship the suzerain's status was referred to as *abbūtu* ("fathership") and the status of the vassal was referred to as *mārūtu* ("sonship"). *ARM* 2.119r.8. Cf. *CAD* 10/1 (M), 321. See for example the fourteenth century B.C. treaty between Shattiwaza of Mittanni and Suppiluliuma I of Hatti, in Beckman, *Hittite Diplomatic Texts*, 6B §3 (p. 49). For additional references and discussion see Weinfeld, "The Covenant of Grant in the Old Testament and in the Ancient Near East," 191–94.

43. For fuller discussion of this command, see Block, "Bearing the Name of the LORD with Honor," 61–72.

Just as Deuteronomy speaks of peoples with more than one name, so the book also speaks of different toponyms representing the same place: Mount Hermon, known to Sidonians as Siryon and to Amorites as Senir (3:9), and Bashan, which is also called "the land of Rephaim" (3:13). However, so far as we know, in neither case does the named entity bear the name of the namer, as is the case with Havvoth-Jair in Deut 3:14, "Jair the Manassite took all the region of Argob, that is, Bashan, as far as the border of the Geshurites and the Maacathites, and called the villages according to his own name, Havvoth-Jair." Jair's action follows the long-standing practice of founders of settlements staking claim to sites by ascribing to them their own personal names.[44] Several analogues to the case of Jair occur elsewhere in the Hebrew Bible:

> And Nobah went and captured Kenath and its villages, and called it Nobah, after his own name. (וַיִּקְרָא לָהּ נֹבַח בִּשְׁמוֹ; Num 32:42)

> And they named the town Dan, after the name of Dan their ancestor (וַיִּקְרְאוּ שֵׁם־הָעִיר דָּן בְּשֵׁם דָּן אֲבִיהֶם), who was born to Israel; but previously the name of the city had been Laish. (Judg 18:29)

By renaming these places with their own names the conquerors claimed (and branded) them as their personal property.[45]

While some places were named after founders or conquerors, some ancient sites were named after deities worshipped there. The most obvious case is Aššur, which was simultaneously the name of a city/city-state and its deity. It is unclear whether Aššur originated as the name of a deity or the name of a place.[46] However, Aššur lacked a clear character or distinct iconographic tradition (unlike other

---

44. In the Pentateuch, see Gen 4:17, where Cain names a town after his son, Enoch, by which he declares Enoch's ownership of/authority over the region.

45. While the context of the naming is not given, presumably the same applies to בְּאֵרֹת בְּנֵי־יַעֲקָן, Beeroth Bene-jaakan, in Deut 10:6, which identifies wells in the desert as the property of the sons of a man named יַעֲקָן, "Jaakan."

46. The toponym (city name) dates back at least to the Early Dynastic III period (ca. 2450 BCE). Thus Postgate, "Royal Ideology and State Administration in Sumer and Akkad," 406. According to Klengel ("The History of Ashur," 22), the name Aššur "probably derives from the name of a local deity; the settlement's patron god, who then gained increasing stature as the city assumed greater importance."

Mesopotamian divinities), he played no role in the Mesopotamian pantheon himself, and was often assimilated to other major deities of the Sumerian and Babylonian pantheons. Therefore, many believe that Aššur was scarcely more than the deified city itself. But as the power of Assyria (called *mat aššur*, "the Land of Aššur") grew, the local deity was transformed into the supreme god of the empire. The close identification of deity and city is reflected in the practice of naming the city as guarantor in some oaths, as if it were a god itself.[47]

Although Aššur presents a rare case of a city and its patron deity bearing the same name, in Mesopotamia and the Levant specific deities were often associated with particular towns, functioning as the town's protector and patron/matron. Divinities' special relationships with specific locations are recognizable in (1) archaeological or textual evidence for the existence of a prominent cult shrine in their honor; (2) a concentration of theophoric personal names involving the name of the god; (3) references to the deities in names and epithets for the place (e.g., "house"/"town" of DN); (4) references to the town in epithets for the deity (e.g., "Baal of Peor"; in Akkadian, Šarrat-Dēr ["Queen of Dēr"], Ishtar of Arbela). If deities were associated with more than one place, this may have reflected local manifestations of a single deity, so that in names like Baal [of] Meon and Baal [of] Peor, the name Baal may identify a single deity, the storm god, to whom devotees of these respective places looked for their security and prosperity. On the other hand, Spencer L. Allen has recently argued that in the cases involving Ishtar each manifestation was considered a deity in her own right.[48]

Although the evidence for theophoric toponyms in the Hebrew Bible is considerable,[49] the contribution of Deuteronomy to the dis-

47. See further, Postgate, "Royal Ideology and State Administration in Sumer and Akkad"; Black and Green, *Gods, Demons and Symbols*, 37–38. On the worship of Aššur, see van Driel, *The Cult of Aššur*; Ebeling, "Aššur," *RLA* 1:196–98.

48. Allen, *The Splintered Divine*.

49. For a listing of these up to the time of David, see de Moor, *The Rise of Yahwism*, 34–38. According to de Moor's classification, twenty-nine of these are Elohistic names, twenty-four are Baalistic, and thirty-eight involve the names of other deities. However, this classification is misleading, since the only truly Elohistic toponym applies to an altar (אֵל אֱלֹהֵי יִשְׂרָאֵל, Gen 33:20); the rest are all El names. Technically El names are not Elohistic, since El and Elohim reflect different morphological developments from the common Semitic noun *il/ilu*. Whereas Elohim represents the plural form of Eloah (אֱלוֹהַּ/, Deut 32:15), the plural of El is Elim (אֵלִים, Exod 15:11; Ps 29:1; 89:7). See further, Block, "God," 336–37.

cussion is limited: עַשְׁתָּרֹת, Ashtaroth, a place in Gilead in the region of Bashan (1:4), and בַּעַל־פְּעוֹר, Baal-Peor (4:3) and בֵּית פְּעוֹר, Beth-Peor (3:29; 4:46; 34:6). Both of these abbreviate בֵּית בַּעַל פְּעוֹר, Beth-Baal-Peor,[50] meaning "the house of the Baal of Peor," analogous to בֵּית בַּעַל מְעוֹן, Beth-Baal-Meon in Josh 13:17.[51] Theophoric toponyms of this form (Baal-GN) are unattested in Canaanite or Egyptian records prior to the Israelite period,[52] but they suggest that the deities involved were revered by the local population and deemed to have a claim on the site.[53]

Moses addressed the Canaanite situation in Deuteronomy 12:2–3: "You must demolish completely all the places where the nations whom you are about to dispossess served their gods, on the mountain heights, on the hills, and under every leafy tree. Break down their altars, smash their pillars, burn their Asherim with fire, and hew down the idols of their gods, and thus blot out their name [שְׁמָם] from their

50. Peor was a mountain in the vicinity of Mount Nebo to which Balak took Balaam in the hopes that he would curse Israel (Num. 23:28). Although technically "Baal of Peor," identifies the local manifestation of Baal as worshiped by the Moabites at this place, Deut 4:3 treats it as a place name, similar to others of this type: Baal-Gad, Baal-Hamon, etc. For these kinds of names, see the articles on these and other names like them in *ABD* 1.550–56.

51. Other place names involving the name/epithet include בַּעַל, Baal (1 Chr 4:33; LXX[B] reads Βαλατ = בַּעֲלָת, as in 1 Kgs 9:18); בָּמוֹת בַּעַל, Bamoth Baal (meaning "high place of Baal," in Moab, in Num 22:41; Josh 13:17); בַּעַל־פְּרָצִים, Baal Perazim (2 Sam 5:20; 1 Chr 14:11); בַּעַל שָׁלִשָׁה, Baal Shalisha (2 Kgs 4:42; cf. 1 Sam 9:4); בַּעַל חֶרְמוֹן, Baal Hermon (Judg 3:3); בַּעַל חָצוֹר, Baal Hazor (2 Sam 13:23; cf. Neh 11:33); בַּעַל תָּמָר, Baal Tamar (Judg 20:33); בַּעֲלָה, Baalah (Josh 15:9, [= Kiriath-jearim], 29); בַּעֲלָת, Baalat (Josh 19:44; 1 Kgs 9:18; 2 Chr 8:6); בְּעָלוֹת, Bealoth (Josh 15:24; 1 Kgs 4:16); בַּעֲלַת בְּאֵר, Baalat Beer (meaning "Baalat of the well," Josh 19:8); הַר־הַבַּעֲלָה, Mount Baalah (Josh 15:11).

52. So also de Moor, *Rise of Yahwism*, 38, n. 24; Isserlin, "Israelite and Pre-Israelite Place-names in Palestine," 135. This conclusion is reinforced by the absence of any Baal-GN names among the toponyms listed and discussed by Aḥituv, *Canaanite Toponyms in Ancient Egyptian Documents*. The absence of Baal-names prior to the Late Bronze Age may suggest that Baal or the name Baal did not achieve widespread popularity until this time. Cf. Rainey, "The Toponymics of Eretz-Israel," 3–4.

53. For a listing of theophoric toponyms up to the time of David, see de Moor, *Rise of Yahwism*, 34–39; Zevit, *The Religions of Ancient Israel*, 592–609. Theophoric toponyms with a *bt*, "house of," prefix also appear in Akkadian texts. E.g., *Bīt-Dagān*, "House of Dagan"; *Bīt-Ishtar*, "House of Ishtar"; *Bīt-Marduk*, "House of Marduk"; *Bīt-Nergal*, "House of Nergal"; on which see Parpola, *Neo-Assyrian Toponyms*, 80–89.

places." Interpreted metaphorically, שְׁמָם, "their name," represents their reputation and the memory of their association with this cult center. However, echoing an earlier statement in Deut 7:5, this reputation/memory can be annihilated (אָבַד) only by demolishing (נָתַץ) their altars (מִזְבְּחוֹת), smashing (שָׁבֵּר) their pillars (מַצֵּבֹת), burning (שָׂרַף) their Asherah poles (אֲשֵׁרִים), and hewing down (גָּדַע) their images (פְּסִילִים).[54] Nevertheless, several features argue for a more literal interpretation.

First, if fixing YHWH's name in 12:2–12 involves the inscription of his name on a place, then these actions probably involve effacing other deities' names from dedicatory inscriptions.

Second, although the verbs differ, Moses' later association of "destroying" (הִשְׁמִיד, cf. אָבַד in 12:2–3) a name with blotting (מָחָה) it out places this action in the same semantic field (9:14).

Third, elsewhere "blotting out" the name is expressly linked to a written record, if not a memorial. Exodus 32:32–34 speaks explicitly about blotting out Moses' name from a document (סֵפֶר) in which YHWH had written it (כָּתַב). Two extra-biblical texts provide illuminating background to the practice of removing persons' names. In a late eighth-century curse inscribed on a city gate memorializing his achievements, Azatiwada wrote:

> Now if a king among kings, or a prince among princes, if any famous human being, effaces the name of Azatiwada (*ymḥ šm 'ztwd*) from this gate and puts [his own] name (*wšt šm*)—or if he covets this city and pulls down this gate, which Azatiwada has made, and makes for himself another gate, and puts his name on it (*wšt šm 'ly*) . . .[55]

A second version of this text inscribed on a statue of Baal, reads as follows:

> Now if a king among kings, or a prince among princes, if any famous human being, orders [men] to efface the name of Azatiwada from the statue of this god (*lmḥt šm 'ztwd bsml '[l] m z*), and puts [his own] name (*wšt šm*) [on it]; or more than

---

54. Cf. the references to blotting out (מָחָה) the names of Israel (9:14; 29:19 [Eng 20]) and Amalek (25:19) from under heaven, and the name of a person who died without having fathered a child (25:9).

55. Cf. the translation by Gibson, *Phoenician Inscriptions*, 50–51; also Lawson Younger, Jr., in *COS* 2.149.

that, if he covets this city and says, I will make another statue,
and put my own name on it (*wšt šm 'ly*).[56]

The similarities between these inscriptions, along with the fact that Azatiwada would inscribe his own name on the city gate and on the image of the deity, testify to the close relationship between the deity, the king, and the place.

Fourth, dedicatory inscriptions from the Levant attest to the practice of inscribing the names of gods on their statues and on foundation stones of temples.[57] Deuteronomy demands that all the names of Canaanite deities be expunged from every cult site because once the people of YHWH invade this land, the other gods' claim to it has terminated.

This evidence provides necessary background for a notion expressed in Deuteronomy twenty-two times in variations of the chosen place formula.[58] While, the first occurrence of the formula is the most complex, nine expressly declare that YHWH will put/set his name at the place that he will choose:

הַמָּקוֹם אֲשֶׁר־יִבְחַר יְהוָה אֱלֹהֵיכֶם מִכָּל־שִׁבְטֵיכֶם לָשׂוּם אֶת־שְׁמוֹ שָׁם לְשִׁכְנוֹ	12:5	the place that YHWH your God will choose out of all your tribes to put his name there to establish it.
הַמָּקוֹם אֲשֶׁר־יִבְחַר יְהוָה אֱלֹהֵיכֶם בּוֹ לְשַׁכֵּן שְׁמוֹ שָׁם	12:11	the place that YHWH your God will choose, to establish his name there.
הַמָּקוֹם אֲשֶׁר יִבְחַר יְהוָה אֱלֹהֶיךָ לָשׂוּם שְׁמוֹ שָׁם	12:21	the place that YHWH your God will choose to set his name there.
הַמָּקוֹם אֲשֶׁר־יִבְחַר לְשַׁכֵּן שְׁמוֹ שָׁם	14:23	the place that he will choose, to establish his name there.

---

56. Cf. the translation by Gibson, *Phoenician Inscriptions*, 54–55.

57. In addition to the statue of Baal cited above, see the tenth-century BCE building inscription of a temple Yaḥimilk dedicated (*COS* 2.146; Gibson, *Phoenician Inscriptions*, 18); the late sixth-century BCE Phoenician inscription discovered in Pyrgi, Italy, dedicated to Astarte (ibid., 154); the Ekron inscription of Akhayus, for the temple of the goddess *PTGYH* (*COS*, 2.64); the mid-fifth century BCE Tema inscription in honor of ṢLM recording the introduction of a new cult and the construction of a new sanctuary (*KAI* §288; Gibson, *Aramaic Inscriptions*, 148–51); from the third-second century BCE the Aramaic and Greek bilingual inscription from Dan, "To the god who is at Dan" (on which see Biran, "Tell Dan Five Years Later," 171, 179–80).

58. Deut 12:5, 11, 14, 18, 21, 26; 14:23, 24, 25; 15:20; 16:2, 6, 7, 11, 15, 16; 17:8, 10; 18:6; 23:17[Eng 16]; 26:2; 31:11.

הַמָּקוֹם אֲשֶׁר יִבְחַר יְהוָה אֱלֹהֶיךָ לְשׂוּם שְׁמוֹ שָׁם	14:24	the place that YHWH your God will choose, to set his name there.
הַמָּקוֹם אֲשֶׁר־יִבְחַר יְהוָה לְשַׁכֵּן שְׁמוֹ שָׁם	16:2	the place that YHWH will choose, to establish his name there.
הַמָּקוֹם אֲשֶׁר־יִבְחַר יְהוָה אֱלֹהֶיךָ לְשַׁכֵּן שְׁמוֹ שָׁם	16:6	the place that YHWH your God will choose, to establish his name there.
הַמָּקוֹם אֲשֶׁר יִבְחַר יְהוָה אֱלֹהֶיךָ לְשַׁכֵּן שְׁמוֹ שָׁם	16:11	the place that YHWH your God will choose, to establish his name there.
הַמָּקוֹם אֲשֶׁר יִבְחַר יְהוָה אֱלֹהֶיךָ לְשַׁכֵּן שְׁמוֹ שָׁם	26:2	the place that YHWH your God will choose, to establish his name there.

Although לְשַׁכֵּן and the hapax form לְשִׁכְנוֹ in 12:5[59] are generally translated something like "to dwell [there]," or "for his dwelling," the substitution of this verb in 12:21 and 14:24, as well as in
the Deuteronomistic History (1 Kgs 9:3; 14:21; 2 Kgs 21:4, 7), suggests it functions as a virtual synonym for שִׂים, "to set, put."[60] This
applies whether לְשַׁכֵּן שְׁמוֹ שָׁם represents an adaptation of a common
Akkadian idiom *šuma šakānu*, "to place his name,"[61] or an unrecog-
nized causative Shapel stem of the verb כון, "to be established" (*ša*
preformative + כון).[62] Accordingly, we should interpret the expression
something like "to place" or "to establish" or even "to stamp" his name
there. The idiom alludes to the custom of a royal builder inscribing
his name in the foundation stone of a palace or monument as a mark
of his claim to this place as his official residence and his authorization
of the building project.[63]

Although Sandra Richter has performed a valuable service in
exploring the contexts in which the Akkadian counterpart, *šumma*

59. The pointing assumes a noun שֶׁכֶן, "dwelling, habitation," from שָׁכַן, "to
dwell."

60. So also Richter, *The Deuteronomistic History and the Name Theology*, 41–105.

61. Thus ibid. and Richter, "The Place of the Name in Deuteronomy," 342–66.

62. Cf. Wächter, "Reste von Šapʿel-Bildungen im Hebräischen," 380–89; Thierry,
"Notes on Hebrew Grammar and Etymology," 1–17; cf. *HALOT* 1496–97.

63. The incongruous plural pronoun in Jeremiah's three-fold repetition of הֵיכַל
יְהוָה הֵיכַל יְהוָה הֵיכַל יְהוָה הֵמָּה, "They are the temple of YHWH, the temple of YHWH,
the temple of YHWH" (Jer 7:4) may be a parody of an inscription above the gate of
the temple: הֵיכַל יְהוָה, "The Temple of YHWH." Note also the emphasis on laying
the foundation stone of the temple in Ezra 3:10 and Hag 2:18. On gods taking the
initiative in temple-building projects in the ancient Near East, see Hurowitz, *I Have
Built You an Exalted House*, 131–68.

šakānu, was used,[64] and in recognizing the biblical formula as an adaptation of this idiom, she pays insufficient attention to its adaptation in the Hebrew Bible. Just as in lexical studies, exploration of etymologies and cognate evidence is important for understanding biblical terms, but in the end context and actual usage are determinative, which means the biblical treatment of this idiom demands closer scrutiny.[65]

The data provided by Deuteronomy on the function of the place that YHWH will choose to stamp his name are illuminating.[66] This will be a place to (1) "seek" (דָּרַשׁ) YHWH (12:5); (2) "see the face of YHWH" (לֵרָאוֹת אֶת־פְּנֵי יְהוָה, 31:11; cf. 16:16);[67] (3) read and hear (קָרָא) the Torah (31:11); (4) learn to fear (יָרֵא) YHWH (14:23; 31:9–13); (5) rejoice (שָׂמַח) before YHWH (12:12, 18; 14:26; 16:11–14; 26:11); (6) eat (אָכַל) before YHWH (12:7, 18; 14:23, 26, 29; 15:20; 18:6–8); (7) present sacrifices to YHWH;[68] (8) celebrate the three great annual pilgrimage festivals: Passover (16:1–8), the Festival of Weeks (Pentecost; 16:9–12); the Festival of Booths (16:13–17; 31:9–13); (9) settle legal disputes before the Levitical priest or the judge (17:8–13); (10) present the offering of firstfruits (רֵאשִׁית כָּל־פְּרִי הָאֲדָמָה אֲשֶׁר תָּבִיא מֵאַרְצְךָ) and recall YHWH's saving and providential grace (26:1–11); (11) demonstrate one's covenant commitment to YHWH through gifts of charity to the marginalized (26:12; cf. 10:12–22); (12) demonstrate communal solidarity by celebrating in

---

64. She notes the following (pp. 136–53): votive inscriptions on images of a donor placed in courtyards of temples as an expression of piety, victory stelae and statuary, building inscriptions (often stamped bricks), foundation deposits (which often featured *šuma šaṭru*, "written name"), and *wall-sikkātus* (clay nails).

65. For a healthy corrective to Richter's preoccupation with extra-biblical monumental evidence, see Hundley, "To Be or Not to Be," 533–55.

66. In trying to establish the significance of לְשַׁכֵּן שְׁמוֹ שָׁם Richter errs in limiting her discussion to occurrences of the place formula that explicitly refer to "his name." The issue is more nuanced than she suggests.

67. For defense of this interpretation, see Tigay, *Deuteronomy*, 159.

68. The general invitation, "You may bring all that I command you," is specified as עוֹלֹתֵיכֶם וְזִבְחֵיכֶם מַעְשְׂרֹתֵיכֶם וּתְרֻמַת יֶדְכֶם וְכֹל מִבְחַר נִדְרֵיכֶם אֲשֶׁר תִּדְּרוּ לַיהוָה, "your whole burnt offerings, and your sacrifices, your tithes and the offering of your hand, and all your chosen votive offerings that you vow to YHWH" (12:11); קָדָשֶׁיךָ אֲשֶׁר־ יִהְיוּ לְךָ וּנְדָרֶיךָ . . . עֹלֹתֶיךָ, "the holy things that are your due and your votive offerings . . . and your whole burnt offerings" (12:26–27); the tithes (מַעְשַׂר) of grain, new wine, and oil, and the firstborn (הַבְּכוֹר) of herds and flocks" (14:22–27); the consecrated firstborn (הַבְּכוֹר) of the herd or flock (15:19–23).

the presence of YHWH with one's children and servants, with Levites and aliens (12:12; 14:27–29; 16:11); and (13) for Levites to serve in the name of YHWH (18:6–8). Obviously the place would function as more than a symbol of YHWH's claim to the land; it would also signify YHWH's delight in his people and his desire to fellowship with them. Indeed, like the tabernacle in the desert, in linking heaven and earth the place would provide a means whereby YHWH could dwell in the land in the midst of his people, on the one hand, and the people could worship in his real—if not physical—presence, on the other.[69]

That the phrase לְשַׁכֵּן שְׁמוֹ שָׁם always occurs in Deuteronomy within the context of the place formula highlights the place's role in providing Israelites constant access to YHWH. Since the Israelites would hear the voice of God and learn to fear him there, the provision of a place enabled and invited them to experience again and again what their ancestors had experienced at Sinai. At the same time, by juxtaposing the first and fullest form of the place formula (12:5) with the charge to delegitimize the claims of other gods by stamping out their names from the land and by imprinting his name on the place that he chooses, YHWH lays exclusive claim to the land and to the devotion of the people. This means that Israel was to reject not only the worship of all other gods (12:2–3; 13:1–19 [Eng 12:32—13:18]), but also the ways in which other peoples served their gods—presumably applying those ways to the worship of YHWH (12:29–31).

Within the Deuteronomic vision of spiritual integrity the singular place signals and symbolizes the radical discontinuity between the essence and practice of the religion of the Canaanites and the Israelites. Deuteronomy 12:5–14 is not so much a law on worship and a command to worship in a certain way, as an invitation to his presence, to enjoy fellowship with him.[70] As Deuteronomy will em-

---

69. Some interpret the association of the "name" with the place formula with an abstracting theological revolution of Deuteronomists combating the ancient notion that the Deity actually resided in the temple. See especially Weinfeld, *Deuteronomy and the Deuteronomic School*, 191–209; Weinfeld, "Deuteronomy, Book of," 175–78. However, as had been the case at Sinai, at the place YHWH chooses to stamp his name he will be simultaneously present in heaven and in the temple. So also Hundley, "To Be or Not to Be," 539–40. For defense of the temple as a provision for YHWH's real presence rather than a place for the name as a hypostatic symbol of YHWH, see Wilson, *Out of the Midst of the Fire.*

70. For fuller discussion, see Block, "The Joy of Worship."

phasize, Israelite religion involved expressions of thanksgiving for YHWH's blessing in providing fertility (6:10–15; 8:6–19; 11:13–17; 26:3, 10–11), as well as pleas for further blessing (26:15). However, Israelite religion was more than a fertility religion and involved more than keeping the gods happy by caring for and feeding them. To the contrary, when they would come to worship YHWH they would eat in his presence! Fundamentally it involved celebrating YHWH's grace in their history (26:5–9), and responding to that grace with ethical righteousness (16:20), and in so doing fulfilling their mission as priestly agents of praise to YHWH and blessing to the world (26:19).[71]

A telling argument against the late (Josianic) date of the book of Deuteronomy or the so-called Deuteronomic Law Code is the absence of any explicit reference in Deuteronomy to Judah, to Jerusalem, to the temple, or to the king's role in building a temple.[72] Until YHWH has given his people rest from all their enemies (12:9–12),[73] the identification of the permanent place for YHWH's name will remain a mystery. But this has not prevented scholars from proposing where that place might be. Acknowledging that the location would not be fixed until David's time, Sandra Richter has proposed that among the later theologians responsible for compiling Deuteronomy 5–27, Mount Ebal was "the first locale where Yahweh had 'placed his name.'"[74] However, this proposal is unconvincing, for several reasons.

First, neither 11:29–32, which anticipates, nor chapter 27, which prescribes the Mount Ebal ritual, speaks of YHWH's name (שֵׁם) or of YHWH choosing (בָּחַר) this place.

Second, Richter's proposal to read the stelae of 27:4–5 as triumphal monuments[75] inscribed with the words and "heroic acts of Yahweh"[76] does not match the realities. On the one hand, Deuteronomy 27 suggests this is to be the Israelites' first cultic observance after they have crossed the Jordan, preceding the conquest of the land, rather

---

71. On which, see Block, "The Privilege of Calling."

72. Contra Pakkala ("The Date of the Oldest Edition of Deuteronomy," 388–401), who finds in these and other features evidence for a Persian date for the oldest portions of the book.

73. Cf. 2 Sam 7:1, 11; 1 Kgs 5:4; 8:56.

74. Richter, "The Place of the Name in Deuteronomy," 366.

75. Ibid., 361.

76. Ibid., 347.

than a commemoration of conquests already achieved. Furthermore, chapter 27 is devoid of any hints of military significance. Rather than providing a focused recitation of YHWH's heroic acts, the inscription in chapter 27 involves "all the words of this Torah" (כָּל־דִּבְרֵי הַתּוֹרָה הַזֹּאת), that is, some version of Moses' exposition of covenant relationship as presented in chapters 5–26.

Third, whereas victory monuments were typically made of stone with the inscriptions chiseled into the rock so they would endure, these stelae consisted of natural stones plastered over, and then inscribed with some sort of ink. Unlike the Deir 'Allah plaster inscriptions, which endured a long time because they were on inside walls,[77] these stelae were out in the open, which meant the inscriptions would be effaced by natural weathering processes in a very short time, thereby neutralizing their monumental function.

Fourth, whereas the place where YHWH stamps his name is presented elsewhere as the place to which the Israelites will come regularly and repeatedly for worship—not military celebrations—the rituals prescribed in Deuteronomy 27 involve a one-time event.

Fifth, the closest analogue to the ritual on Mount Ebal is found, not in extra-biblical accounts of the erection of victory or votive stelae, but in the inner-biblical Sinai narrative. The association of whole burnt offerings and peace offerings with stelae links this event with Exod 24:1–11. As in our text, there the sacrifices are associated with twelve pillars representing the tribes of Israel (v. 4) and eating in the presence of Yahweh (v. 11). Like the rituals at Sinai, this ceremony is covenantal. Through the ritual at Sinai YHWH's earlier promise to establish (הֵקִים) with Abraham's descendants the covenant he had made with the ancestor (Gen 17:7) was fulfilled, and his descendants were formally constituted the covenant people of YHWH. However, that event did not fulfill completely the agenda declared to Moses at the time of his call (Exod 3:8) and reiterated many times thereafter (e.g., Exod 6:2–8). In Deuteronomy Moses declared repeatedly that Yahweh's purpose in rescuing Israel from Egypt was to give his people the land he had sworn to the ancestors.[78] The Sinai event had sealed

77. On the Deir 'Allah inscriptions, see, Hoftijzer and van der Kooij, *Aramaic Texts from Deir 'Allah*; Hoftijzer and van der Kooij, *The Balaam Text from Deir 'Allah Re-Evaluated*; Hackett, *The Balaam Text from Deir 'Allah*.

78. Deut 1:8, 35; 6:10, 18, 23; 7:13; 8:1; 10:11; 11:9, 21; 19:8; 26:3; 28:11; 30:20; 31:7, 20, 21, 23.

the bipartite relationship between people and deity, but the third party was missing.

According to the original plan the third member should have been incorporated into the scheme within months after Israel left Horeb. However, because of the people's rebellion at Kadesh Barnea, the completion of the triangle had been delayed for forty years. By eating the covenant meal in the presence of Yahweh (27:7) *in the land he has given them,* the Israelites celebrated the completion of the triangle.

Seventh, the function of this ritual is suggested by the expression, בָּאֵר הֵיטֵב. English translations generally follow the meaning of באר in rabbinic writings[79] by rendering the phrase something like "very distinctly" (NAS; cf. NJPS), "very plainly" (ESV, RSV), or "very clearly" (NRS, NIV). However, as in 1:5, where the narrator applied בֵּאֵר to Moses' oral proclamation rather than the transcription of a text, this phrase speaks more to the purpose of the inscription than the nature of the script. The Hebrew word is cognate to Akkadian *burru,* "to confirm," that is, "put a legal document in force."[80] Inscribing the text on these pillars not only transforms the Torah of Moses into a monument, but also represents a critical phase in the ritual by which the covenant relationship involving Yahweh, the people, and the land is made legally binding. Performed as soon as the Israelites enter the land, the ceremonies envisioned here signal the beginning of the full functioning of the tripartite relationship.

Given Moses' predictions that YHWH will choose a place to stamp with his name, on the one hand, and the frequency of toponyms involving the names of Baal and other divinities, on the other, it is remarkable that of the 502 place names in the Hebrew Bible not a single one has YHWH as the theophore.[81] Several Yahwistic analogues to toponyms like Baal-peor ("Baal of Peor," Deut 4:3;

---

79. See Jastrow, *Dictionary of the Targumim,* 135.

80. See Schaper, "The 'Publication' of Legal Texts in Ancient Judah," 230; G. Braulik and N. Lohfink, "Deuteronomium 1,5," 49. *CAD* (2 [1965], 127) defines *burru* as "to establish the true legal situation (ownership, amounts, liability, etc.) by a legal procedure involving an oath."

81. So also Hess, *Israelite Religions,* 274. De Moor (*Rise of Yahwism,* 38) observes that altars designated YHWH-yireh (יְהוָה יִרְאֶה, "Yahweh will provide," Gen 22:14) and YHWH-shalom (יְהוָה שָׁלוֹם, "YHWH is peace," Judg 6:24) represent the closest the Hebrew Bible comes to Yahwistic place names.

FIGURE 7: The Triadic Covenantal Relationship
Involving Deity, People, and Territory

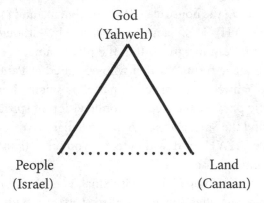

God
(Yahweh)

People   Land
(Israel)   (Canaan)

Hos 9:10) and Baal-meon ("Baal of Meon," Num 32:38) occur in
the Hebrew Bible, and several have surfaced in inscriptions from
Israelite territory. Regarding the former, we may note expressions like
"Yahweh of Sinai" (Deut 33:2; cf. Judg 5:5; Ps 68:9 [Eng 8]), "Yahweh
of Mount Paran" (Deut 33:2; Hab 3:3), "Yahweh of Edom" (Judg 5:4),
and "Yahweh of Teman" (Hab 3:3),[82] which could potentially support
a sort of poly-Yahwism involving geographically distinct Yahwehs,
analogous to the poly-Baalism reflected in Baalistic toponyms.[83]
Support for such perceptions in Israel may be drawn from names like:
יהוה ה[ה]תמן, "YHWH of the Southland/Teman,"[84] and יהוה שמרן,
"YHWH of Samaria," that have surfaced in eighth-century BCE
jar fragment inscriptions from Kuntillet 'Ajrud.[85] We may specu-

82. One might also imagine "Yahweh Sebaoth of Jerusalem," "Yahweh of Bethel,"
"Yahweh of Hebron," "Yahweh of Samaria," etc.

83. Thus Allen, *The Splintered Divine*.

84. This epithet has surfaced on two eighth-century BCE jar fragments discovered at Kuntillet 'Ajrûd.

85. For the former, see KAjr 19:5-6 and KAjr 20:1, in Dobbs-Allsopp, *Hebrew
Inscriptions*, 293–96; for the latter, see KAjr 18:2, in ibid., 290. These texts have been
translated as follows:

> Utterance of 'Ashyaw the king: "Say to Yehallel and to Yaw'asah and
> to [. . .]: 'I bless you by Yahweh of Samaria and his asherah!'"

> [. . .] to Yahweh of the Teman and his asherah. And may he grant
> [?] everything that he asks from the compassionate god [. . .], and
> may he grant according to his needs all that he asks! . . . Utterance

late that like Baal-Peor (an abbreviation for Beth-Baal-Peor, "the house of Baal at Peor") these names reflect the existence of shrines to YHWH at these sites that may have been known as בית יהוה [ה]תמן, "the house of YHWH of Teman," and בית יהוה שמרן, "the house of YHWH of Samaria," respectively. Although the divine name has not been integrated into the place name, in a syncretistic context the move from "Yahweh who appeared at Paran" to "a god who is the Yahweh of a particular place," is small. However we interpret these phrases, the Deuteronomic vision of spiritual integrity generally and the Shemaʿ in 6:4–5 in particular leave no room either for multiple YHWHs or devotion to any god other than YHWH, the redeemer and savior of Israel.[86]

The association of YHWH with Sinai, Paran, Edom, and Teman above draws our attention to an alleged extra-biblical occurrence of the Tetragrammaton as a toponym. A fourteenth-century BCE topographical list of Pharaoh Amenophis III contains the phrase *t3 š3 sw yhw*, which may be translated either as "Yhw in the land of the Shasu," or "the Shasu-land of Yhw."[87] For more than a half century some have argued that *yhw* represents the Tetragrammaton, and that here the name of the God of Israel is used as a toponym.[88] While the

---

of ʿAmaryaw, "Say to my lord: 'Is it well with you? I bless you by Yahweh of Teman and his asherah. May he bless you and keep you, and may he be with my lord!'"

[. . . May] he prolong [their] days, and be satisfied [. . .] Yahweh of the Teman has dealt favorably [with . . .]

Thus McCarter, *COS* 2:171–72. For discussion of these texts see Smith, *The Early History of God*, 118–25; Albertz, *The History of Israelite Religion*, 1:206; Day, *Yahweh and the Gods and Goddesses of Canaan*, 49–52. This perception of Yahweh compares with Mesopotamian references to Ishtar of Arbela, Ishtar of Nineveh, Ishtar of Akkad (*ANET*, 205); Egyptian references to Amon-Re in Thebes, Amon-Re in Heliopolis, etc.; and biblical references to Baal of Peor, Baal of Gad, Baal of Tamar, Baal of Maon, Baal of Hermon, Baal of Hazor, etc. These gods were worshiped in many different places, perhaps as local manifestations of the one deity.

86. See further, Block, "How Many is God?" 73–97; Smith, *God in Translation*, 143–47.

87. For the text, see Kitchen, *Ramesside Inscriptions*, Series A, vol. 2, 75 (§56:96). Kitchen renders the name, Yahiwa. Weinfeld translates the phrase, "the land of the nomad [tribes] of YHWH." See "The Tribal League at Sinai," 304.

88. Noll writes, "Yahu is a shortened form of the divine name Yahweh, a kind of nickname. It was not uncommon for places to be named after the god worshiped

word seems to function as a toponym rather than a personal name,[89] it is also possible that it reflects an early awareness of YHWH in this region.[90] However, because the Egyptian texts are so fragmentary, all such identifications are speculative.[91]

Even if *yhw* in this Egyptian text is historically linked with the name of the Israelite deity, the fact remains that despite Deuteronomy's repeated declaration that YHWH would imprint his name and his presence on a place, that place is never identified in the book, and the deity's name never functions as a toponym in the Hebrew Bible—or does it? The book of Ezekiel ends with a remarkable vision of an ide-

---

in the area. Apparently there were some Yahweh worshipers living on the southern edges of Canaan in the Late Bronze Age," *Canaan and Israel in Antiquity*, 122. This identification is often marshaled to defend the notion that Yahwism originated in the desert south of Israel. For discussion and bibliography, see Mettinger, *In Search of God*, 24–28; van der Toorn, "Yahweh," 911–12; Redford, *Egypt, Canaan, and Israel in Ancient Times*, 272–74; Smith, *God in Translation*, 96–97 n. 22; Görg, "Jahwe—ein Toponym," 7–14; Lemaire, *The Birth of Monotheism*, 23.

89. So also Hasel, *Domination and Resistance*, 231.

90. Cf. Hess, *Israelite Religions*, 159.

91. Ben Gad HaCohen ("Shasu Land YHW and the Tribe of Judah") suggests the name may be associated with Petra. Kenneth A. Kitchen dismisses such speculation out of hand:

> No. 96 read as *Yhw*, has elicited much comment, because Grdseloff (*RHJE* 1 [1944], 81–82) ingeniously compared it with the biblical name of deity, YHWH, and then speculated that YHWH had thus originated in S. Transjordan (at this place?) and linked this to the old Kenite hypothesis of some bygone Old Testament scholars. In this, he soon found an uncritical following (listed in part by Astour, *Festschrift Edel*, 1979, 21 n. 25). But all this remains, alas, just a tissue of unsupported speculation. The location of *Yhw* is wholly unknown, anywhere in Sinai, Negeb, Edom, S. Syria. Its link with the name YHWH remains tenuous (no final *h* or equivalent *w/y*), and one cannot just pile up one gossamer hypothesis upon another (Kenite or otherwise) without some firm support. Contrast the treatment by Astour, 21. A quite different and more rational solution for the nature of this name was offered by M. Weippert, *ZAW* 84 (1972), 491, n.144. Namely, that this *Yhw* is an abbreviated form of a place-name of the type having a prefixed verb-form, + complement such as *el*. One may mention others such known in Egyptian lists, such as *Yashup-el*, or biblical *Yiptah-el*—here, *Yhw* may be an abbreviated form from *Yahu-el*, or the like (Kitchen, *Ramesside Inscriptions Translated and Annotated*, Series B: Notes and Comments, vol. 2, *Ramesses II*, Royal Inscriptions Inscriptions, 129).

alized future for the triangular relationship involving YHWH, Israel, and the land. Having envisioned YHWH's return to his temple, the society reconstructed under the leadership of the Zadokite priesthood, and the tribes occupying the lands assigned to them, the vision ends with a picture of a city in the heart of the land, offering free access to all Israel through twelve gates named after the tribes. The book closes with a remarkable announcement: וְשֵׁם־הָעִיר מִיּוֹם יְהוָה שָׁמָּה, "And the name of the city from that day will be 'YHWH Shammah [YHWH is there]!'" (48:35). Ezekiel was not alone in announcing the renaming of the city. Several decades earlier, Jeremiah had looked beyond the judgment of faithless Israel and envisioned a restoration that burst the boundaries of the nation and the significance of Jerusalem as he knew it (Jer 3:17):

בָּעֵת הַהִיא יִקְרְאוּ לִירוּשָׁלִַם כִּסֵּא יְהוָה	At that time Jerusalem shall be called the throne of YHWH,
וְנִקְווּ אֵלֶיהָ כָל־הַגּוֹיִם	and all nations shall gather to it,
לְשֵׁם יְהוָה לִירוּשָׁלִָם	to the name of YHWH, to Jerusalem,
וְלֹא־יֵלְכוּ עוֹד אַחֲרֵי שְׁרִרוּת לִבָּם הָרָע:	and they shall no longer stubbornly follow their own evil heart.

Bearing the Divine Name: The Professional Dimension

One more dimension of bearing the name in Deuteronomy calls for brief attention, viz., the verbal invocation of YHWH's name. On the one hand, YHWH invited/authorized all Israelites to invoke his name in oaths (6:13; 10:20). In the highly litigious ancient Near Eastern world, oaths were especially important to reinforce and confirm declarations of all sorts, especially in legal contexts and in the contexts of political agreements and treaties. Oaths functioned as oral equivalents to stamping written documents with the seal of the higher authority, thereby invoking the deity as the guarantor of the declaration. Whereas others would swear by the life of several or even many gods, the Israelites were to swear only in YHWH's name.

On the other hand, YHWH authorized priests and prophets to speak in his name. The utterances of the former involved two types of activities. Deuteronomy 18:7 speaks generally of Levitical priests from the outlying towns coming to the central sanctuary, authorizing them to minister in the name of YHWH (שֵׁרֵת בְּשֵׁם יְהוָה), alongside their Levitical kinsfolk who stand before YHWH. According to Deut

10:8, having set them aside as custodians of the covenant, YHWH assigned the tribe of Levi the duties of carrying the ark of the covenant of Yahweh,[92] standing before him,[93] serving him,[94] and blessing the people in his name.[95] This statement is echoed in 1 Chr 23:13:

Deuteronomy 10:8	1 Chronicles 23:13
בְּעֵת הַהִוא הִבְדִּיל יְהוָה אֶת־שֵׁבֶט הַלֵּוִי	וַיִּבָּדֵל אַהֲרֹן . . . הוּא־וּבָנָיו
לָשֵׂאת אֶת־אֲרוֹן בְּרִית־יְהוָה	לְהַקְדִּישׁוֹ קֹדֶשׁ קָדָשִׁים . . . עַד־עוֹלָם
לַעֲמֹד לִפְנֵי יְהוָה	לְהַקְטִיר לִפְנֵי יְהוָה
לְשָׁרְתוֹ	לְשָׁרְתוֹ
וּלְבָרֵךְ בִּשְׁמוֹ עַד הַיּוֹם הַזֶּה	וּלְבָרֵךְ בִּשְׁמוֹ עַד־עוֹלָם
At that time YHWH set apart the tribe of Levi	Aaron was set apart . . . he and his sons
to carry the ark of the covenant of YHWH	to dedicate the most holy things . . . forever
to stand before YHWH	to present offerings before YHWH
to minister to him	to minister to him
and to bless in his name to this day.	and to bless in his name forever.

92. Numbers 4:1–15 and 10:21 specify the Kohathite branch of the Levitical family for this responsibility. Deuteronomy is not overly concerned about the distinctions between priests and Levites, hence the references to "the Levitical priests" (הַכֹּהֲנִים הַלְוִיִּם: 17:9, 18; 18:1; 24:8; 27:9, and elsewhere, Josh 3:3; 8:33; Jer 33:18, 21), "the priests, the sons of Levi" (הַכֹּהֲנִים בְּנֵי לֵוִי: 31:9), or simply "the Levites" (as in 18:8, הַלְוִיִּם הָעֹמְדִים שָׁם לִפְנֵי יְהוָה, "the Levites who stand there before YHWH" (18:7; cf. 27:14; 31:25). The task of physically carrying the ark applied until the construction of the temple as the permanent residence for the ark. Cf. 1 Sam 6:15; 2 Sam 15:24.

93. This is official court language, signifying authorization to enter the presence of the king in order to minister to him and/or in order to receive a commission from him to dispense to the people (cf. Dan 1:4). With respect to God, the expression is used of the heavenly host standing at Yahweh's right and left hand (2 Chr 18:18). Moses applies it to prophets in Deut 18:5 (cf. Jer 15:1; 18:20; 23:18; 1 Kgs 17:1; 18:15) and Levitical priests (10:8; 18:7; cf. Zech 3:1; 2 Chr 29:11).

94. The verb שֵׁרֵת, "to serve, to minister to," involves primarily cultic service, like the presentation of offerings and sacrifices on the altar—which Num 18:7 and Ezek 44:15–16 restrict to priests—but it also concerns general maintenance of the tabernacle/temple as Yahweh's residence (Num 18:1–6; Ezek 44:11).

95. Although Num 6:22 and 1 Chr 23:13 associate this function specifically with Aaron and his descendants, neither text precludes other Levites performing this service; if kings could bless the people in the name of Yahweh (2 Sam 6:18; 1 Kgs 8:14, 55), surely Levites could as well (10:8).

While not limited to this, presumably the blessings involved the pronouncement of the Aaronic blessing found in Num 6:24–26 (cf. Lev 9:22),[96] by which act they "put YHWH's name on the sons of Israel,"[97] and thereby claim them as YHWH's own and as potential targets of divine blessing. To bless in the name of YHWH means to pronounce a benediction on YHWH's behalf and with his authority, in effect stamping the utterance with his name. Psalm 24:3–5 may reflect this type of priestly service. Instructing the people on the prerequisites to acceptable worship, verse 4 refers to a blessing and righteousness that worshipers receive from YHWH. Since the former involves a verbal utterance—apparently by the priest—this is probably also the case with the latter. In the spirit of Deut 6:25, to the person who has clean hands and a pure heart, who has not done obeisance to vain gods, and who has not sworn deceitfully, speaking on YHWH's behalf the priest declares, "You are righteous."[98]

A second type of divinely authorized priestly utterance involved legal pronouncements. Although neither explicitly associates the name of YHWH with the utterance, two Deuteronomic texts imply pronouncements in the name of YHWH. Deuteronomy 17:8–13 calls on the Israelites to bring legal cases that cannot be resolved through ordinary means to the Levitical priest who is in office at the central sanctuary; he serves as the final court of appeal. Since he stands at the sanctuary and serves YHWH their God there, his pronouncements are to be accepted as divine verdicts. To reject the verdict is the height of presumption (הֵזִיד), calling for the death penalty in order to purge the evil from Israel. This interpretation is reinforced by 21:1–9, which involves a technical procedure for dealing with an insoluble crime. While the elders of the town are to take the initiative in such

96. The significance of this blessing in ancient Israel is reflected in two silver amulets from the seventh century BCE found in Jerusalem, inscribed with this blessing. See Barkay, *Ketef Hinnom*, 29–31. A syncretistic eight-century B.C.E. version of the blessing from northeastern Sinai reads: "I bless you by Yahweh of Teman and his Asherah. May he bless you and keep you, and may he be with my lord." As translated by McCarter, *COS* 2.172; cf. Meshel, *Kuntillet Ajrud*, 20.

97. וְשָׂמוּ אֶת־שְׁמִי עַל־בְּנֵי יִשְׂרָאֵל. As noted earlier, Deuteronomy applies the inscription on the medallion of the high priest (Exod 28:36) to Israel as a whole with the phrase, עַם־קָדֹשׁ לַיהוָה אֱלֹהֶיךָ, "a holy people, belonging to Yahweh your God" (Deut 26:19; cf. 7:6, 14:2, 21).

98. Cf. Ezek 18:9. Although Deut 17:14–20 is silent on this role for the king, as king and royal patron of the cult, David would bless the people in the name of YHWH (2 Sam 6:18; 1 Chr 16:2).

cases, the ritual is to be performed in the presence of Levitical priests, whom YHWH has chosen to serve him and to bless in his name. In every impossible dispute (רִיב) and case of assault (נֶגַע) the utterance (עַל־פִּיהֶם, lit., "according to their mouth") is to be determinative, presumably because it has been spoken "in the name of YHWH" (בְּשֵׁם יְהוָה) that is, it bears his name and comes with his stamp of approval/authorization.

Deuteronomy's vision of verbal utterances bearing YHWH's name is not limited to priestly declarations. In Deut 18:15–22 YHWH promises to raise up a prophet who will speak in his name. According to verse 18b this means YHWH will put his words in the prophet's mouth and he will speak to the people all that YHWH commands him. YHWH will personally hold the people accountable for heeding the prophet's words as if they had come from his own mouth. However, prophets who speak presumptuously (יָזִיד) in YHWH's name (when YHWH has not authorized/charged them to speak), who speak in the name of other gods, or who make predictions in YHWH's name and the predictions that fail to materialize, are false prophets. While the punishment for the last offense is unstated, the first two are capital crimes; those prophets will die.[99] In keeping with the Deuteronomic vision of spiritual integrity for the people and the land, true Israelite prophecies bear the name of YHWH, and YHWH alone. They may not bear the stamp of any other deity.

In later texts, the divine stamp of approval on prophetic utterances is reflected in a series of formulas, like the citation formula, "Thus has the Lord YHWH declared" (כֹּה אָמַר אֲדֹנָי יְהוִה, Ezek 2:4), the summons formula, "Now hear the word of YHWH" (וְעַתָּה שְׁמַע דְּבַר־יְהוָה, Amos 7:16), or the oral signatory formula, "the declaration of the Lord YHWH" (נְאֻם אֲדֹנָי יְהוִה, Ezek 5:11). On the king's behalf royal officials would stamp documents as authentic and authoritative with seals declaring their relationship to the king.[100]

---

99. In 13:2–6 [Eng 1–5] Moses presents a slightly different case without references to YHWH's name. A prophet or dreamer who tries to get the people to go after other gods is a counselor of rebellion against YHWH, Israel's savior and redeemer, and must be executed.

100. E.g., the Megiddo seal, לשמע עבד ירבעם, "Belonging to Shema' servant of Jeroboam" and the Tel-en-Nasbeh seal, ליאזניהו עבד המלך, "Belonging to Ja'azaniah servant of the King" (for photographs of both, see Cogan and Tadmor, *II Kings*, Figures 12(a) and 12(c) respectively); and the bulla, לגדליהו עבד המלך, "Belonging to Gedaliah, servant of the king" (Avigad, *Hebrew Bullae*, #5 [p. 24]).

This is obviously impossible with oral utterances made in the name of a superior, but the formula, "the declaration of YHWH" (נְאֻם יְהוָה) functioned as an oral signature with which prophets stamped their utterances. Ezekiel 13:3–9 illustrates well the problem posed by false prophets who claimed authority to use the "seal" with YHWH's name:

Thus has the Lord YHWH declared [כֹּה אָמַר אֲדֹנָי יְהוִה]:
"Woe to the foolish prophets, who follow their own impulse, even though they have not seen a thing. Your prophets, O Israel, have lived like jackals among ruins. You have not gone up into the breaches, nor repaired the wall around the house of Israel, that it might stand in the battle, on the day of YHWH.

Those who say, 'The declaration of YHWH' [נְאֻם יְהוָה], have envisioned emptiness and deceptive divination. Even though YHWH has not commissioned them, they expect him to fulfill the pronouncement! Surely you have envisioned an empty vision and declared a deceptive divination—you, who say 'The declaration of YHWH' [נְאֻם יְהוָה], when I have not even spoken."

Therefore, thus has the Lord YHWH declared: "Because you have made empty pronouncements, and have envisioned lies—therefore, I am challenging you!"—the declaration of the Lord YHWH [נְאֻם אֲדֹנָי יְהוִה]. "My hand will come upon those prophets who envision emptiness and who divine lies:

In the company of my people, they will not be found,
And in the register of the house of Israel,
they will not be recorded;
And to the land of Israel, they will not come back.
Then you will know that I am the Lord YHWH."[101]

Everything about these prophets was false: their message, their tone, their claim to speak for YHWH; and their use of the signatory formula, when they were never authorized to do so.[102] In so doing they bore his name in vain.

---

101. As translated in Block, *Ezekiel Chapters 1–24*, 396–97.

102. See also the reference to swearing and blessing falsely in the name of Yahweh in note 2 above.

Conclusion

The incomparability of YHWH is a common theme in the Hebrew Bible.[103] The confessions of foreigners like Jethro (Exod 18:10–11) and Rahab (Josh 2:9–11) testify to the effectiveness of YHWH's great deeds associated with the rescue of the Israelites from Egyptian bondage in highlighting the distinctions between YHWH, the God of Israel, and the gods worshipped by other peoples.[104] The question that concerns Moses in Deuteronomy is not so much whether or not the nations recognize YHWH's incomparability, but whether or not the Israelites will commit themselves exclusively to this incomparable YHWH by fearing him alone, walking only in his ways, loving him alone, serving only him, and proving it with full-bodied and whole-hearted obedience to his will (Deut 6:4–5; 10:12). This exclusive devotion demanded by YHWH distinguished Israelite religion radically from the religions of the surrounding peoples. Professionally, this requirement was to be acknowledged by kings who ruled in his name alone, priests who served the people cultically and pastorally in his name alone, and prophets who spoke only in his name. As a people, the Israelites were to love and serve him with their entire beings (heart/mind, body, resources; Deut 6:4; 10:12), walk in all his ways (הָלַךְ בְּכָל־דְּרָכָיו) and not after other gods (הָלַךְ אַחֲרֵי אֱלֹהִים; 6:14; 8:19; 11:28; 13:3 [Eng 2]; 28:14), and swear by his name alone (בִּשְׁמוֹ תִּשָּׁבֵעַ; 6:13; 10:20). The stamp of YHWH's name on Israel symbolized his claim on them, a claim that tolerated no other brands, no other allegiances. While YHWH had already declared his claim to the Promised Land (Lev 25:23), Moses declares that at some future date his exclusive geographic claim would be symbolized by the stamp of his name on the place that he would choose. To this place YHWH's people could come for celebration, fellowship, and spiritual renewal, and from this place his rule and his blessing would radiate throughout the land as Israelites extended his righteous rule (32:4) with ethical conduct in pursuit of "righteousness, only righteousness" (צֶדֶק צֶדֶק תִּרְדֹּף, 16:20).

---

103. Labuschagne, *The Incomparability of Yahweh in the Old Testament.*

104. Note YHWH's declared aim that Israel, the Egyptians, and the world recognize his distinction from other all gods (Exod 8:6, 22 [Eng 10, 22]; 9:14, 29; 10:2). According to Exod 11:7, these actions also served the corresponding goal of demonstrating the distinction that YHWH drew between Israel and the other peoples (represented by Egypt).

Unlike the claims made by the gods of other lands and other peoples, YHWH's claims were exclusive. He demanded that the names of all other gods be obliterated from their land, their memory (12:3), and their lips,[105] and that their lives be governed by his will alone. Anything less represented ungrateful compromise at best and faithless idolatry at worst. To be stamped with the name of YHWH but to submit to other gods and to live like other peoples signified vain and empty bearing of his name. To live in the land stamped by his name but live like the Canaanites and do obeisance to their gods betrayed his holy name. For prophets and priests to speak or serve in the name of other gods signified a betrayal of his calling.

How well did the Israelites respond to this high and holy demand? Their history is a history of failure. Although YHWH and his servant Moses pleaded for unqualified and whole-hearted fidelity, they anticipated Israel's corporate betrayal of their calling (31:16–21, 26–29; 32:15–22). How quickly spiritual recidivism would take root, sprout, and flourish is indicated by the historian in Judg 2:10–13:

> And all that generation also were gathered to their fathers. Then another generation arose after them who did not know YHWH or the actions he had performed for Israel. So the descendants of Israel committed that which was evil in YHWH's sight; they served the Baals. They abandoned YHWH, the God of their fathers, who had brought them out of the land of Egypt. They pursued other gods, [chosen] from among the gods of the peoples who surrounded them, and they prostrated themselves before them. Thus they provoked YHWH to anger. They abandoned YHWH and served the Baals and the Ashtaroth.

This infidelity is symbolized by the persistence of toponyms that bore the names of other gods until the days of the nation's demise at the hands of the Assyrians and the Babylonians. Strikingly, whereas among theophoric place names associated with the rest of the tribes El and Baal names predominated, of the seven places assigned to the Levites six appear to have included the names of other deities.[106]

---

105. Cf. Exod 23:13; Josh 23:7; Hos 2:19 [Eng 17]; Ps 16:4.

106. Levitical cities with theophoric names certainly derived from pagan deities: Beth Shemesh (בֵּית שֶׁמֶשׁ, Josh 21:16); Anathoth (עֲנָתוֹת), Josh 21:18), Beth-Horon (בֵּית חוֹרֹן, Josh 21:22); Be-Eshterah (בְּעֶשְׁתְּרָה, undoubtedly a contraction of בֵּית עַשְׁתָּרָה, "House of Ashtarte," Josh 21:27). Levitical cities with theophoric names

Apparently cultic centers devoted to these deities were singled out for the Levite allotments, perhaps suggesting that they were to lead the way in expunging their names from those places. Inasmuch as those original names are preserved in the Hebrew Bible, obviously the spiritual leaders of Israel failed to heed Moses' charge in Deut 12:3. Given the behavior of the Levite in Judges 17–18, this is not entirely surprising. In later times, Hezekiah and Josiah would seek to restore exclusive devotion to YHWH by applying Moses' injunctions literally.[107] Although the Deuteronomistic Historian expresses no explicit interest in the names of pagan deities tied to cult centers, Josiah's defilement of those installations by demolishing them (נָתַץ), grinding them to dust (דָּקַק), burning the remains (שָׂרַף), and dumping (שָׁלַךְ) the ashes over graves or running water may have been intended to wipe out the memory of their names (2 Kgs 23:6–15; cf. Deut 7:5; 12:3).

In keeping with Moses' vision of YHWH as the only true God (Deut 4:35, 39; 10:17–21; 32:1–43), centuries later David would celebrate the extension of his exclusive claims beyond Israel to the entire cosmos:

23 Sing to YHWH, all the earth!
Tell of his salvation from day to day.
24 Declare his glory among the nations,
his marvelous works among all the peoples!
25 For great is YHWH, and greatly to be praised,
and he is to be revered above all gods.
26 For all the gods of the peoples are idols,
but YHWH made the heavens.
27 Splendor and majesty are before him;
strength and joy are in his place.
28 Ascribe to YHWH, O clans of the peoples,
ascribe to YHWH glory and strength!
29 Ascribe to YHWH the glory due his name;
bring an offering and come before him!
Prostrate before YHWH in the splendor of holiness;
30 tremble before him, all the earth;
Yes, the world is established; it shall never be moved.

possibly derived from pagan deities: Kibzaim (קִבְצַיִם, Josh 21:22; however, ים may be the name of the god of the sea [Yamm, in Ugaritic texts], in which case the name means something like "Yamm has gathered"); Jokneam קָנְעָם, Josh 21:34; apparently a corruption of יָקְמְעָם, "May 'Am raise up/establish"; cf. 1 Chr 6:53).

107. 2 Kgs 18:4, 22 and 23:4–24, respectively.

³¹ Let the heavens be glad, and let the earth rejoice,
      and let them say among the nations, "YHWH reigns!"
³² Let the sea roar, and all that fills it;
      let the field exult, and everything in it!
³³ Then shall the trees of the forest sing for joy
      before YHWH,
      for he comes to judge the earth.
³⁴ Oh give thanks to YHWH, for he is good;
      for his steadfast love endures forever!
³⁵ Say also: "Save us, O God of our salvation,
      and gather and deliver us from among the nations,
      that we may give thanks to your holy name,
      and glory in your praise.
³⁶ Blessed be YHWH, the God of Israel,
      from everlasting to everlasting!"
      (1 Chr 16:23–36; adapted from ESV)

Inspired by David's vision, Solomon would build a temple for YHWH, "in order that all the peoples of the earth may know your name (שְׁמֶךָ) and fear you, as do your people Israel, and that they may know that your name is read on this house (שִׁמְךָ נִקְרָא עַל־הַבַּיִת הַזֶּה) that I have built" (1 Kgs 8:43).[108] Presumably above the entrance to the temple compound the builders inscribed the words, היכל יהוה, "The Temple of YHWH" (Jer 7:4).[109] This was not only YHWH's authorized dwelling place, but also the symbol of his claim upon his land and his people for the world to recognize.

The missiological function of YHWH's name imprinted on his people and on the building that served as his earthly residence is clear. His exclusive claims to his people and their mandate as a kingdom of priests and a holy nation (Exod 19:4–6) would be fulfilled only to the extent that Israel would demonstrate unqualified commitment to him (Deut 6:4), and that the land itself would have only one name stamped on it—the name of YHWH. Fast forwarding the reel to the present day, this remains the case. As the people of God, we are baptized into Christ (Rom 6:3–4; Gal 3:27) and branded

108. Apart from the Exodus narratives (Exod 7:5; 14:4, 8), statements like this highlighting universal revelatory goals occur only three additional times in Old Testament narratives: in association with the crossing of the Jordan (Josh 4:21–24), David's triumph over Goliath (1 Sam 17:46), and Hezekiah's victory over the Assyrians (2 Kgs 19:19).

109. Cf. n. 59 above.

with his name (Acts 11:26; 26:28; 1 Pet 4:16), and as the temple of the Holy Spirit and the living God, he demands the undiluted and full-bodied allegiance of individual Christians (1 Cor 6:19–20) and the church corporately (2 Cor 6:14–18). The God of Israel and Lord of the church will not share either his glory or our devotion with Belial (Greek Βελιάρ; Hebrew בְּלִיַּעַל. [Deut 13:14 (Eng 13)]) or any other godlet (Greek εἴδωλον; Hebrew אֱלִילִים [Ps 96:5]). May we all bear the name of the Lord with honor, and may the world read his name, and his name alone, on this temple in which he dwells.

9

"In Spirit and in Truth"
The Mosaic Vision of Worship[1]

Introduction

THESE DAYS IF PEOPLE ask you what kind of church you attend, they probably do not have in mind your denomination, but the worship style; is it traditional, liturgical, or contemporary? In the past the differences in worship have revolved around the use of musical instruments in worship, but it extended to other matters as well: the use of creeds, formal benedictions, confessions of sin, or prepared prayers. In our concern to satisfy people's liturgical and musical tastes, I sometimes wonder if we have explored seriously enough what the Scriptures have to say about acceptable worship. Yes, we acknowledge the legacy of Robert Webber in the Ancient-Future Faith movement, which seeks to recover the richness and profundity of early Christian worship. However, in evangelicals' recent fascination with post-New Testament practices and perspectives we observe an increasing tendency to accept early worship forms as authoritative and decreasing attention to the theology of worship of the Scriptures. Indeed in some circles the Reformation principle of *sola scriptura* is threatened by enthusiasm to recover the worship of the early church, and practices become normative even when they lack explicit biblical warrant.[2]

1. This is an expanded version of a paper presented to the Biblical Worship Section of the Evangelical Theological Society in Atlanta, November 18, 2010.

2. The Gloria Patri is an interesting case. The original wording of the first part of

But even when we agree that the Scriptures alone should be our ultimate authority for Christian faith we are divided as to which Scriptures we should appeal. Should our worship be regulated by the whole Bible or are only the teachings and practices of the New Testament determinative?[3] While rarely explicitly declared, the latter is implied by many scholars who write on this subject. In what I consider to be one of the most important books on worship from a biblical perspective, *Engaging with God: A Biblical Theology of Worship,* one of David Peterson's declared goals is "to expose the discontinuity between the Testaments" on the subject of worship.[4] Although the book is presented as a "biblical theology of worship," and although the Old Testament is three times the length of the New Testament, and probably contains ten times as much information on worship, Peterson disposes of its treatment of the subject in fifty-six pages, while devoting almost two hundred pages to the New Testament. For

---

the doxology, *Gloria Patri per Filium in Spiritu Sancto* ("Glory to the Father through the Son in the Holy Spirit"), was modeled on the formula for baptism (Matt 28:19). It reflects the New Testament picture more closely than the version with which we are familiar:

Δόξα Πατρὶ καὶ Υἱῷ καὶ Πνεύματι
καὶ νῦν καὶ ἀεὶ καὶ εἰς τοὺς αἰῶνας των αἰώνων Ἀμὴν

Gloria Patri, et Filio, et Spiritui Sancto.
Sicut erat in principio, et nunc, et semper, et in sæcula sæculorum. Amen.

Glory be to the Father, and to the Son and to the Holy Spirit;
as it was in the beginning, is now, and ever shall be, world without end. Amen.

The modification of the first line represents a fourth-century CE response to Arians, who claimed that since Jesus was begotten the Son was neither eternal nor equal in divinity with the Father. By replacing the prepositions "through" and "in" with conjunctions "and," the post-Nicene Church sought to ensure a proper stress on the co-equality of each person of the Holy Trinity—despite the fact that the Holy Spirit is never addressed directly in the New Testament, either in prayer or in praise, and that his role is to direct people's attention to the Son. The urge to treat the Holy Spirit as object of worship is extra-biblical, deriving, not from Scripture, but from philosophical and theological deduction. It assumes that since Father, Son, and Holy Spirit are equally divine, they are to be equally worshiped.

3. For a helpful introduction to this subject, see Farley, "What is "Biblical" Worship?" 591–613.

4. Peterson, *Engaging with God,* 24.

Peterson, the Old Testament's focus on place, festivals, and priestly rituals provides a foil against which to interpret New Testament worship, which is centered on a person, involves all of life, and, when it speaks of Christians gathering, focuses on edification.[5] The problem also appears in John Piper's work. In a sermon titled "Worship God!"[6] Piper contrasts Old Testament and New Testament worship, asserting that Old Testament worship was external, involving form and ritual, while New Testament worship concerns internal spiritual experience.[7] But this perception of a radical contrast between Old and New Testament worship has a long history in Protestantism. Luther said, "If any would not sing and talk of what Christ has wrought for us, he shows thereby that he does not really believe." However, Luther misunderstood Old Testament worship completely when he added, "and that he belongs not into the New Testament, which is an era of joy, but into the Old, which produces not the spirit of joy, but of unhappiness and discontent."[8]

Such generalizations are misleading on several counts. First, they underestimate the liturgical nature of worship in the New Testament. What can be more cultic and formal than the Lord's Supper, the worship experience *par excellence* prescribed by Jesus, or the ritual of baptism, called for in the Great Commission (Matt 28:19)? Acts

---

5. Similar perspectives are reflected in Carson's essay, "Worship under the Word," 11–63. Although he cautions against exaggerating the differences between the forms of worship under the Mosaic and the new covenants, this is what he does when he uses Rom 12:1–2 to illustrate the change in the language of worship, which under the old covenant was bound up with Temple and priestly service, but which under the new is transported away from the cultus (ibid., 37); and when, in his presentation of Christian worship he speaks of the New Testament as our guide (ibid., 44). This comment implies that the practice of first-century Christians as described and commanded in the NT alone provides the norms for Christian worship, a point observed also by Farley, "What is Biblical Worship?" 595–96.

6. November 9, 1997. Accessed April 24, 2010 from http://www.desiringgod .org/ResourceLibrary/Sermons/ByDate/1997/1016_Worship_God/.

7. He declares, "You can see what is happening in the NT. Worship is being significantly de-institutionalized, de-localized, de-ritualized. The whole thrust is being taken off of ceremony and seasons and places and forms; and is being shifted to what is happening in the heart—not just on Sunday, but every day and all the time in all of life."

8. In his preface to the Velentin Babst Gesangbuch (1545), as cited in W. E. Buzsin, "Luther on Music," *Musical Quarterly* 32 (1946) 83.

2:41–42 describes the early church engaged in the external activities of baptism, instruction, fellowship, breaking bread, and prayer.

Second, they misrepresent the shape of true worship as it is presented in the Old Testament. Carson is certainly correct when he interprets Jesus' prediction in John 4:21–24 of a day when the focus of worship will shift from the place to the manner of worship and suggesting that "in spirit and in truth" (ἐν πνεύματι καὶ ἀληθείᾳ) is "a way of saying that we must worship God *by means of Christ*. In him the reality has dawned and the shadows are being swept away (cf. Heb 8:13)."[9] Peterson is also correct in suggesting that the worship "in spirit and in truth" of which Jesus spoke contrasts "with the symbolic and typical," represented by Old Testament forms. However, his portrayal of worship "in truth" as "real and genuine worship" rendered by "true worshippers" is problematic.[10] In ancient Israel the worship of many was true, that is, it was both real and genuine. The forms may have involved replica actions of heavenly realities, but they were divinely revealed and the worship was true and authentic. Peterson is also correct when he says that worship "in spirit" refers to the Holy Spirit, "who regenerates us, brings new life, and confirms us in the truth." However, if this represents a change, then we must admit that in ancient Israel worshipers were unregenerate, they lacked the new life, and they were not confirmed in the truth. But this does not seem to match the image of Caleb (Num 14:24; Deut 1:36; Josh 14:9), or David, who authored so many of the Psalms, or Isaiah in Isaiah 6.

John Piper's interpretation of Jesus' statement is even more problematic: "I take 'in spirit' to mean that this true worship is carried along by the Holy Spirit and is happening mainly as an inward, spiritual event, not mainly as an outward bodily event. And I take 'in truth' to mean that this true worship is a response to true views of God and is shaped and guided by true views of God."[11] If this is correct, and if Jesus' comment speaks of the contrast between Old Testament and New Testament worship, then we would have to say that in ancient Israel (1) true worship carried along by the Spirit was totally lacking, (2) worship was primarily a matter of external actions,

---

9. Carson, "Worship under the Word," 37.

10. Peterson, *Engaging with God*, 98–99.

11. Piper, "Worship God!"

rather than an inward spiritual event, and (3) the Israelites lacked true views of God that would have guided true worship.

It seems that by driving these wedges between the Testaments we have overlooked significant continuities and mistakenly retrojected on ancient Israel problems within the Judaisms of Jesus' day and of the apostolic age. We have not allowed the Old Testament to speak for itself and have denied the true worshipers in Israel the hope that YHWH had offered them with his gracious revelation. My task in this chapter is to explore worship in one small portion of the Old Testament, the book of Deuteronomy. When I try to let this book speak with its own voice on the subject of worship I begin to doubt the wisdom or validity of this dichotomizing of Old Testament worship as external and cultic and New Testament worship as internal and spiritual.

Deuteronomy as a Worship Book

The translators of the Septuagint sent the interpretation of the book of Deuteronomy down an unfortunate track when they named the fifth book of the Pentateuch Τὸ Δευτερονόμιον, "second law,"[12] instead of translating the Hebrew title, הַדְּבָרִים, as οἱ Λόγοι, meaning "the words," or סֵפֶר דְּבָרִים as Τὸ Βιβλίον τῶν Λόγων, "The Book of Words," and when they decided to translate the Hebrew word תּוֹרָה as νόμος rather than διδαχή or διδασκαλία, "teaching, instruction."[13] Whether or not νόμος meant "law" in the third century BCE,[14] later readers have treated this book primarily as a legislative document and in so doing overlooked its true pastoral intent and genre. The book does indeed contain many statutes and ordinances, but these are subservient to the pastoral and rhetorical agenda, which is to inspire the Israelites to gratitude for YHWH's grace, and to promote fear, faith, and covenant commitment (love) that will be demonstrated in lives of joyful obedience. Deuteronomy is actually cast as a collection of

---

12. The form of the name seems to be derived from Deut 17:18, where Hebrew מִשְׁנֵה הַתּוֹרָה, "a copy of the Torah," is misinterpreted as τὸ δευτερονόμιον, "second law."

13. Deut 1:5; 4:8, 44; 17:11, 18, 19; 27:3, 8, 26; 28:58, 61; 29:20, 28[Eng 21, 29]; 30:10; 31:9, 11, 12, 24, 26; 32:46; 33:4, 10.

14. There is some debate whether νόμος actually bore the narrow sense of "law," in the third century BCE, or whether its scope was broader, more akin to Hebrew תּוֹרָה. See Gutbrod, "Nomos," 1046–47.

Moses' valedictory sermons prior to his death on Mount Nebo.[15] The book recounts the last worship service officiated by Moses, a covenant renewal service on the Plains of Moab.[16] As a record of worship it reflects a gathering as concerned with edification and instruction as any that Peterson finds in the New Testament.[17]

The structure of chapters 12–26, which scholars generally mislabel as the Deuteronomic Law Code, reinforces the perception of the book of Deuteronomy as a worship document. These chapters do indeed contain many specific regulations governing Israel's life in the Promised Land, and the heading in 12:1 leads readers to expect a formal series of laws comparable to those found in the Book of the Covenant. However, in tone and style much of this material bears a closer resemblance to Moses' preaching in chapters 6–11, especially chapter 7, than to the regulations of the Covenant Code (Exod 20:22—23:19) or the Instructions on Holiness of Leviticus (17:1—26:2), and certainly than to Mesopotamian laws.[18]

Deuteronomy on Worship

But what has the book of Deuteronomy actually to say about worship? I propose to answer this question under four headings: (1) the place of the cult and ritual in Deuteronomy; (2) the place of the *place* of worship in Deuteronomy; (3) the function of cultic worship in Deuteronomy; (4) the nature of true and spiritual worship in Deuteronomy.

---

15. This conclusion is confirmed not only by the pervasively hortatory style of the addresses, but also by the verbs used to described what Moses is doing in this book: לָמַד, "to teach" (4:1, 5, 10, 14; 6:1; 31:19, 22); דִּבֶּר, "to speak" (1:1, 3, 18; 4:45; 5:1, 31; 31:30); as for the Israelites, they are to "learn" (לָמַד) them: 5:1; 17:19(?); 31:12; and "teach" (לָמַד) them: 5:31; 11:19; שָׁנַן (6:7).

16. The book includes transcripts of Moses' three sermons (1:6—4:40; 5:1b—26:19, 28:1–69[Eng 29:1]; 29:1 [Eng 2]—30:20), instructions for a covenantal ritual at Gerizim and Ebal (27:1–26), a hymn (cast as Israel's national anthem (32:1–43), and a closing benediction for each of the tribes (33:1–29).

17. Peterson, *Engaging with God*, 196, 202, 206–21, 257–50, 287.

18. The literary boundaries of this section are set by the heading in Deut 12:1 and the conclusion in 26:16–19, which create an effective frame around 12:2—26:15. Within this framework Moses' instructions exhibit a remarkable structural similarity to the Book of the Covenant:

The Place of the Cult and Ritual in Deuteronomy

It is clear that Deuteronomy was not written as a manual on worship practice. Unlike Exodus 25–31 (which prescribes the construction and ornamentation of the tabernacle, including the dressing of the priest) and Leviticus 1–16 (which prescribes in detail Israel's sacrificial procedures [Lev 1–7], the consecration and conduct of priests [Lev 8–10], the boundaries of ritual purity and impurity [Lev 11–15], and the rituals of the Day of Atonement [Lev 16]), Deuteronomy spends little time on cultic procedures. To be sure, in his second address Moses devotes some time to cultic events and practices.

TABLE 8: The Annual Festivals and Offerings in Israel's Liturgical System

Passover and Unleavened Bread	16:1–8
Shavuoth (Festival of Weeks)	16:9–12
Sukkoth (Festival of Booths)	16:13–15; 31:10–13
Offerings	
זִבְחֵיכֶם ("sacrifices")	12:6, 11, 27; 18:3; 32:38; 33:19
עֹלֹת ("whole burnt offerings")	12:6, 11, 13–14, 27; 27:6[18]
שְׁלָמִים ("fellowship, peace offerings")	27:7
מַעְשְׂרֹת ("tithes")	12:6, 11, 17; 14:22–29; 26:12–15
נְדָרִים ("votive offerings")	12:6, 11, 17, 26; 23:19, 22–24[Eng 18, 21–23]
תְּרוּמָה ("sacred contribution")	12:6, 11, 17

Exodus 20:22—23:19	Deuteronomy 12:2—26:15
A Principles of Worship (20:23–26), highlighting Israel's cultic expression of devotion to YHWH	A Principles of Worship (12:2—16:17), highlighting Israel's cultic expression of devotion to YHWH
B Casuistic and Apodictic Laws (21:1—23:13), highlighting Israel's ethical expression of devotion to YHWH	B Casuistic and Apodictic Instruction (16:18—25:19), highlighting Israel's ethical and civil expression of devotion to YHWH
A' Principles of Worship (23:14–19), highlighting Israel's cultic expression of devotion to YHWH	A' Principles of Worship (26:1–15), highlighting Israel's cultic expression of devotion to YHWH

נְדָבָה ("freewill offering")	12:6, 17; 16:10; 23:25[Eng 24]
בְּכֹרֹת ("firstborn offering")	12:6, 17; 14:23; 15:19–23
נָסִיךְ ("libation")	32:38
רֵאשִׁית ("firstfruits")	18:4; 26:2–11

Other Rituals and Regulations

Priestly prebends	18:1–8
The heifer ritual	21:1–9
The covenant renewal ritual	27:1–26

However, these texts express little interest in ritual procedures. Indeed if Deuteronomy were our sole source on cultic matters it would be impossible to reconstruct the forms of Israel's rituals. The exceptions are special ceremonies involving the slaughter of the heifer over a running stream (21:1–9), the offering of firstfruits (26:1–11), and the covenant ceremony at Mounts Gerizim and Ebal (27:1–26). However, the first is not concerned with regular worship, but involves a graciously revealed special ritual to purge the community of bloodguilt in murder cases where the guilty person cannot be identified. The second involves a liturgical ritual, complete with instructions for the manipulation of an offering and a prescribed creedal utterance by the worshiper to accompany the offering. However, even here the emphasis is clearly on covenantal theology and the blessing of covenant relationship. Like the consecration of the firstborn in 15:19–23, the harvest of the firstfruits symbolizes YHWH's delight in fellowship with his people and offers a regular venue for thanksgiving for YHWH's gracious provision of fruit for the people's labor, but especially for his fulfillment of his promises to the ancestors and his original redemption of Israel. As in earlier references to the sacrifices and festivals, the focus is not on the ritual itself but on the profound theology underlying Israel's status as the people of YHWH. The third involves a one-time event integrating the Promised Land into the tripartite covenantal relationship involving YHWH, the people, and the land.[19]

---

19. On the interpretation of 27:1–26, see Block, *Deuteronomy*, 623–39.

The Place of the Place of Worship in Deuteronomy

The importance of place in Israel's past and present in Deuteronomy can scarcely be overestimated.[20] But Moses also looks forward to Israel occupying her place in the land promised to the ancestors,[21] and to YHWH taking his place at the place (מָקוֹם) he would choose to establish his name. This is the place that concerns us, for this would be the place where Israel would worship him.

In Deuteronomy Moses refers to the place that YHWH would choose to establish his name twenty-one times.[22] The "place formula" occurs in a variety of forms, ranging from the most elemental, "the place that he will choose" (16:16; 31:11), to the most complex, "the place that YHWH your God will choose out of all your tribes to put his name and to establish it" (12:5). This most complex form—which is the first in the book—makes four fundamental assertions concerning "the place." (1) YHWH, the God of Israel, will choose the place.[23] (2) It will be chosen from within the territorial tribal allotments.[24]

20. In Moses' recollection, Egypt was the place of YHWH's multiplication of the population in fulfillment of the promises to the ancestors, but also the place of oppression and ultimate redemption (1:30; 4:34; 6:21; 10:22; 11:3; 16:12; 24:18; 26:5–8); Sinai/Horeb was the place of divine revelation and covenant (4:9–15; 5:2; 18:16; 28:69[Eng 29:1]), but also of Israel's failure (9:7–21) and YHWH's gracious covenant renewal (9:25—10:5); the desert was a place of providential care (1:31; 8:15–16), but also of testing (8:2–6) and failure (1:19–46; 6:16; 9:22–24); the Plain of Moab was a place of covenant renewal (11:26–28; 26:16–19; 28:69—29:20[Eng 29:1–21]; 30:11–20) and Moses' farewell (31:1—34:12). On the importance of time and place in Deuteronomy, see McConville and Millar, *Time and Place in Deuteronomy*.

21. Deut 1:8, 21, 35; 4:1; 6:3, 10; 6:18, 23; 7:13; 8:1; 9:5; 10:11; 11:9, 21; 12:1; 19:8; 26:3, 15; 27:3; 28:11; 29:24[Eng 25]; 30:5, 20; 31:7, 16, 20.

22. Deut 12:5, 11, 14, 18, 21, 26; 14:23, 24, 25; 15:20; 16:2, 6, 7, 11, 15, 16; 17:8, 10; 18:6; 26:2; 31:11. For variations/ echoes of the formula in later writings, see Josh 9:27; 2 Kgs 21:7; 23:27; Jer 7:12; Ezra 6:12; Neh 1:9.

23. Moses does not say how that choice would be made or communicated, but the location was revealed to David through Gad the prophet (2 Sam 24:18–25; 1 Chr 21:18). The present promise was obviously in the mind of the psalmists in Pss 78:68 and 132:13–14. On the initiative of deities in ancient Near Eastern accounts of temple construction, see Hurowitz, *"I Have Built You an Exalted House,"* 135–67.

24. Predicted in Numbers 34 and fulfilled by Joshua in Joshua 14–19. With hindsight we can recognize three distinct phases in the nation's religious history, each involving centralized worship at a single primary sanctuary but at different places: (1) wherever the nation camped during their desert wanderings; (2) at a series of locations in the land of Canaan during the nation's transition from tribal government to a monarchy; Mount Ebal/Shechem (Deut 27; Josh 8:30–35; 24), Bethel

(3) It will bear YHWH's name. The expression speaks of divine ownership: just as a person who bears the name of YHWH is recognized as belonging to YHWH,[25] so the place bearing the imprint of his name is recognized as his possession[26] and alludes to the practice of inscribing the name of the founder of a building on the foundation stone. YHWH hereby validates the location and declares it to be a locale where he could be worshiped and confidently invoked.[27] (4) The place will be the goal of Israel's pilgrimages. Whereas else-

---

(Judg 20:26–27), Shiloh (Judg 21:19–21; 1 Sam 1–3; Jer 7:12–14; Ps 78:60); and (3) at a permanent location after the transition was complete. The successive interpretation of "the place that YHWH will choose" has been well argued by Wenham, "Deuteronomy and the Central Sanctuary"; McConville, "Time, Place, and the Deuteronomic Altar-Law," 89–139; idem, *Law and Theology in Deuteronomy*, 98–35.

25. On which, see Block, "Bearing the Name of the LORD with Honor," 61–72. Cf. Exod 20:7; Deut 5:11; Isa 44:5. Isaiah 18:7 speaks of the temple as the place of YHWH's name. Note also the references to "building a house for the name of YHWH" (2 Sam 7:13; 1 Kgs 3:2; 5:17–19[Eng 3–5]; 8:17–20, 44, 48).

26. For equivalent expressions in Akkadian texts, see EA 287:60–63 (*ANET* 488; cf. EA 288:5, *ANET* 488); in an Egyptian text, Rameses III refers to building a temple for Amon "as the vested property of your name" (*ANET* 261). Here the expression is equivalent to "the place where YHWH causes [people] to remember his name" in Exod 20:24, "the place on which my name is called/read," which later always refers specifically to the city of Jerusalem (Jer 25:29) or the temple/house of YHWH (1 Kgs 8:43; Jer 7:10, 11, 14, 30; 32:34; 34:15). The same expression (קְרָא שֵׁם עַל) is used of Israel as the elect people of YHWH in Deut 28:10 and 2 Chr 7:14, and is applied to a prophet in Jer 15:16, and the elect nations in Amos 9:12; Isa 63:19 notes the nations are not called by God's name. See further above, pp. 253–60.

27. John van Seters rightly associates the "name" with the Ark of the Covenant, since it contained the tablets of the covenant, in the preamble of which YHWH had imprinted his own name. When YHWH chose Jerusalem as the place to set his name, the city was designated as the place for the ark to rest. See *The Biblical Saga of King David*, 235. On the inscription of a name on the foundation stone of a temple for its validation, see McBride, *The Deuteronomic Name Theology*, 93–94. The translation of לְשַׁכֵּן שְׁמוֹ, "to establish his name," assumes that שׂוּם, "to set, place," and שַׁכֵּן, "to establish," are virtual synonyms, and that שַׁכֵּן is a shapel form of כּוּן, "to establish," rather than a piel infinitive of שָׁכֵן, "to dwell." Thus Brockelmann, *Grundriss der vergleichenden Grammatik der semitischen Sprachen*, 1:522. Much of the evidence for this position derives from Akkadian counterparts to the Hebrew expression. See McBride, *Deuteronomic Name Theology*, 204–10; Richter, *The Deuteronomistic History and the Name Theology*; idem, "The Place of the Name in Deuteronomy," 342–66. LXX translates, ἐπικληθῆναι, "for his name to be invoked there." Recognizing the oddity, the Masoretes pointed the word as if from שָׁכֵן, "to dwell," and attached it to the following verb, "you shall seek his dwelling place." The Targums read "to make his Shekinah dwell there." For discussion of the textual and grammatical issues involved, see Tov, *Textual Criticism of the Hebrew Bible*, 42; McCarthy, *BHQ*, 85*–86.*

where the verb דָּרַשׁ, "to seek," usually speaks of looking for something, or enquiring, or even caring for, that is, to seek someone else's
welfare (11:12), here the idiom דָּרַשׁ אֶל־הַמָּקוֹם literally, "to seek to the
place," means "to make a pilgrimage to the place," or "to visit the place
with spiritual intent."[28]

Given the frequency of the place formula in Deuteronomy, it is
easy to become fixated with geography, and forget that the place represents something much greater. In the ancient world temples were
not merely monuments that people would visit; they were viewed
as residences for deities. Frequent association with the phrases
לִפְנֵי יְהוָה, "before YHWH,"[29] and אֶת־יְהוָה, "with YHWH" (16:16;
17:12; 31:11) demonstrates that this would be the case also for "the
place that YHWH would choose." Deuteronomy's emphasis on "the
place" highlights the availability and personal presence of the One
who actually dwells in heaven (4:39),[30] but who condescends to take
up residence on earth for the purpose of communing with his people.[31] When people would make pilgrimages to the place, they would
come for an encounter and audience with YHWH.

28. Cf. Tigay, *Deuteronomy*, 120. See also Amos 5:5, and Isa 11:10, "you may
make a pilgrimage to the place" (דָּרַשׁ אֶל).

29. 10:8; 12:7, 12, 18; 14:23, 26; 15:20; 16:11; 18:7; 19:17; 24:4, 13; 26:5, 10, 13;
27:7; 29:9, 14[Eng 10, 15]; cf. earlier references to events "before YHWH": 1:45 (at
Kadesh Barnea the people wept before YHWH); 4:10 (at Horeb the people stood
before YHWH); 6:25 (people are recognized as righteous before because of their
obedience); 9:18, 25 (Moses fell down [חִתְנַפֵּל] before YHWH to intercede for the
people). For a thorough discussion of the significance of לִפְנֵי יְהוָה, "before YHWH,"
in Deuteronomy, see Wilson, *Out Of The Midst Of The Fire*, 142–97.

30. As Solomon recognized repeatedly in his prayer of dedication for the place
that is stamped with the name of YHWH: 1 Kgs 8:23, 30, 32, 34, 36, 39, 43, 45, 49.

31. A deeply entrenched scholarly tradition interprets the temple as the residence for the name of YHWH (שֵׁם יְהוָה) as a late theological abstraction of earlier
perceptions of real presence. According to Moshe Weinfeld, Deuteronomy is not
only a remarkable literary achievement, but represents a profound monument to
the theological revolution advocated by Josianic circles. This revolution attempted
to eliminate other shrines and to centralize all worship of YHWH in Jerusalem, as
well as to "secularize," "demythologize," and "spiritualize" the religion. It sought to
replace traditional images of divine corporeality and divine enthronement in the
temple with more abstract and spiritual notions reflected in the "name theology" of
the book. In this new religious world sacrifices are no longer institutional and corporate matters, but personal expressions of faith, and the tithe is no longer "holy to
YHWH," but remains the possession of the owner (14:22–27). See further Weinfeld,
"Deuteronomy, Book of," 1775–78. In recent years this interpretation has come un-

The Function of Cultic Worship in Deuteronomy

The significance of this conclusion is magnified when we examine specifically what YHWH invited the Israelites to *do* "before his face." Limiting ourselves initially to the occurrences of the place formula, we observe that the Israelites were invited to come there to "see the face of YHWH" (31:11; cf. 16:16), to hear the Torah read (31:11) and thereby learn to fear YHWH (14:23; 31:9–13), to celebrate the three great annual pilgrimage festivals,[32] to present their offerings and recall YHWH's saving and providential grace (26:1–11), to demonstrate their covenant commitment to YHWH horizontally by gifts of charity to the marginalized (26:12; cf. 10:12–22), to demonstrate communal solidarity by celebrating with their children, servants, the Levites, and the alien (12:12; 14:27–29; 16:11), and to settle legal disputes before the Levitical priest/judge (17:8–13). This was also the place where Levites would serve in the name of YHWH, standing before him, and blessing the people in his name (10:8; 18:6–8).

Many today view Israel's worship as involving obligatory cultic actions demanded by YHWH to satisfy his need for honor, which the people dutifully performed in response to divine commands. All males were compelled to go to the central shrine three times a year to observe the festivals of Passover/Unleavened Bread, Weeks, and Booths (16:1–17), and if they could drag the females in their families and their neighbors with them so much the better. Judging by the picture painted by Deuteronomy, one could scarcely be farther from the truth.

The attitudinal foundations are laid in 12:2–14.[33] Although many refer to this text as the Deuteronomic altar law,[34] and most

---

der increasing scrutiny. See especially Richter, *The Deuteronomistic History and the Name Theology*; Vogt, *Deuteronomic Theology and the Significance of Torah*; Wilson, *Out Of The Midst Of The Fire*; Wilson, "Central Sanctuary or Local Settlements?" 323–40.

32. Passover (16:1–8), Festival of Weeks (Pentecost, 16:9–12), Festival of Booths (16:13–17; 31:9–13).

33. For fuller discussion of this text, see Block, "The Joy of Worship," 98–117. On worship as joyful celebration, see Weinfeld, *Deuteronomy and the Deuteronomic School*, 210–24; Braulik, "The Joy of the Feast," 27–65; idem, "Commemoration of Passion and Feast of Joy," 67–85; Willis, "'Eat and Rejoice Before the Lord," 276–94.

34. However, not only does a reference to Israel's "altar" (מִזְבֵּחַ) not appear until verse 27, but the designation "law," is also much too legal. Speaking for YHWH,

translations treat this unit as a series of legal prescriptions, its genre is established by the hortatory sermonic injunctions that punctuate it (vv. 4, 8–9, 13–14). Indeed, many of the verbs should probably be interpreted modally rather than as imperatives, which greatly diminishes its legal flavor greatly:

> But you *may* make pilgrimages [lit. "seek"] to the place YHWH your God will choose from among all your tribes to put his Name there to establish it. To that place you *may come*; there you *may bring* your burnt offerings and sacrifices, your tithes and special gifts, what you have vowed to give and your freewill offerings, and the firstborn of your herds and flocks. There, in the presence of YHWH your God, you and your families *may* eat and you *may* celebrate in everything you have put your hand to, because YHWH your God has blessed you.
> (vv. 5–7)

Translating the text this way yields a profoundly positive picture and flies in the face of common perceptions in several respects. First, as already noted, more than an order from on high, this is *an invitation* to the Israelites to make regular pilgrimages to the place where YHWH resides.

Second, the Israelites are invited to come to/enter the place where YHWH resides. Many translations render the verb בּוֹא as "go," but this obscures the intent. Speaking on behalf of YHWH, Moses says, "There you may come/enter."[35] The verb presents the Israelites' movement from the perspective of the person at the destination, rather than a person sending them off.[36] This is the Old Testament equivalent to Jesus' invitations, "Come to me all you that labor and are loaded down" (Matt 11:28), and "If any are thirsty, let them come

---

Moses invites his people to continuous and repeated fellowship with him. YHWH's provision of a place ensures that future Israelites will have regular access to himself, just as the exodus generation had at Sinai. Compare not only the emphasis in the Exodus narratives on Sinai as a place where Israel would "serve" YHWH (עָבַד, Exod 3:12; 4:23; 7:16, 26[Eng 8:1]; 8:16[Eng 20]; 9:1, 13; 10:3, 7–8, 11, 24, 26; 12:31), offer sacrifices to him (זָבַח, Exod 3:18; 5:3, 8, 17; 8:4, 21–25[Eng 8, 25–29]; 10:25), and celebrate a festival in his honor (חָגַג, Exod 5:1; cf. 10:9), but also YHWH's opening words to Israel in Exod 19:4, "You yourselves have seen what I did to the Egyptians, and how I bore you on eagles' wings *and brought* (הֵבִיא) *you to myself.*"

35. "To go" would have been expressed with הָלַךְ.

36. The opposite of בּוֹא, "to come, enter," is יָצָא, "to go out" (cf. 28:6, 19).

to me and drink" (John 7:37). True Israelite worship occurred in God's presence by his gracious invitation.

Third, the Israelites are invited to bring (הֵבִיא) all their offerings to YHWH (vv. 6, 11). Again Moses represents the person offering the invitation at the destination rather than the source.[37] His catalogue of seven types of offerings reflects his enthusiasm: "whole burnt offerings," "animal sacrifices," "tithes," "specially dedicated donations," "votive offerings," "freewill offerings," and "the firstborn of herds and flocks." The list is obviously not exhaustive, but representative of the whole of the Israelite cultic system of fellowship with YHWH.

Fourth, the Israelites are invited to eat there in the presence of YHWH.[38] As elsewhere in ancient Near Eastern and biblical contexts, eating together was a ritual act of fellowship and communion, often the culminating event of a covenant-making ritual.[39] However, unlike pagan offerings that were presented as food for the gods, here the focus is on the offerings as food for the worshipers. The Israelites' God will host his vassals at this banquet table, but he will not eat with them.[40]

Fifth, the Israelites are invited to celebrate the blessing of YHWH on their work. Whereas verbs for joy and celebration occur in the Sinai regulations only in Lev 23:40, the second address in Deuteronomy sets the mood of worship with the verb שָׂמַח, "to rejoice," various forms of which occur eight times in connection with appearing before YHWH.[41]

---

37. So also verse 11. Taking the offering to a place might have been expressed with נָשָׂא, "to carry," as in verse 26.

38. On "eating before YHWH," see Wilson, *Out of the Midst of the Fire*, 161–65.

39. Gen 31:54; Exod 24:5–11.

40. In Exod 18:12 Moses, Aaron, and the elders of Israel eat with Jethro "before God." Compare Uriah's eating before David (2 Sam 11:13), Adonijah's supporters eating before him (1 Kgs 1:25), and Jehoiachin's eating "before" his overlord, the king of Babylon (2 Kgs 25:29//Jer 52:33). In Ezek 44:3, the prince (נָשִׂיא) eats "before YHWH." According to Exod 24:10–11, at Sinai/Horeb the elders observed the glorious presence of YHWH as they ate and drank. This compares with the banquet Joseph prepared for his brothers (Gen 43:26–34). He and his brothers were served separately for cultural reasons (v. 32), but the seating arrangement reflected their social relationship. Not only did the brothers sit in rank according to age, but they sat "before" (לִפְנֵי), rather than "with," Joseph (v. 33).

41. Deut 12:7, 12, 18; 14:26; 16:11, 14–15; 26:11; to which should be added 27:7, the context of which sets the agenda for the first worship service of the type en-

Sixth, Moses extends the privilege of access to all. Going beyond the Israelites' experience at Sinai—where only Moses, Aaron, and the elders had eaten in the presence of God (vv. 12, 18; 31:10–12)—he encourages heads of households to bring with them their sons and daughters, their male and female servants, as well as landless Levites and aliens, and widows and the fatherless within their gates (i.e., their communities; 12:18; 16:11, 14; 26:11). True worship not only celebrates the vertical relationship graciously established by YHWH, but also manifests itself in horizontal charity toward the economically vulnerable.

Having discovered Deuteronomy's disposition toward worship, we may now recognize the profound theological significance of other texts. In the sequel to 12:1–13, Moses emphasizes that offerings to be presented to YHWH may not be eaten in the local communities; they must be eaten at the central sanctuary (vv. 14–19). Nevertheless, if the Israelites desire to eat meat where they live, they may do so freely, provided the meat is from ritually clean animals (animals of the type acceptable as sacrifices to YHWH), and the sanctity of the animals' life is protected by draining the blood (vv. 20–28). In a sense every slaughter is a sacrifice and every meal is worship. Accordingly, the so-called food laws in verses 14:1–21 function as an invitation to YHWH's privileged people to dine at his table. There the emphasis is not on foods prohibited, but on the full range of foods available to YHWH's covenant people. Identified as his "sons," "a holy people belonging to YHWH" (עַם קָדוֹשׁ לַיהוָה), chosen (בָּחַר) to be his "special treasure" (עַם סְגֻלָּה), Israelites are invited to eat precisely those foods that YHWH accepts as offerings.

We should not interpret the call for the annual tithe in 14:22–29 merely or even primarily as a burden or a duty placed upon the Israelites. On the contrary, YHWH's blessing of the fields and herds provides occasions for him to invite them to come and eat in his

---

visioned in this address in the Promised Land at Mount Ebal. The root also occurs in 24:5 and 33:18 of rejoicing in other circumstances. It seems that Moses has seized upon the phrase found in the legislation concerning the Festival of Booths in Lev 23:40, "and you shall rejoice before YHWH your God," and made it normative for the regular worship that transpires before YHWH at presentation of the tithe (14:21–27), Festival of Weeks (16:9–12), Festival of Booths (16:13–17), the presentation of the firstfruits (26:1–11), and the celebration of entrance into the Promised Land (27:1–8).

presence. In fact, he finds such delight in fellowship with them that he makes it as easy as possible for them to participate freely. Those for whom distance from the central sanctuary renders it impractical to carry the tithe physically may come to the sanctuary with silver and purchase all the food they want (כֹּל אֲשֶׁר תִּשְׁאָלְךָ נַפְשֶׁךָ, v. 26). Meanwhile those with means must ensure that the privilege and satisfaction of eating in YHWH's presence is open to all: Levites, aliens, the fatherless, widows (vv. 27–29).

Similar considerations characterize the offering of the firstborn (15:19–23). As in 12:5–14 and 14:22–29, here the key verbs should probably be interpreted modally:

> Set apart for YHWH your God every firstborn male of your herds and flocks. Do not put the firstborn of your oxen to work, and do not shear the firstborn of your sheep. Each year you and your family *may* eat them in the presence of YHWH your God at the place he will choose. If an animal has a defect, is lame or blind, or has any serious flaw, you must not sacrifice it to YHWH your God. You *may* eat it in your own towns. Both the ceremonially unclean and the clean *may* eat it, as if it were gazelle or deer.

The divine demand for the firstborn was not to be viewed as an intrusive and burdensome duty. On the contrary, the consecration of the animal to YHWH symbolized Israel's privileged status as YHWH's firstborn among the nations. Furthermore, the birth of the first offspring to each ewe or heifer reminded the people of YHWH's delight in their company. Each new birth represented his open invitation to come and eat in his presence.

This positive spin on the sacrifices climaxes in 26:1–15, where Moses finally offers some detail on the ritual to be followed when people present their offerings to YHWH—in this case the firstfruits of the field. We may easily imagine similar rituals performed by devotees of the fertility gods of Baal and Asherah. However, Moses will not allow Israel's rituals to degenerate to mere fertility religion. This annual event offers another occasion for the people to celebrate YHWH's grace in their history as well. In fact, the creed they are to recite in the context of this ritual touches on the offering presented only at the very end. After presenting the offering to the priest and affirming, "I declare today to YHWH your God that I have come to the land YHWH swore to our forefathers to give us" (v. 3), they are to say:

> My father was a wandering Aramaean; he went down into Egypt with a few people and lived there and became a great nation, powerful and numerous. But the Egyptians mistreated us and made us suffer, putting us to hard labor. Then we cried out to YHWH, the God of our fathers, and YHWH heard our voice and saw our misery, toil and oppression. So YHWH brought us out of Egypt with a mighty hand and an outstretched arm, with great terror and with miraculous signs and wonders. He brought us to this place and gave us this land, a land flowing with milk and honey; and now I bring the firstfruits of the soil that you, O YHWH, have given me. (26:5–10)

The emphasis is on YHWH's historical demonstration of grace in the nation's salvation and his provision of this good land. Commenting on John 4:23–24, Carson says, "Christian worship is new covenant worship; it is gospel-inspired worship; it is Christ-centered worship; it is cross-focused worship."[42] However, we may well ask how revolutionary this is. When we let Deuteronomy make its own case, we discover that true Israelite worship was covenant worship; it was gospel-inspired worship; it was YHWH-centered worship; it was redemption-focused worship.

And this raises the question: what really is *new* in the worship envisioned by Jesus in John 4:21–24? Is it that worship "in spirit and in truth" has never happened before? Or is it that with the coming of Christ worship "in spirit and in truth" takes on a new dimension? It seems best to relate the newness to Jesus' incarnation and his personal presence among his people. In the past YHWH's grace and his delight in fellowship with his people had been symbolized by the tabernacle and the temple, to which the people could come and celebrate his grace in his presence. YHWH delighted in worship there when it was practiced by true worshipers. However, Jesus is the embodiment of the divine resident of that temple. In the light of his becoming flesh and dwelling among us (John 1:14), the physical temple has become superfluous. The heavenly reality of which the temple and its rituals were shadows and replicas has come down. From now on true worship of the Father happens when believers' worship focuses on Christ. In that sense the incarnation signals a turn in the history of humanity generally and the climax of salvation history in particular.

42. Carson, "Worship under the Word," 37.

The Nature of True and Spiritual Worship in Deuteronomy

To this point I have focused on formal cultic worship. Far from being a burden to unfortunate Israelites, with their clear understanding of the will of their God, which included the details of their religious rituals, the Israelites were the envy of the nations (Deut 4:5–8). They possessed a divinely revealed cultic system that actually worked;[43] through the replica actions associated with the temple, the benefits of the sacrifice of Christ—slain before the foundation of the world[44]— were applied to them. Although the blood of the bulls and goats they offered did not remove their sin (Heb 10:4), when they offered them in faith and with integrity they were actually forgiven. But was this all there was to true worship in the Old Testament? The book of Deuteronomy is clear that this was not the case.

If true worship involves *reverential acts of homage and submission before the divine sovereign in response to his gracious revelation of himself and in accordance with his will,*[45] then this involves all of life. In fact, if the life is not in order, then no ritual will have any positive effect. The prophets knew the gradations of acceptable acts of worship well. To Saul, Samuel declared: "Has YHWH as great delight in burnt offerings and sacrifices, as in obeying the voice of YHWH? Look, to obey is better than sacrifice, and to listen [is preferable to] the fat of rams" (1 Sam 15:22). And hear the eighth-century BCE prophet Amos:

> I hate, I despise your feasts,
> and I take no delight in your solemn assemblies.
> Even though you offer me your burnt offerings and grain offerings,
> I will not accept them;
> and the peace offerings of your fattened animals,
> I will not look upon them.
> Take away from me the noise of your songs;
> to the melody of your harps I will not listen.
> But let justice roll down like waters,
> and righteousness like an ever-flowing stream.
> (Amos 5:21–24, ESV)

43. Note the repeated promises of forgiveness, "and he shall be forgiven!" in the instructions concerning sacrificial rituals in Lev 4:20, 26, 31, 35; 5:10, 13, 16, 18; 6:7; 19:22; and the psalmist's celebration in Ps 32:1.

44. Cf. John 17:24; Eph 1:4; Heb 4:3; 1 Pet 1:20; Rev 13:8; 17:8.

45. For full development of this thesis, see Block, *For the Glory of God.*

Similar perspectives are expressed in other well-known texts in the prophets[46] and the Psalms (Pss 15, 24). These inspired writers are unanimous in insisting that true worship begins in everyday life; true piety is not demonstrated primarily in impressive ritual, but in walking humbly with God and acting with justice and *hesed* toward others (Mic 6:6–8).

However, in elevating ethical living above liturgical worship these prophets and psalmists were scarcely breaking new ground. Micah's comment concerning what is good and what YHWH requires (דָּרַשׁ) of his people (Mic 6:8) recalls a question Moses had asked centuries earlier: "And now, Israel, what does YHWH your God ask (שָׁאַל) of you?" (Deut 10:12a). Many in our day expect an answer something like, "To perform the rituals as specified and to be scrupulous in the presentation of your offerings," or "To keep all the commands of YHWH." However, Moses takes the discussion in a completely different direction. His answer in 10:12b—11:1 consists of three parts, each of which provides an ethical response. We may illustrate the structure of this text in tabular form as illustrated in Table 9.

TABLE 9: What Does YHWH Require of His People?
The Three-Part Answer of Deuteronomy 10:12–21

The Issue		So what does YHWH your God ask of you? (10:12a)		
		I	II	III
The Requirement		*You shall fear YHWH your God, walk in all his ways, love him, and serve YHWH your God with all your heart and with all your soul, and keep the commands and statutes of YHWH, which I am commanding you today for your good. (10:12b–13)*	*Circumcise therefore the foreskin of your heart, and be no longer stubborn. (10:16)*	*You shall fear YHWH your God. You shall serve him and hold fast to him, and by his name you shall swear. (10:20)*
The Basis of the Requirement	The Doxology	Behold, to YHWH your God belong heaven and the heaven of heavens, the earth with all that is in it. (10:14)	For YHWH your God is God of gods and Lord of lords, the great, the mighty, and the awesome God, who is not partial and takes no bribe. (10:17)	He is your praise. He is your God, who has done for you these great and terrifying things that your eyes have seen. (10:21)
	The Application	Yet YHWH set his heart in love on your fathers and chose their offspring after them, you above all peoples, as you are this day. (10:15)	He executes justice for the fatherless and the widow, and demonstrates love for the sojourner, by giving him food and clothing. So demonstrate love for the sojourner, therefore, for you were sojourners in the land of Egypt. (10:18–19)	Your fathers went down to Egypt seventy persons, and now YHWH your God has made you as numerous as the stars of heaven. (10:22)
The Conclusion		You shall therefore demonstrate love for YHWH your God, keeping his charge, his statutes, his rules, and his commands always. (11:1)		

While each answer emphasizes the proper disposition and fundamental covenant commitment to YHWH as the divine requirement, the prophetic perspective is most explicit in the first (vv. 12b–13). The statement involves five key verbs, all of which we hear repeatedly in the book: (1) fear YHWH your God;[47] (2) walk in all his ways;[48] (3) love YHWH your God;[49] (4) serve YHWH your God with your whole being;[50] (5) keep the commands and decrees of YHWH.[51] This combination of demands captures in a nutshell the message of Deuteronomy, especially as it relates to the worshipful human response to divine grace. The response called for involves fundamental dispositions (fear, love) and active expressions (walk, serve, keep), but it says nothing explicitly about cultic service (which would be subsumed under the larger rubrics of serving YHWH and keeping his commands). In Deuteronomy's view, attitude and action are interrelated. Without fear and love, walking, serving, and keeping all the commands become legalistic, deontological performances of duty. Without walking, serving, and keeping all the commands, fear and love are useless and dead.[52] In ascribing pride of place to "reverent awe" (or "awed trust"; יָרֵא), Moses reinforces his own emphasis elsewhere and prepares for the fundamental tenet of biblical wisdom: "The fear of YHWH is the first principle of wisdom."[53] By placing "love" in the middle, Moses ensures the centrality of the Supreme Command, to "love YHWH your God with all your heart and being and resources" (6:5). Furthermore, by associating "love" (אָהֵב) with walking, serving, and keeping, Moses buttresses the Deuteronomic understanding of the word as "covenant commitment demonstrated

---

47. Cf. 4:10; 5:29; 6:2, 13, 24; 8:6; 10:20; 13:5, 12[Eng 4, 11]; 14:23; 17:13, 19; 19:20; 31:12–13.

48. Cf. 5:33; 6:7; 8:6; 10:12; 11:22; 13:5–6[Eng 4–5]; 19:9; 26:17; 28:9; 30:16.

49. Cf. 6:5; 11:1, 13, 22; 13:4[Eng 4]; 19:9; 30:6, 16, 20.

50. Cf. 6:13; 10:20; 11:13; 13:5[Eng 4]; also 28:47.

51. Cf. 4:2, 6, 40; 5:10, 29; 6:2, 17; 7:9, 12; 8:2, 6, 11; 10:13; 11:1, 8; 13:5, 19[Eng 4, 18]; 17:19; 19:9; 26:17–18; 27:1; 28:9, 45; 29:8[Eng 9]; 30:10, 16.

52. "Fear and love" express covenant commitment, which may be viewed as the Mosaic counterpart to the New Testament πίστις. James has caught the spirit of this text precisely in Jas 2:14–26; on which, see Stein, "'Saved by Faith [Alone]' in Paul Versus 'Not Saved by Faith Alone' in James," 4–19.

53. Job 28:28; Ps 111:10; Prov 1:7; 9:10; 15:33; Eccl 12:13. Cf. Prov 15:16; 19:23; 22:4, etc.

in action in the interests of the other person." [54] The phrase "to walk in the ways of YHWH" is delightfully ambiguous, meaning either "to live as YHWH has revealed we should live," or "to live as YHWH himself lives," that is, to emulate his character and actions.[55] "To serve YHWH" (LXX λατρεύω) does not refer primarily to cultic service (which should be λειτουργέω in LXX),[56] but to living as faithful vassals of YHWH.[57] The addition of "with all your heart/mind (לֵב) and with all your being (נֶפֶשׁ)" reinforces this interpretation.

But what does this kind of "vassaldom" look like? The best clue is found in Deuteronomy 6:4–5, which these modifiers echo:

---

54. Cf. Malamat, "You Shall Love Your Neighbor as Yourself," 112–14; idem, "Love Your Neighbor as Yourself," 50–51.

55. This ethical principle is known as *imitatio dei*, "the imitation of God." Cf. 12:17–19, which calls for compassion and justice toward the vulnerable, just as YHWH exercises compassion and justice. See also Lev 19:2, which calls YHWH's people to be holy as YHWH their God is holy.

56. Concerning Rom 12:1 and New Testament worship, Piper writes ("Worship God!"):

> When Paul uses it [λατρεύω = Hebrew עָבַד] for Christian worship he goes out of his way to make sure that we know he means not a localized or outward form for worship practice but a non-localized, spiritual experience. In fact, he takes it so far as to treat virtually all of life as an act of worship when lived in the right spirit . . . And in Romans 12:1 Paul urges Christians to "present your bodies as living and holy sacrifices acceptable to God which is your spiritual worship."
>
> So even when Paul uses an Old Testament word for worship, he takes pains to let us know that what he has in mind is not mainly a localized or external event of worship but an internal, spiritual experience—so much so that he sees all of life and ministry as an expression of that inner experience of worship.

The same may be said of Moses' use of Hebrew עָבַד (LXX λατρεύω). Cf. Peterson's discussion of this word in *Engaging with God*, 66–67.

57. The word עָבַד occurs frequently in the exodus and plague narratives of Exodus 3–10 of what the Israelites would do at Sinai (3:12; 4:23; 7:16, 26 [Eng 8:1]; 8:16 [Eng 20]; 9:1, 13; 10:3, 7, 8, 11, 24, 26; 12:31). Perhaps because 5:1 and 8:25, 28 [Eng 29, 32] indicate that the activities at Sinai will include cultic service, many translations render עָבַד as "worship." However, this is somewhat misleading. The focus of the events at Sinai is on rituals by which the Israelites, who had been "slaves" (עֲבָדִים) of Pharaoh become "vassals" (עֲבָדִים) of YHWH. Cf. 14:12, where the people declare their preference of slavery to Pharaoh over death in the desert as YHWH's duped servants.

Hear, O Israel! Our God is YHWH! YHWH alone![58]
So you shall love (אָהֵב) YHWH with all your לֵב
and with all your נֶפֶשׁ and with all your מְאֹד.

In verse 5 Moses explains explicitly what he means by exclusive allegiance to YHWH with a triad of qualifiers for "love": with one's whole לֵב, נֶפֶשׁ, and מְאֹד. The traditional rendering, "with all your heart, soul, and strength," is slightly misleading with respect to each element and obscures the profundity of this statement. We should not interpret this verse as a Greek psychological statement confirming some sort of tripartite anthropology. Rather, this is Moses' call for absolute and singular devotion to YHWH, as called for by verse 4.[59] Proceeding from the inside out, these expressions represent three concentric circles, each representing a sphere of human existence, as illustrated in the following diagram:

FIGURE 7: The Literary Interpretation of Deuteronomy 6:5

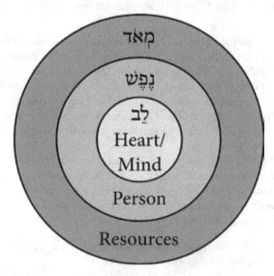

Each of the expressions calls for brief comment. As the Hebrew word for both the seat of thought and of emotion, לֵב serves com-

---

58. For defense of this interpretation, see Block, "How Many Is God?" 73–97.
59. McBride, "The Yoke of the Kingdom," 273–306.

prehensively for one's inner being.[60] The word נֶפֶשׁ[61] refers to one's entire person. The third word, מְאֹד, carries the broader sense of "resources,"[62] which would include not only physical strength, but also economic or social strength, and even the physical resources one owns: house, fields, livestock, family, and servants. Everything is to be devoted to YHWH; nothing may be kept for oneself or devoted to another god. The progression and concentricity in the vocabulary now becomes apparent. Beginning with the inner being, Moses moves to the whole person, and then to all that one claims as one's own, as he calls on Israelites to love God without reservation or qualification.[63] Covenant commitment must be rooted in the heart, but then extend to every level of one's being and to all of life.

This understanding adds texture and intensity to Deut 10:12: to serve YHWH with one's whole being is to sacrifice one's very self to the will of God. But it also provides perspective on Rom 12:1, which turns out to be neither revolutionary nor new. On the contrary, Paul has recaptured precisely the Mosaic vision of whole-hearted and whole-bodied worship involving all of life: "I appeal to you therefore, brothers and sisters, by the mercies of God, to present your bodies

60. Which explains why, when Mark reports Jesus' quotation of this verse in 12:30, he actually cites four Greek words: καρδία (= Hebrew לֵב), ψυχή (= Hebrew נֶפֶשׁ), διάνοια (= Hebrew לֵב), and ἰσχύς (= Hebrew מְאֹד).

61. The word denotes fundamentally "throat, gullet," but the word is used in a variety of derived metaphorical senses: "appetite/desire" (Prov 23:2; Eccl 6:7), "life" (Gen 9:5; 2 Sam 23:17; Jonah 2:6[Eng 5]). Note especially Deut 12:23, "But be sure you do not eat the blood, because the blood is the life (נֶפֶשׁ), and you must not eat the life (נֶפֶשׁ) with the meat (בָּשָׂר)." Note also the merismic use of נֶפֶשׁ and בָּשָׂר ("body and being") for totality in Isa 10:18. In Job 2:4–6, the adversary is permitted to touch Job's בָּשָׂר but not his נֶפֶשׁ. The word may also refer to a person as a "living being" (Ezek 4:14; etc.); the whole self (Lev 26:11); even a corpse, that is, a body without life/breath (Lev 21:11). See further Fredericks, "נפשׁ," 133–34.

62. The common rendering of מְאֹד, as "strength," follows the lead of the Septuagint, which reads δύναμις, "power" (ἰσχύς in Mark 12:30). Only here and in 2 Kgs 23:25 (which echoes this statement) is this word used as a noun; elsewhere it always functions adverbially, meaning "greatly, exceedingly." Cognate adjectival expressions occur in both Ugaritic (*mad/mid*, "great, strong, much;" *Kirta* 1.ii.35 [Parker, *Ugaritic Narrative Poetry*, 15]; *Baal Cycle* 10.v.15 [*Ugaritic Narrative Poetry*, 130]) and Akkadian (*mādum*, "many, numerous," and *ma'du* "quantity, fullness," from the verb *mâdum*, "to become numerous," *AHw* 573). Cf. *HALOT* 2:538.

63. The serial use of three words expresses the superlative degree. Just as "iniquity, rebellion, and sin" in Exod 34:7 refers to "every conceivable sin," so "heart, being, and resources" refers to every part of a person.

(σώματα) as a living sacrifice, holy (θυσίαν ζῶσαν ἁγίαν εὐάρεστον) and acceptable to God, which is your reasonable/logical service (λογικὴν λατρείαν)."

We obscure the echo of Deut 10:12 and open the door to a false dichotomy between Old Testament and New Testament worship if we translate λογικὴν λατρείαν as "spiritual worship" (ESV, NRS) or "your spiritual act of worship" (NIV). The translators of the Authorized Version got it right when they rendered the phrase as "reasonable service," provided by "service" we understand whole-bodied and whole-hearted vassaldom: all of life devoted to God. This is exactly what Paul develops in Romans 12–15 as the logical and reasonable primarily ethical response to the redemption we have received through the cross (Rom 1–11), even as Israel's whole-hearted and whole-bodied vassaldom demonstrated in obedience was the logical and reasonable response to YHWH's magnificent acts of redemption (Deut 4:32–40).

And with this we turn to the last infinitive phrase of Deut 10:12–13: YHWH asks Israel to keep his commands (מִצְוֹת) and his ordinances (חֻקֹּת) today—for their own good. The last phrase announces the bonus. True worship is expressed in everyday obedience to the revealed will of God for the pleasure and glory of God, but in the end Moses declares that it turns out to be for Israel's own good. As given at Sinai and expounded in Deuteronomy the law was not intended as an instrument of death but of *life*. Having rescued Israel from the bondage of Egypt and defeated the forces of evil and darkness with signs and wonders, and in anticipation of delivering the Promised Land into their hands, YHWH commanded Israel to do all these statutes, to fear YHWH their God, for their good always, that he might preserve them alive, as they were at the time of Moses' address. And they would be considered righteous, if they would keep the entire command before YHWH their God, as he commanded them (Deut 6:22–25). Like the blessing and the declaration of righteousness in Ps 24:5, this is the true benefit of worship that pleases God. Those who fear YHWH, walk in his ways, demonstrate love for him, and serve him alone concretize their vassaldom in scrupulous but joyful obedience, and for having done so will hear the most welcome words from YHWH's lips: "Well done, good and faithful vassal. You have been faithful; enter into the joy of your suzerain" (Matt 25:21, 23).

The links between fearing and loving God, and walking in his ways, faithfully serving him, and concrete obedience are not merely outdated fossils of Old Testament worship that are eliminated or even transformed in the New Testament; they are fundamental to New Testament worship as well. Jesus told his disciples, "If you love me [i.e., are covenantally committed to me], you will keep my commands" (John 14:15), and the one who demonstrates love for Jesus by keeping his commands is assured of the love of the Father (John 14:21, 23; 15:10).

Conclusion

We are all grateful to Martin Luther for having rediscovered the gospel of salvation by grace alone through faith alone in Christ alone. However, we are less pleased with the wedge he drove between Old Testament faith and New Testament faith with his law-gospel contrast—undoubtedly the result of his struggles with Roman Catholicism and his mistaken identification of its works-based righteousness with Old Testament religion. But Luther's influence on this count is pervasive to this day. Theologians and biblical scholars continue to be fixated on the discontinuities between Old and New Testaments. The book of Hebrews does indeed declare that with the coming of Christ some aspects of worship have changed drastically. With the incarnation and with Jesus Christ's sacrificial death, heavenly redemptive realities have happened on earth, and there is no longer any need to participate in shadow rituals associated with the temple. The liturgical forms of worship have certainly changed. However, when we read the Old Testament for its own message, and not merely as a foil against which to read the New Testament, we discover that that the underlying theology of worship is identical: *True worship involves reverential acts of submission and homage before the divine Sovereign in response to his revelation of himself and in accordance with his will.* As in Christian worship, for the faithful in ancient Israel, worship "in spirit and in truth" was driven by God's animating, inspiring, and empowering Spirit;[64] it was addressed to the one true and

---

64. On the one hand the role of the Holy Spirit in tabernacle worship does not receive much attention in Exodus and Leviticus. However, as in archaeological excavations, absence of evidence is not evidence of absence. On the other hand, the role of the Spirit in the construction of the tabernacle is instructive: the craftsman who built the tabernacle was filled with the Spirit of God (Exod 28:3; 31:3; 35:31), and those who contributed spontaneously and voluntarily to the project are characterized as persons "whose heart impelled them" (נְשָׂא לִבּוֹ) and "whose heart/spirit moved them" (נָדַב לִבּוֹ/נְדָבָה רוּחוֹ; Exod 25:2; 35:5, 21–22, 26, 29; cf. 36:2).

living God; it was the human response to God's gracious redemption, his call to covenant relationship, and his revelation of his will; it was fundamentally a matter of the heart, but was expressed concretely in life—full-bodied and whole-hearted service of God—and only secondarily in ritual actions. And the latter were viewed not merely as obligations imposed by an overwhelming Deity, but as privileges and opportunities for personal and corporate fellowship with God.

The time has come for a new generation of biblical scholars, theologians, and pastors to begin focusing on the continuities between Old and New; Israel's faith and Christian faith; and most significantly YHWH, the God of Israel, and Jesus Christ, the Lord of the church. Until we have reconnected the Testaments, not only will the only Bible that Jesus and the apostles had remain a dead book for the church, but God's single historical plan of redemption will continue to be misunderstood. Jesus does not offer an alternative way to God, replacing the failed program of the Old Testament. God never fails! His plans never collapse; nor do they need to be repaired. The life offered to believers in Jesus is not another gospel. It represents the climax and fulfillment of the plan that God started with Israel, whom he chose to be vehicles of grace and glory. Because of the work of Christ, Christians may worship the Father in spirit and in truth; and because of this same work of Christ, slain before the foundation of the world, ancient Israelites could worship the Father in spirit and in truth as well. In the book of Deuteronomy Moses has mapped out his exciting vision of what that sort of worship should have looked like before Christ.[65]

65. I am grateful to Myrto Theocharous, Matthew Patton, and Charlie Trimm for reading an earlier draft of this paper and giving me extremely helpful feedback. I am also grateful to Stanley Porter and Mark Boda, who invited me to participate in the Bingham Colloquium, June 4–5, 2010, and for the responses to a version of my paper by attendees. Of course, any infelicities in substance and argumentation are my own responsibility.

Bibliography

Ackerman, Susan. "The Personal is Political: Covenantal and Affectionate Love (*āhēb, āhăbâ*) in the Hebrew Bible." *Vetus Testamentum* 52 (2002) 437–58.

Ahituv, Shmuel. *Canaanite Toponyms in Ancient Egyptian Documents.* Jerusalem: Magnes, 1984.

Aland, K. et al. *Novum Testamentum Graece et Latine.* 26th ed. Stuttgart: Deutsche Bibelgesellschaft, 1986.

Albertz, Rainer. *A History of Israelite Religion in the Old Testament Period.* Translated by J. Bowden. 2 vols. OTL. Louisville: Westminster John Knox, 1994.

Albright, W. F. "Discussion." In *City Invincible: A Symposium on Urbanization and Cultural Development in the Ancient Near East,* edited by C. H. Kraeling and R. M. Adams, 94–123. Chicago: University of Chicago Press, 1960.

———. *From Stone Age to Christianity: Monotheism and the Historical Process.* 2nd ed. Garden City, NY: Doubleday, 1957.

———. *YHWH and the Gods of Canaan: A Historical Analysis of Two Contrasting Faiths.* Garden City, NY: Doubleday, 1968.

Allen, David M. "Deuteronomic Re-Presentation in a Word of Exhortation: An Assessment of the Paraenetic Function of Deuteronomy in the letter to the Hebrews." PhD diss., University of Edinburgh, 2007.

Allen, Leslie C. *Psalms 101–150.* Word Biblical Commentary 21. Waco, TX: Word, 1983.

Allen, Spencer L. "The Splintered Divine: A Study of Ishtar, Baal, and Yahweh Divine Names and Divine Multiplicity in the Ancient Near East." PhD diss., University of Pennsylvania, 2011.

Alt, Albrecht. "The Origins of Israelite Law." In *Essays in Old Testament History and Religion,* translated by R. A. Wilson, 101–71. Garden City, NY: Doubleday, 1967.

Alter, Robert. *The Art of Biblical Poetry.* New York: Basic Books, 1987.

Amir, Y. "The Decalogue according to Philo." In *The Ten Commandments in History and Tradition,* edited by Ben-Zion Segal, 121–60. Jerusalem: Magnes, 1990.

Andersen, Francis I. *The Hebrew Verbless Clause in the Pentateuch.* Journal of Biblical Literature Monograph Series 14. Nashville: Abingdon, 1970.

Arnold, Bill T. "Deuteronomy as the *Ipsissima Vox* of Moses." *Journal of Theological Interpretation* 4 (2010) 53–74.

Austin, J. L. *How to Do Things with Words.* 2nd ed. Edited by J. O. Urmson and M. Sbisà. Cambridge: Harvard University Press, 1975.

Averbeck, Richard E. "זבח." In *New International Dictionary of Old Testament Theology & Exegesis*. Edited by Willem VanGemeren, 1:1066–73. Grand Rapids: Zondervan, 1997

———. "מִנְחָה." In *New International Dictionary of Old Testament Theology & Exegesis*. Edited by Willem VanGemeren, 2:978–90. Grand Rapids: Zondervan, 1997.

———. "עָלָה." In *New International Dictionary of Old Testament Theology & Exegesis*. Edited by Willem VanGemeren, 3:407–15. Grand Rapids: Zondervan, 1997.

———. "שָׁלֵם." In *New International Dictionary of Old Testament Theology & Exegesis*. Edited by Willem VanGemeren, 4:135–43. Grand Rapids: Zondervan, 1997.

Avigad, N. *Hebrew Bullae from the Time of Jeremiah: Remnants of a Burnt Archive.* Jerusalem: Israel Exploration Society, 1986.

———. "Jerahmeel and Baruch." *Biblical Archaeologist* 42 (1979) 114–18.

Baillet, M. *Les "Petites Grottes" de Qumrân. Exploration de la falaise. Les grottes 2Q, 3Q, 5Q, 6Q, 7Q à 10Q.* Discoveries in the Judaean Desert 3. Oxford: Clarendon, 1962.

Baly, D. "The Geography of Monotheism." In *Translating and Understanding the Old Testament: Essays in Honor of Herbert Gordon May*, edited by H. T. Frank and W. L. Reed, 253–78. Nashville: Abingdon, 1970.

Barkay, G. *Ketef Hinnom: A Treasure Facing Jerusalem's Walls.* Jerusalem: Israel Museum, 1986.

Barr, James. *The Concept of Biblical Theology: An Old Testament Perspective.* Minneapolis: Fortress, 1999.

Bass, B. M., editor. *Stogdill's Handbook of Leadership.* Rev. ed. New York: Free Press, 1981.

Bauckham, Richard."James and the Jerusalem Church." In *The Book of Acts in Its Palestinian Setting.* Vol. 4 of *The Acts of the Apostles in Its First Century Setting*, 459–67. Grand Rapids: Eerdmans, 1995.

———. "James and the Gentiles (Acts 15:13–21)." In *History, Literature, and Society in the Book of Acts.* Edited by Ben Witherington, 154–84. Cambridge: Cambridge University Press, 1966.

Beale, G. K. *The Book of Revelation.* New International Greek Testament Commentary. Grand Rapids: Eerdmans, 1999.

Beckman, Gary. *Hittite Diplomatic Texts.* Edited by Harry A. Hoffner Jr. 2nd ed. Society of Biblical Literature Writings from the Ancient World 7. Atlanta: Scholars, 1999.

Bell, Richard H. "Deuteronomy 32 and the Origin of the Jealousy Motif in Romans 9–11." In *Provoked to Jealousy: The Origin and Purpose of the Jealousy Motif in Romans 9–11*, 200–85. Wissenschaftliche Untersuchungen zum Neuen Testament 2/63. Tübingen: Mohr (Siebeck), 1994.

Bennis, Warren G. "About the Teal Trust." No pages. Online: http://www.teal.org.uk/about.htm.

———. "Leadership Theory and Administrative Behavior: The Problems of Authority." *Administrative Science Quarterly* 4 (1959) 259–301.

Benz, F. L. *Personal Names in the Phoenician and Punic Inscriptions.* Studia Pohl 8. Rome: Pontifical Biblical Institute, 1972.

Bergen, Robert D. "Preaching Old Testament Law." In *Reclaiming the Prophetic Mantle: Preaching the Old Testament Faithfully*, edited by G. L. Klein, 51–69. Nashville: Broadman, 1992.

Berger, P.-R."Der Kyros-Kylinder mit dem Zusatzfragment BIN II Nr. 32 und die akkadischen Personennamen im Danielbuch." *Zeitschrift für Assyriologie* 64 (1975) 219–34.

Bergey, R. "The Song of Moses (Deuteronomy 32.1–43) and Isaianic Prophecies: A Case of Early Intertextuality?" *Journal for the Study of the Old Testament* 28 (2003) 33–54.

Berlin, E., and M. Z. Brettler. *The Jewish Study Bible*. Oxford: Oxford University Press, 2004.

Berry, R. J. *The Care of Creation: Focusing Concern and Action*. Downers Grove, IL: InterVarsity, 2000.

———, editor. *Environmental Stewardship: Critical Perspectives—Past and Present*. New York: Continuum, 2006.

Betz, O. "στίγμα." In *Theological Dictionary of the New Testament*. Edited by G. Kittel and G. Friedrich, and translated by G. W. Bromiley, 7:657–64. Grand Rapids: Eerdmans, 1971.

Biran, Avraham. "Tell Dan Five Years Later." *Biblical Archaeologist* 43 (1980) 168–82.

Black, Jeremy, and Anthony Green. *Gods, Demons and Symbols of Ancient Mesopotamia: An Illustrated Dictionary*. London: British Museum, 1992.

Blenkinsopp, J. *Prophecy and Canon: A Contribution to the Study of Jewish Origins*. South Bend, IN: University of Notre Dame Press, 1977.

———. *The Pentateuch: An Introduction to the First Five Books of the Bible*. New York: Doubleday, 1992.

Block, Daniel I. "Bearing the Name of the LORD with Honor." In *How I Love Your Torah, O LORD!*, 61–72. Eugene, OR: Cascade Books, 2011.

———. *The Book of Ezekiel Chapters 1–24*. New International Commentary on the Old Testament. Grand Rapids: Eerdmans, 1997.

———. *The Book of Ezekiel Chapters 25–48*. New International Commentary on the Old Testament. Grand Rapids: Eerdmans, 1998.

———. *Deuteronomy*. New International Version Application Commentary. Grand Rapids: Zondervan, 2012.

———. "Divine Abandonment: Ezekiel's Adaptation of an Ancient Near Eastern Motif." In *Perspectives on Ezekiel: Theology and Anthropology*, edited by Margaret S. Odell and John T. Strong, 15–42. Society of Biblical Literature Symposium Series 9. Atlanta: Scholars, 2000.

———. *For the Glory of God: Recovering a Biblical Theology of Worship for the Church*. Grand Rapids: Baker, forthcoming.

———. "God." In *Dictionary of the Old Testament: Historical Pentateuch*, edited by B. T. Arnold and H. G. M. Williamson, 336–55. Downers Grove, IL: InterVarsity, 2005.

———. *The Gods of the Nations: Studies in Ancient Near Eastern National Theology*. Rev. ed. Evangelical Theological Society Monographs. Grand Rapids: Baker, 2000.

———. *How I Love Your Torah, O LORD! Studies in the Book of Deuteronomy*. Eugene, OR: Cascade, 2011.

———. "How Many is God? An Investigation into the Meaning of Deuteronomy 6:4–5." In *How I Love Your Torah, O LORD! Studies in the Book of Deuteronomy,* 73–97. Eugene, OR: Cascade Books, 2011.

———. "The Joy of Worship: The Mosaic Invitation to the Presence of God Deut 12:1–14." In *How I Love Your Torah, O LORD! Studies in the Book of Deuteronomy,* 98–117. Eugene, OR: Cascade Books, 2011.

———. *Judges, Ruth.* NAC. Nashville: Broadman & Holman, 1999.

———. "Leadership, Leader, Old Testament." In *New Interpreter's Dictionary of the Bible.* Edited by K. D. Sakenfeld, 3:620–26. Nashville: Abingdon, 2008.

———. "Marriage and Family in Ancient Israel." In *Marriage and Family in the Biblical World,* edited by K. Campbell, 33–102. Downers Grove, IL: InterVarsity, 2003.

———. "My Servant David: Ancient Israel's Vision of the Messiah." In *Israel's Messiah in the Bible and the Dead Sea Scrolls,* edited by Richard. S. Hess and M. Daniel Carroll R., 17–56. Grand Rapids: Baker, 2003.

———. "Nations." In *New International Dictionary of Old Testament Theology & Exegesis.* Edited by Willem VanGemeren, 4:966–72. Grand Rapids: Zondervan, 1997.

———. "The Privilege of Calling: The Mosaic Paradigm for Missions (Deut 26:16–19)." In *How I Love Your Torah, O LORD! Studies in the Book of Deuteronomy,* 140–61. Eugene, OR: Cascade, 2011.

———. "Sojourner; Alien; Stranger." In *International Standard Bible Encyclopedia.* Rev. ed. Edited by G. Bromiley, 4:561–64. Grand Rapids: Eerdmans, 1988.

———. "To Serve and to Keep: Toward a Biblical Understanding of Humanity's Responsibility in the Face of the Biodiversity Crisis." In *Keeping God's Earth: Creation Care and the Global Environment.* Edited by Daniel I. Block and Noah J. Toly, 116–42. Downers Grove, IL: InterVarsity, 2010.

———. "Unspeakable Crimes: The Abuse of Women in the Book of Judges." *The Southern Baptist Theological Journal* 2 (1998) 46–55.

———. "Who do Commentators say 'the Lord' is? The Scandalous Rock of Romans 10:13." In *On the Writing of New Testament Commentaries. Festschrift for Grant R. Osborne on the occasion of his 70th birthday.* Edited by Stanley E. Porter and Eckhard J. Schnabel. Leiden: Brill (forthcoming, 2012).

———. "'You Shall Not Covet Your Neighbor's Wife: A Study in Deuteronomic Domestic Ideology." *Journal of the Evangelical Theological Society* 53 (2010) 449–474.

Blum, E. *Studien zur Komposition des Pentateuch.* Beihefte zur Zeitschrift für die alttestamentliche Wissenschaft 189. Berlin: de Gruyter, 1990.

Bord, L. J., and D. Hamidović. "Écoute Israël (Deut. VI 4)." *Vetus Testamentum* 52 (2002) 13–29.

Borowski, O. *Every Living Thing: Daily Use of Animals in Ancient Israel.* Walnut Creek, CA: AltaMira, 1998.

Boston, James R. "The Song of Moses: Deuteronomy 32:1–43." PhD diss., Union Theological Seminary, 1966.

———. "The Wisdom Influence upon the Song of Moses." *Journal of Biblical Literature* 87 (1968) 198–202.

Botterweck, G. J., and H. Ringgren, editors. *Theological Dictionary of the Old Testament.* Translated by J. T. Willis, G. W. Bromiley, and D. E. Green. 15 vols. Grand Rapids: Eerdmans, 1974–.

Bouma-Prediger, S. *For the Beauty of the Earth: A Christian Vision for Creation Care*. Grand Rapids: Baker, 2001.

Braulik, Georg. "Die Abfolge der Gesetze in Deuteronomium 12–26 und der Dekalog." In *Das Deuteronomium: Entstehung, Gestalt und Botschaft*, 252–72. Ephemerides theologicae lovanienses 68. Leuven: Leuven University Press, 1985.

———. "Commemoration of Passion and Feast of Joy." In *The Theology of Deuteronomy: Collected Essays of Georg Braulik, O.S.B.* Translated by U. Lindblad, 67–85. Bibal Collected Essays 2. N. Richmond Hills, TX: Bibal, 1994.

———. *Die deuteronomischen Gesetze und der Dekalog*. Stuttgarter Bibelstudien 145. Stuttgart: Katholisches Bibelwerk, 1991.

———. "Gesetz als Evangelium: Rechtfertigung und Begnadigung nach der deuteronomischen Tora." *Zeitschrift für Theologie und Kirche* 79 (1982) 127–60.

———. "The Joy of the Feast." In *The Theology of Deuteronomy: Collected Essays of Georg Braulik*. Translated by U. Lindblad, 27–65. Bibal Collected Essays 2. N. Richland Hills, TX: Bibal, 1994.

———. "Law as Gospel: Justification and Pardon according to the Deuteronomic Torah." *Interpretation* 38 (1984) 5–14.

———. "The Sequence of the Laws in Deuteronomy 12–26." In *A Song of Power and the Power of Song: Essays on the Book of Deuteronomy*, edited by D. L. Christensen, translated by L. M. Maloney, 313–35. Studies in Biblical Theology 3. Winona Lake, IN: Eisenbrauns, 1993.

———. "Wisdom, Divine Presence and Law: Reflections on the Kerygma of Deut 4:5–8." In *The Theology of Deuteronomy: Collected Essays of Georg Braulik, O.S.B.* Translated by U. Lindblad, 1–25. Bibal Collected Essays 2. N. Richmond Hills, TX: Bibal, 1994.

Braulik, G., and N. Lohfink, "Deuteronomium 1,5 באר את־התורה הזאת: 'er verlieh dieser Tora Rechtskraft.'" In *Textarbeit: Studien zu Texten und ihrer Rezeption aus dem Alten Testament und der Umwelt Israels: Festschrift für Peter Weimar zur Vollendung seines 60. Lebensjahres mit Beiträgen von Freunden, Schülern und Kollegen*, edited by K. Kiesow and T. Meurer, 35–51. Alter Orient und Altes Testament 294. Münster: Ugarit, 2003.

Breuer, Mordechai. "Dividing the Decalogue into Verses and Commands." In *The Ten Commandments in History and Tradition*, edited by Ben-Zion Segal and Gershon Levi, 291–330. Jerusalem: Magnes, 1990.

Brichto, H. C. *Toward a Grammar of Biblical Poetics*. Oxford: Oxford University Press, 1992.

Briggs, C. A. *A Critical and Exegetical Commentary on the Book of Psalms*. International Critical Commentary. Edinburgh: T. & T. Clark, 1907.

Briggs, Richard S. "Speech-Act Theory." In *Dictionary for Theological Interpretation of the Bible*, edited by K. J. Vanhoozer et al., 763–66. Grand Rapids: Baker, 2005.

———. *Words in Action: Speech Act Theory and Biblical Interpretation: Toward a Hermeneutic of Self-Involvement*. Edinburgh: T. & T. Clark, 2001.

Brinkman, John A. et al. "*sikiltu*." *The Assyrian Dictionary of the Oriental Institute of the University of Chicago*. Vol. 15, 244–45. Chicago: University of Chicago Press, 1956.

Bristow, M. J., editor. *National Anthems of the World.* 11th ed. London: Weidenfeld & Nicholson, 2006.

Britt, Brian M. "Deuteronomy 31–32 as a Textual Memorial." *Biblical Interpretation* 8 (2000) 358–74.

———. *Rewriting Moses: The Narrative Eclipse of the Text.* Journal for the Study of the Old TestamentSup 402. Gender, Culture, Theory 14. London: T. & T. Clark, 2005.

Brockelmann, C. *Grundriss der vergleichenden Grammatik der semitischen Sprachen.* 2 vols. 1908. Reprint, Hildesheim: G. Olms, 1961.

Bronner, L. *The Stories of Elijah and Elisha as Polemics against Baal Worship.* Leiden: Brill, 1968.

Brown, F., S. R. Driver, and C. A. Briggs. *A Hebrew and English Lexicon of the Old Testament.* Oxford: Clarendon, 1907.

Brown, W. P., ed. *The Ten Commandments: The Reciprocity of Faithfulness.* Louisville, KY: Westminster/John Knox, 2004.

Bulmer, R. "The Uncleanness of the Birds of Leviticus and Deuteronomy." *Man* 24 (1989) 304–21.

Bunimovitz, Shlomo, and Zvi Lederman. "Beth-Shemesh." In *The New Encyclopedia of Archaeological Excavationsin the Holy Land.* 4 volumes. Edited by Ephraim Stern, 1:249–53. New York: Simon & Schuster, 1993.

Buzsin, Walter. "Luther on Misic." *Musical Quarterly* 32 (1946) 80–97.

Calvin, John. *Commentaries on the Four Last Books of Moses.* Translated by Charles William Bingham. Grand Rapids: Eerdmans, 1950.

———. *Institutes of the Christian Religion.* Edited by J. T. McNeill. Library of Christian Classics. London: SCM, 1961.

———. *John Calvin's Sermons on the Ten Commandments.* Edited and translated by B. W. Farley. Grand Rapids: Baker, 1980.

Carson, D. A. "Worship under the Word." In *Worship by the Book.* Edited by D. A. Carson, 11–63. Grand Rapids: Eerdmans, 2002.

Cassuto, Umberto. "The Prophet Hosea and the Books of the Pentateuch." In *Biblical and Oriental Studies.* Vol. 1, 79–100. Jerusalem: Magnes, 1973.

———. "The Song of Moses (Deuteronomy Chapter xxxii 1–43)." In *Biblical and Oriental Studies.* Vol. 1, 41–46 Jerusalem: Magnes, 1973.

———. *A Commentary on the Book of Exodus.* Translated by I. Abrahams. Jerusalem: Magnes, 1967.

Chan, Kim-Kwong. "You Shall Not Eat These Abominable Things: An Examination of Different Interpretations on Deuteronomy 14:3–20." *East Asia Journal of Theology* 3 (1985) 95–104.

Chaney, M. L. "'Coveting Your Neighbor's House' in Social Context." In *The Ten Commandments: The Reciprocity of Faithfulness.* Edited by W. P. Brown, 302–18. Louisville, KY: Westminster/John Knox, 2004.

Chapman, David W. "Marriage and Family in Second Temple Judaism." In *Marriage and Family in the Biblical World,* edited by K. M. Campbell, 183–239. Downers Grove, IL: InterVarsity, 2003.

Childs, Brevard S. *The Book of Exodus: A Critical Theological Commentary.* Old Testament Library. Philadelphia: Westminster, 1974.

———. *Introduction to the Old Testament as Scripture.* Philadelphia: Fortress, 1985.

Christensen, D. L., and M. Narucki. "The Mosaic Authorship of the Pentateuch." *Journal of the Evangelical Theological Society* 32 (1989) 465–71.

Christensen, Duane. *Deuteronomy 21:10—34:12.* Word Biblical Commentary 6B. Nashville: Nelson, 2002.

Clarke, Ernest G. *Targum Pseudo-Jonathan: Deuteronomy.* Aramaic Bible 5B. Collegeville, MN: Liturgical, 1998.

Clines, David J. A. "The Ten Commandments, Reading from Left to Right." In *Interested Parties: The Ideology of Writers and Readers in the Hebrew Bible,* 25–48. Journal for the Study of the Old Testament Supplement Series 205; Sheffield, UK: Sheffield Academic, 2009.

———. "The Ten Commandments, Reading from Left to Right." In *Words Remembered, Texts Renewed: Essays in Honour of John F. A. Sawyer,* edited by J. H. G. Davies and W. G. E. Watson, 96–112. Journal for the Study of the Old Testament Supplement Series 195. Sheffield, UK: Sheffield Academic, 1995.

———, ed. *Dictionary of Classical Hebrew.* 7 vols. to date. Sheffield, UK: Sheffield Academic, 1993–.

Coats, George W. *Moses: Heroic Man, Man of God.* Journal for the Study of the Old Testament Supplement Series 57. Sheffield, UK: JSOT, 1988.

Cogan, M., and H. Tadmor. *II Kings: A New Translation with Introduction and Commentary.* Anchor Bible 11. Garden City, NY: Doubleday, 1988.

Collon, D. *The Seal Impressions from Tell Atchana/Alalakh.* Alter Orient und Altes Testament 27. Neukirchen-Vluyn: Neukirchener, 1975.

Coogan, M. D., ed. *The New Oxford Annotated Bible.* 3rd ed. Oxford: Oxford University Press, 2001.

Costecalde, C. B. *Aux origins du sacré biblique.* Paris: Letouzey & Ané, 1986.

Cowley, A. E., ed. *Aramaic Papyri of the Fifth Century B.C.* London: Clarendon, 1923.

Craig, J. A. *Assyrian and Babylonian Religious Texts.* Vol. 1. Leipzig: Hinrichs, 1895.

Craigie, Peter C. *The Book of Deuteronomy.* New International Commentary on the Old Testament. Grand Rapids: Eerdmans, 1976.

———. "The Comparison of Hebrew Poetry: Psalm 104 in the Light of Egyptian and Ugaritic Poetry." *Semitics* 4 (1974) 10–21.

Cribb, Bryan H. *Speaking on the Brink of Sheol: Form and Message of Old Testament Death Stories.* Piscataway, NJ: Gorgias, 2009.

Crüsemann, F. *Bewahrung der Freiheit: Das Thema des Dekalogs in sozialgeschichtlicher Perspektive.* Kaiser Traktate 78. München: Kaiser, 1983.

———. *The Torah: Theology and Social History of Old Testament Law.* Translated by A. W. Mahnke. Minneapolis, MN: Fortress, 1996.

Curtis, Edward M. "Idol, Idolatry." In *Anchor Bible Dictionary,* edited by D. N. Freedman, 3:376–81. Garden City, NY: Doubleday, 1992.

Dahood, M. "Yahweh our God is the Unique." In *Ras Shamra Parallels,* vol. 1, edited by L. R. Fisher. Analecta orientalia 49. Rome: Pontifical Biblical Institute, 1972.

Dalley, Stephanie. "Erra and Ishum." In *The Context of Scripture.* Vol. 1, *Canonical Compositions from the Biblical World.* Edited by Hallo, W. W. and K. L. Younger, 404–16. Leiden: Brill, 1997.

Dandamaev, Muhammad A. *Slavery in Babylonia: From Nabopolassar to Alexander the Great (626–331 B.C.).* Edited by M. A. Powell and D. B. Weisberg, and translated by V. A. Powell. DeKalb, IL: Northern Illinois University Press, 1984.

Davidson, R. "Which Torah Laws Should Gentile Christians Obey? The Relationship between Leviticus 17–18 and Acts 15." Paper presented to the Evangelical Theological Society, San Diego, November 15, 2007.

Davies, Graham. "A Samaritan Inscription with an Expanded Text of the Shema." *Palestine Exploration Quarterly* 131 (1999) 3-19.

Davies, John. *Royal Priesthood: Literary and Intertextual Perspectives on an Image of Israel in Exodus 19.6.* Library Hebrew Bible/Old Testament Studies. New York: Continuum, 2004.

Day, John. "New Light on the Mythological Background of the Allusion to Resheph in Habakkuk III 5." *Vetus Testamentum* 29 (1979) 259-74.

————. *Yahweh and the Gods and Goddesses of Canaan.* Journal for the Study of the Old Testament Studies 265. Sheffield, UK: Sheffield Academic, 2000.

De Moor, Johannes C. *The Rise of Yahwism: The Roots of Israelite Monotheism.* Rev. and enlarged ed. Bibliotheca ephemiridum theologicarum lovaniensium 91. Leuven: Leuven University Press, 1997.

De Wette, W. M. L. "Dissertatio critico-exegetica qua Deuteronomium a propribus pentateuchi libris diversum, alius cuiusdam recentioris auctoris opus esse monstratur."Doctoral dissertation. Jena, 1805.

DeRouchie, Jason S. *A Call to Covenant Love: Text Grammar and Literary Structure in Deuteronomy 5–11.* Gorgias Dissertations 30. Piscataway, NJ: Gorgias, 2007.

Dick, M. B. "Worshiping Idols: What Isaiah Didn't Know." *Bible Review* 18.2 (2002) 30-37.

Dijkstra, Meindert. "Moses, the Man of God." In *The Interpretation of Exodus: Studies in Honour of Cornelis Houtman,* edited by Riemer Roukema, 17–36. Biblical Exegesis and Theology 44. Leuven: Peeters, 2006.

Dobbs-Allsopp, F. W., et al, *Hebrew Inscriptions: Texts from the Biblical Period of the Monarchy with Concordance.* New Haven, CT: Yale University Press, 2005.

Donbaz, V. "An Old Assyrian Treaty from Kültepe." *Journal of Cuneiform Studies* 57 (2005) 63–68.

Donner, H. and W. Röllig. *Kanaanäische und aramäische Inschriften.* 2nd ed. 3 vols. Wiesbaden: Harrassowitz, 1966–69.

Douglas, J. D., ed. *The Illustrated Bible Dictionary.* 3 vols. Downers Grove, IL: InterVarsity, 1980.

Douglas, Mary. *Purity and Danger: An Analysis of the Concepts of Pollution and Taboo.* New York: Ark, 1984.

Driver, S. R. *A Critical and Exegetical Commentary on Deuteronomy.* International Critical Commentary. Edinburgh: T. & T. Clark, 1902.

Drucker, P. "Forward: Not Enough Generals Were Killed." In *The Leader of the Future,* edited by F. Hesselbein, M. Goldsmith, and R. Beckhard, vii. San Francisco: Jossey-Bass, 1996.

Duff, Nancy. "Should the Ten Commandments Be Posted in the Public Realm? Why the Bible and the Constitution Say, 'No.'" In *The Ten Commandments: Reciprocity of Faithfulness,* edited by W. P. Brown, 159–70. Louisville, KY: Westminster/John Knox, 2004.

Dunn, James D. G. *Christology in the Making: An Inquiry into the Origins of the Doctrine of the Incarnation.* London: SCM, 1980.

Durham, John I. *Exodus.* Word Biblical Commentary 3. Waco, TX: Word, 1987.

Ebeling, E. "Aššur." In *Reallexikon der Assyriologie und Vorderasiatischen Archäologie*, edited by M. P. Streck, 1:196–98. Berlin: DeGruyter, 1975.

Eissfeldt, O. *Das Lied Moses Deuteronomium 32 1–43 und das Lehrgedicht Asaphs Psalm 78 samt einer Analyse der Umgebung des Mose-Liedes*. Beihefte zur Zeitschrift für die alttestamentliche Wissenschaft 104/5. Berlin: Akademie, 1958.

Exum, J. Cheryl, and H. G. M. Williamson. *Reading from Right to Left: Essays in Honor of David J. A. Clines*. London: Sheffield Academic, 2003.

Falk, Ze'ev W. *Hebrew Law in Biblical Times*. 2nd ed. Provo, UT: Brigham Young University Press, 2001.

Farley, Michael A. "What is "Biblical" Worship? Biblical Hermeneutics and Evangelical Theologies of Worship," *Journal of the Evangelical Theological Society* 51 (2008) 591–613.

Finsterbusch, Karin. "Bezüge zwischen Aussagen von Dtn 6,4–9 und 6,10–25." *Zeitschrift für die alttestamentliche Wissenschaft* 114 (2002) 433–37.

Firmage, Edwin. "Zoology (Animal Profiles)." In *Anchor Bible Dictionary*, edited by D. N. Freedman, 6:1136–37. Garden City, NY: Doubleday, 1992.

Fishbane, M. *Biblical Interpretation in Ancient Israel*. Oxford: Clarendon, 1985.

Fleming, Daniel E. "The Etymological Origins of the Hebrew *nābîʾ*: The One Who Invokes God." *Catholic Biblical Quarterly* 55 (1993) 217–24.

———. *The Installation of Baal's High Priestess at Emar*. Harvard Semitic Studies 42. Atlanta: Scholars, 1992.

Fokkelman, J. P. *Major Poems of the Hebrew Bible at the Interface of Hermeneutics and Structural Analysis*. Vol. 1, *Ex. 15, Deut 32, and Job 3*. Studia Semitica Neerlandica. Assen, Netherlands: Van Gorcum, 1998.

Follingstad, C. M. *Deictic Viewpoint in Biblical Hebrew Text: A Syntagmatic and Paradigmatic Analysis of the Particle* כי. Dallas, Texas: SIL, 2001.

Ford, J. Massyngberde. *Revelation: A New Translation with Introduction and Commentary*. Anchor Bible 38. Garden City, NY: Doubleday, 1975.

Fossum, Jarl E. "Son of God." In *Dictionary of Deities and Demons in the Bible*, edited by K. van der Toorn, B. Becking, and P. W. van der Horst, 788–94. Rev. ed. Leiden: Brill, 1999.

Foster, B. R. "Animals in Mesopotamian Literature." In *A History of the Animal World in the Ancient Near East*, edited by B. J. Collins, 271–88. Handbuch der Orientalistik I/64. Leiden: Brill, 2002.

———. *Before the Muses: An Anthology of Akkadian Literature*. 2 vols. Bethesda, Maryland: CDL, 1993.

Foster, Paul. "Why did Matthew get the *Shema* wrong? A Study of Matthew 22:37." *Journal of Biblical Literature* 133 (2003) 309–33.

Foster, Richard J. *The Challenge of the Disciplined Life: Christian Reflections on Money, Sex & Power*. Rev. ed. San Francisco: Harper & Row, 1989.

Fox, Michael. *Character and Ideology in the Book of Esther*. Columbia, SC: University of South Carolina Press, 1991.

Fredericks, D. C. "נֶפֶשׁ." In *New International Dictionary of Old Testament Theology & Exegesis*, edited by Willem VanGemeren, 3:133–34. Grand Rapids: Zondervan, 1997.

Freedman, D. N. "Pentateuch." In *The Interpreter's Dictionary of the Bible*, edited by G. A. Buttrick, 3:711–27. Nashville: Abingdon, 1964.

————. *The Nine Commandments: Uncovering the Pattern of Crime and Punishment in the Hebrew Bible.* New York: Doubleday, 2000.

————. "Pentateuch." In *The Interpreter's Dictionary of the Bible*, edited by G. A. Buttrick, 3:711-27. Nashville: Abingdon, 1964.

Freedman, Mordechai A. "Israel's Response in Hosea 2:17b: 'You are My Husband.'" *Journal of Biblical Literature* 99 (1980) 199–204.

Fritz, Volkmar. "Temple Architecture: What Can Archaeology Tell Us about Solomon's Temple?" *Biblical Archaeology Review* 13.4 (1987) 38–49.

Fyall, R. S. *Now My Eyes See You: Images of Creation and Evil in the Book of Job.* New Studies in Biblical Theology 12. Downers Grove, IL: InterVarsity, 2002.

Geisler, Norman L., ed. *Inerrancy.* Grand Rapids: Zondervan, 1979.

Geller, Stephen. *Parallelism in Early Biblical Poetry.* Missoula, MT: Scholars, 1979.

Gentry, Peter. "No One Holy, Like the Lord." Faculty address delivered at the Southern Baptist Theological Seminary, September 9, 2010. Accessible at file:///E:/Gentry/no-one-holy-like-the-lord%20Faculty%20Address%20Gentry.htm.

Gerstenberger, E. "תועב *t'b*, pi. to abhor." In *Theological Lexicon of the Old Testament*, edited by E. Jenni and C. Westermann, and translated by M. E. Biddle, 3:1428–31. Peabody, ME: Hendrickson, 1997.

————. *Wesen und Herkunft des "Apodiktischen Rechts."* Wissenschaftliche Monographien zum Alten und Neuen Testament 20. Neukirchen: Neukirchener, 1965.

Gibson, J. C. L. *Textbook of Syrian Semitic Inscriptions.* Vol. 2, *Aramaic Inscriptions.* Oxford: Clarendon, 1975.

————. *Textbook of Syrian Semitic Inscriptions.* Vol. 3, *Phoenician Inscriptions Including Inscriptions from the Mixed Dialect of Arslan Tash.* Oxford: Clarendon, 1982.

Gile, Jason. "Ezekiel 16 and the Song of Moses: A Prophetic Transformation?" *Journal of Biblical Literature* 130 (2011) 87–108.

Giles, Terry, and William J. Doan. *Twice Used Songs: Performance Criticism of the Songs of Ancient Israel.* Peabody, ME: Hendrickson, 2009.

Görg, Manfred. "Jahwe—ein Toponym." *Biblische Notizen* 1 (1976) 7-14.

Goldingay, J. *Daniel.* Word Biblical Commentary 30. Dallas, TX: Word, 1989.

Goody, J. *The Logic of Writing and the Organization of Society.* Cambridge: Cambridge University Press, 1986.

Gordon, Cyrus H. "His Name is 'One.'" *Journal of Near Eastern Studies* 29 (1970) 198–99.

Gosse, B. "Deutéronome 32,1-43 et les redaction des livre d'Ezéchiel et d'Isaïe." *Zeitschrift für die alttestamentliche Wissenschaft* 107 (1995) 110–17.

Gottlieb, R. S. *A Greener Faith: Religious Environmentalism and Our Planet's Future.* Oxford: Oxford University Press, 2006.

Gowan, Donald E. *Theology of the Prophetic Books: The Death and Resurrection of Israel.* Louisville, KY: Westminster/John Knox, 1998.

Grant, Jamie A. *The King as Exemplar: The Function of Deuteronomy's Kingship Law in the Shaping of the Book of Psalms.* Atlanta: Society of Biblical Literature, 2004.

Greenberg, Moshe. "Biblical Reality toward Power: Ideal and Reality in Law and Prophets." In *Religion and Law: Biblical-Judaic and Islamic Perspectives*, edited by E. B. Firmage et al., 101–12. Winona Lake, IN: Eisenbrauns, 1990.

———. "Decalogue (The Ten Commandments)." In *Encyclopaedia Judaica.* 2nd ed. Edited by Fred Skolnik, 5:520–25. Farmington Hills, MI: Gale, 2007.

———. "Hebrew *segulla*: Akkadian *sikiltu.*" *Journal of the American Oriental Society* 71 (1951) 172–74.

———. "The Vision of Jerusalem in Ezekiel 8–11: A Holistic Interpretation." In *The Divine Helmsman: Studies on God's Control of Human Events.* Festschrift Lou H. Silverman, edited by J. L. Crenshaw and S. Sandmel, 143–64. New York: Ktav, 1980.

Grisanti, M. A. "שָׁקַץ." In *New International Dictionary of Old Testament Theology & Exegesis,* edited by Willem VanGemeren, 5:243–46. Grand Rapids: Zondervan, 1997.

Gröndahl, F. *Die Personnenamen der Texte aus Ugarit.* Studia Pohl 1. Rome: Pontifical Biblical Institute, 1967.

Grosheide, F. W. *Commentary on the First Epistle to the Corinthians.* New International Commentary on the New Testament. Grand Rapids: Eerdmans, 1953.

Grudem, Wayne. *Systematic Theology: An Introduction to Biblical Doctrine.* Grand Rapids: Zondervan, 1994.

Guillaume, A. "Is 44:5 in the Light of the Elephantine Papyri." *Expository Times* 32 (1920–21) 377–79.

Guest, Steven Ward. "Deuteronomy 26:16-19 as the Central Focus." PhD diss., Southern Baptist Theological Seminary, 2009.

Guinness, O., and J. Seel, eds. *No God but God: Breaking with the Idols of Our Age.* Chicago: Moody, 1992.

Gutbrod, W. "νόμος." In *Theological Dictionary of the New Testament,* edited by G. Kittel, and translated by G. W. Bromiley, 4:1022–91. Grand Rapids: Eerdmans, 1967.

Hackett, JoAnn. *The Balaam Text from Deir 'Alla.* Harvard Semitic Monographs 19. Atlanta: Scholars, 1984.

HaCohen, David Ben-Gad. "Shasu Land, YHW, and the Tribe of Judah." Paper delivered to the Society of Biblical Literature. San Francisco, November 21, 2011.

Hafemann, Scott J. *Paul, Moses, and the History of Israel: The Letter / Spirit Contrast and the Argument from Scripture in 2 Corinthians 3.* Tübingen: Mohr (Siebeck), 1995.

Hague, S. T. "אָרוֹן." In *New International Dictionary of Old Testament Theology & Exegesis,* edited by Willem VanGemeren, 1:500–10. Grand Rapids: Zondervan, 1997.

Hallo, W. W. and K. L. Younger, eds. *The Context of Scripture.* 3 Vols. Leiden: Brill, 1997–2002.

Hamilton, G. J. "Alphabet." Unpublished and undated paper.

———. "Development of the Early Alphabet." PhD diss., Harvard University, 1985.

Haran, Menahem. "Book-Scrolls in Israel in Pre-exilic Times." *Journal of Jewish Studies* 33 (1982) 161–73.

———. "Seething a Kid in Its Mother's Milk." *Journal of Jewish Studies* 30 (1979) 23–35.

Harrelson, W. *The Ten Commandments and Human Rights.* Rev. ed. Macon, GA: Mercer, 1997.

Harrison, R. K. *Introduction to the Old Testament.* Grand Rapids: Eerdmans, 1969.

Hartley, John E. "Clean and Unclean." In *International Standard Bible Encyclopedia.* Rev. ed. Edited by G. W. Bromiley, 1:718–23. Grand Rapids, Michgan: Eerdmans, 1979.

———. *Leviticus.* Word Biblical Commentary 4. Dallas, TX: Word, 1992.

Hartman, L. F. and S. D. Sperling. "God, Names of." In *Encyclopaedia Judaica.* 2nd ed. Edited by F. Skolnik, 7:672–76. Farmington Hills, MI: Gale, 2007.

Hartsock, Nancy C. M. *Money, Sex and Power: Toward a Feminist Historical Materialism.* New York: Longman, 1983.

Hasel, G. "The Polemic Nature of the Genesis Cosmology." *Evangelical Quarterly* 46 (1974) 81–102.

Hasel, Michael G. *Domination and Resistance: Egyptian Military Activity in the Southern Levant, 1300–1185 B.C.E.* Probleme der Ägyptologie 11. Leiden: Brill, 1998.

Healey, J. F. "Dagon." In *Dictionary of Deities and Demons in the Bible,* edited by K. van der Toorn, B. Becking, and P. W. van der Horst, 216–19. Rev. ed. Leiden: Brill, 1999.

———. "Tirash תירוש." In *Dictionary of Deities and Demons in the Bible,* edited by K. van der Toorn, B. Becking, and P. W. van der Horst, 871–72. Rev. ed. Leiden: Brill, 1999.

Heidel, A. *The Babylonian Genesis.* 2nd ed. Chicago: University of Chicago Press, 1954.

Herrmann, W. "El." In *Dictionary of Deities and Demons in the Bible,* edited by K. van der Toorn, B. Becking, and P. W. van der Horst, 274–80. Rev. ed. Leiden: Brill, 1999.

———. "Jahwe und des Menschen Liebe zu ihm zu Dtn. VI 4." *Vetus Testamentum* 50 (2000) 47–54.

———. "Rider Upon the Clouds." In *Dictionary of Deities and Demons in the Bible,* edited by K. van der Toorn, B. Becking, and P. W. van der Horst, 703–5. Rev. ed. Leiden: Brill, 1999.

Hess, Richard S. *Amarna Personal Names.* American School of Oriental Research Dissertation Series 9. Winona Lake, IN: Eisenbrauns, 1996.

———. *Israelite Religions: An Archaeological and Biblical Survey.* Grand Rapids: Baker, 2007.

Hill, A. E. "רָמַס." In *New International Dictionary of Old Testament Theology & Exegesis.* Edited by Willem VanGemeren, 3:1126–27. Grand Rapids: Zondervan, 1997.

Himbaza, I. *Le Décalogue et l'histoire du texte: Etudes des formes textuelles du Décalogue et leurs implications dans l'histoire du texte de l'Ancien Testament.* Orbis biblicus et orientalis 207. Göttingen: Vandenhoeck & Ruprecht, 2004.

Hoffman, Joel M. *In the Beginning: A Short History of the Hebrew Language.* New York: New York University Press, 2004.

Hoftijzer, J. and K. Jongeling. *Dictionary of the North-West Semitic Inscriptions.* New York: Brill, 1995.

Hoftijzer, J., and G. van der Kooij. *Aramaic Texts from Deir ʿAllah.* Documenta et Monumenta Orientis Antiqui 19. Ledien: Brill, 1976.

———. *The Balaam Text from Deir Alla Re-Evaluated: Proceedings of the International Symposium Held at Leiden 21–24 August 1989.* Leiden: Brill, 1991.

Holladay, W. "Jeremiah and Moses: Further Observations." *Journal of Biblical Literature* 85 (1966) 17–27.

Hossfeld, F.-L. *Der Dekalog: Seine späten Fassungen, die originale Komposition und seine Vorstufen.* Orbis biblicus et orientalis 45. Göttingen: Vandenhoeck & Ruprecht, 1982.

Houston, Walter. *Purity and Monotheism: Clean and Unclean Animals in Biblical Law.* Journal for the Study of the Old Testament Supplement Series 140. Sheffield, UK: Sheffield Academic, 1993.

Huehnergard, J. "On the Etymology and Meaning of Hebrew *nabi*." *Eretz-Israel* 26 (1999) 88*–93*.

Huffmon, H. B. *Amorite Personal Names in the Mari texts: A Structural and Lexical Study.* Baltimore, MD: John Hopkins University Press, 1965.

———. "The Covenant Lawsuit in the Prophets." *Journal of Biblical Literature* 78 (1959) 285–95.

Hugenberger, Gordon. *Marriage as a Covenant: Biblical Law and Ethics as Developed from Malachi.* Biblical Studies Library. Winona Lake, IN: Eisenbrauns, 1998.

Hundley, Michael. "To Be or Not to Be: A Reexamination of Name Language in Deuteronomy and the Deuteronomistic History," *Vetus Testamentum* 59 (2009) 533–55.

Hurowitz, Victor (Avigdor). *I Have Built You an Exalted House: Temple Building in the Bible in the Light of Mesopotamian and Northwest Semitic Writings.* Journal for the Study of the Old Testament Supplement Series 115. Sheffield, UK: Sheffield Academic, 1992.

Hurtado, Larry W. *One God One Lord: Early Christian Devotion and Ancient Jewish Monotheism.* London: SCM, 1988.

Hutter, M. "Adam als Gärtner und König (Gen 2:8, 15)." *Biblische Zeitschrift* 30 (1986) 258–62.

Hwang, Jerry. *The Rhetoric of Remembrance: A Investigation of the "Fathers" in Deuteronomy.* Siphrut: Literaturre and Theology of the Hebrew Scriptures. Winona Lake, IN: Eisenbreauns, forthcoming.

Isserlin, B. S. J. "Israelite and Pre-Israelite Place-names in Palestine: A Historical and Geographical Sketch." *Palestine Exploration Quarterly* 89 (July–Dec. 1957) 133–44.

Jackley, John L. *Below the Beltway: Money, Sex, Power, and Other Fundamentals of Democracy in the Nation's Capital.* Washington, DC: Regnery, 1996.

Jackson, B. S. "A Feminist Reading of the Decalogue(s)." *Biblica* 87 (2006) 542–54.

Jacobs, L. "Shema, Reading of." In *Encyclopeaedia Judaica.* 2nd ed. Edited by Fred Skolnik, 14:1370–74. Farmington Hills, MI: Gale, 2007.

Janzen, J. G. "On the Most Important Word in the Shema (Deuteronomy VI 4–5)." *Vetus Testamentum* 37 (1987) 280–300.

———. "The Claim of the Shema." *Encounter* 59 (1998) 243–57.

Janzen, W. *Old Testament Ethics: A Paradigmatic Approach.* Louisville, KY: Westminster/John Knox, 1994.

Jastrow, M. *A Dictionary of the Targumim, Talmud Babli, Yerushalmi and Midrashic Literature.* New York: Judaica, 1971.

Jenni, E. "אָדוֹן *ādôn*." In *Theological Lexicon of the Old Testament,* edited by E. Jenni and C. Westermann, and translated by M. E. Biddle, 1:23–29. Peabody, ME, Hendrickson,1997.

Jepsen, Alfred. "Beiträge zur Auslegung und Geschichte des Dekalogs." *Zeitschrift für die alttestamentliche Wissenschaft* 149 (1967) 277–304.

Johnson, Robert M. "'The Least of the Commandments': Deuteronomy 22:6–7 in Rabbinic Judaism and Early Christianity." *Andrews University Seminary Studies* 20 (1982) 205–15.

Johnstone, W. "The Ten Commandments: Some Recent Interpretations." *Expository Times* 100 (1989) 453–59, 461.

Josberger, Rebekah. "Between Rule and Responsibility: The Role of the *āb* as Agent of Righteousness in Deuteronomy's Domestic Ideology." PhD diss., the Southern Baptist Theological Seminary, Louisville, KY, 2007.

Josephus, Flavius. *Jewish Antiquities.* Loeb Classical Library. Cambridge: Harvard University Press, 1978.

Joüon, Paul. *A Grammar of Biblical Hebrew.* Translated by T. Muraoka. Subsidia Biblica 14/I–14/II. Rome: Editrice Pontificio Istituto Biblio, 1991.

Kaiser, Walter C., Jr. "The Current Crisis in Exegesis and the Apostolic Use of Deuteronomy 25:4 in 1 Corinthians 9:8–10." *Journal of the Evangelical Theological Society* 21 (1978) 3–18.

———. "Leviticus." In *The New Interpreter's Bible,* edited by L. E. Keck, et al., 1:985–1191. Nashville: Abingdon, 1994.

Kalluveetil, Paul. *Declaration and Covenant: A Comprehensive Review of Covenant Formulae from the Old Testament and the Ancient Near East.* Rome: Biblical Institute Press, 1982.

Kaufman, Stephen. "The Structure of the Deuteronomic Law." *Maarav* 1 (1979) 105–58.

Keel, O. *Das Böcklein in der Milch seiner Mutter und Verwandtes im Lichte eines altorientalischen Bild-motifs.* Orbis biblicus et orientalis 33. Freiburg: Universitäsverlag, 1980.

———. *Jahwe-Visionen und Siegelkunst: Eine neue Deutung der Majestätschilderung in Jes 6, Ez 1 und Sach 4.* Stuttgarter biblische Beiträge 84/85. Stuttgart: Katholisches Bibelwerk, 1977.

———. *The Symbolism of the Biblical World: Ancient Near Eastern Iconography and the Book of Psalms.* Translated by T. J. Hallett. New York: Seabury, 1978.

Keiser, T. A. "The Song of Moses as a Basis for Isaiah's Prophecy." *Vetus Testamentum* 55 (2005) 486–500.

Kellermann, D. "עָלָה." In *Theological Dictionary of the Old Testament,* edited by G. J. Botterweck and H. Ringgren, and translated D. E. Green, 11:97–113. Grand Rapids: Eerdmans, 2001.

Keneally, Thomas. *Moses the Lawgiver.* New York: Harper & Row, 1975.

King, P. J. and L. E. Stager. *Life in Biblical Israel.* Library of Ancient Israel. Louisville, KY: Westminster/John Knox, 2001.

Kitchen, Kenneth A. *On the Reliability of the Old Testament.* Grand Rapids: Eerdmans, 2003.

———. *Ramesside Inscriptions Translated and Annotated.* Series A: Translations, vol. 2. *Ramesses II, Royal Inscriptions.* Oxford: Blackwell, 1996.

———. *Ramesside Inscriptions Translated and Annotated,* Series B: Notes and Comments, vol. 2, *Ramesses II, Royal Inscriptions.* Oxford: Blackwell, 1999.

Kittel, R. *Geschichte des Volkes Israel.* 6th ed. Stuttgart: Kohlhammer, 1932.

Klengel, Horst. "The History of Ashur in the Third and Second Millennia B.C.E." In *Discoveries at Ashur on the Tigris: Assyrian Origins: Antiquities in the*

Vorderasiatisches Museum, Berlin, edited by P. O. Harper, et al. New York: Metropolitan Museum of Art, 1995.

Kline, Meredith G. "The Two Tablets of the Covenant." *Westminster Theological Journal* 22 (1960) 133–46.

Knierim, R. "The Composition of the Pentateuch." In *The Task of Old Testament Theology: Substance, Method, and Cases*, 351–79. Grand Rapids: Eerdmans, 1995.

————. *The Task of Old Testament Theology: Substance, Method, and Cases: Essays*. Grand Rapids: Eerdmans, 1995.

Knoppers, Gary. "Rethinking the Relationship between Deuteronomy and the Deuteronomistic History." *Catholic Biblical Quarterly* 63 (2002) 393–415.

————. "The Deuteronomist and the Deuteronomic Law of the King: A Re-examination of a Relationship." *Zeitschrift für die alttestamentliche Wissenschaft* 108 (1996) 329–46.

Koehler, Ludwig and Walter Baumgartner. *The Hebrew and Aramaic Lexicon of the Old Testament*. Translated and edited by M. E. J. Richardson. Leiden: Brill, 2001.

Kooij, A. van der. "The Ending of the Song of Moses: On the Pre-Masoretic Version of Deut 32:43." In *Studies in Deuteronomy in Honour of C. J. Labuschagne*, edited by F. G. Martínez, 93–100. Vetus Testamentum Supplement Series 53. Leiden: Brill, 1994.

Kornfeld, W. "קדשׁ qdš." In *Theological Dictionary of the Old Testament*, edited by G. J. Botterweck and H. Ringgren, and translated by G. W. Bromiley, 12:521–30. Grand Rapids: Eerdmans, 1964.

———— . "Reine und unreine Tiere im Alten Testament." *Kairos* 7 (1965) 134–47.

Köstenberger, Andreas. *God, Marriage, and Family: Rebuilding the Biblical Foundation*. Wheaton, IL: Crossway, 2004.

Kruse, Colin G. "Law." In *New Dictionary of Biblical Theology: Exploring the Unity and Diversity of Scripture*, edited by T. D. Alexander, et al., 629–36. Downers Grove, IL: InterVarsity, 2000.

Kugel, J. L. "Poetry." In *Harper's Bible Dictionary*, edited by Paul J. Achtemeier, 804–6. San Francisco: Harper & Row, 1985.

————. *The Idea of Biblical Poetry: Parallelism and Its History*. Baltimore, MD: Johns Hopkins University Press, 2004.

Kühlewein, J. "בַּעַל ba'al owner." In *Theological Lexicon of the Old Testament*, edited by E. Jenni and C. Westermann, and translated by M. E. Biddle, 1:247–51. Peabody, ME: Hendrickson, 1997.

Kuntz, P. G. *The Ten Commandments in History: Mosaic Paradigms for a Well-Ordered Society*. Grand Rapids: Eerdmans, 2004.

Labuschagne, C. J. *The Incomparability of Yahweh in the Old Testament*. Pretoria Oriental Series 5. Leiden: Brill, 1966.

————. "קָרָא qr' to call." In *Theological Lexicon of the Old Testament*, edited by E. Jenni and C. Westermann, and translated by M. E. Biddle, 3:1158–64. Peabody, MA: Hendrickson, 1997.

————. "The Song of Moses in Deuteronomy 32—Logotechnical Analysis." Online: http://www.labuschagne.nl/2b.deut32.pdf.

————. "The Song of Moses: Its Framework and Structure." In *Dructu Oris Sui: Essays in Honour of A. van Selms*, edited by I. H. Eybers et al., 85–98. Leiden: Brill, 1971.

————. "'You Shall not Boil a Kid in its Mother's Milk': A New Proposal for the Origin of the Prohibition." In *The Scriptures and the Scrolls*, edited by F. G. Martínez, 6–17. Vetus Testamentum Supplement Series 49. Leiden: Brill, 1992.

Lambert, W. G. "Ancestors, Authors, and Canonicity." *Journal of Cuneiform Studies* 11 (1957) 1–14.

————. *Babylonian Wisdom Literature*. Oxford: Clarendon, 1960.

————. "A Catalogue of Texts and Authors." *Journal of Cuneiform Studies* 16.3 (1962) 59–77.

————. "The Cosmology of Sumer and Babylon." In *Ancient Cosmologies*, edited by C. Blacker and M. Loewe, 42–62. London: Allen & Unwin, 1975.

————. "Himmel." In *Reallexikon der Assyriologie und Vorderasiatischen Archäologie*, edited by M. P. Streck, 4:411–12. Berlin: DeGruyter, 1975.

Lang, B. "The Number Ten and the Antiquity of the Fathers: A New Interpretation of the Decalogue." *Zeitschrift für die alttestamentliche Wissenschaft* 118 (2006) 218–38.

Langdon, Stephen. *Babylonian Penitential Psalms*. Paris: Geuthner, 1927.

Leaney, A. R. C. *The Rule of Qumran and its Meaning*. New Testament Library. London: SCM, 1966.

Lee, Andrew. "The Narrative Function of the Song of Moses in the Contents of Deuteronomy and Genesis-Kings." PhD diss., University of Gloucestershire, 2010.

Lee, Won. "The Exclusion of Moses from the Promised Land: A Conceptual Approach." In *The Changing Face of Form Criticism for the Twenty-first Century*, edited by Marvin A. Sweeney and Ehud Ben Zvi, 217–39. Grand Rapids: Eerdmans, 2003.

Leibert, Julius. *The Lawgiver*. New York: Exposition, 1953.

Leichty, Earle. "The Colophon." In *Studies Presented to A. Leo Oppenheim*, edited by Robert D. Biggs and John A. Brinkman, 147–54. Chicago: Chicago University Press, 1964.

Leiman, S. Z. *The Canonization of Hebrew Scripture: The Talmudic and Midrashic Evidence*. 2nd ed. Transactions of the Connecticut Academy of Arts and Sciences. New Haven: Connecticut Academy of Arts and Sciences, 1991.

Lemaire, André. *The Birth of Monotheism: The Rise and Disappearance of Yahwism*. Washington, DC: Biblical Archaeology Society, 2007.

————. "Writing and Writing Materials." In *Anchor Bible Dictionary*, edited by D. N. Freedman, 6:999–1008. Garden City, NY: Doubleday, 1992.

Leuchter, Mark. "Why is the Song of Moses in the Book of Deuteronomy?" *Vetus Testamentum* 57 (2007) 295–317.

Levinson, Bernard M. *Deuteronomy and the Hermeneutics of Legal Innovation*. Oxford: Oxford University Press, 1998.

Lewis, T. J. "Teraphim תרפים." In *Dictionary of Deities and Demons in the Bible*. Edited by K. van der Toorn, B. Becking, and P. W. van der Horst, 844–50. Rev. ed. Leiden: Brill, 1999.

Liddell, H. G. and R. Scott. *A Greek-English Lexicon*. Rev. ed. Edited by H. S. Jones and R. McKenzie. Oxford: Clarendon, 1996.

Liedke, G. "חקק *ḥqq* einritzen, festsetzen." In *Theologisches Handwörterbuch zum Alten Testament*, edited by E. Jenni and C. Westerman, 1:626–34. Munich: Kaiser, 1971.

Lienhard, S. J. *Exodus, Leviticus, Numbers, Deuteronomy.* Ancient Christian Commentary on Scripture. Old Testament 3. Downers Grove, IL: InterVarsity, 2001.

Lim, Johnson Teng Kok. "The Sin of Moses in Deuteronomy." *Asia Journal of Theology* 17 (2001) 250–66.

Littauer, M. A. and J. H. Crouwel. "Chariots." In *Anchor Bible Dictionary,* edited by D. N. Freedman, 1:888–92. Garden City, NY: Doubleday, 1992.

Lohfink, N. "אֶחָד *'echādh.*" In *Theological Dictionary of the Old Testament,* edited by G. J. Botterweck and H. Ringgren, and translated by G. W. Bromiley, 1:196. Grand Rapids: Eerdmans, 1964.

———. "Der Bundesschluss im Land Moab: Redaktionsgeschichtliches zu Dt 28,69–32,47." *Biblische Zeitschrift* 6 (1962) 32–56.

———. "Dt 26,17–19 und die 'Bundesformel.'" In *Studien zum Deuteronomium und zur deuteronomischen Literatur I,* 228–35. Stuttgarter biblische Aufsatzbände 8. Stuttgart: Katholisches Bibelwerk, 1990.

———. *Great Themes from the Old Testament.* Translated by R. Walls. Edinburgh: T. & T. Clark, 1982.

———. "Kennt das Alte Testament einen Unterschied von 'Gebot' und 'Gesetz'? Zur biblelteologischen Einstufung des Dekalogs." *Jahrbuch für Biblische Theologie* 4 (1989) 63–89.

———. "Zur deuteronomischen Zentralizationsformel." *Biblica* 65 (1984) 297–329.

———. "Zur Fabel in Dtn 31–32." In *Konsequente Traditionsgeschichte: Festschrift für Klaus Baltzer zum 65. Geburtstag.* Edited by R. Bartelmus, T. Krüger, and H. Utschneider, 255–79. Orbis biblicus et orientalis 126. Freiburg: Universitätsverlag, 1993.

Lohfink, N. and G. Braulik. "Deuteronomium 4,13 und der Horebbund." In *Für immer verbündet: Studien zur Bundestheologie der Bibel,* edited by C. Dohmen and C. Frevel, 27–36. Stuttgarter Bibelstudien 211. Stuttgart: Katholisches Bibelwerk, 2007.

Lohse, B., *Martin Luther's Theology.* Minneapolis, MN: Fortress, 1999.

Lord, Carnes. *The Modern Prince: What Leaders Need to Know Now.* 2nd ed. New Haven, CT: Yale University Press, 2003.

Loretz, O. "Die *Einzigkeit* Jahwes (Dtn 6,4) im Licht der ugaritischen Baal-Mythos." In *Vom Alten Orient zum Alten Testament: Festschrift W. F. von Soden.* Edited by M. Dietrich and O. Loretz, 215–304. Neukirchen-Vluyn: Neukirchener, 1995.

———. *Ugarit-Texte und Thronbesteigigungspsalmen: Die Metamorphose des Regenspenders Baal-Jahwe (Ps 24, 7–10; 29; 47; 93; 95–100 sowie Ps 77, 17–20; 114).* Ugaritisch-biblische Literatur 7. Münster: Ugarit, 1988.

Lunn, Nicholas. *Word-Order Variation in Biblical Hebrew Poetry: Differentiating Pragmatics and Poetics.* Paternoster Biblical Monographs. Eugene, OR; Wipf & Stock, 2006.

Luther, Martin. *Lectures on Deuteronomy.* Luther's Works 9. Minneapolis, MN: Concordia, 1960.

Luyten, Jos. "Primeval and Eschatological Overtones in the Song of Moses (Dt 32, 1–43)." In *Das Deuteronomium.* Edited by N. Lohfink, 341–47. Leuven: Leuven University Press, 1985.

Malamat, Abraham. "'Love Your Neighbor as Yourself': What it Really Means." *Biblical Archaeology Review* 16.4 (1990) 50–51.

————. "'You Shall Love Your Neighbor As Yourself': A Case of Misinterpretation?" In *Die Hebräische Bibel und ihre zweifache Nachgeschichte: Festschrift für Rolf Rendtorff zum 65. Geburtstag*, edited by E. Blum et al., 111–15. Neukirchen-Vluyn: Neukirchener, 1990.

Maraqten, M. *Die semitischen Personennamen in den alt-und reischsaramäischen Inschriften aus Vorderasien.* Hildesheim: Olms, 1988.

Martens, E. A. "Accessing Theological Readings of a Biblical Book." *Andrews University Seminary Studies* 34 (1996) 223–37.

Martin, Ralph P. *James*. Word Biblical Commentary 48. Waco, TX: Word, 1988.

Martínez, Florentino G. and Eibert J. C. Tigchelaar. *The Dead Sea Scrolls Study Edition*. Leiden: Brill, 1997.

Maxwell, J. C. *The 21 Irrefutable Laws of Leadership: Follow Them and People Will Follow You.* Nashville: Nelson, 1998.

Mayes, A. D. H. *Deuteronomy*. New Century Bible. Grand Rapids: Eerdmans, 1981.

McBride, S. Dean, Jr. "Polity of the People of God: The Book of Deuteronomy." *Interpretation* 41 (1987) 229–44.

————. "The Yoke of the Kingdom: An Exposition of Deut. 6:4–5." *Interpretation* 27 (1973) 273–306.

McCarter, P. K., Jr., *I Samuel: A New Translation with Introduction, Notes and Commentary.* Anchor Bible 8. Garden City, NY: Doubleday, 1980.

McCarthy, Carmel, ed. *Deuteronomy*. Biblia Hebraica Quinta 5. Stuttgart: Deutsche Bibelgesellschaft, 2007.

McConville, J. G. *Deuteronomy*. Apollos Old Testament Commentary. Downers Grove, IL: InterVarsity, 2002.

————. *Grace in the End: A Study in Deuteronomic Theology.* Grand Rapids: Zondervan, 1993.

————. *Law and Theology in Deuteronomy.* Sheffield, UK: JSOT, 1984.

————. "Singular Address in the Deuteronomic Law and the Politics of Legal Administration." *Journal for the Study of the Old Testament* 97 (2002) 19–36.

McConville, J. Gordon, and J. G. Millar. *Time and Place in Deuteronomy.* Journal for the Study of the Old Testament Supplement Series 179. Sheffield Academic, 1984.

McKenzie, S. L. "Deuteronomistic History." In *Anchor Bible Dictionary*, edited by D. N. Freedman, 2:160–68. Garden City, NY: Doubleday, 1992.

Meier, S. A. *Speaking of Speaking: Marking Direct Discourse in the Hebrew Bible.* Vetus Testamentum Supplement Series 46. Leiden: Brill, 1992.

Mendenhall, George. "The Conflict Between Value Systems and Social Control." In *Unity and Diversity: Essays on the History, Literature, and Religion of the Ancient Near East*, edited by J. J. M. Roberts, 169–80. Baltimore, MD: Johns Hopkins University Press, 1975.

Merrill, Eugene H. *Deuteronomy*. New American Commentary. Nashville: Broadman & Holman, 1994.

Merwe, C. H. J. van der, J. A. Naudé, and J. H. Kroeze. *A Biblical Hebrew Reference Grammar.* Biblical Languages: Hebrew 3. Sheffield, UK: Sheffield Academic, 2004.

Meshel, Z. *Kuntillet Ajrud.* Jerusalem: Israel Museum, 1978.

Mettinger, Tryggve N. D. *In Search of God: The Meaning and Message of the Everlasting Names.* Translated by F. H. Cryer. Philadelphia: Fortress, 1987.

———. *No Graven Image? Israelite Aniconism in Its Ancient Near Easter Context.* Coniectanea biblica Old Testament Series 42. Stockholm: Almqvist & Wiksell International, 1995.

Milgrom, Jacob. "Profane Slaughter and a Formulaic Key to the Composition of Deuteronomy." *Hebrew Union College Annual* 47 (1976) 1–17.

Millar, J. G. "Living at the Place of Decision: Time and Place in the Framework of Deuteronomy." In *Time and Place in Deuteronomy,* J. G. Millar and J. G. McConville, 15–88. Journal for the Study of the Old Testament Supplement Series 179. Sheffield, UK: Sheffield Academic, 1994.

———. *Now Choose Life.* Grand Rapids: Eerdmans, 1998.

Millard, Alan R. "Books in the Late Bronze Age in the Levant." In *Past Links: Studies in the Languages and Cultures of the Ancient Near East. Fs. Anson Rainey,* edited by S. Izre'el et al., 171–81. Israel Oriental Studies 18. Winona Lake, IN: Eisenbrauns, 1998.

———. "Daniel 1–6 and History." *Evangelical Quarterly* 49 (1977) 67–73.

———. "Mass Communication and Scriptural Proclamation: The First Step." *Evangelical Quarterly* 2 (1978) 67–70.

———. "La prophetie et l'ecriture—Israël, Aram, Assyrie." *Revue de l'histoire des religions* 202 (1985) 125–44.

———. *Reading and Writing in the Time of Jesus.* Sheffield, UK: Sheffield Academic, 2000.

Miller, Cynthia L. "Pivotal Issues in Analyzing the Verbless Clause." In *The Verbless Clause in Biblical Hebrew: Linguistic Approaches,* edited by Cynthia L. Miller. Winona Lake, IN: Eisenbrauns, 1999.

Miller, J. W. *The Origins of the Bible. Rethinking Canon History.* New York: Paulist, 1994.

Miller, P. D. *Deuteronomy.* Interpretation. Louisville, KY: John Knox, 1990.

———. "Deuteronomy and the Psalms: Evoking a Biblical Conversation." *Journal of Biblical Literature* 118 (1999) 3–18.

———. "'Moses My Servant': The Deuteronomic Portrait of Moses." *Interpretation* 41 (1987) 245–55.

———. "The Place of the Decalogue in the Old Testament and Its Law." In *The Way of the Lord: Essays in Old Testament Theology,* 3–16. Grand Rapids: Eerdmans, 2004.

———. "The Sufficiency and Insufficiency of the Commandments." In *The Way of the Lord: Essays in Old Testament Theology,* 17–36. Grand Rapids: Eerdmans, 2004.

———. *The Ten Commandments.* Interpretation. Louisville, KY: Westminster/ John Knox, 2009.

Miller, Robert D., II. "The 'Biography' of Moses in the Pentateuch." In *Illuminating Moses: A History of Reception,* edited by Jane Beal. Commentaria Series. Leiden: Brill, forthcoming.

Moberly, R. W. L. "Toward an Interpretation of the Shema." In *Theological Exegesis: Essays in Honor of Brevard S. Childs,* edited by C. Seitz and K. Greene-McCreight, 124–44. Grand Rapids: Eerdmans, 1999.

———. "Yahweh is One: The Translation of the Shema." In *Studies in the Pentateuch,* edited by J. A. Emerton, 209–15. Vetus Testamentum Supplement Series 41. Leiden: Brill, 1990.

Monson, John. "The New 'Ain Dara Temple: Closest Solomonic Parallel." *Biblical Archaeology Review* 26.3 (2000) 20–35, 67.

Moo, Douglas J. "Nature in the New Creation: New Testament Eschatology and the Environment." *Journal of the Evangelical Theological Society* 49 (2006) 449–88.

Moore, Russell D. "After Patriarchy, What? Why Egalitarians Are Winning the Gender Debate." *Journal of the Evangelical Theological Society* 49 (2006) 569–76.

Moskala, J. *The Laws of Clean and Unclean Animals in Leviticus 11: Their Nature, Theology, and Rationale (An Intertextual Study).* Adventist Theological Society Dissertation Series. Berrien Springs, MI: Adventist Theological Society, 2000.

Murphy, Frederick J. *Early Judaism: The Exile to the Time of Jesus.* Peabody, ME: Hendrickson, 2002.

Mutius, H.-G. von. "Sprachliche und religionsgeschichtliche Anmerkungen zu einer neu publizierten samaritanischen Textfassung von Deuteronomium 6,4." *Biblische Notizen* 101 (2000) 23–26.

Nelson, R. *Deuteronomy.* Old Testament Library. Louisville, KY: Westminster/John Knox, 2002;

Neusner, Jacob. *The Treasury of Judaism: A New Collection and Translation of Essential Texts. The Life Cycle, Vol. 2.* Studies in Judaism. Lanham, MD: University Press of America, 2008.

New International Webster's Comprehensive Dictionary of the English Language. Deluxe Encyclopedic Edition. Naples, Florida: Trident, 1996.

Nicholson, E. W. *Deuteronomy and Tradition: Literary and Historical Problems in the Book of Deuteronomy.* Philadelphia: Fortress, 1967.

———. *God and His People: Covenant Theology in the Old Testament.* Oxford: Clarendon, 1986.

Niehaus, J. J. "The Deuteronomic Style: An Examination of the Deuteronomic Style in the Light of Ancient Near Eastern Literature." Unpublished manuscript, 1985.

Nielsen, E. "The Song of Moses (DT 322): A Structural Analysis." *Ephemerides theologicae Lovaniensis* 71 (1996): 5-22.

———. *The Ten Commandments in New Perspective: A Traditio-historical Approach.* Studies in Biblical Theology, 2nd Series 7. Naperville, IL: Allenson, 1968.

———. "'Weil Jahwe unser Gott ein Jahwe ist' (Dtn. 6,4f)." In *Law, History, and Tradition: Selected Essays by Eduard Nielsen,* 106–18. Copenhagen: Gads, 1983.

Nigosian, Solomon A. "Linguistic Patterns of Deuteronomy 32." *Biblica* 78 (1997) 206–24.

———. "The Song of Moses (DT 32) A Structural Analysis." *Ephemerides theologicae Lovanienses* 72 (1996) 5-22.

Nissinen, Martii. *Prophets and Prophecy in the Ancient Near East.* Atlanta: Society of Biblical Literature, 2003.

Nohrnberg, James. *Like Unto Moses: The Constituting of an Interruption.* Bloomington, IN: Indiana University Press, 1995.

Noll, K. L. *Canaan and Israel in Antiquity: An Introduction.* Sheffield, UK: Sheffield Academic, 2001.

Noonan, J. T., Jr. "The Muzzled Ox." *Jewish Quarterly Review* 70 (1980) 172–75.

Noth, Martin. *The Deuteronomistic History.* Translated by D. Orton. Journal for the Study of the Old Testament Supplement Series 15. Sheffield, UK: JSOT, 1981.

———. *Überlieferungsgeschichtliche Studien.* 2nd ed. Tübingen: Niemeyer, 1957.

Olson, Dennis T. *Deuteronomy and the Death of Moses: A Theological Reading.* Overtures to Biblical Theology. Minneapolis, MN: Fortress, 1994.

Oppenheim, A. Leo. *Ancient Mesopotamia: Portrait of a Dead Civilization.* Rev. ed. Chicago: University of Chicago Press, 1977.

Otto, Eckart. *Das Deuteronomium.* Beihefte zur Zeitschrift für die alttestamentliche Wissenschaft 284. Berlin: de Gruyter, 1999.

———. "Mose der erste Schriftgelehrte: Deuteronomium 1,5 in der Fabel des Pentateuch." In *L'Ecrit et L'Esprit: Etudes d'Histoire du texte et de théologie biblique en hommage à Adrian Schenker,* edited by D. Böhler, I Himbaza, and P. Hugo, 273–84. Orbis biblicus et orientalis 214. Göttingen: Vandenhoeck & Ruprecht, 2005.

———. "Revisions in the Legal History of Covenant Code, Deuteronomy, Holiness Code and the Legal Hermeneutics of the Torah." Paper delivered to the Society of Biblical Literature, New Orleans, November 23, 2009.

———. *Theologische Ethik des Alten Testaments.* Theologische Wissenschaft 3/2. Stuttgart: Kohlhammer, 1994.

Oxford English Dictionary. Compact Edition. Oxford: Oxford University Press, 1971.

Pakkala, Juha. "The Date of the Oldest Edition of Deuteronomy." *Zeitschrift für die alttestamentliche Wissenschaft* 121 (2009) 388–401.

Pardee, D. "Dawn and Dusk (The Birth of the Gracious and Beautiful Gods)." In *The Context of Scripture,* edited by W. W. Hallo, vol. 1, 274–83. Leiden: Brill, 1997.

Parker, S. B., ed. *Ugaritic Narrative Poetry.* Society of Biblical Literature Writings from the Ancient World 9; Atlanta: Scholars, 1997.

Parpola, Simo. "The King as God's Son and Chosen One." In *Assyrian Prophecies.* State Archives of Assyria 9. Helsinki: Helsinki University Press, 1997.

———. *Letters from Assyrian and Babylonian Scholars.* State Archives of Assyria 10. Helsinki: Helsinki University Press, 1993.

———. *Neo-Assyrian Toponyms.* Alter Orient und Altes Testament 6. Neukirchen: Neukirchener, 1970.

Parpola, S. and K. Watanabe. *Neo-Assyrian Treaties and Loyalty Oaths.* State Archives of Assyria 9. Helsinki: Helsinki University Press, 1988.

Patrick, Dale. *Old Testament Law.* Atlanta: John Knox, 1985.

Perlitt, L. *Bundestheologie im Alten Testament.* Wissenschaftliche Monographien zum Alten und Neuen Testament 36. Neikirchen-Vluyn: Neukirchener, 1969.

Peters, George. *Biblical Theology of Missions.* Chicago: Moody, 1972.

Peterson, David. *Engaging with God: A Biblical Theology of Worship.* Downers Grove, IL: InterVarsity, 1992.

Phillips, Anthony. *Ancient Israel's Criminal Law: A New Approach to the Decalogue.* New York: Schocken, 1970.

———. "The Decalogue: Ancient Israel's Criminal Law." In *Essays on Biblical Law,* 2–24. London: T. & T. Clark, 2002.

———. "A Fresh Look at the Sinai Pericope." In *Essays on Biblical Law,* 25–48. London: T. & T. Clark, 2002.

Philo. *De Specialibus Legibus.* In *Philonis Alexandrini opera quae supersunt,* 5:1–265. Reprint. Berlin: de Gruyter, 1962.

———. *On the Decalogue.* Loeb Classical Library. Cambridge: Harvard University Press, 1984.

Piper, John. "Worship God. http://www.desiringgod.org/ResourceLibrary/ Sermons/ByDate/1997/1016_Worship_God/.

Pleins, J. David. *The Social Visions of the Hebrew Bible: A Theological Introduction.* Louisville, KY: Westminster/John Knox, 2001.

Pohlmann, K.-P. *Ezechiel Studien: Zur Redaktionsgeschichte des Buches und zur Frage nach den ältesten Texten.* Beihefte zur Zeitschrift für die alttestamentliche Wissenschaft 202. Berlin: de Gruyter, 1992.

Polaski, Donald C. "Moses' Final Examination: The Book of Deuteronomy." In *Postmodern Interpretations of the Bible—A Reader,* edited by A. K. M. Adam, 29–41. St. Louis, MO: Chalice, 2001.

Polzin, R. *Moses and the Deuteronomist: A Literary Study of the Deuteronomistic History.* New York: Seabury, 1980.

Porten, Bezalel. *Archives from Elephantine.* Berkeley, CA: University of California Press, 1968.

Postgate, J. N. "Royal Ideology and State Administration in Sumer and Akkad. "*Civilizations of the Ancient Near East,* ed. J. M. Sasson, 395-411. Peabody, MA: Hendrickson, 1995.

Pressler, Carolyn. *The View of Women Found in the Deuteronomic Family Laws.* Beihefte zur Zeitschrift für die alttestamentliche Wissenschaft 216. Berlin: de Gruyter, 1993.

Preuss, H. D. "גִּלּוּלִים." In *Theological Dictionary of the Old Testament,* edited by G. J. Botterweck and H. Ringgren, and translated by G. W. Bromiley, 3:1–5. Grand Rapids, Eerdmans, 1965.

———. *Die Verspottung fremder Religionen im Alten Testament.* Beihefte zur Zeitschrift für die alttestamentliche Wissenschaft 12. Stuttgart: Kohlhammer, 1971.

Pritchard, James B., ed. *Ancient Near Eastern Texts Relating to the Old Testament.* 3rd ed. Princeton: Princeton University Press, 1969.

Propp, W. H. C. *Exodus 19–40: A New Translation with Introduction and Commentary.* Anchor Bible 2A. Garden City, NY: Doubleday, 2006.

Qimron, Elisha. "The Biblical Lexicon in the Light of the Dead Sea Scrolls." *Dead Sea Discoveries* 2 (1995) 296–98.

Rabinowitz, L. I. "Cosmology." In *Encyclopaedia Judaica.* 2nd ed. Edited by F. Skolnik, 5:231–32. Farmington Hills, MI: Gale, 2007.

Rad, G. von. *Deuteronomy: A Commentary.* Old Testament Library. Philadelphia: Westminster, 1966.

———. *The Problem of the Hexateuch and Other Studies.* London: SCM, 1966.

———. *Studies in Deuteronomy.* Studies in Biblical Theology 9. London: SCM, 1953.

Rainey, A. F. "The Toponymics of Eretz-Israel." *Bulletin of the American School of Oriental Research* 231 (1978) 1–17.

Ratner, R. and B. Zuckerman. "'A Kid in Milk?': New photographs of KTU 1:23, line 14." *Hebrew Union College Annual* 57 (1986) 15–60.

Redford, Donald B. *Egypt, Canaan, and Israel in Ancient Times.* Princeton, NJ: Princeton University Press, 1992.

———. "Hyksos." In *Anchor Bible Dictionary,* edited by D. N. Freedman, 3:341–44. Garden City, NY: Doubleday, 1992.

Reines, Alvin J. "Commandments, The 613." In *Encyclopaedia Judaica.* 2nd ed. Edited by F. Skolnik, 5:760–83. Farmington Hills, MI: Gale, 2007.

Rendsburg, G. A. "The Mock of Baal in 1 Kgs 18:27." *Catholic Biblical Quarterly* 50 (1988) 414–17.

Rendtorff, Rolf. *The Covenant Formula: An Exegetical and Theological Investigation.* Translated by M. Kohl. Edinburgh: T. & T. Clark, 1998.

Richter, Sandra. *The Deuteronomistic History and the Name Theology: lešakkēn šemô šām in the Bible and the Ancient Near East.* Beihefte zur Zeitschrift für die alttestamentliche Wissenschaft 318. Berlin: de Gruyter, 2002.

———. "The Place of the Name in Deuteronomy." *Vetus Testamentum* 57 (2007) 342–66.

Ringgren, H. "Monotheism." In *The Interpreter's Dictionary of the Bible.* Supplementary Volume, edited by K. Crim, 602–4. Nashville: Abingdon, 1978.

Rodd, Cyril S. *Glimpses of a Strange Land: Studies in Old Testament Ethics.* Edinburgh: T. & T. Clark, 2001.

Rofé, A. "The End of the Song of Moses (Deuteronomy 32:43)." In *Liebe und Gebot: Studien zum Deuteronomium, Festschrift zum 70. Geburtstag von Lothar Perlitt.* Ed. R. G. Kratz, and H. Spieckermann, 164–72. Göttingen: Vandenhoeck & Ruprecht, 2000.

———. "The Tenth Commandment in the Light of Four Deuteronomic Laws." In *The Ten Commandments in History and Tradition*, edited by Ben-Zion Segal and G. Levi, 45–54. Jerusalem: Magnes, 1990.

Römer, Thomas. "Moses outside the Torah and the Construction of a Diaspora Identity." *Journal of Hellenic Studies* 8 (2008) 1–12.

Rose, M. *5. Mose 12–25: Einführung und Gesetze.* Zürcher Bibel-kommentare. Zurich: Theologischer, 1994.

Rösel, Martin. "Names of God." In *Encyclopedia of the Dead Sea Scrolls*, edited by L. H. Schiffman and J. C. VanderKam, 2:600–602. Oxford: Oxford University Press, 2000.

Rosenfield, Paul. *The Club Rules. Power, Money, Sex and Fear: How it Works in Hollywood.* New York: Warner, 1992.

Roth, Martha. T. *Law Collections from Mesopotamia and Asia Minor.* 2nd ed. Society of Biblical Literature Writings from the Ancient World 6. Atlanta: Scholars, 1997.

Rubin, Gretchen Craft. *Power Money Fame Sex: A User's Guide.* New York: Atria, 2001.

Rudman, D. "When Gods Go Hungry: Mesopotamian Rite Clarifies Puzzling Prophecy." *Bible Review* 18.3 (2002) 37–39.

Safrai, Shmuel and Michael Avi-Yonah. "Temple: Structure." In *Encyclopaedia Judaica.* 2nd ed. Edited by F. Skolnik, 19:611–16. Farmington Hills, MI: Gale, 2007.

Saggs, H. W. F. *The Greatness That was Babylon: A Sketch of the Ancient Civilization of the Tigris-Euphrates Valley.* London: Sidgwick & Jackson, 1962.

Sailhamer, John H. *The Pentateuch as Narrative: A Biblical Theological Commentary.* Library of Biblical Interpretation. Grand Rapids: Zondervan, 1992.

Salveson, Allison. "Early Syriac, Greek and Latin Views of the Decalogue." In *The Decalogue through the Centuries: From the Hebrew Scriptures to Benedict XVI*, edited by J. Greenman and T. Larsen. Louisville, KY: Westminster/John Knox, forth-coming.

Sanders, Deion. *Power, Money & Sex: How Success Almost Ruined My Life.* Nashville: Word, 1999.

Sanders, James A. *Torah and Canon*. Philadelphia: Fortress, 1972.

Sanders, P. *The Provenance of Deuteronomy 32*. Old Testament Studies 37. Leiden: Brill, 1996.

Sandy, D. Brent. *Plowshares & Pruning Hooks: Rethinking the Language of Biblical Prophecy and Apocalyptic*. Downers Grove, IL: InterVarsity, 2002.

Sawyer, John F. A. *Sacred Languages and Sacred Texts*. New York: Routledge, 1999.

Schaper, J. "The 'Publication' of Legal Texts in Ancient Judah." In *The Pentateuch as Torah: New Models for Understanding Its Promulgation and Acceptance*, edited by G. N. Knoppers and B. M. Levinson, 225–36. Winona Lake, IN: Eisenbrauns, 2007.

Schiffman, L. H. "Phylacteries and Mezuzot." In *Encyclopedia of the Dead Sea Scrolls*, edited by L. H. Schiffman and J. C. VanderKam, 2:675–77. Oxford: Oxford University Press, 2000.

———. "Some Laws Pertaining to Animals in Temple Scroll Column 52." In *Legal Texts and Legal Issues: Proceedings of the Second Meeting of the International Organization for Qumran Studies Cambridge 1995: Published in Honour of Joseph M. Baumgarten*. Edited by M. Bernstein, 167–78. Studies on the Texts of the Desert of Judah 23. Leiden: Brill, 1997.

Schmid, Herbert. *Die Gestalt des Mose: Probleme atlttestamentlicher Forschung unter Berücksichtigung der Pentateuchkrise*. Erträge der Forschung 237. Darmstadt: Wissenschaftliche Buchgesellschaft, 1986.

Schmidt, Werner H. *Die Zehn Gebote im Rahmen alttestamentlicher Ethik*. Erträge der Forschung 281. Darmstadt: Wissenschaftliche Buchgesellschaft, 1993.

Schreiner, Thomas R. *The Law and Its Fulfillment: A Pauline Theology of Law*. Grand Rapids: Baker, 1993.

———. *Romans*. Baker Exegetical Commentary on the New Testament. Grand Rapids: Baker, 1998.

Scurlock, JoAnn. "Animal Sacrifice in Ancient Mesopotamian Religion." In *History of the Animal World in the Ancient Near East*. Edited by Billie Jean Collins, 389–97. Handbook of Oriental Studies 64. Leiden: Brill, 2002.

Searle, John. *Speech Acts: An Essay in the Philosophy of Language*. Cambridge: Cambridge University Press, 1969.

Segal, Ben-Zion, and G. Levi, eds. *The Ten Commandments in History and Tradition*. Jerusalem: Magnes, 1990.

Segal, Eliezer. "Justice, Mercy, and a Bird's Nest." *Journal of Jewish Studies* 42 (1991) 176–95.

Seitz, G. *Redaktionsgeschichtliche Studien zum Deuteronomium*. Beiträge zur Wissenschaft vom Alten und Neuen Testament 93. Stuttgart: Kohlhammer, 1971.

Seters, John van. *The Biblical Saga of King David*. Winona Lake: Eisenbrauns, 2009.

Seux, M. J. *Épithètes royales akkadiennes et sumériennes*. Paris: Letouzey et Ané, 1967.

Simian-Yofre, H. "עוד." In *Theological Dictionary of the Old Testament*, edited by G. J. Botterweck and H. Ringgren, and translated by D. W. Scott, 10:495–515. Grand Rapids: Eerdmans, 1999.

Sivan, H. *Between Woman, Man, and God: A New Interpretation of the Ten Commandments*. Journal for the Study of the Old Testament Supplement Series 401. London: T. & T. Clark, 2004.

Ska, Jean-Louis. "From History Writing to Library Building: The End of History and the Birth of the Book." In *The Pentateuch as Torah: New Models for*

Understanding Its Promulgation and Acceptance, edited by G. N. Knoppers and B. M. Levinson, 145–69. Winona Lake, IN: Eisenbrauns, 2007.

Skehan, Patrick W. "A Fragment of the 'Song of Moses' (Deut 32) from Qumran." *Bulletin of the American Schools of Oriental Research* 136 (1954) 12–15.

———. "The Structure of the Song of Moses in Deuteronomy (Deut 32:1–43)." *Catholic Biblical Quarterly* 13 (1951) 153–63.

Skehan, Patrick W., and Alexander A. di Lella. *The Wisdom of Ben Sira: A New Translation with Notes.* Anchor Bible. New York: Doubleday, 1987.

Smend, Rudolf. *Die Bundesformel.* Theologische Studien 68. Zurich: EVZ, 1963.

Smircich, L. and G. Morgan. "Leadership: The Management of Meaning." *Journal of Applied Behavioral Science* 18 (1982) 257–73.

Smith, Mark S. *The Early History of God: YHWH and Other Deities in Ancient Israel.* San Francisco: Harper & Row, 1987.

———. *God in Translation: Deities in Cross-Cultural Discourse in the Biblical World.* Forschungen zum Alten Testament 57. Tübingen: Mohr Siebeck, 2008.

———. "Matters of Space and Time in Exodus and Numbers." In *Theological Exegesis: Essays in Honor of Brevard S. Childs*, edited by C. Seitz and K. Greene-McKnight, 182–207. Grand Rapids: Eerdmans, 1999.

Soden, W. von, ed. *Akkadisches Handwörterbuch.* 3 vols. Wiesbaden: Karrassowitz, 1965–81.

Sohn, Seock-Tae. *The Divine Election of Israel.* Grand Rapids: Eerdmans, 1991.

———. "'I Will Be Your God and You Will Be My People': The Origin and Background of the Covenant Formula." In *Ancient Near Eastern, Biblical, and Judaic Studies in Honor of Baruch A. Levine*, edited by R. Chazan, W. W. Hallo, and L. H. Schiffman, 355–72. Winona Lake, IN: Eisenbrauns, 1999.

Sonnet, Jean-Pierre. *The Book Within the Book: Writing in Deuteronomy.* Leiden: Brill, 1997.

Sonsino, Rifat. "Forms of Biblical Law." In *Anchor Bible Dictionary*, edited by D. N. Freedman, 4:252–54. Garden City, NY: Doubleday, 1992.

Spronk, Klaas. "The Picture of Moses in the History of Interpretation." In *The Interpretation of Exodus: Studies in Honour of Cornelis Houtman*, edited by R. Roukema, et al., 253–64. Leuven: Peeters, 2006.

Stamm, J. J. *The Ten Commandments in Recent Research.* Studies in Biblical Theology. 2nd Series 2. Naperville, IL: Allenson, 1967.

Stein, Robert. "'Saved by Faith [Alone]' in Paul versus 'Not Saved by Faith Alone' in James." *Southern Baptist Journal of Theology* 4/3 (2000) 4–19.

Stephens, Ferris J. "Prayer to Every God." In *Ancient Near Eastern Texts Relating to the Old Testament.* Edited by J. B. Pritchard, 391–92. 3rd ed. Princeton: Princeton University Press, 1969.

Stern, Ephraim, ed. *The New Encyclopedia of Archaeological Excavations in the Holy Land.* 4 volumes. New York: Simon & Schuster, 1993.

Stewart, David A. *Money, Power, and Sex.* New York: Libra, 1965.

Stolz, F. "Monotheismus in Israel." In *Monotheismus im alten Israel und seiner Umwelt*, edited by O. Keel, 163–74. Biblische Beiträge 14. Fribourg: Schweizerisches Katholisches Bibelwerk, 1980.

Stuart, D. K. *Exodus.* New American Commentary 2. Nashville: Broadman & Holman, 2006.

———. *Studies in Early Hebrew Meter.* Missoula, Montana: Scholars, 1976.

Thierry, G. J. "Notes on Hebrew Grammar and Etymology." *Oudtestamentische Studiën* 9 (1951) 1–17.

Thiessen, Matthew. "The Form and Function of the Song of Moses (Deuteronomy 32:1–43)." *Journal of Biblical Literature* 123 (2004) 401–24.

Thompson, J. A. *The Book of Jeremiah*. New International Commentary on the Old Testament. Grand Rapids: Eerdmans, 1980.

———. *Deuteronomy: An Introduction and Commentary*. Tyndale Old Testament Commentaries. Downers Grove, IL: InterVarsity, 1974.

Tigay, J. *Deuteronomy*. Jewish Publication Society Torah Commentary. Philadelphia: Jewish Publication Society, 1996.

———. *You Shall Have No Other Gods: Israelite Religion in the Light of Hebrew Inscriptions*. Harvard Semitic Monographs 31. Atlanta: Scholars, 1986.

Toly, Noah J., and Daniel I. Block, editors. *Keeping God's Earth: The Global Environment in Biblical Perspective*. Downers Grove, IL: InterVarsity, 2010.

Toorn, Karel van der. *Scribal Culture and the Making of the Hebrew Bible*. Cambridge: Harvard University Press, 2007.

———. "Sheger." In *Dictionary of Deities and Demons in the Bible*, edited by K. van der Toorn, B. Becking, and P. W. van der Horst, 760–62. Rev. ed. Leiden: Brill, 1999.

———. "Yahweh." In *Dictionary of Deities and Demons in the Bible*, edited by K. van der Toorn, B. Becking, and P. W. van der Horst, 910–19. Rev. ed. Leiden: Brill, 1999.

Tov, Emanuel. *Textual Criticism of the Hebrew Bible*. 2nd rev. ed. Minneapolis, MN: Fortress, 2001.

Trible, Phyllis. *Texts of Terror: Literary-Feminist Readings of Biblical Narratives*. Overtures to Biblical Theology. Philadelphia: Fortress, 1984.

Turner, Philip. *Sex, Money and Power: An Essay on Christian Ethics*. Cambridge, MA: Cowley, 1985.

Uehlinger, C. "Leviathan." In *Dictionary of Deities and Demons in the Bible*, edited by K. van der Toorn, B. Becking, and P. W. van der Horst, 511–15. Rev. ed. Leiden: Brill, 1999.

Van Driel, G. *The Cult of Aššur*. Studia Semitica Neerlandica. Assen: van Gorcum, 1969.

Van Dyke, Fred, ed. *Redeeming Creation: The Biblical Basis for Environmental Stewardship*. Downers Grove, IL: InterVarsity, 1996.

VanderKam, J. C. *The Dead Sea Scrolls Today*. Grand Rapids: Eerdmans, 1994.

VanGemeren, Willem, ed. *New International Dictionary of Old Testament Theology & Exegesis*. 5 vols. Grand Rapids: Zondervan, 1997.

Vanhoozer, Kevin J. *Is There a Meaning in This Text? The Bible, the Reader, and the Morality of Literary Knowledge*. Grand Rapids: Zondervan, 1998.

Veijola, T. "Höre Israel! Der Sinn und Hintergrund von Deuteronomium VI 4–9." *Vetus Testamentum* 42 (1992) 528–41.

Vermes, Geza. "Pre-Mishnaic Jewish Worship and the Phylacteries from the Dead Sea." *Vetus Testamentum* 9 (1959) 65–72.

Vogt, Peter. *Deuteronomic Theology and the Significance of Torah: A Reappraisal*. Winona Lake, IN: Eisenbrauns, 2006.

Vokes, F. E. "Creeds in the New Testament." *Studia Evangelica* 6 (1973) 582–84.

————. "The Ten Commandments in the New Testament and in First Century Judaism." In *Studia Evangelica 5*, edited by F. L. Cross, 146–54. Berlin: Akademie, 1968.

Vriezen, T. C. "Das hiph'il von *'āmar* in Deut 26,17.18." *Jaarbericht van het Vooraziatische-Egyptisch Geselschap Ex oriente lux* 17 (1964) 207–10.

Wächter, Ludwig. "Reste von Šap'el-Bildungen im Hebräischen." *Zeitschrift für die alttestamentliche Wissenschaft* 83 (1971) 380–89.

Walker, C. and M. B. Dick, "The Induction of the Cult Image in Ancient Mesopotamia: The Mesopotamian *mispî* Ritual." In *Born in Heaven, Made on Earth: The Making of the Cult Image in the Ancient Near East*, edited by M. B. Dick, 55–121. Winona Lake, IN: Eisenbrauns, 1999.

Waltke, Bruce K. "Canonical Process Approach to the Psalms." In *Tradition and Testament: Essays in Honor of Charles Lee Feinberg*, edited by J. S. Feinberg and P. D. Feinberg, 3–19. Chicago: Moody, 1981.

————. "Oral Tradition." In *A Tribute to Gleason Archer: Essays on the Old Testament*, edited by W. C. Kaiser, Jr. and R. F. Youngblood, 17–34. Chicago: Moody, 1986.

Waltke, Bruce K., with Charles Yu. *An Old Testament Theology: An Exegetical, Canonical, and Thematic Approach*. Grand Rapids: Zondervan, 2007.

Walton, John H. "Interpreting the Bible as an Ancient Near Eastern Document." In *Israel: Ancient Kingdom or Late Invention*, edited by Daniel I. Block, 298–327. Nashville: Broadman & Holman, 2008.

————. "The Place of the *hutqaṭṭēl* within the D-Stem Group and Its Implications in Deuteronomy 24:4." *Hebrew Studies* 32 (1991) 7–17.

Watanabe, C. E. *Animal Symbolism in Mesopotamia: A Contextual Approach.* Wiener Offene Orientalistik 1. Vienna: Institute für Orientalistik, University of Vienna, 2002.

Watts, James W. "The Legal Characterization of Moses in the Rhetoric of the Pentateuch." *Journal of Biblical Literature* 117 (1998) 415–26.

————. *Psalm and Story: Inset Hymns in Hebrew Narrative*. Sheffield, UK: JSOT, 1992.

————. *Reading Law: The Rhetorical Shaping of the Pentateuch*. Biblical Seminar 59. Sheffield, UK: Sheffield Academic, 1999.

————. "Rhetorical Strategy in the Composition of the Pentateuch." *Journal for the Study of the Old Testament* 68 (1995) 3–22.

Weinfeld, Moshe. "The Covenant of Grant in the Old Testament and in the Ancient Near East." *Journal of the American Oriental Society* 90.2 (1970) 184–203.

————. "The Decalogue: Its Significance, Uniqueness, and Place in Israel's Tradition." In *Religion and Law: Biblical-Judaic and Islamic Perspectives*, edited by E. B. Firmage et al., 3–47. Winona Lake, IN: Eisenbrauns, 1990.

————. "Deuteronomy, Book of." In *Anchor Bible Dictionary*, edited by D. N. Freedman, 2:168–83. Garden City, NY: Doubleday, 1992.

————. *Deuteronomy 1–11: A New Translation with Introduction and Commentary.* Anchor Bible 5. Garden City, NY: Doubleday, 1991.

————. *Deuteronomy and the Deuteronomic School*. 1972. Reprint. Winona Lake, IN: Eisenbrauns, 1992.

————. "Divine Intervention in War in Ancient Israel and in the Ancient Near East." In *History, Historiography and Interpretation: Studies in Biblical and*

Cuneiform Literature, edited by Hayim Tadmor and M Weinfeld, 124–31. Jerusalem: Magnes, 1983.

———. "Social and Cultic Institutions in the Priestly Source against Their Ancient Near Eastern Background." *Proceedings of the Eighth World Congress of Jewish Studies* (1983) 105–11.

———. "The Tribal League at Sinai." In *Ancient Israelite Religion: Essays in Honor of Frank Moore Cross*. Edited by P. D. Miller, P. D. Hanson, and S. D. McBride, pp. 303-14. Philadelphia: Fortress, 1987.

———. "The Uniqueness of the Decalogue and Its Place in Jewish Tradition." In *The Ten Commandments in History and Tradition*, edited by Ben-Zion Segal and G. Levi, 1–44. Jerusalem: Magnes, 1990.

Weiss, Meir. "The Decalogue in Prophetic Literature." In *The Ten Commandments in History and Tradition*, edited by Ben-Zion Segal, 67–81. Jerusalem: Magnes, 1990.

Weitzman, S. *Song and Story in Biblical Narrative: The History of a Literary Convention in Ancient Israel*. Indianapolis, IN: Indiana University Press, 1997.

Wellhausen, J. *Die Composition des Hexateuchs und der historischen Bücher des Alten Testaments*. Berlin: Reimer, 1889.

———. *Prolegomena to the History of Israel*. 1885. Reprint. Cleveland: World, 1957.

Wells, Tom and Fred Zaspel. *New Covenant Theology: Description, Definition, Defense*. Frederick, MD: New Covenant Media, 2002.

Wenham, Gordon J. *The Book of Leviticus*. New International Commentary on the Old Testament. Grand Rapids: Eerdmans, 1979.

———. "Deuteronomy and the Central Sanctuary." *Tyndale Bulletin* 22 (1971) 103–18.

———. "The Ethics of the Psalms." In *Interpreting the Psalms: Issues and Approaches*, edited by D. Firth and P. S. Johnston, 175–94. Downers Grove, IL: InterVarsity, 2005.

Wennberg, Robert N. *God, Humans, and Animals: An Invitation to Enlarge Our Moral Universe*. Grand Rapids: Eerdmans, 2003.

Westbrook, Raymond. "Prohibition on Restoration of Marriage in Deuteronomy 24:1–4." In *Studies in Bible 1986*, edited by S. Japhet, 387–405. Scripta hierosolymitana 31; Jerusalem: Magnes, 1986.

Wevers, John William. *Notes on the Greek Text of Deuteronomy*. Society of Biblical Literature Septuagin and Cognate Studies 39. Atlanta: Scholars, 1995.

Whitekettle, R. "Where the Wild Things Are: Primary Level Taxa in Israelite Zoological Thought." *Journal for the Study of the Old Testament* 93 (2001) 17–37.

Whitelam, K. W. "Israelite Kingship: The Royal Ideology and Its Opponents." In *The World of Ancient Israel: Sociological, Anthropological and Political Perspectives*, edited by R. E. Clements, 119–39. Cambridge: Cambridge University Press, 1991.

Widengren, Geo. *The Ascension of the Apostle and the Heavenly Book*. Uppsala: Lundequistska Bokhandeln, 1950.

Wiebe, J. M. "The Form, Setting and Meaning of the Song of Moses." *Studia Biblica et Theologica* 17 (1989) 119–63.

Wilkinson, L., ed. *Earthkeeping in the Nineties: Stewardship of Creation*. 3rd ed. Eugene, OR: Wipf & Stock, 2003.

Will, George. "Ending the 'Feminization' of Politics." *Courier Journal* (January 29, 2004) A7.

Williamson, P. R. "Covenant." In *Dictionary of the Old Testament: Pentateuch*, edited by T. D. Alexander and D. W. Baker, 139–55. Downers Grove, IL: InterVarsity, 2003.

Willis, T. M. "'Eat and Rejoice Before the Lord': The Optimism of Worship in the Deuteronomic Code." In *Worship and the Hebrew Bible: Essays in Honour of John T. Willis*, edited by Rick R. Marrs, 276–94. Journal for the Study of the Old Testament Supplement Series 284. Sheffield, UK: JSOT, 1999.

Wilson, Gerald H. *Psalms Volume 1*. The New International Version Application Commentary. Grand Rapids: Zondervan, 2002.

Wilson, Ian. "Central Sanctuary or Local Settlement?: The Location of the Triennial Tithe Declaration (Dtn 26, 13–15)." *Zeitschrift für die Alttestamentliche Wissenschaft* 120/3 (2008) 232–40.

———. "Merely a Container? The Ark in Deuteronomy." In *Temple and Worship in Biblical Israel*, edited by J. Day, 212–49. London: T. & T. Clark, 2007.

———. *Out of the Midst of the Fire*. Society of Biblical Literature Dissertation Series 151. Atlants: Scholars, 1995.

Wolde, Ellen van. "Does *'innâ* Denote Rape? A Semantic Analysis of a Controversial Word." *Vetus Testamentum* 52 (2002) 528–44.

Wright, Christopher J. H. *Deuteronomy*. New International Biblical Commentary. Peabody, ME: Hendrickson, 1996.

———. *An Eye for an Eye: The Place of Old Testament Ethics Today*. Downers Grove, IL: InterVarsity, 1983.

———. *God's People in God's Land: Family, Land, and Property in the Old Testament*. Grand Rapids: Eerdmans, 1990.

———. *The Mission of God: Unlocking the Bible's Grand Narrative*. Downers Grove, IL: InterVarsity, 2006.

———. *Old Testament Ethics for the People of God*. Downers Grove, IL: InterVarsity, 2004.

———. "Ten Commandments." In *International Standard Bible Encyclopedia*. Rev. ed. Edited by G. W. Bromiley, 4:786–90. Grand Rapids: Eerdmans, 1988.

———. *Walking in the Ways of the Lord: The Ethical Authority of the Old Testament*. Downers Grove, IL: InterVarsity, 1995.

Wright, G. E. "The Lawsuit of God: A Form-Critical Study of Deuteronomy 32." In *Israel's Prophetic Heritage*, edited by B. W. Anderson et al., 26–67. New York: Harper: 1962.

Wright, J. E. *The Early History of Heaven*. New York: Oxford University Press, 2000.

Wright, N. T. *The Climax of the Covenant: Christ and the Law in Pauline Theology*. Minneapolis, MN: Fortress, 1993.

———. "Monotheism, Christology and Ethics: 1 Corinthians 8." In *The Climax of the Covenant: Christ and the Law in Pauline Theology*, 120–36. Edinburgh: T. & T. Clark, 1991.

Würthwein, Ernst. *The Text of the Old Testament*. Translated by E. F. Rhodes, 2nd ed. Grand Rapids: Eerdmans, 1995.

Wyatt, N. "Astarte." In *Dictionary of Deities and Demons in the Bible*, edited by K. van der Toorn, B. Becking, and P. W. van der Horst, 109–14. Rev. ed. Leiden: Brill, 1999.

————. "Oil יצהר." In *Dictionary of Deities and Demons in the Bible*, edited by K. van der Toorn, B. Becking, and P. W. van der Horst, 640. Rev. ed. Leiden: Brill, 1999.

————. *Religious Texts from Ugarit: The Words of Ilimilku and His Colleagues.* Biblical Seminar 53. Sheffield, UK: Sheffield Academic, 1998.

Xella, P. "Resheph." In *Dictionary of Deities and Demons in the Bible*, edited by K. van der Toorn, B. Becking, and P. W. van der Horst, 700–703. Rev. ed. Leiden: Brill, 1999.

Yadin, Y. "New Gleanings on Resheph from Ugarit." In *Biblical and Related Studies Presented to Samuel Iwry*, edited by Ann Kort and Scott Morschauser, 259–74. Winona Lake, IN: Eisenbrauns, 1985.

Yeivin, I. *Introduction to the Tiberian Masorah.* Translated and edited by E. J. Revell. Masoretic Studies 5. Missoula, MT: Scholars, 1980.

Zevit, Ziony. "Jewish Biblical Theology: Whence? Why? And Whither?" *Hebrew Union College Annual* 76 (2005) 289–340.

————. *The Religions of Ancient Israel: A Synthesis of Parallactic Approaches.* New York: Continuum, 2001.

Index of Scripture References

Index of Extracanonical Literature

Index of Modern Authors

Index of Selected Subjects